W9-BRN-201

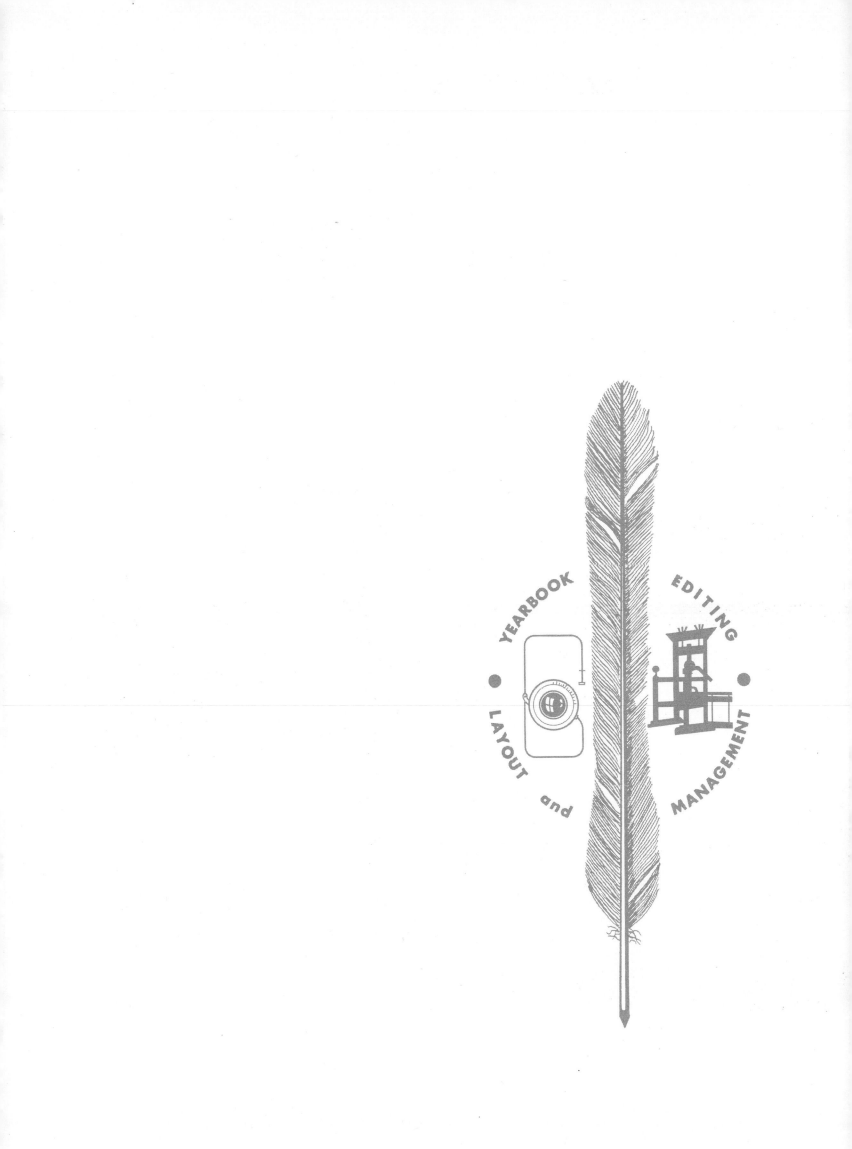

YEARBOOK LAYOUT and EDITING MANAGEMENT

Photo by Don Richards

YEARBOOK Editing, Layout, and Management

C. J. MEDLIN

**Professor Emeritus of Journalism
and Director of Student Publications, Inc.,
Kansas State University**

 Iowa State University Press, Ames, Iowa

© 1966 The Iowa State University Press
All rights reserved. Printed in the U.S.A.
Code # 1799

First edition, 1966
Second printing, 1967

Library of Congress Catalog Card Number: 66—22970

Color by Don Richards

Photo by Bob Hankins

The natural color photographs shown in in this section are reproduced from color separation negatives furnished by courtesy of the 1965 Royal Purple, Kansas State University. It is regretted that color pictures from other schools could not be used, but because of the expense involved it was not practical. However, the examples used are excellent and demonstrate the fine results being achieved in color printing in school annuals.

Preface

THE SCHOOL YEARBOOK STAFF often takes over its job with little or no experience in book publishing. Invariably the staff faces a multitude of problems that must be solved quickly and intelligently if the yearbook it produces is to be a successful venture.

School press associations, workshops, yearbook conventions, magazines for student journalists, and companies that produce school annuals are all valuable sources of information. Frequently, however, their information is not immediately available to help solve the day-by-day problems of yearbook production.

This book has been designed to fill the need for readily available information on all the basic problems of publishing a school annual. It is a production handbook for faculty advisers and all student staff members, and it is designed to serve as a textbook for courses in yearbook editing and supervision of school publications.

The author expresses deep gratitude to these members of the Kansas State University staff: Dr. Lowell Brandner for valuable advice and for editing the entire manuscript; Professor Jack Backer for editorial assistance in selecting examples of illustrations; and to Mrs. Anita Johnson and Mrs. Jan Hedrick, secretaries to Student Publications, Inc., for typing the manuscripts. Special thanks are extended to the late Professor Hallam Walker Davis, Professor Ralph R. Lashbrook, Professor Byron E. Ellis, and Professor George R. Eaton who encouraged, advised, and helped the author in the publication of two previous books, *School Yearbook Editing and Management* and *Yearbook Layout*. Some of the material printed in those two books is repeated in this book.

Grateful acknowledgment is also made to many individuals and concerns who made this book possible: Director Merritt Bailey and associates at the Iowa State University Press for generous cooperation and suggestions in printing; Lawrence E. Blaker of the Studio Royal, Manhattan, Kansas; and David R. Von Riesen, Kansas State University Photographic Services, for many suggestions and pictures.

The author is also particularly indebted to the National Scholastic Press Association, University of Minnesota, for much valuable information, to Professor Fred L. Kildow, director of the association, and to Mrs. Lucille Kildow and Mr. and Mrs. C. J. Leabo for their generous and helpful efforts in supplying material requested.

Special thanks are extended to staff members and advisers of the many yearbooks whose materials are quoted and reproduced in this book. The indulgence of some staffs is requested for my not always selecting the best layouts they contributed. Because the aim is to show interesting and effective techniques from all sections of an annual, it was sometimes necessary to select pages imperfect in some respects, but illustrating interesting and outstanding results in the areas being discussed. Credit lines identifying the annuals and the schools publishing them accompany the illustrations.

The author would like to give individual credit to each of the scores of photographers, editors, writers, advisers, artists, printers, engravers, and many others whose work is reproduced in this book, but that would be an endless task. He can only say, sincere thanks to all who have made a contribution.

C. J. MEDLIN

Photo by Don Richards

Table of Contents

A significant color picture of a beloved campus landmark will strengthen the annual and heighten its function as a memory book. Carefully select the spot and be sure photograph used is of high quality.

Achieving a School Yearbook's Functions

WHAT IS THE COMPELLING FORCE that causes more than twenty million students to "lay their money on the line" each year for a copy of their school yearbook?

It's the glow of satisfaction each one gets when he sees his picture with his name beside it in the annual. It gives him a sense of *identity*. Looking at his likeness there with all the others, he has a feeling of belonging. This sense of identity helps make him want to be a better citizen. This sense of identity is very important. Anyone wants respect from his friends or acquaintances. He hesitates to do anything shameful. The annual proudly proclaims the accomplishments of each student and identifies him with his picture.

Today more than thirty thousand schools in the United States publish yearbooks annually at an estimated cost of one-hundred million dollars![1]

[1] Estimated from information furnished by the National Scholastic Press Association, University of Minnesota, Minneapolis, and American Yearbook Company, Topeka, Kansas.

These books touch intimately the lives of millions of students, their parents, and friends. The well-planned and carefully edited yearbook records in enduring form the accomplishments of each student in the school.

Annuals Forced To Discontinue Publication

At one time some school administrators and boards of education forced annuals to discontinue publication. In many cases both sides of the issue were not heard. The annual was allowed no advocate, no champion. One school principal who prided himself on killing the yearbook—usually in a different school each year—remarked in exasperation, "A yearbook has more lives than a cat." Happily a principal of this kind is a rarity today. Most administrators and school boards recognize the value of the annual to the school and community, and many of the schools where annuals were discontinued are now producing books again.

Photo by Don Richards

Six Functions of the Annual

What is it that gives an annual more lives than a cat? What do students and their families prize in the annual? What functions give it vitality? A careful study of the modern yearbook reveals that it has six important functions. To fulfill these functions it must:

1. Be a memory book, with pictures of every student and teacher in the school accurately identified.
2. Tell a complete history of one year of school life.
3. Promote morale in the school.
4. Be a usable book of reference.
5. Give worthwhile educational training to student staff members.
6. Build goodwill for the school by giving a true and comprehensive picture of what the institution is trying to accomplish.

How Yearbooks Got Started

A clearer understanding of the functions of the annual or yearbook can be obtained by a brief glance at its history and development. In the early years it was a memory album for seniors only. In the beginning seniors exchanged pictures. Some pasted them into albums together with newspaper clippings to serve as a reminder of school days. Some such procedure still exists in a few small schools.

Eventually printed yearbooks came into being. In the late 1880's, the use of halftones was developed, and the more progressive schools adopted this new method of photo reproduction in their publications. Tremendous possibilities were opened to enterprising editors with this new device for picture reproduction. However, editors did not start immediately to produce streamlined books similar to those now being printed. It was too much to expect yearbooks to change overnight. Most annuals continued to be senior memory books, with the addition of views and a few snapshots. After all, they were produced to a large extent by students who had little or no experience in the publishing business, and who were carrying a full assignment of school work in addition to their editorial duties.

The Annual as a Memory Book

Today the chief function of the yearbook is the same as it was before printed annuals made their appearance. It should still be a memory book, a family album of the school. Students still want pictures of themselves and their friends. Close studies of yearbook sales prove that the number of copies purchased *depends upon the number of people whose pictures appear in the book*. Every student whose picture appears is almost a sure purchaser. He can say to his family and friends, "Yes, that's my picture. Not a thing of beauty, perhaps, but it's there." That student feels he belongs. If he has to say, "No, there isn't a picture of me in the book," he feels unimportant and insignificant. The book has not fulfilled its function for that student.

Getting Pictures of All Students

How are you as editor of a school annual going to get pictures of all students and teachers in the book? There are several ways. Often individual pictures of each student in the senior, junior, sophomore, and freshman classes are printed in panels. If this is impractical, because of the size of the book or the cost to each student, individual pictures of seniors can be used and group pictures can be taken of the underclassmen.

Frequently, staffs in large high schools and colleges find that the underclass organization is not very closely knit. Hence many high schools find it easier to get pictures of homeroom groups. The universities often depend upon individual or group pictures of fraternities and dormitories to take the place of underclass panels.

An excellent opportunity to add pictures is afforded by the organization section. Each organization, whether in a university or high school, wants a panel or group picture of adequate size showing all its members. This, of course, can be supplemented with activity pictures to be discussed later. Pictures showing all members of each organization in school are double assurance that everyone will appear at least once in the annual.

Get Pictures of Late Enrollees

Some schools insure getting pictures of all students in the class section by paying for the photographs, from yearbook or school funds, for any student who cannot afford to pay for his own picture. These students are contacted on a personal basis, and the photographer usually makes a special price to the annual for this work.

In many instances, the photographer comes to the school and takes all the pictures of classes and organizations over a period of two or three days. To include pictures of all students who were absent during this period, and also to picture those who enter school later in the year, a page near the back of the annual often is devoted to one or more group pictures, taken during the spring, of "absentee and new students." The next best thing to getting a picture of a student in the annual is to list his name as "member not pictured" with the class or organization to which he belongs.

Most families in the United States have a treasured, well-worn copy of a school annual that automatically opens at a certain page. On that page is a picture of a son or daughter, even though he or she may be only in some club or group picture. But that makes the school annual a worthy school project. That gives it life beyond its own year. It gives permanence to each year of school life.

The yearbook is nearly unique among books in that it is one of the select few which *all* owners keep throughout their lives. It is one of the few books they own which increases in value, as anyone can prove by trying to buy at five times its cost any privately owned annual which is ten or more years old.

Complete History of One Year of School Life

The development of the second function of the annual—telling a complete history of one year of school life—has been a slow and sometimes a confused process. Definite progress has not always resulted from some of the experiments tried, but excellent general improvement has resulted from the efforts of the many editors, faculty advisers, and school administrators who have made definite contributions.

State and national school press associations have given invaluable help by sponsoring conventions, yearbook contests, and instruction books. Professional magazines, published for teachers and students interested in journalism and the graphic arts, have pointed the way with timely and worthwhile articles on yearbook production in all its phases.

Contributions of the thousands of photographers, engravers, artists, printers, cover makers, and paper manufacturers who do the work on annuals should not be underestimated. Anyone truly familiar with the many hours spent by individuals of the graphic arts industry instructing and helping annual staffs long after the "whistle has blown" knows they are sincerely interested in more useful books and finer examples of good book production.

Get Complete Coverage

In editing the yearbook you are faced with the difficult problem of compiling a history of the school year while that history is being made. Events that seem important the day they happen often have little historical value. The fact that the leading halfback reports to football practice Tuesday afternoon with an injury that may keep him out of the important game of the year is a good news item, but the result of the game is more significant to the editor of the annual. You must separate the wheat from the chaff, the significant from the insignificant. It is more important to record the names of students who were elected to the honor society than to tell of the banquet they had on May 20.

What are some of the important things that should be included in the yearbook? The book must have some introductory or opening pages. Perhaps the title page and a table of contents are the only ones absolutely necessary. The late George Sargent called the title page "the door to the book." It should give the name of the annual, the year published, the publisher, school, town, and state. Many times this complete introduction is omitted, and the reader must then search through several pages to find the name of the school, the town, the state, and year of publication. A detailed discussion of opening pages is made in a later chapter. They are highly important.

Good View Sets the Scene

At least one good view of the main school building as students generally approach it should appear early in the book. This reproduction will be more attractive if it shows students entering or leaving the building. One picture might serve for a small high school, but several pictures will be necessary to identify a large university and give the proper setting. Views carefully identified or interpreted by good cutlines will have added interest for the reader. If the book is to be a complete history of the school year, it must show students in classrooms, laboratories, shops, or other places of curricular activity, and indicate actual class procedure. Every reader wants to know what and where.

Faculty pictures can be easily worked into the section portraying the work of the school by use of individual photographs, panels, and group pictures, or the teachers can be shown in classrooms or laboratory pictures. Sometimes they are shown with the organizations they sponsor.

Sports coverage is good in most yearbooks. In fact, it usually is the most popular section in the annual. Editors must be careful to give a complete picture of the athletic program. Some attention ought to be given to activities of second teams, freshmen, scrubs, intramurals, and girls' sports, so that proper balance is maintained. Copy should be interesting, lively, and unbiased. Tell the story of the game or season regardless of its success or disappointment. Give due credit to opposing teams and emphasize the highlights of the game. An accurate, complete, and easy-to-find record of scores of every sport is important.

Cover Extracurricular Activities

The extracurricular activities of students and faculty members are important parts of the history of the year. It is sometimes difficult to distinguish between an organization and an activity, and there is probably no definite dividing line. The significant thing is to include all of them. It is a definite achievement when a student wins a scholarship, is elected to an honor society, makes the debate team, orchestra, band, or livestock judging team, fills a leading post on the yearbook or newspaper staff, takes part in a school play, is a cheerleader, or in any other way proves that he is a valuable citizen in the school community. It is your job to pass out the palm of praise for success in all fields of school endeavor.

In the school life section, sometimes called the feature or snapshot section, editors have a real chance to tell their story by emphasizing the highlights of the school year with pictures that recall events, such as special assemblies, rallies, trips, traditions, homecoming celebrations, pep functions, open house, rush week, registration, and many others. Candid shots which record current fads, fashions, and habits of students lend interest.

The snapshots, or news pictures, should portray events and not feature individuals. These reproductions are more effective if they are large enough so people and objects can be recognized easily. Good headlines, copy, and captions can do much to complete the story the pictures attempt to tell.

How To Cover the Complete Year

The problem of presenting the complete story of the year is difficult to solve. In most cases the final deadline for copy is eight or ten weeks before delivery of the book to the school. This much time is needed by the printer to print and bind the annual. Thus, if the yearbook is to be delivered to students at commencement time, as was once the universal practice, it is impossible to include many important events that happen during the last two or three months of the school year.

In an effort to solve this problem, some schools have adopted the practice of covering the year from early spring of the previous year to early spring of the current year. This plan is not completely satisfactory, especially to seniors, because many of their significant achievements and important activities are omitted. For various reasons some schools still follow this plan.

Supplement for Spring Events

Many schools print a supplement of 8, 16, or 32 pages covering the late spring events. The supplement is either given or mailed to the subscriber to be inserted in the back of his annual. Some printers have devised ingenious methods for the insertions, such as a large envelope glued to the inside back cover to hold the extra pages, or a sensitized tape that can be applied to the back cover or end sheet to hold the supplement in place and thus make it a more permanent part of the yearbook.

Summer Delivery of the Annual

A growing number of schools each year elect to have their yearbook delivered in the summer or early fall, following spring commencement. Thus they can cover one entire school year. To encourage "summer" delivery of books some printers allow a discount from their regular price.

While the latter plan has many advantages, it also creates some problems such as requiring the staff and adviser to spend some time after the school term is over in preparing final copy, reading proof, delivering the annuals, and sometimes collecting accounts. The plan works satisfactorily in high schools and small colleges where most of the students live in the immediate community. Some have special parties during the summer or early fall and each student gets his book then.

However, large universities have found that mailing books to seniors and other students who do not return to the school is extremely expensive. This is particularly true if the book contains advertising or if the student lives or is employed in a foreign country. The postage required to mail a yearbook weighing seven pounds and carrying advertising, from New York to Los Angeles, is $2.00 (without advertisements, 40 cents). The cost of insurance is 10 cents per book, and wrapping and addressing will perhaps total 25 cents. This makes a total cost of mailing the book, if it carries advertising, $2.35 per subscriber. This additional cost of delivering the annual to its owner should be given careful consideration before the plan is adopted.

Promote Morale at the School

Too few yearbook staffs are making an all-out effort to cover all the outstanding accomplishments of the school, its students, and faculty members. Many of the accomplishments will be covered if a good job is done in fulfilling the two functions previously discussed. You have an opportunity to make a real contribution in developing this particular purpose of your annual.

It is, of course, important to tell about the school's accomplishment in sports, and give credit to the students and coaches who made it possible. And most annuals do a good job in this area. However, it's just as important to picture outstanding results achieved in the field of music, debate, judging, and particularly scholastic honors and outstanding research. Some of these are announced without much fanfare and often late in the year. You need to provide space and be alert to cover them.

If you give proper emphasis to the school's accomplishments, you will find that pride and allegiance suddenly blossom. The school will make a long stride towards worthwhile goals, pride, dignity, citizenship, togetherness, and spirit.

The Annual as a Book of Reference

"Why should the yearbook be a reference book? Why add more to an already heavy job?" These questions are being asked by yearbook planners, according to Mrs. Lucille Kildow, yearbook judge in charge of the National Scholastic Press Association and the Associated Collegiate Press Critical Service.[2] She said:

> To answer them, let's consider where school personnel and outside readers go to find facts and data regarding your school and activities. They go to your yearbook, don't they? And how do they find what they are looking for? Do they use the page-flipping, hit-or-miss, trial-and-error method? Or have yearbook planners been foresighted in their anticipation of the readers' needs and desires? In short, how effective is the book as a reference aid?

Yearbooks have come a long way since the above questions were asked. Most staffs have accepted the responsibility for making their annual

[2] Mrs. Lucille Kildow in *Scholastic Editor*, Vol. 36, No. 6, March 1957.

a usable book of reference. How is this accomplished?

If your annual is to be a book of reference, it must contain the information the user expects to find in a complete yearbook. It ought to have pictures of all students and teachers carefully identified, as well as a complete history of the school year.

To be a usable reference book, it should be arranged in a logical order with a table of contents giving the page number of each section or chapter. Most important, it must have a complete index giving the page numbers where pictures and information can be found on each individual, organization, activity, or event. This means that most pages must be numbered. Avoid skipping page numbers on more than four or five consecutive pages because of layout plans. Detailed instructions are given later in this book on how to prepare the table of contents and index.

Educational Value of the Yearbook

The educational value of the school yearbook to staff members can be classified into two general categories: the technical know-how of the publishing business, and training in general business methods. The training thus acquired can be used in almost any business or profession the students may later enter. There are few fields of endeavor in which this knowledge cannot be used.

There are innumerable instances of staff members who, because of the inspiration and knowledge acquired from working on the yearbook, have later become top-flight executives with newspapers, magazines, house organs, advertising agencies, publishing houses, and engraving companies. Many student photographers and artists, because of their experience on the yearbook staff, have later become leaders in these fields.

The business training acquired from selling books and advertising, estimating and controlling budgets, managing offices and keeping records, cooperating with staff members, and dealing with the public cannot be overestimated. The faculty adviser and other teachers should constantly remember that students will benefit from actually doing the jobs to which they have been assigned on the annual.

In many cases, especially as deadline dates approach, it would be simpler and quicker for the adviser to take matters into his or her own hands and order cuts, make layouts, instruct the printer, and even write the copy and the picture captions.

In some cases this may be necessary if contract requirements are to be met. In most cases it is not. A carefully planned production schedule will leave time to instruct the student staff members in their jobs and leave them sufficient time to complete all assignments.

Student editors and business managers can help in this educational process. The widest possible allocation of jobs, in general, is to be desired. In most cases the editors and managers have at least a fair understanding of all processes involved in the publication. In some cases the editor, and possibly the business manager, are the only ones who really understand the job. In these cases the yearbook is not serving its full purpose.

It is the job of the adviser to teach students to assume responsibility. The successful production of the annual requires skill in dividing and allocating responsibility and authority among others.

However, the adviser must remember that the educational value to the staff is distinctly, sharply subordinated to the goal of giving the school the finest, most worthwhile book within its means. The educational training afforded staff members is purely a by-product. The experience has high value only as it produces a good book. The staff member who has only a small part in producing a really fine book will get better training than the editor-in-chief of a slovenly, fumbling, amateurish product. The adviser must assume the responsibility of producing a good book as well as affording staff members a worthwhile educational experience.

"Top Scholars Choose Journalism"

The significance of the educational training gained by students working on school publications is pointed out in an article in the November, 1965, issue of *The Quill*. Using the headline quoted above, Patrick W. Kennedy, assistant to the director of the Newspaper Fund of the *Wall Street*

Journal, says in part:

High school journalism—the dumping ground for scholastic misfits.
Right?
Wrong! ! !
The day is approaching when high school students with weak grades in English or poor attitudes toward learning no longer will be assigned to the journalism class or permitted on the staff of the school newspaper. A rags-to-riches journalism story is being written in high schools across the nation.
Behind this optimistic prediction by the Newspaper Fund is the disclosure that:

Eighty of 121 of the 1965 Presidential Scholars selected journalism as a major high school activity.
Student newspapers are gaining stature in high schools, homes, and communities through responsible performance.
More boys are becoming interested in scholastic journalism because of an interest in writing.
More students see opportunities for public service in the adult careers of journalists.
For those unfamiliar with the term Presidential Scholars, the designation goes to superior high school students, selected by a presidential commission, for highest performance potential. The first scholars were selected in 1964.
A breakdown on the 1965 students' journalism activities from figures furnished by The Commission on Presidential Scholars reveals that:
Forty students were editors or staff members of school newspapers.
Thirty-two students have written for professional newspapers or magazines, state or national high school anthologies.
Thirty students have won awards or prizes for creative writing.
Twenty-five students were editors or staff members of school yearbooks.
Sixteen students were editors or staff members of school literary magazines.[3]

The message is clear. If you have persons in your school who doubt the value of educational training gained by students working on the annual, see that they get the message. They will be more willing to cooperate if they know the facts.

The Annual as Public Relations Tool

The importance of the yearbook as a public relations vehicle was emphasized in comments by Gerald Barker, director of public relations, Washburn University, Topeka, at a publications conference in September, 1965, for college administrators and publications personnel from Kansas colleges.

Mr. Barker said colleges have four general publics: students, alumni, prospective students, and parents.

With this introduction, Barker presented what he said are the four most important publications on a college campus. They are: the catalog, the student newspaper, the alumni magazine, and the college yearbook. He pointed out the important uses for the first three publications and then said this about college yearbooks:

This is the most important vehicle of all. This is the supreme effort. This is the epitome of what actually is accomplished by students on the campus. This is not a weekly issue, it's an annual. Catalogs are thrown away when they are out of date, but here is something which is in date, which remains current for as long as a person

---

[3] Copyright by *The Quill*, 1965, reprinted with permission.

lives. We keep a complete file in our office and we refer to them constantly.

This is why I believe that the major budgetary resources should go into a campus yearbook. It is perpetuating the very thing for which you stand, for which you exist.

There is no reason why everyone shouldn't buy one, shouldn't have one, because you will discover when you have been out of school as long as some of us have been that you will look back in the yearbook and say, "this couldn't have happened," but it did and because of the record which is maintained in the yearbook, it is there for as long as life itself.

So of these four (public relations) instruments, the annual is the number one publication. It goes to the students, to families, to high school reading rooms. We try to place them in professional offices so that people waiting can look at them. They will find out more about Washburn University and remember it longer than through any other communication.

Building Goodwill for the School

The yearbook, if it gives a true and comprehensive picture of what the school is trying to accomplish, can do much to sell students, parents, and other supporters on the school's value to the community, the state, and the nation.

Too often, even in small communities, the general public gets the impression that students spend most of their time "whooping-it-up" for athletic contests, going to dances, or racing around town in "hot-rod" cars. They seldom have the opportunity to observe the long hours put in by students in classrooms, laboratories, libraries, or in home study. If the yearbook brings to the attention of all who read it the worthwhile scholastic accomplishments of the school, in addition to extracurricular activities, it aids in building goodwill for the school. If the voters of the community are well informed about the real opportunities offered by the school to the young people of the community, they are more willing to vote bonds and pay taxes to provide needed improvements and adequate support of the school. The annual provides one of the most effective ways of presenting these needs to the community.

Annuals to Prospective Students

Perhaps private schools were the first to recognize the public relations value of the yearbook. The private schools place much emphasis on their educational activities, and devote considerable space to showing beautiful campus views as well as telling a complete history of the year. The yearbook is often sent to prospective students to tell them the advantages of that particular institution. The traveling representatives of private schools make use of the annual to present their institution in a favorable light to prospective donors as well as regular supporters of the institution.

Many of the more progressive tax-supported state colleges and universities have recognized the value of the school annual in showing prospective students and taxpayers of the state what the schools are doing. Often several hundred copies of the annual are purchased and sent to high school libraries and prominent state officials. Students attending the colleges are urged to show copies of their annuals to high school seniors and influential citizens in their home communities. Deans, heads of departments, and coaches use the yearbook in discussing the merits of their institution when interviewing prospective students.

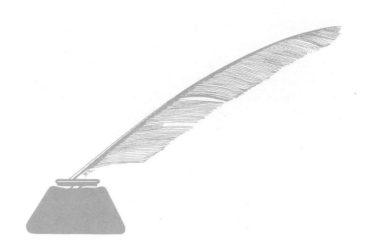

Thousands of staff members get training each summer in yearbook workshops throughout the nation. This picture is reproduced by courtesy of the 1965 Wildcat, published by high school students at the Kansas State University Publications Workshop in Manhattan.

Chapter 2

Selecting and Training the Staff

THE HEAD OF THE SCHOOL, whether college president or high school principal, is an unofficial member of the annual staff who has much to do with its success or failure. By sympathetic cooperation and assistance he can smooth the path for the annual staff, or he can use delaying tactics that will make it virtually impossible to publish a truly representative yearbook.

The situation has been well stated by Laurence R. Campbell in his booklet, *A Principal's Guide to High School Journalism*, published by Quill and Scroll Foundation, Northwestern University. Dr. Campbell says:

Education costs money. How well every principal realizes this fact. No matter where he turns he discovers needs that stretch all his financial resources. Hence, he is usually glad to discover an activity that pays its own way if given a fair chance.

Just what is meant by a fair chance? Simply this: no publication staff should be expected to achieve results—educationally or financially—if it is hampered and hamstrung by policies or rulings that make it impossible to finance its program.

Like the professional newspaper, student publications have two chief sources of revenue—circulation and advertising. True, there are miscellaneous sources, too. With few exceptions, a well-organized business staff can raise adequate funds unless low ceilings are put on subscriptions and advertising. . . .

Usually school publications indicate that a school has a good principal. If a school newspaper or yearbook is a failure, often the principal must share much of the blame. Thus, the principal has a great responsibility in developing the possibilities of scholastic journalism.

The same statements are true when applied to colleges and college administrators. How, then, can the school administrator help the annual staff?

First, he can see that the members of the staff get an early start by providing for the appointment or election of the editor and the business manager early in the spring, more than a year before they are to publish the annual. There are many important events to be covered after the current annual goes to press, if the book is to be a complete history of one year of school life. A certain cotton planter once remarked, "It takes 13 months out of the year to raise a cotton crop." It takes at least 15 months out of the year to produce a successful annual.

Give Staff a Place To Work

Second, the school or college should provide an office or room where the staff can do its work, just as space is provided for the band and the orchestra to practice and for the athletic teams to perform. If an office is provided, the work on the annual can be done during activity periods when students have free hours, or after school. The staff will have a place to work and can make progress each day. This is essential if the undertaking is to succeed and if the book is to come out on time. It is necessary for the staff to have desks, typewriters, filing cabinets, a camera, and other equipment.

Often the commercial department of a school has 20 to 40 typewriters that are used a few hours

a day, but no typewriter is made available for the yearbook staff. The same is true of darkrooms and other school facilities. It is sometimes difficult for the school administrator, because of crowded conditions in the schools, to allocate suitable quarters for the annual, but an equitable division of space can be made if the head of the school is interested in seeing that the annual staff is given a fair chance for success.

Appointment of Adviser

Third, the principal or president can appoint some faculty member who has had sufficient training to advise the annual staff. If there is no one in the school qualified to do the job, he should follow the same plan used in securing an athletic coach or music supervisor. If the school has a journalism teacher, he is usually the one best qualified to do the job, but his teaching load should be reduced. Sometimes in a large high school or college, the head adviser is in charge of the editorial or production end of the annual, and assistant advisers are appointed from the bookkeeping or business school to advise the business staff. Often some member of the faculty aids in taking and processing pictures. However, one adviser should be in general charge of the production of the book and be responsible for the proper coordination of all departments.

The adviser should be encouraged by the school administration to attend publication conventions and university summer courses on yearbook production. He should be given credit for work done during vacation months on magazines, newspapers, or in publishing houses. Many improvements are being made each year in the graphic arts industries, and the adviser who is to do a good job must keep abreast of the times.

Work of the Adviser

The position of adviser to the yearbook staff is a difficult one. To do a good job will probably require more time, preparation, and study than any two courses he will have to teach. It is important that he do a thorough job, as his professional advancement and standing in the school and community will be determined in no small degree by the results he obtains.

The position of adviser is comparable in many respects to that of the publisher of a newspaper or magazine who employs an editor and business manager to do the detail work. His job is to see that the work of the staff is properly coordinated, that the book published is a good one,

that it be delivered on time, and that there is enough money to pay the bills. To accomplish this he must have a thorough grasp of the entire problem. The task will not be too difficult if the adviser has had proper training in English, journalism, social science, business, etc. If he has had experience working on a newspaper, magazine, or for a publishing house, so much the better. The school administrator should take all these things into consideration when employing a teacher who is to be the adviser. If the adviser has not had training along these lines, he can often arrange to attend summer sessions of journalism schools, or take work in a field that will give him the information he needs. Several large universities have summer short courses on yearbook production that are a great help to advisers.

If the adviser is appointed on short notice and feels he needs information on the production of the annual, he can obtain it by writing the state and national school press associations. The schools of journalism located in the state where the adviser is employed often can suggest books that will give the desired information.

Place Responsibility on the Staff

The adviser should place responsibility directly on the shoulders of the editor and business manager. Students will do a much better job if they are given responsibility. Often the job will not be done exactly as the adviser had visualized, but in a surprising number of instances the staff members will turn out something just as good and sometimes better. The adviser should discuss in detail with the editor and business manager all the major projects to be carried out. He should not be the boss who gives orders, but should see that the editor and business manager make all assignments to their respective assistants and assume responsibility for execution of the assignments.

The adviser should attend all staff meetings and discuss beforehand with the editor and manager what is to be done in the meeting. The meeting can be conducted by the editor or manager. The work to be done should be carefully outlined for the other members of the staff. A staff meeting must not be allowed to deteriorate into a debating society. It is the place to coordinate the efforts of the entire staff for the job to be done.

Censorship of the Annual

The adviser should not act as a censor. If members of the staff are properly trained, they will have too much pride in their book and school

adviser should tell the editor there are certain things that he must watch in accepting copy for the book. First, copyrighted material that has appeared in books, magazines, and other publications cannot be reprinted without permission of the publisher. Second, postal regulations forbid mailing publications containing obscene material. Third, the libel laws prohibit written defamation of character.

If the editor is taught to understand the standards of good taste and fair play, there should be no need of faculty censorship. It is necessary to impress upon the staff the importance of accuracy in the annual, because after it is printed there is no chance to run a correction, as is done by newspapers when errors appear.

"Yearbooks Can Be Sued—for Plenty"

Some concise advice regarding libel laws is offered by Dr. Dwight Bentel, head of the department of journalism and advertising at San Jose State College, San Jose, Calif., and published in the *Illinois High School Journalist*. He says in part:

In the eyes of the law, the school publication looks like any other.

There's no reason to tremble at the thought. A fair-minded and responsible student staffer who conscientiously practices the Golden Rule usually will circumvent the dangers of libel or copyright.

Most of the laws are based on easily discernible matters of right and wrong: In common decency one doesn't maliciously or carelessly defame anyone.

One doesn't steal copyrighted material for publication, or material which hasn't been copyrighted but is the unpublished property of an individual, for use in the newspaper or yearbook.

As a matter of simple courtesy, one doesn't use another person's picture in an advertisement without first getting that person's permission.

In the area of libel there's another safeguard working for the student journalist. Most libel suits are a by-product of crime reporting. Student publications don't ordinarily "cover" crime.

So . . . while any number of stinging or biting laws may stalk outside the publications' office windows, they don't often get inside.

Sometimes, of course, they do. Last year a million-dollar libel suit was filed against a Long Island printer, a Long Island school board, and a high school principal, because of a caption under a girl's picture in a yearbook. . . .

Some specific advice for yearbook editors is included in the article as follows:

Yearbook Captions. It sometimes happens that after a yearbook has identified the senior "most likely to succeed," "the biggest political wheel," "the warmest smile," it takes an uncomplimentary turn and discovers less commendable qualities among its constituency. At best this is a cruel practice. It also can be dangerous legally. So can captions under pictures in the life section that take a defamatory twist for the sake of "humor" or informality. Witness the million-dollar libel action in Long Island.

The student staffer should be aware of other restrictive laws which also affect his journalistic endeavors.

Copyright. A literary or artistic creation belongs to its creator. A person's property right in his literary or artistic creation is fully protected by the law before it has been published, just as though it has been copyrighted. Copyright is his protection after publication. Fine, imprisonment, or both can be the fate of the person who illegally uses the material in either case.

The protection applies only to the literary or artistic creation itself, not to the idea or the facts it incorporates. It is the literary style which may not be copied; information cannot be copyrighted. A person may rewrite and publish an article in his own style and own words, using all of the facts included in a copyrighted piece, without violating the copyright.

The law permits the press "reasonable use" in quoting copyrighted material. For books or magazine articles this means sufficient quotation to convey the sense or nature of the article short of actually injuring its value.

Right of Privacy. A person has a right to freedom from unwarranted invasion of his private life and affairs. The law protecting such right is comparatively new, hence to a large extent, ill-defined.

The photographer has been the principal offender. A camera-over-the-transom or sneak-a-picture approach to yearbook journalism or the insensitive portrayal of a person in a distressing or embarrassing situation, is instinctively avoided by the mature staffer regardless of any vagueness in the law protecting the victim. In short, the photographer will avoid trouble simply by being a lady or gentleman.

There is, however, one point at which privacy law is nailed down bonny-tight. A person's photograph may not be used in an advertisement without his consent. To show the captain of the track team, unbeknownst to him, running to buy a hot dog at the local beanery may please the advertiser. But it may make the runner's bosom heave from something other than shortness of breath. He will have no trouble finding an attorney who is sympathetic.[1]

Course in Yearbook Production Required

Many yearbook advisers who have journalism training insist that a regular credit course be required of major members of the annual staff. One effective plan is to arrange a course so that one hour a week can be given to recitation and two or three hours to laboratory work. In schools where a journalism course is already offered, it is an easy matter to divide the class so some of its members are assigned to work on the annual and others on the school newspaper.

Probably the greatest single advantage of having a class in yearbook production is the better

---

[1] Reprinted by permission of the author and the *Illinois High School Journalist*, University of Illinois, Urbana.

possibility of producing the book on schedule. When the class meets two or three times a week, there is no excuse for duplication of effort. Each individual can be given an assignment that needs to be done and one he has the ability to do. Thus an intelligent division of work expedites the production of the book. Most advisers who teach a course in yearbook production find it makes the job of advising easier and produces a better yearbook.

Workshops for Yearbook Staffs

At least one college or university in nearly every state conducts a workshop each summer for high school yearbook and newspaper staffs. The major project for yearbook staff members is to plan in detail the yearbook to be published by their school during the following year. Instruction in layout, writing, editing, photography, and the business aspects are also covered. Some of the workshops produce model annuals during the session and students have an opportunity to get practical experience in producing the book. The University of Minnesota conducts a workshop for college yearbook staffs each summer.

Workshops and Courses for Advisers

Summer workshops for advisers are held at several universities. In some cases the advisers are invited to the same workshop attended by their staffs. However, if credit is to be earned, they usually are required to attend special classes limited to individuals having college standing. Of course, many advisers take regular courses in journalism summer sessions or night schools to earn credit for advanced degrees or to get instruction that they feel they need as yearbook advisers.

Wall Street Journal Fellowships

The *Wall Street Journal* awards fellowships to high school journalism teachers and advisers for summer study. The magnitude of this program is illustrated by the following news release by the *Wall Street Journal*, April 25, 1963.

Summer study grants for 434 high school journalism teachers and publications advisers were announced today by The Newspaper Fund.
Teachers from 46 states, Washington, D.C., and the Philippine Islands will share the study fellowships which represent an investment of $153,000 by The Newspaper Fund.
Under The Fund's sponsorship, these teachers will spend up to 12 weeks studying scholastic and professional journalism problems and techniques at 46 colleges and universities.
The Newspaper Fund was established to interest young people in journalism careers. It seeks to improve students' knowledge of the profession by introducing their teachers to the latest developments in scholastic and professional journalism. Since 1959 more than 1,700 teachers have received these graduate school fellowship grants, according to Paul S. Swensson, executive director.

Selecting the Editor and Business Manager

Perhaps the most satisfactory method of selecting the editor and the business manager of the annual is appointment by a publications board. Many schools have a board of publications composed of students and faculty, with the students usually in the majority. Quite often in a large school the dean of the journalism school is chairman of the board, and the faculty adviser should be a member. From three to ten students usually are elected members of the board at the general school election. In a small school the board could be composed of the principal, faculty adviser, and one representative from each of the four classes.

In addition to electing the editor and the business manager, the board often determines general policies of the annual, approves important contracts, and also may direct other publications in the school. Student members of the board are often better judges of student ability than are faculty members. However, because of their lack of experience they are often more harsh in judging fellow students than are the faculty members. Then, too, student members of the board can be a great aid to publications because they have a better chance to know community opinion about the annual.

Most boards require a candidate for one of the major positions on the staff to have at least one year's experience working on the annual. Many capable editors and managers have served three full years on the staff before being elected to a major position. Even if the book is published by the senior class, there is no valid reason why minor staff positions cannot be held by students from the lower classes. It is fair neither to the student elected nor to the school to appoint an editor or manager who has had no previous experience on the publication. Editors are faced with a maze of problems of writing, editing, illustrating, financing, and producing the annual that cannot be successfully and efficiently handled by anyone who is new to such work.

Written Applications Required

Often the board of publications requires the

candidate for an executive position on the year-book to write a letter of application stating his qualifications in detail. The board should receive letters of recommendation or interview the editor, business manager, and faculty adviser under whom the applicant has worked. It is a good idea to check the applicant's grades, interview his major instructors, and talk with school executives to secure all the information possible about his ability and initiative.

Some schools have application blanks for applicants to fill out. Shown in Figure 2.1 is the application form used by the Board of Student Publications, Kansas State University.

Applicants for the positions of editor and business manager must realize the importance and scope of their work and the amount of time required to do the job. They should agree to make their work on the book their major activity for the year. Other activities must be limited so that plenty of time is available to work on the annual and to direct the efforts of their assistants.

There are probably other satisfactory methods of selecting the editor and the business manager of the annual. However, there are three distinct advantages in the method outlined. First, it assures the selection of a student with previous experience in publishing the annual. Second, the selection is the combined judgment of several persons who have studied the qualifications of the various applicants. Third, a board representing the entire school is in a much better position than the adviser or school administrator to outline general policies, and if need arises, to remove from office appointees who are not satisfactory.

The board must be careful not to hamper the annual staff with petty regulations or attempts to dictate how the editor and business manager shall carry on the business of publishing. As soon as the appointments have been made, the general policy outlined, and the major contracts approved, the responsibility for publishing the annual should be placed upon the shoulders of the editor and faculty adviser, and the board should step into the picture only in case of an emergency.

Duties of the Editor

Election to editorship of the annual is a distinct honor for the student chosen, but like election to any important position, it entails duties and responsibilities. While the public is willing to give the editor credit for a job well done, it also feels free to criticize. The editor must immediately recognize his responsibility to the entire

school and see that nothing is included in the book that gives special consideration to any political party, organization, or clique to which he may belong.

No absolute distinction can be made between the duties of the editor and the business manager. On some phases they must work hand in hand if the book is to be a success. In general, the editor is the production manager, and the business manager is in charge of circulation and finance.

The editor should exercise great care in selecting editorial assistants. The editor, together with the faculty adviser, can check the ability of all available applicants to determine each one's ability to do the job to which he will be assigned. The editor must be careful not to appoint members to his staff because they happen to be personal friends and want the job because of the honor attached. Each member of the staff worthy of the name has an important and necessary job to do. If he fails, the editor or some other member of the staff must step into the breach. This is sometimes difficult because the editor has other duties.

These are general duties of the editor as production manager:

1. Selecting and supervising the work of editorial assistants.
2. Preparing the budget (with the business manager).
3. Planning the book.
4. Letting contracts (with the business manager, adviser, and publications board).
5. Getting pictures to tell the story.
6. Making layouts and preparing copy.
7. Planning and executing a production schedule that will insure delivery of the annual on time.

Tryouts for Staff Positions

Some editors have adopted the policy of having tryouts for positions on the staff. When this is possible, it is a good plan. However, the appointment of assistants should not be delayed too long, otherwise most of the capable students will be working on the staffs of the school paper or other school publications and will not be available for work on the annual.

The size of the book will, of course, determine the number of assistants needed to do the job. Editorial assistants for a medium-sized annual are two or three assistant or associate editors, a photographic editor, administration editor, class editor, organizations editor, feature editor, sports editor, and student photographer.

KANSAS STATE UNIVERSITY
BOARD OF STUDENT PUBLICATIONS
(This form is to be accompanied by a letter stating qualifications in detail.)

NOTE

Date ...., 19.....

Applications for Royal Purple or Collegian executive positions filled by the Board of Student Publications of Kansas State University are made with the understanding that mem of the business staff who are paid for their work agree not to solicit advertising or do other advertising work for any other publication, within the city limits of Manhattan, during the period for which they are employed. This prohibition includes vacation periods. The Board of Student Publications reserves the right to discharge any executive or other employee, for cause, at any time.

I, ... hereby apply for the position of .... for the .... I am carrying .... hours during the current semester and expect to earn at least as many points as the number of hours carried (required for eligibility for this position).

My grade point average in all college work up to the beginning of this semester, was .... for .... hours. After this semester, I expect to have .... hours of college work left to complete for graduation.

My major field (curriculum) in college work is .... and I am particularly interested in the following minor fields: ....

....

My journalistic experience or background includes the following:
1. Experience on Student Publications (give years of service in any capacity, staff positions held, etc.)

....

....

....

2. Experience on other publications (give name of publication, capacity in which you worked,—executive experience as well as other):

....

....

....

3. College journalism courses taken, if any, and grades in those courses:

....

....

....

4. Other special qualifications not covered above:

....

....

....

In making this application, I understand that the executives of student publications are representatives of the Board of Student Publications and as such responsible to the Board, which in turn represents the entire college and its student body. If I am selected, therefore, I expect to keep in mind the fact that the publication represents the entire student body, both on the campus and in the eyes of the people of the state.

SIGNED ....

Manhattan Address ....

Telephone ....

REFERENCES
Following are the names of references who are acquainted with my background and capabilities (at least three, more if you wish).

NAME	ADDRESS	OCCUPATION
1	....	....
2	....	....
3	....	....
4	....	....

FIGURE 2.1. A form of this kind requires the applicant to list his qualifications in an orderly manner and list three references. The last paragraph helps him to realize his responsibility to the annual and the school.

At least two or three of the assistant editors should be selected from the lower classes so they will be getting experience to aid in publishing future yearbooks. Assistant editors should be capable of writing copy, headlines and cutlines, editing copy, and reading proof. The section editors should work on the book from the very beginning of the school year. The editor can show each section editor the plans for his part of the book. The section editor can aid in obtaining the photographs and identifications, and can be in an excellent position to write the copy needed when the section goes to the printer. A large university book sometimes has as many as 100 persons working on the yearbook staff. For example, the sports editor might need several assistants to complete the job on time. He may have different assistants in charge of major, minor, intramural, and women's sports. Other large sections or chapters of the book also may require several individuals to do the job. Often 15 or 20 persons are needed to do typing, filing, and mounting of photographs, to issue photo and other receipts, to prepare an index of the book, and to do needed office work. However, if the work is departmentalized with a capable section editor in charge of each chapter in the book, much greater efficiency is assured, and many of the details of the undertaking are taken off the shoulders of the editor.

The editor should have time to read every line of copy that goes into the book, because he, and he alone, is held responsible for the job. He ought to outline to each assistant in detail the kind of copy he wants and insist that it be written as wanted. Above all, he must insist upon accuracy, accuracy, accuracy. He can inspire the staff to do a good job by his industry, efficiency, and enthusiasm. He should give praise for work well done, and if some writer does an excellent job, reward him with a by-line.

Duties of the Business Manager

It may sometimes seem to the business manager of an annual that most of the honors for the production of a good book go to the editor, but the business manager has just as important a job and often is kept busy doing it long after the editorial staff has written the last line of copy and sent the last proof back to the printer.

He must exercise the same judgment as the editor in selecting his assistants and can use many of the same methods.

Business assistants required for efficient production of a medium-sized annual are two or three assistant managers, a circulation manager, advertising manager, office manager, and bookkeeper.

Most of the assistants listed will need several persons to help them. The circulation manager, even in a small school, will require a circulation assistant in each class to sell the annuals and collect the money. In a large university he often has as many as 50 salesmen in the different schools, organizations, and dormitories.

His general duties can be summarized as:

1. Selecting and supervising the work of business assistants.
2. Preparing the budget (with the editor and the adviser).
3. Letting contracts (with the editor).
4. Conducting book sales campaign.
5. Selling advertising and preparing it for the printer.
6. Exploiting all sources of revenue as planned in the budget.
7. Supervising bookkeeping and business records.
8. Distributing the annual and closing up the book affairs.

Get Experienced Printer

The staff must select a printer who not only has the know-how of book printing but who also has the equipment and trained workmen to do the job. The printer will do most of his work after the photographs have been taken and the copy written. In spite of this, the complete plans for the book should be discussed in detail with him while this work is still in the preliminary stages.

Work Out Detailed Specifications

Printing and binding is the largest single item of expense in producing the annual. It is necessary to establish what this cost will be before definite plans can progress very far. The only way the printer can estimate the cost of his work is to know in detail the kind of book wanted. It is usually advantageous to the staff to contract with the printer to do the complete job of printing and binding the book, as well as furnishing the paper and covers. A written contract should be drawn up and signed, covering these details:

1. The number of books to be printed.
2. Number of pages, trimmed size of page, type size of page, and size of type to be used.
3. Quality and weight of paper to be used.
4. Special sections to be printed in more than one color.
5. Method of binding.
6. Kind of covers to be used.
7. Conditions to be met for delivery.
8. Price for extra copies and extra pages, and deductions for fewer copies and fewer pages.
9. Total amount to be paid and terms of payment.

Number of Books To Be Printed

It is seldom possible to tell the printer the exact number of books wanted until after the book sales campaign has been conducted. This campaign should be conducted soon after school opens in the fall. It is usually safe to estimate about the same number of books that have been sold on the average for the previous three or four years. The printer can be advised of the exact number of books wanted several months before the delivery date. He should be notified in plenty of time so he can order the number of covers and the quantity of paper needed, and estimate the time required in the print shop and bindery.

Number and Size of Pages To Be Printed

The number of pages the book is to contain will have to be estimated in the same manner as number of books wanted. The exact number can be specified after the staff has had a chance to see how the estimated budget is being met. The detailed budget is discussed in a later chapter.

There are three page sizes commonly used in printing annuals. They are 9 by 12 inches, 8½ by 11 inches, and 7¾ by 10⅝ inches. Sizes given are the finished or trimmed size of the pages. These sizes are used most frequently because they can be printed 4, 8, or 16 pages at a time, and then folded and trimmed with minimum waste.

Sample Printing Contract

Printers specializing in yearbook production have printed contracts outlining the conditions under which they propose to work with the staff. Shown in Figure 2.2 is a contract used by one of the yearbook specialists. Before signing any contract the editor, business manager, adviser, and in most cases a school administrator should read it carefully and understand all terms of the agreement.

General terms of the agreement are outlined in the left-hand column of the contract, Figure 2.2. The specifications and price to be charged for your particular annual can be entered in the right-hand column. It's important that all the specifications be covered fully and in a manner that both parties to the contract understand.

In the item-by-item discussion of the specifications that follows, an effort is made to point out where the detailed specifications can be entered in the contract, Figure 2.2. The blanks to be filled in are in the right-hand column and have been numbered 1 through 11 and are referred to by

number only as detailed specifications are discussed. The number of books and pages wanted can be entered under item 3 and trim size of pages under item 2.

Kind of Composition

An important factor determining the price charged for your annual, as well as its general appearance, is the method used by the printer to reproduce the copy you write for the yearbook. The two methods commonly used in printing yearbooks are linotype composition and "cold type" composition.

The two methods are discussed in detail in the chapter on layout. If you are not familiar with printing, you should study the information presented in that chapter carefully before placing your printing contract. This book is an example of linotype composition, except for examples reproduced to show the cold type method. The next paragraph is an example of cold type composition with justified margins.

Each year the senior journalism class accepts the responsibility of writing and editing the school paper and annual. In order to do a better job, the class has divided itself into two staffs. The majority of the students work on the BOOSTER with Mary Sullivan as editor-in-chief, and another group works with Carol O'Neal, TURNERITE editor-in-chief. The work of both staffs is under the guidance and sponsorship of Mr. Jack Knowles.

This class has an atmosphere all its own with typewriters beating out the history of your school and cameras catching its spirit in action. It's a class where experience is the real teacher. It is a place where students get an opportunity to write, to explore the field of journalism, and to bring their experience to life for the benefit of the school, the community, and their fellow classmates.

The following paragraph is an example of cold type composition with unjustified margins.

THE SWEETHEART BALL, the first of the two annual formal dances, was held on the evening of January 28. The spacious mess hall, transformed for the occasion into a fairyland of hearts and flowers, was filled to capacity. The music was furnished by the Freddy-Joe Orchestra. Faculty members, Cadets and their dates pronounced the affair one of the best ever held on the campus.

The second formal dance will be the Military Ball just before graduation.

The kind of composition purchased should be entered under item No. 1 of the sample contract.

Miss
Mrs.
Ship to Mr. _____ Title_____
                          Please Print

School_____ Phone_____ Date_____

Street Address_____ City_____ State_____

Yearbook Title_____ Year_____ Date Seniors Leave_____ Shipping Date_____

THE AGREEMENT IS:

Subject to approval of the Company and changes must be in writing and approved by the school and American Yearbook Company. No verbal agreements are binding.

All materials and complete instructions will be provided to the school. Layouts are to be prepared in accordance with Company's copy preparation instructions.

Specifications on number of copies, type of paper and color of end sheets, additional color, and complete cover information are due on or before the following dates: November 15 if books ship before June 30; February 15 if books ship after July 1.

THE COMPANY exercises no control over contents; therefore, the customer agrees to indemnify and hold harmless the printer from any decree or judgment sustained against the printer based upon any civil claim or action on the grounds that any material in the yearbook violates any copyright, proprietary right or contains any matter that is libelous or scandalous or invades any person's right to privacy. The customer also agrees, upon reasonable notice from the printer, to defend any civil demand, claim, action or proceeding that may be brought or asserted against the printer.

TERMS: The school agrees to pay $2.00 deposit for each book ordered at the time of the first copy deadline, and an additional $2.00 per book or 50% of the balance due on the final copy deadline.

SHIPMENT will be made according to terms of the Copy Schedule (which is subject to the approval of the school) providing copy has been received on time according to the schedule. All shipments are F.O.B. plant and will be shipped C.O.D. unless consignment is requested and approved by the company credit department prior to the shipping date.

THE COMPANY shall not be liable for delays or losses caused by strikes, accidents, government restrictions, acts of God, or other causes beyond their control, and such delays shall not constitute a breach of contract.

ADDITIONAL SERVICE CHARGES: Overprints, reverses and mortices, $1.50 per page, if used on more than 5% of total pages; vertical headlines, 75¢ each; pictures in excess of 49 per page (64 per page 9 x 12 trim size), 5¢ each. Company art work and corrective work on school prepared copy will be charged for on an hourly basis. President Program, Bleed pages $2.00 per page additional.

_____

_____
(Signature) Student Editor or Business Manager

_____
(Signature) Yearbook Adviser

I hereby agree to receive merchandise and remit full payment as per this agreement.

_____
(Signature) School Administrator

_____
(Signature) Representative

SPECIFICATIONS AND PRICES

1. Program __Linotype_____

2. Trim Size __9 x 12 Page__ Trim Size

3. Copies __1,000__ Pages __200_____ $ __Included__

4. Covers __Special Embossed_____ ⎫
   ☒ Stiff ☐ Padded   ⎬ _____
                                   ⎭

5. Binding:
   ☐ Side Stitched ☐ Saddle Stitched   _____
   ☒ Smythe-Sewed ☐ _____

6. End Sheets __Process Color Printed____ _____

7. Paper __100# No. 1 Enamel_____ _____

8. Proofs __Page Proofs (Pictures with type)__

9. Additional Specifications _____ _____
   __16 Pages of Duotone (2 colors) and__ _____
   __2 Pages of 4 Color Process_____ _____

   _____ _____

10. _____ TOTAL $ __2,695.00__

TYPE OF COPY SCHEDULE

11. Final Copy due March 1st, 1965 _____

EDI-KIT INFORMATION

F-P-or Multiples
Ship Kit_____ or ☐ August
                  (Date)

To_____

Include: Quantity

☐ Subscription Receipts   _____

☐ Advertising Section Materials _____

☐ Division Page Manual   ☐ Art Manuals

Regent Programs: Mounting Boards: ☐ Oversize ☐ Page Size

SPECIAL INSTRUCTIONS

Correspond with_____

_____

_____

SALES	TIME TABLE	KIT	SPECS	COPY ACK	FILE

11-63/600/29   THIS COPY TO PLANT

FIGURE 2.2. This is a common form of contract used by printers specializing in school yearbook printing and binding. It should be read carefully by the staff and the adviser and its terms clearly understood before signing.

The printer sometimes wants to know the type size to be used if he is to make a close estimate of the cost of printing the book. For instance, it requires 12 lines of 6-point type to fill a space one inch high, but only six lines of 12-point type to fill the same space. Then, too, many more characters must be set to fill the line if the smaller size type is used.

The printer may want to know the type area of the page so he can estimate the cost of setting the type to fill this space. He also should be shown the dummy, and his attention should be called to any illustrations that are to bleed or extend outside the type page. Illustrations that have to be arranged for special layouts of this kind often require extra work by the printer. In some cases a larger size sheet of paper must be purchased to permit the bleeding of many illustrations in the printed book.

Galley Proofs or Page Proofs

The contract should make clear whether the printer is to furnish proofs to the staff. It should also clarify whether galley or page proofs are to be sent. Galley proof is a trial impression of composed type to check against the original manuscript to find and correct errors or to make changes. Page proof includes not only the impression of all type but an impression of all illustrations as well. It shows all elements of the page arranged exactly as they are to appear in the finished book. While pulling proofs costs money and slows production, most staffs feel that it is worth whatever it costs to check the accuracy of each page before the book goes to press. The kind of proofs agreed upon can be noted under item 8.

Quality and Weight of Paper

It is usually safest to specify Number 1 enamel, the best grade of enamel paper. However, Number 2 enamel is sometimes used and often is quite satisfactory. It has been estimated by yearbook printers that the difference between the cost of Number 1 enamel and Number 3 enamel for the yearbook is usually less than 1½ per cent of the total budget. It would seem wise, therefore, to get a good grade of paper, as the quality of paper will greatly determine how clearly the photographs will be reproduced.

Most yearbooks are printed on 80- or 100-pound stock, usually referred to as "substance 80 lb." or "substance 100 lb.," and commonly written in contracts as:

"Paper Stock to be 25 by 38-80 (substance 80 lb.) Number 1 enamel."

This means that one ream (500 sheets) of the paper cut to 25 by 38 inches will weigh 80 lbs.

The weight of the paper determines the thickness of the sheet. Thus, a book printed on 100-lb. enamel would be 25 per cent thicker than the same book printed on 80-lb. paper. Most printers maintain that just as good an impression can be made on 80-lb. paper as on 100-lb. paper, and this probably is true. Sometimes, however, the staff will specify 100-lb. paper to increase the thickness of the book. They will, of course, have to pay 25 per cent more for the paper used (for the same number of pages) since paper is sold on the basis of weight. In some instances 70- or 120-lb. paper is used in printing annuals. The weight and grade of paper selected would be entered under item 7.

Special Sections Printed in Color

To enhance the beauty and appeal of year books, the opening pages, division pages, and sometimes other sections of the book are printed in two, three, or four colors. The printer must have this information when estimating the cost of the job. Books usually are printed in signatures of 4, 8, 16, or 32 pages. This means that one sheet of paper will fold to make 4, 8, 16, or 32 consecutive pages of the finished book. Thus, pages to be printed in more than one color cannot be "dropped in" at any point desired by the editor without increasing the printing cost. The printer can assist the staff in arranging the color work so that it can be printed and inserted in the book at the lowest possible cost. For example, suppose the printer has a press that will print 16 pages on one sheet of paper (or in one signature), and the staff desires to have the opening section of eight pages and four division sheets printed in the same three colors (black is called a color in the printing trade). How can this be done most economically?

The printer probably would print the entire 16 pages in one signature. He would arrange the pages so that the first eight (opening pages) could be trimmed from the remainder of the printed signature and folded to make pages one to eight inclusive. He would then trim each of the four division sheets so they could be "tipped-in" at designated points in the book. A "tip-in" usually is one sheet, such as a division page, which is "tipped" or glued to a preceding or following signature in the book (or between pages eight and nine of a 16-page signature) before it is bound into a whole. This is hand work and adds materially to the cost of printing the book. The dummy should be carefully planned and paged so the color inserts will come at the end or in the middle of the printed signature. If this is not done it will be necessary for the printer to slit the folded form by hand to tip-in the division page. This again increases costs and slows production. In planning the dummy it sometimes is necessary to add or eliminate a few pages in some sections of the book so the color inserts can be economically tipped-in at the end, beginning, or middle of a signature. Color printing specifications can be entered under item 9 on the contract.

Specify Method of Binding

There are four common methods of binding yearbooks:
1. Saddle-stitched binding.
2. Side-wire stitched binding.
3. Spiral binding.
4. Smythe-sewed binding.

Saddle-stitched Binding

The saddle-stitched method of binding usually is used on books having only a few pages and a flexible cardboard or heavy paper cover. One of the advantages of this type of binding is that the pages of the book can be opened out flat when being read. This is not possible with books that are side-wire stitched. The printer must know that the book is to be saddle-stitched before a single form is printed. This is imperative because the printer will have to place the first eight pages in the book on the same signature with the last eight pages in the book (if 16-page signatures are being used). Succeeding signatures would have to be handled in the same way. After all the signatures have been printed and folded, the first signature (containing the first and last eight pages in the book) is opened flat at pages 8 and 9. The second signature is opened in the same way and placed on top of the first signature. Succeeding signatures are manipulated in the same manner, until all signatures are in order. Using a wire-stitching machine, two or three wire staples are then forced through all the signatures in the gutter of the book. These staples also pass through the cover at the same time and are clenched. Thus, all the signatures are attached to the cover forming the finished book or booklet.

Side-Wire Stitched Binding

The side-wire stitched method of binding is used on small high school annuals and on a few college yearbooks. It is probably the most economical method of binding books with too many pages to permit saddle stitching. However, the book cannot be opened out flat at the binding edge, and from this standpoint is not so satisfactory as the other methods of binding mentioned. If the book is to be side-wire stitched, the folded signatures are placed in order, one on top of the other (they are not opened in the middle). The cover is then creased and fitted around the book. Often glue is applied along the binding edge before the cover is placed in position. A wire-stitching machine then forces wire staples through the cover and the assembled pages front to back, about one-fourth inch from the binding edge. These staples are clenched by the machine, completing the operation. This method of binding is usually most satisfactory if a pliable cover stock is used. It is difficult to do a first-class job by this method with a stiff cover.

Spiral Binding Method

The spiral binding method is not used extensively on yearbooks. Printed signatures of the book are placed in order in the same manner employed for side-wire stitching. The front and back lids of the cover are put in position. The cover is not joined around the binding edge of the book. A machine is used to punch or cut slots through the cover and printed signatures about one-fourth inch from the binding edge. About one-eighth inch is then trimmed from the binding edge, so all pages will be separated. Coiled wire or plastic is then threaded through the slots to hold the cover and pages in place. This method of binding is economical and allows the pages of the book to be opened out flat. It is not advisable to print too near the binding edges of pages, as some of the printed material would be destroyed when holes for binding are punched. This method of binding is not so substantial as some of the other methods, but will give excellent service if the book is handled with care.

Smythe-sewed Binding Most Satisfactory

Smythe-sewed binding, of which this book is an example, is the most satisfactory method of binding an annual. It is durable, allows easy opening of the book, and usually is employed when a stiff cover is used. The durability of the sewed binding depends upon how well the forms are sewed to the cloth which holds them together. This cloth is then carried over to the front and back lid of the cover and glued underneath the fly leaf. It is a good plan, on books containing many pages, to specify that heavy re-enforcing tapes be sewed to the forms and glued under the end sheet in addition to the cloth joint.

Side-stitched Book Hard To Open

McCain sewed or side-stitched binding is sometimes used on small annuals to save money but the results achieved are not very satisfactory. The signatures are arranged in the same manner as for side-wire stitched binding but are sewed with thread instead of being wire stitched. The book cannot be opened out flat at the binding edge and this is not so satisfactory as the Smythe-sewed binding discussed above. Type of binding can be entered under item 5.

Specify Kind of Cover Wanted

The printer must know the kind of cover wanted for the annual if he is to estimate the cost of this item. There are many types of covers available. The printer usually can show samples and give approximate costs of the various kinds. Since the yearbook is a memory book and will be kept by the owner for many years, it is well to purchase as good a cover as the budget will allow. Small yearbooks are sometimes bound in tough, flexible cardboard covers. These are manufactured in many colors and finishes.

Stiff Binding Commonly Used

The most satisfactory cover for the annual is a stiff binding similar to that used on textbooks, novels, and other books kept and used over a period of years. The weight or thickness of the binding board selected is usually determined by the number of pages in the annual. The more pages the book contains, the thicker the binding board needed to properly protect it.

Four Kinds of Covers Offered

The four ordinary classifications of covers offered to the yearbook staff are: special embossed, standard embossed, silk screened, and lithographed or printed. These classifications are determined by the method used in applying to the cover the design and lettering desired by the staff. The printer can show the different kinds of covers available at the time the contract is let. The classification of cover selected can be entered under item 4.

The color selected for the cover should be in harmony with the general color scheme of the annual. The lettering and any printed or embossed design used on the cover will be more effective if it employs the same style of lettering and art work as the theme or general plan of the book.

Printed End Sheets Often Used

Specifications concerning the printing of end sheets should be entered under item 6. The end sheets, folded sheets of heavy paper used to fasten the bound pages of the book to the cover, are often printed in one or more colors.

Conditions for Delivery

The specifications should give the date the books are to be delivered. To meet this delivery date, the printer must have the copy at definitely scheduled times. When the schedule is set up, it must be followed. If the staff is three or four days late getting copy to the printer, the delivery of the books may be delayed several weeks because the printer may have other jobs scheduled for the presses and the bindery and would have to cease working on the annual until it can again be worked into his production schedule.

The printer must have the copy in plenty of time if he is to do a good job of printing and binding the yearbook. He knows better than anyone else how much time will be required to do the job. Some printers demand that all copy for the yearbook be delivered to them several months before the delivery date of the book. You are not justified in entering into an agreement of this kind without making a serious effort to find a printer who can do the job in less time. After all, you owe a responsibility to the purchasers of the book. Students buying the annual have a right to expect the book to give as complete a history of the school year as possible. If copy must be delivered several months before the book is distributed, only the activities of the first half of the year can be covered adequately.

Final Copy Deadline

The price charged for yearbook printing is contingent upon when final copy is received by the printer. For example, if the final deadline for a spring delivery book is set as February 15, the discount from the regular price might be as much as 5 or 10 per cent. However, few staffs are willing to miss the coverage of most of the second semester happenings. The final copy date can be entered under item 11.

Extra Pages and Extra Copies

It usually is not possible to specify the exact number of books and pages wanted at the time the contract is made with the printer. The agreement should have a clause stating the price for additional books and also the amount to be deducted for fewer books than specified in the contract. It is standard practice to state the price for additional signatures of eight or 16 pages, and the deductions from the contract price are made on the same basis. However, the printer must know the number of books and number of pages wanted before covers and paper are ordered and before the first form is printed.

Terms of Payment

The contract will set forth the total amount to be paid the printer for work and materials furnished. Since the printer usually is the last concern to work on the annual and hence the last to be paid, he is justified in demanding satisfactory guarantee of payment or in shipping the books C.O.D. The terms of payment and time of shipment of the yearbook are covered, in the sample contract Figure 2.2, under "Terms" and "Shipment" in the left-hand column. The total amount to be paid can be entered at the bottom of the right-hand column, item 10.

Letterpress Specifications

The specifications and contract just discussed are for an annual printed by offset. However, the same specifications can be used for yearbooks printed by the letterpress method, except it will be necessary to remember that all illustrations and pictures will require separate engravings. The cost of these engravings must be added to the printing quotation. Usually a separate contract is made directly with an engraving company.

Select Printer Who Will Do Good Job

Selecting your printer and letting the contract for the printing of your annual is one of the most important decisions you will make during the entire year. Subscribers to the yearbook expect you to do a complete and accurate job of editing. They also expect you to select a printer who will do a first-class job of printing.

Yearbook staffs and advisers and administrators sometimes become too interested in saving money. To save money and get out an inferior annual is no virtue. You owe it to the school and to yourself to hire a printer who has demonstrated his ability to do the best job possible with the pictures and copy you will furnish. You need to work out a contract that will cover all of the niceties that are required to make a first-class yearbook and one that the school can be proud of.

When the school board lets a contract for a new high school building, the taxpayers expect a beautiful building providing all the classrooms, laboratories, and equipment needed to provide superior educational opportunities for the students of the community. The students who selected you to edit their annual expect you to spend the money they provide to get out the best book you can. You were elected to *get out* a yearbook not liquidate it. Remember, "The yearbook is like a diamond; it's forever!" It needs to be elegant.

Building Staff Morale

One of the most effective ways to build staff morale is to give some kind of special recognition near the end of the year to staff members who have done meritorious work on the annual. A certificate, or better still, a gold key or pin can be presented to these students at a special banquet or assembly. The gold key seems to be more prized by the students, and the fact that the pins are worn with pride encourages other students to try for this special recognition.

The students to be thus honored can be nominated by the editor, business manager, and faculty adviser with the approval of the board of publications. Adequate publicity should be given in the local and school newspapers and, of course, the students' names and pictures ought to appear in the annual. The individuals who receive special recognition must be selected with the greatest of care and with absolute fairness, or the purpose for which the award is being made will lose its significance. All staff members should know early in the year the basis on which the selections are made. The plan of the *Royal Purple*, Kansas State University, Manhattan, is to have the editor and business manager rate each student on the respective staffs, using an appraisal form developed for the purpose. The adviser fills out the same form for all students on the staff. Thus the opinion of the individuals who should know about the work of each student is a matter of record.

The appraisal form used to rate the editorial staff is shown in Figure 2.3, and the one for the business staff in Figure 2.4. These forms can be posted in the yearbook office in the fall so all workers will know the requirements for winning an award. Just being on the staff does not win the award; only excellence is rewarded.

Maintain Staff Morale

Of course, the most effective way to maintain staff morale is to builld a tradition of high performance and success by producing the best annual possible year after year. Several schools in America have built great traditions for winning sports teams. Too few have done as well in the field of publications.

Building a tradition of success in producing outstanding yearbooks is a slow and arduous task. In the beginning the esprit de corps will be as a small trickle of water in a dry creek, but can become as a mighty river if properly nurtured. The goal can be accomplished by selecting staff members of fine ability and high character and by constantly feeding their imagination with the wine of high resolve to live in the tradition of the editors who have gone before.

"Yes, it's easy to maintain staff morale and win high ratings after the tradition has been established but we don't have anything to build on," is the complaint of some staffs. Do you really want to produce the best yearbook your school ever had? Do you want to win an All-American or Medalist rating? It's not easy. But high ratings are not the exclusive property of rich schools or those with long traditions of winning.

That honor goes to the staff that's willing to work all year, including all summer and during school vacations. It requires not only hard work and long hours, but knowledge about what makes a good yearbook. It demands enthusiasm, talent, and even diplomacy.

After you have finished reading this textbook or attended a workshop, don't stop studying or working. Get other textbooks, instruction books, subscribe to scholastic magazines, and study good yearbooks from other schools. Have frequent meetings with your staff and assign each member something to do or study. Meet often with your photographer and printer. They can help you to plan and produce the kind of a book that will be a winner.

Royal Purple Editorial

(Circle your opinion on each item)

	1 Poor	2 Below Average	3 Average	4 Above Average	5 Outstanding
1. Ability to produce good results while working under pressure	1	2	3	4	5
2. Initiative (Does this person take intelligent action on his own, or wait to be told what to do?)	1	2	3	4	5
3. Acceptance of responsibility (Does this person willingly take over difficult and important assignments and show a willingness to be judged on the merits of his own work, or does he try to dodge such assignments and pass responsibility to others?)	1	2	3	4	5
4. Influence on fellow workers (Does this person tend to inspire others to work harder and produce better results, or is his presence a discordant factor?)	1	2	3	4	5
5. Adaptability to varied assignments	1	2	3	4	5
6. Contribution beyond the requirements of his job	1	2	3	4	5
7. Speed in completing assignments	1	2	3	4	5
8. Thoroughness and accuracy in copywriting	1	2	3	4	5
9. Meeting deadlines	1	2	3	4	5
10. Understanding of the mechanical problems bearing on yearbook work	1	2	3	4	5
11. Attention to routine details	1	2	3	4	5
12. Ability to understand and to follow instructions	1	2	3	4	5

Appraisal Form
for K-Key Awards

Name of Student
Being Appraised_____

Royal Purple Business

(Circle your opinion on each item)

	1 Poor	2 Below Average	3 Average	4 Above Average	5 Outstanding
1. Ability to produce good results while working under pressure	1	2	3	4	5
2. Initiative (Does this person take intelligent action on his own, or wait to be told what to do?)	1	2	3	4	5
3. Acceptance of responsibility (Does this person willingly take over difficult and important assignments and show a willingness to be judged on the merits of his own work or docs he try to dodge such assignments and pass responsibility to others?)	1	2	3	4	5
4. Influence on fellow workers (Does this person tend to inspire others to work harder and produce better results, or is his presence a discordant factor?)	1	2	3	4	5
5. Meeting deadlines	1	2	3	4	5
6. Contribution beyond the requirements of the job	1	2	3	4	5
7. Effort to improve own work	1	2	3	4	5

MARK FOR OFFICE STAFF ONLY:

8. Competence in following instructions	1	2	3	4	5
9. Accuracy	1	2	3	4	5
10. Regular in attendance	1	2	3	4	5

MARK FOR BUSINESS STAFF ONLY:

8. Ability to make layouts that truly visualize the finished advertisement	1	2	3	4	5
9. Understanding of mechanical problems bearing on advertising	1	2	3	4	5
10. Attendance at meetings	1	2	3	4	5

FIGURE 2.3. (shown on the opposite page). The appraisal form for editorial workers requires the editor and adviser to rate each worker in 12 categories. The grade can range from one to five points in each category.

FIGURE 2.4. Appraisal form for business staff requires each student be rated in ten categories. The first seven are the same for all, while three categories are for office workers, and three for advertising staff members.

Chapter 3

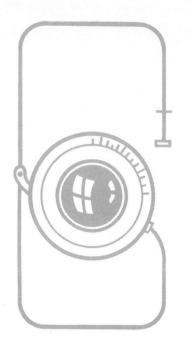

There are many kinds of pictures that help tell the story of the school year. Getting the right ones requires skill, patience, and careful planning. This dramatic picture is a fine example of what is needed. Courtesy of the 1965 Gopher, University of Minnesota, Minneapolis.

Getting Pictures That Tell the Story

PICTURES ARE the basic ingredient of an annual. To make your publication outstanding today, you need good photographs more than ever before. The pictures should be true, literate, and as interpretive as the written word. They must convey *exact* meaning to the reader. Readers, exposed to thousands of pictures in newspapers and magazines and to dramatic scenes on TV, will quickly recognize dull and uninteresting pictures. Thus every member of the staff who has anything to do with planning coverage of events, the kind of picture to be taken, how it will be displayed on the page, and finally what the copy and cutline will say needs to know what gives a photograph interest and impact.

A complaint often heard is that photographers are temperamental. Yes, they are temperamental; so are yearbook editors and advisers. They are human beings. If they are not temperamental, they probably don't care enough about excellence. You need to remember that good pictures are taken by people, not cameras. If a published picture is to achieve its goal, there must be

intelligent cooperation among all staff members concerned all the way along the line. Don't let some lazy person ruin a good idea just because he is not doing his job. Get someone who cares.

Photographer Must Be on Job

Getting satisfactory pictures of news events or significant happenings is much more difficult than covering the same events as a news reporter. The reporter, if he is delayed, can almost always find out what has happened, and write his story. The photographer, on the other hand, must be there when it happens, and be in position to get a picture that will tell the story.

If interesting and complete pictorial coverage of the important events of the year is to be obtained, someone with a camera must "cover the waterfront" at all hours of the day and night. If the school's flashy halfback breaks away for a 60-yard touchdown run against an old rival, the yearbook photographer must be ready on the sidelines or near the end zone with a camera. The teams will not run through the play a second time just so a picture can be taken.

Pictorial Quality

Sparkling reproductions and beautiful printing cannot be expected unless you have top quality photographs to start with. The printer can make slight improvements in the reproduction qualities of some photographs, but he must use an expensive process of air brushing, retouching, and re-etching. Yearbook editors seldom resort to this process because of the expense. Photographs seldom look as attractive on the finished pages as they do before going through the printing process. Some of the detail is usually lost even by the best printers.

Photographs with detail in both the highlights and shadows will reproduce best. Prints that show too much contrast often have a chalky appearance in the highlights, while the shadows are too dark. All prints should be made on glossy paper. Uniform contrast is necessary in all pictures used in a composite cut, such as a snapshot page or class panel. It is important to reject any prints that have brown, gray, or yellow tones. Black tones reproduce best.

Good Equipment Needed

A cardinal rule for yearbook staffs to remember is that their yearbook can be only as good as the pictures it contains. Many otherwise good yearbooks have been disappointing because the staffs accepted pictures that were poor in quality. Some of the more common defects to watch out for are: under- or overexposure, out of focus, poor composition of the subject, scratches, fingerprints, and other marks due to careless handling during processing.

"Many pictures used in publications are too small, dull, dark, and have no impact," according to Clifton C. Edom, a leading teacher of photography and professor of journalism, University of Missouri.

Under ideal conditions, good quality pictures can be produced with relatively inexpensive equipment. However, the pictorial coverage by the yearbook usually requires meeting all kinds of adverse conditions, thus demanding more photographic equipment than many smaller schools own. One solution to this is to employ a commercial photographer to take pictures for the annual.

Individual class pictures and large group pictures are often taken by a commercial photographer. It usually is not satisfactory to have activity or news pictures taken by a commercial photographer because he is not available when interesting and spontaneous events occur. Then, too, it robs students of an excellent opportunity to learn to take pictures and to thus contribute to the yearbook and the school.

Therefore, you may decide to purchase equipment, a few pieces at a time, as funds permit. This plan is recommended, especially if the school has a faculty member capable of supervising and training student photographers. No amount of expensive equipment will produce good pictures, however, unless persons who use the equipment thoroughly understand its operation. For this reason, look for versatility and simplicity of operation when buying photographic equipment.

Basic Types of Cameras Available

Three basic types of cameras are used extensively by news and yearbook photographers. Each camera has a distinct purpose but is able to take a variety of pictures.

Advantages and Disadvantages of the Press 4x5

The 4x5 in. press camera is probably the most famous and for many years was standard equipment for all press photographers. It is still being used by many newspaper and yearbook photographers. It was one of the first to be equipped with a flash gun, making it possible to take pictures under almost all conditions.

The press camera is excellent for taking views and small or medium-sized groups. It is adaptable to certain types of action and individual shots. It provides a large 4x5 in. negative which is helpful for retouching and quick processing. It uses cut film or film packs, making it possible to take and develop one or more pictures at a time instead of waiting until a complete roll has been exposed. Properly used, this camera will produce high quality photographs. It is a tough, durable camera and will give years of service when properly cared for.

The chief disadvantage of the 4x5 in. press camera is that it is expensive, both to buy and to operate. It gives good results when you have time to compose the picture, but it is difficult to handle in crowded areas and to use for quick action or candid shots. It is heavy to carry and often the photographer does not have it with him when it is needed to get pictures of unexpected events.

35mm Camera Popular

The 35-millimeter camera has caught the enthusiasm of amateurs as well as many professional photographers. It is light and easy to handle. Many enthusiasts carry one with them at all times, to be ready to take pictures at a moment's notice. It has a large film capacity—20 to 36 exposures per roll. Because the film is small and inexpensive, the cameraman can take several shots of each event, thus increasing his chances of getting an outstanding pictures. The 35mm, because of the many different kinds of lenses available for the expensive models, has a scope that larger cameras cannot equal. Many pictures required by an annual can be taken with a 35mm camera and available light.

The 35mm is a delicate piece of equipment to operate and is too complicated for any but the most dedicated amateurs. It is a camera that should be owned and cared for by one person rather than being available for use by several different individuals. Its biggest drawback is the difficulty of properly processing the tiny film and getting satisfactory enlargement prints. The negative must be handled with extreme care to avoid scratches, dust damage, and grain—any one of which can ruin the final results.

Twin-Lens Reflex Most Versatile

The twin-lens reflex $2\frac{1}{4}$x$2\frac{1}{4}$ in. camera incorporates many of the good points of the two cameras just discussed and has few of the drawbacks mentioned. It is lightweight and easy to handle. Many models are inexpensive to buy and to operate. The film produced is large enough to insure satisfactory enlargements. It chief disadvantage is that often a flash must be used. However, if the camera is equipped to use an electronic flash, the cost is not great. Then, too, with the ad-

FIGURE 3.1. This series of shots covers the introduction of the homecoming queen. Note the versatility of results with the 35mm camera, which recorded close-ups of individuals as well as mob scenes all in perfect focus.

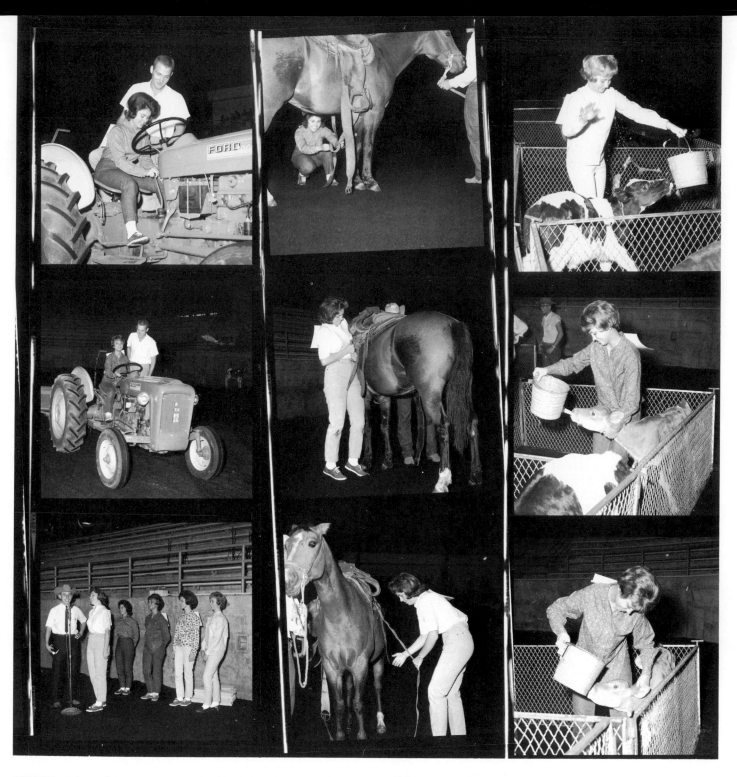

FIGURE 3.2. This series of contact prints was taken with a 2¼ x 2¼ with-lens reflex camera and illustrates its ability for detail. The three pictures in the right-hand column show satisfactory action shots.

vent of film with an ASA of 400 or more, flash is becoming much less necessary for this type of camera. It is probably the basic camera that should be purchased for a yearbook staff; other types can be added as money is available. Shown in Figure 3.1 are contact prints made from 35mm film, and Figure 3.2 shows 2¼x2¼ in. contact prints.

Order Enlargements Promptly

As soon as contact prints are received, the editor should study them carefully, select the ones wanted, and order the enlargements. Study the contact prints through a magnifying glass or reading glass for imperfections and to determine if individuals pictured have satisfactory facial expressions. Check to see that eyes are open. Sometimes you will want the photographer to enlarge only a part of the picture and you must so indicate.

Many Photographers Furnish Own Camera

Today thousands of students own their own photographic equipment including cameras with an assortment of lenses, light meters, flash guns, and almost anything that's manufactured for professional photographers. Many yearbooks now depend upon the best of such students to take practically all of the activity shots as well as group and candid shots.

A plan that works well in most schools is to recruit three or four of the most talented camera owners as staff members. Actually many are semi-professionals and have been taking and selling pictures of parties, weddings, and other activities in the school and community for several years. Some even "string" for newspapers and press associations.

If this plan is to be used, some additional equipment may be needed in the darkroom for processing the pictures. The darkroom should be carefully supervised by a faculty member to see that it is kept in first-class condition and that each student has a specified time to use the facility.

Prints Often Purchased by Staff

As an incentive, most yearbooks pay the student photographer for each picture used in the publication. If he furnishes his own film, paper, and developer the price usually ranges from $2.00 to $3.00 per print depending on the size enlargement required. More, of course, is paid for color work. This method of getting pictures for the annual is growing in popularity each year, and is producing excellent results at less cost than buying cameras and equipment for the staff.

Formal and Informal Pictures

Pictures required for a yearbook fall into two general classifications, formal and informal.

FIGURE 3.3. Uniform head sizes and a neutral gray background make the entire panel pleasing in appearance. Leaving a uniform amount of space around each head is also effective.

FIGURE 3.4. This group of 38 is properly arranged and posed on a specially constructed platform. The face of each individual is plainly visible and large enough to be easily recognized and properly identified.

Sometimes they are classified as "studio" and "action" shots. Individual photographs to be used in a class section usually are more satisfactory if a neutral or light gray background is used as shown in Figure 3.3. The gray background contrasts well with hair, face, and clothing. Much better detail comes in both highlights and darker portions of the portrait than if a white or black background is used.

A uniform head-size for all pictures used in a composite panel must be adopted if expense and time are to be cut to the minimum, and if the finished engraving is to look good. The photographer can insure uniform head-size on all class pictures by using some device to measure the distance from the point of the chin to the eyebrows when the image of the subject is reflected on the ground glass of his camera. Some photographers prefer to have the distance from the chin to top of the head the same in all pictures. This plan, too, gives good results.

Some schools use individual pictures arranged in panels for the organization section. This is satisfactory if all students in school have photographs taken for use in the class section. In many schools only the seniors appear in the class section. If individual pictures are demanded for organizations in these schools, many students will not have pictures taken because of the high cost of individual portraits. If group pictures are taken of organizations, the cost to each individual will be

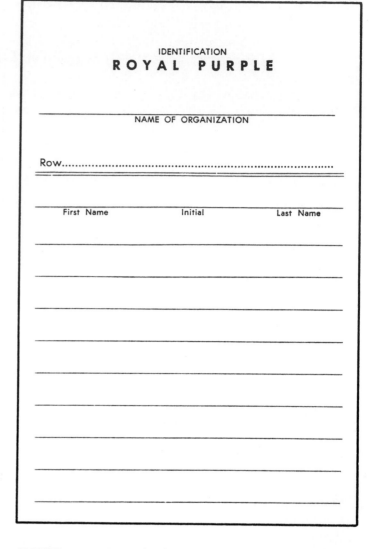

FIGURE 3.5. Printed identification slips like this, attached to clipboards, can be passed simultaneously down each row in a group (from right to left) just before a group picture is taken and after the individuals have been arranged as they will appear in the picture.

FIGURE 3.6. This group of 17 is arranged informally around a table. Each face is visible and large enough to be recognized. This kind of arrangement adds variety.

FIGURE 3.7. Catching the happy mood of the moment, as in this informal group, gives the annual impact.

small, and more students will have their pictures in the annual. This plan will make a more complete memory book and increase book sales.

Arrangements of Large Groups

Large groups should be posed so all faces will be as large as possible in the limited space provided. The individuals in the group to be photographed must be arranged so the heads of those in each successive row will appear between the heads of those in the row directly in front. In photographing large groups, best results can be achieved in a studio or room set aside for this purpose. A platform constructed as a series of stairsteps is essential for the best results. Such a platform 18 feet long, containing four steps, will accommodate a group of about 60. The steps should be approximately 10 inches wide and each succeeding step about 11 inches higher than the one in front. This arrangement will force the individuals in each succeeding row to stand close to the row in front of them and also bring the heads to the proper height so they will not be hidden

from the camera. This compact arrangement makes it possible to get the people in both the front and back rows in sharp focus. Few studios are equipped with a camera that will get a good picture of more than 60 persons at one time. Best results will be obtained by dividing large organizations or classes into groups of 40 to 50 students. Then the faces will be large enough to be easily recognized when the picture is reproduced in the book. An example of an excellent arrangement of a large group is shown in Figure 3.4. A time-saving method of obtaining identification of every individual in each group is shown in Figure 3.5.

Informal Group Pictures

Informal pictures of small groups add interest and variety to the book. As many as 15 to 20 persons can be photographed effectively in an informal shot if care is taken to pose the group properly, as illustrated in Figures 3.6 and 3.7. The group can be shown engaged in some project sponsored by the organization, or pictured in the club's meeting place or living quarters. In an effort to get informal pictures, do not forget that the chief purpose of the organization space in the book is to show pictures of all members in such a manner that they can easily be recognized and identified.

FIGURE 3.8. "Gamma Phis yell their way to first place in the fall Pep Coordinating Council noise-making contest," according to the cutline in the *Royal Purple*. The photographer had to be alert to get this shot.

FIGURE 3.9. When a homecoming queen is introduced to the crowd by a U.S. Senator, the cameraman who gets the picture has planned every detail well in advance.

Informal pictures defeat their purpose if the faces of individuals are partly hidden, or if they are so small individual members cannot be recognized. Some books use informal or action pictures depicting the activities of organizations in addition to a group picture showing the entire membership. This is an excellent plan and adds life and interest to the section.

Pictures of Big Events

If the book is to tell a complete history of the school year, pictures must be taken of all the big events. These are sometimes called news pictures, but they also should have historical significance. The picture should be large enough to show what is happening, and the significant highlights of the event should be pictured. Event pictures will have greater interest to the reader of the annual if they create an impact on his mind, arouse his emotions, or cause him to recall interesting and pleasing happenings in which he or his friends had a part. Pictures that catch the wild enthusiasm of the participants, the radiant smile of the beauty queen, or recall such big events as a pep rally or commencement, will help make the annual a real memory book. Examples of pictures of this type are shown in Figures 3.8 to 3.11.

FIGURE 3.10. "On a chilly Halloween eve, the torch-bearer lights the bonfire for the Homecoming rally," reads the cutline. The photographer who got this picture has a sense of the dramatic and knows his camera.

Insuring Pictorial Coverage

Definite plans must be made well in advance of all events if satisfactory pictorial coverage is to be obtained. A meeting at a definite time each week is necessary to plan for all pictures that can be taken during the week. The editor of the book, photographic editor, student photographers, and faculty adviser should attend all meetings. It is sometimes desirable to have one or more section editors present, especially if plans are to be made for extensive coverage of the section of the book in which a particular editor is vitally interested. In general, the committee must be kept small so definite plans can be made without too much delay. It must be a *working* committee.

Before attending the meeting each member should make a list of all the events scheduled for the coming week. This information can be obtained by reading the school paper, the local papers, by inquiring at the office of the principal or dean of students, and from any news tips the individual members of the committee can get

about events not formally scheduled or announced. All members of the yearbook staff should be instructed to watch for spontaneous events and get in touch with the editor as quickly as possible so pictures can be obtained.

Select Events To Be Covered

With lists of all events scheduled for the week, the committee can select the events it wants covered. It is not enough to tell the photographer to cover a football game. The editor must consult his dummy and instruct the photographer on the type of picture wanted. Suppose one of the events to be covered during the week is the homecoming game. The annual should include not only action pictures of the game, but the color and pageantry connected with the football spectacle. Picture possibilities include marching bands, pep rallies, yelling rooters, cheerleaders in action, coaches on the sidelines, the team rushing onto the field, crowning of the homecoming queen, stunts during half time, press box scenes, visiting dignitaries, etc. It is difficult to get all these pictures during one game, and there would not be space in the annual to print all of them if they were taken. So it is up to the editor to select the features he wants photographed for the homecoming game and plan in detail with the photographer the best way to get them.

More effective pictures of an event are obtained when the editor and photographer discuss in detail with the person in charge of the event what will happen, when, and where it will occur. If this information is obtained well in advance, the cameraman can arrange to be at a strategic place to shoot the dramatic picture needed for the annual. Usually the person in charge of the event will be glad to cooperate and will help stage a good picture.

Bread-and-Butter Pictures

When plans have been completed to cover all the important events during the week, the committee can then make plans to get as many as possible of the non-event pictures (such as those shown in Figures 3.12 through 3.17) that are necessary to complete the yearbook. Compile, from the dummy, a list of the required pictures. In the beginning the list will be long, calling for pictures of the school buildings, students in classrooms and laboratories, faculty members, seniors, underclassmen, organizations, clubs, publications, fraternity houses, and many others. Such pictures usually can be taken at the convenience of the photographer, but some should be taken each week. In setting up a production schedule for the book, certain forms or sections of the annual must go to the printer early. Pictures for these sections are the first ones assigned to photographers. Checking the dummy often reveals that only one or two more pictures are needed to complete a page or section. These pictures are given top priority on the list of pictures to be taken that week.

Complete Arrangements for Each Picture

When it is decided what non-event, or time-

FIGURE 3.11. A sudden blast of wind, and later rain, caught these sedate marchers in unfamiliar garb. Most of the photographers laughed, but the boy who had the last laugh got this shot which was published.

FIGURE 3.12. A classroom shot similiar to this can be taken any time by getting permission of the teacher in advance and looking the situation over carefully for the best position from which to take it.

less, pictures are to be taken during the week, some member of the staff must make arrangements to get the individuals to be photographed to the proper place at the appointed time. For example, suppose ten organization groups can be accommodated at the studio during the week. The photographic editor or some responsible member of the staff must work out plans with the photographer when each group is to appear and how the group is to be arranged so the picture will fit the layout. Someone should be at the studio to get identifications of all members in the group. After plans have been completed at the studio, the president of each organization must be notified in ample time so he can get word to all members of his organization to be at the studio at the appointed time. Often he will want to instruct the members how to dress. Sometimes the organization is allowed to make its appointments directly with the studio, but even if this is done, the staff must have a definite understanding with the photographer regarding the kind of picture wanted.

Better and more usable pictures are obtained when definite plans with all parties concerned are made in advance. Often a telephone call will do the job if the picture wanted is a candid shot of a teacher, or an informal photograph of a committee. Once arrangements are made, it is up to the staff photographer to be on the job at the appointed time.

FIGURE 3.13. Take several shots in the library so you will have a choice. A tall perpendicular picture similar to this will add variety to your page layouts.

45

Care of Prints and Negatives

Negatives of all pictures should be developed as soon as possible after they are taken and preferably within a week. If the processing is done promptly, the photographer will know what results he is getting. He can determine if he is using the proper lens opening, timing, lighting, and if he is the proper distance from the subject. Sometimes the camera may not be working properly and needs adjustment or repair. If undeveloped negatives are allowed to pile up, this may not be revealed until many worthless pictures are shot.

All negatives and prints must be handled with care to obtain the best results. Commercial photographers who make pictures for the book will retain ownership and take care of the negatives. If the student photographer processes the pictures he takes, a file can be provided for keeping the negatives in good condition. Each negative is numbered in the margin with ink. The negative can then be placed in an envelope bearing the same number and filed in numerical order. If many pictures are to be used, a catalog is necessary to record the number of each negative and a short, identifying description. Contact prints are

FIGURE 3.14. Why not get pictures of that popular professor, the superintendent, and the principal the first week of school? Then you will have them when needed.

FIGURE 3.15. Some of the first bread-and-butter pictures you should take are of the editor of the yearbook or newspaper and the student body president. This is the editor of the yearbook, and the typewriter and pictures in the foreground add just the right atmosphere.

made from all negatives and delivered to the editor. Each print should have, written on the back, the negative number and any identification obtained when the shot was made. A very soft pencil must be used for this, because if much pressure is exerted when writing on the back of a print, it will make the print useless for reproduction. The number on the print is important. Often the editor will require an enlargement to fit the page layout, and the photographer can find the negative easily in his file if the proper number is given.

All prints must be handled carefully, by the edges, so no fingerprints will show when plates are made. Since prints usually have a tendency to curl, they should be placed under a stack of books for about 24 hours. They can then be filed, if it is not possible to send them immediately to the publisher. Prints should go to the printer as soon as possible, for they sometimes fade or turn brown or yellow. Then, too, the printer can start production as soon as pictures are received.

Requirements of a Good Picture

The editor, faculty adviser, photographic editor, and staff photographer should all have a thorough understanding of what constitutes a good picture and gives it a story-telling quality. A careful study of photographs in leading picture magazines, newspapers, and good yearbooks will reveal many of the requirements.

When the cameraman goes on an assignment, it is a good plan for someone to go with him to aid in posing the picture and to help plan the best method of covering the event. Often it is necessary for the assistant to prevent someone from walking between the camera and the subject to be photographed. Sometimes he must hold a chair or a stepladder for the cameraman so he can see over the heads of the crowd. Just before the picture is made, the photographer is busily concerned with adjusting his camera, and the assistant, if he knows his job, can see that all individuals to be photographed are posed as they should be. He may note that someone is looking directly at the camera or has moved slightly so that he will not be in the picture. He can take care of these details quickly.

FIGURE 3.16. It's obvious that this is no $350,000 fraternity house, but the photographer made it distinctive by shooting it from exactly the right place. Take all views early before frost as they usually photograph better before the leaves come down. Posing people in the pictures adds interest.

FIGURE. 3.17. Watch any building construction on your campus. Pick a day when something interesting is happening and get into the right spot so you can take a dramatic picture.

The photographer is focusing the camera the instant before snapping the picture and sometimes cannot see all the subjects clearly. It is up to the assistant to tip him off by a prearranged word or sign when to snap the picture. An alert assistant can be of great help in keeping the individual or individuals from freezing up just before the picture is made. He can engage them in conversation and take their minds off having their picture taken. In semi-posed pictures of this kind the photographer must strive for an off-guard effect.

Get Identifications for Pictures

The assistant can be helpful, too, in getting identifications of persons in the picture or making some notation describing the event, where it took

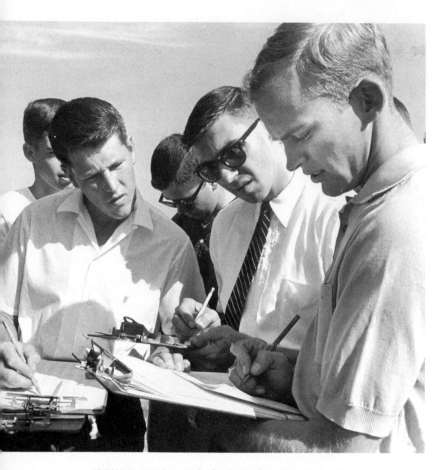

FIGURE 3.18. Tabulating the final results of a cross-country meet requires a lot of work and concentration; the photographer caught them in this close-up of a coach and his assistants.

FIGURE 3.19. "With the instrument of her trade, Jo Mapes, a folksinger for ten years, appears in Hootenany USA," reads the cutline in the *Royal Purple*. This picture with black background is a fine example of simplicity.

place, and the significance of the picture. But whether the photographer has an assistant or not, identifications should be obtained *when the picture is taken*. Besides his camera, a photographer should have a pencil and a notebook, or small cards, as a standard part of his equipment.

Many pictures for yearbooks are of spontaneous events where identification of individuals is not necessary. In semi-posed pictures, however, where a few persons are the center of interest, it may be desirable to identify those in the photograph. Then it is absolutely necessary that their names be obtained before the picture is taken. This insures getting them in the same order they will be in the picture. A lot of time can be wasted trying to find someone to identify all the persons in a photograph. Invariably, there is at least one person whom no one seems to know.

Strive for Simplicity

The photographer should make an effort, in most cases, to keep the picture simple. He ought to get as close to the subject as possible and eliminate individuals who do not add to the story. He must try to keep away from complicated or confusing backgrounds that detract. The effectiveness of simplicity is well illustrated in Figures 3.18 and 3.19.

Atmosphere Pictures

Although simplicity should be the keynote in most pictures, the reverse is sometimes true. The story behind the picture may be told in the background, in the interest of the onlookers, or the size of the crowd. The importance of pictures of this kind is shown in Figures 3.20 and 3.21. In a yearbook, pictures of this type usually have more appeal than the same kind of pictures used in a magazine of national circulation, because the story they tell reaches into the reader's life—he understands their significance.

Spontaneous Events

Spontaneous happenings offer opportunities to get pictures that have real impact on the reader's mind. Staff members often miss spontaneous pictures because they follow the dummy too closely and are not aware of the importance of spontaneous happenings. The dummy should not be followed so rigidly that it becomes a straitjacket. The plan can usually be changed to accommodate any picture that has real significance. The pictures in Figures 3.22 and 3.23 show spontaneous events.

FIGURE 3.20. Derby Darling candidates bring out plenty of interested spectators as well as a clown. The purpose of this picture is to recall the event to the reader, not to picture the winner.

FIGURE 3.21. This atmosphere picture is the exact opposite of simplicity. Its purpose is to help the reader recall the times he was one of the 12,500 screaming fans who stormed the fieldhouse for basketball games.

FIGURE 3.22. Flashcard manipulators go berserk and throw away several hundred dollars worth of cards when their team makes an unexpected touchdown. Only an alert photographer would have his camera pointed in the right direction to get such a picture.

Candid Shots

Candid shots of one person are usually hard to get, because the person having his picture taken is likely to freeze up just before the shot is made. Best results are obtained when candid pictures are snapped at an instant when the subject is off guard, perfectly relaxed, and natural. The cameraman's assistant can be a real help in obtaining pictures of this kind, if he will chat with the subject being photographed and keep the subject's mind off posing for the picture. Figures 3.24 to 3.26 inclusive are examples of good candid shots.

Available-Light Pictures

Fast film now being marketed by several film manufacturers helps one get good candid shots. This high-speed film for both cut and roll film cameras is used extensively by press and commercial photographers, who often take pictures indoors without flash bulbs or other lighting equipment.

Available- or existing-light pictures, as photographers call them, are not new, but they have become considerably more popular in recent years. This has been due partly to improved film and partly to their increased use by pictorial magazines and newspapers. They have a naturalness that is hard to capture in pictures where harsh

FIGURE 3.23. "Screams of delight run through the ranks of the Pi Phis at Interfraternity Sing after they were announced winner of the sorority division," states the cutline. Sidelights of this kind add impact.

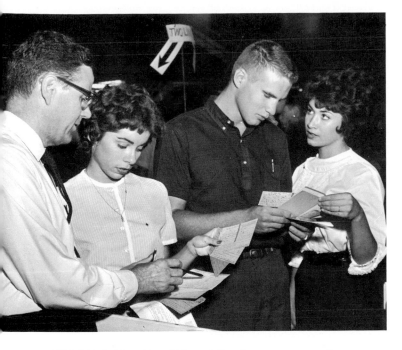

FIGURE 3.25. Bewildered freshmen at enrollment get help, and how! Candid shots of this type are much more effective than posed pictures.

FIGURE 3.24. The candid cameraman was there, as friends of Terry Biery congratulate him after he was announced Favorite Man on Campus at the Sadie Hawkins Dance. They are too happy and thrilled to know that a picture is being taken.

FIGURE 3.26. Working his way into the group around the hand warmer, the yearbook photographer came up with this outstanding picture.

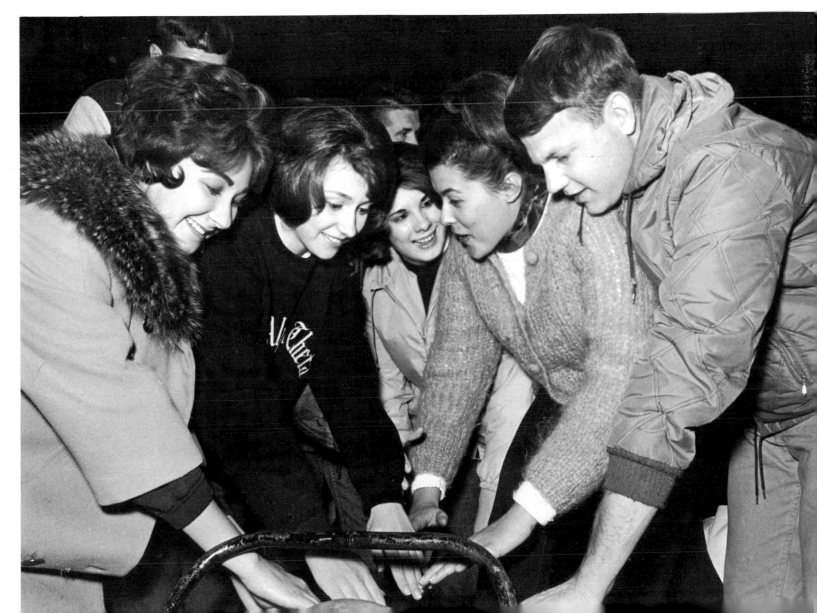

FIGURE 3.27. Surrounded by reporters, rival coaches discuss the basketball game their teams just finished.

However, the photographer was able to get this outstanding shot by using available light.

lighting is used. Examples of pictures taken under adverse conditions by available light are shown in Figures 3.27 to 3.29.

Of course, when fast film is used, the manufacturer's recommendations on both exposure and development should be followed explicitly, and the advice of an expert should be sought regarding the camera's suitability for this type of film.

Action Pictures of Athletic Events

The cameraman has no opportunity to pose action shots of athletic events. The most newsworthy picture usually is one showing the winning touchdown in a football game, the winning goal in basketball or a home run with the bases loaded in baseball. This is seldom possible because the game moves so fast that the photographer cannot always be in the proper position to get the shot. He should get as close to the action as the rules will permit and safety will allow. He must have his camera directed at the spot where he thinks the action will take place, and must have it set for the proper timing, lens opening, and focus to catch the action clearly.

Because of the speed with which he must operate, and other factors involved, many of the pictures taken will not be satisfactory. However, the results improve with practice. One sports

FIGURE 3.28. Action-packed rodeo pictures taken inside a pavilion or fieldhouse present a difficult problem. Usually the shots taken by available light give the best results, as shown in this calf-roping scene.

52

FIGURE 3.29. Four O'Clock Forum speakers tackle varied topics, such as Goldwater and Conservatism. Note the interesting facial expressions captured in this available-light shot.

FIGURE 3.30. Catching a pass for the winning touchdown is a dramatic moment in the game. Clarity of detail and the crowd in the background contribute to the effectiveness of this picture.

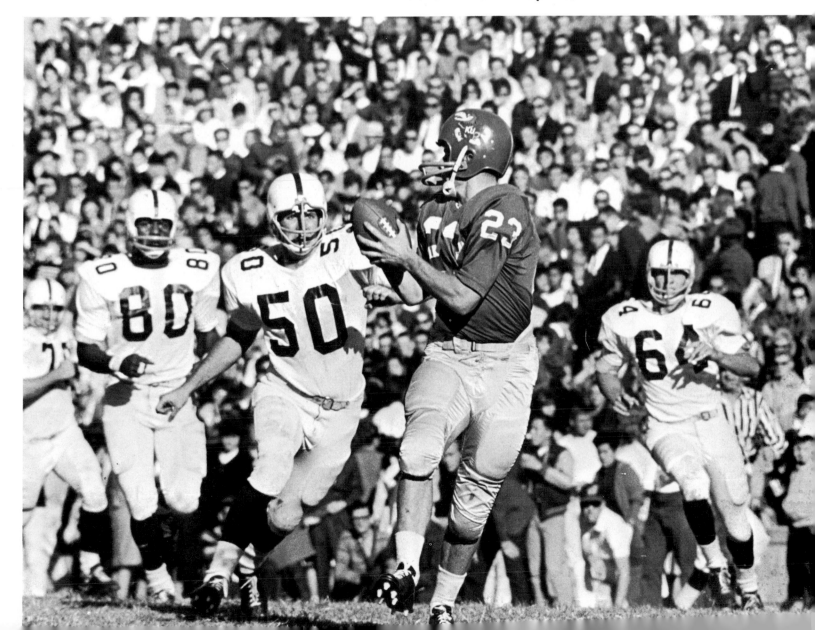

FIGURE 3.31. Anchor-man Dale Alexander breaks the tape at the finish line of the mile relay. Interested team members in background and the leaning official all contribute to the impact of the picture.

FIGURE 3.32. Opponents strain to get the initial lead at the starting line of a cross-country race. This interesting picture caused many comments by students who had never seen the start of a race—only the finish.

photographer compared snapping action pictures to shooting ducks. He said, "You have to lead 'em a little." Meaning, of course, that the camera should be directed slightly ahead of the play as it requires an instant to snap the picture.

In addition to the usual action pictures of sports events, some editors are using pictures showing dramatic lighting effects, sidelights of the game, and particularly shots of historical significance. Examples of effective sports pictures are shown in Figures 3.30 to 3.35 inclusive.

Posed and Semi-posed Pictures

A large percentage of the activity pictures used in the book are either posed or semi-posed. Very often a pressing crowd will prevent a photographer from getting a picture of an individual receiving an award or being crowned. Sometimes pictures are missed because the photographer forgot to pull a slide. When this happens, it is necessary to pose the participants for the benefit of the photographer so the action can be captured on film.

Other pictures falling into this category in-

FIGURE 3.33. Taut, straining muscles are evident as the giant center snatches a rebound. Pictures of this kind reproduce well in the yearbook and lend variety.

FIGURE 3.34. Will the attempted tip-in go through the hoop? This picture shows dramatic action, and the garish lights and shadows add another dimension.

clude portraits of queen candidates, pictures of outstanding students, shots of publication staff members, etc. These pictures can be natural, although they are obviously posed. Figures 3.36 to 3.40 inclusive are examples.

The Picture Story

The picture story has become increasingly popular in recent years. The yearbook, since it is largely a picture publication, can use this technique to good advantage for certain events. Sometimes a school affair will be so important that a series of pictures is justified and would best portray the event.

A picture story, however, is more than a hodge-podge of pictures taken at random. It needs to be planned, just as a writer plans a story. It should have a beginning, build up to a climax, and have an ending. In other words, the reader should be able to tell from the series of pictures what the story is about, with only minimum text.

It is necessary, then, to give a little forethought to a story to be told with pictures. Instead of telling the photographer to "go get a bunch of pictures," the editor should explain how the story fits in with the rest of the book, what it is supposed to portray, and what type of pictures are wanted. The photographer will be better prepared to get pictures to fit the story if he is given advance briefing.

Not all events that occur during the school year are important enough to warrant a series of pictures. The yearbook covers an entire year, and if several events are given unusual prominence by picture stories, some lesser event probably will be omitted. Therefore, the best subjects for picture stories are those in which the largest number of the students and faculty participate.

Picture magazines sometimes use a central figure in a picture story and follow his progress

FIGURE 3.35. "Jumping-Jill" cheerleader soars into the atmosphere in this interesting shot. Sidelights of this kind are appreciated more by many readers than are action pictures that they often do not understand.

FIGURE 3.36. "An imported jumping horse is admired after his demonstration"—an excellent posed picture.

from the beginning to the end. For a yearbook, however, it is usually best not to select one person for the main character of a story, because it places him in a position of too much prominence. Then, too, the story usually is one that is familiar to all students.

The amount of text needed with the picture story depends somewhat on what is being portrayed. There are few exceptions to the rule that every picture needs some explanation. Even though the picture story should be self-explanatory to be most effective, some text is needed to make the story absolutely clear. Many picture stories require both cutlines and accompanying text. Some need only cutlines to explain the story. A few picture stories can get by with only one or two words below each picture, but that is the exception rather than the rule. Examples of interesting picture stories are shown following the chapters on copy writing and layout.

Mood Pictures Add Impact

Recording the mood of an occasion in pictures adds interest to a yearbook. Catching the enthusiasm of the crowd, the smile of a beauty queen, or the concentration of a group at work are the goals to be sought.

Usually pictures of violence, pain, grief, and unhappiness are omitted from the annual. An effort is made to recall accomplishments and

FIGURE 3.37. Alumni, returning to Boyd Hall for homecoming, are asked to pose for a picture. The camera angle distorted the size of the girl's hand so it is a focal point and it should be cropped away if the layout in the annual will permit. It's such a good picture it should be used even if the hand cannot be eliminated.

FIGURE 3.39. After being named Miss K-State-Manhattan, Jan Buenning accepts congratulations of friends! This "insurance" picture was taken after the coronation —just in case it might be needed.

FIGURE 3.38. Feature editor of *Royal Purple* smiles at the right time as he poses for this shot.

happy events. However, pictures of plays, operas, and skits sometimes depict murder, sadness, and many other emotions. Figures 3.41 to 3.43 illustrate such pictures.

If You Want To Be a Photographer, Study Photography

No effort is made in this discussion to instruct photographers on how to operate a camera or process film and prints. That is something that each photographer must learn by diligent study and long practice. Taking a course or several courses in photography is an ideal way to start to learn. Many colleges and quite a few high schools offer such courses. However, if you live in an area where no courses are offered, you might want to investigate the possibility of attending a summer workshop for yearbook photographers offered by colleges in almost every state. Such a course usually includes some elementary instruction and practice.

One of the best ways to learn is to work for a good photographer. Try to get a part-time job or summer job with the photographer in your hometown. Work at every job possible. Don't be afraid to go to work early and stay late if it's necessary to do so. Get your employer to suggest books and literature you can study at night.

If none of the above possibilities is available and you still want to be a photographer, get some books on the subject from the library, read photography magazines, or ask a college about home-study photography courses. Many newsstands carry photography magazines. Then, too,

FIGURE 3.40. If this picture was not posed after the crowning, the photographer had an excellent location.

FIGURE 3.41. This picture, depicting violence, is from a one-act play satirizing the Russian court system.

most manufacturers of photographic equipment publish booklets and complete information instructions on how to use their products. It's amazing how much you can learn about almost any kind of equipment by careful study of the instructions that come with the product—too few people read them.

Mastering photography requires hard study, practice, and everlasting perseverance. Buy a camera, use it every day, and develop a fierce pride in the pictures you take. Don't be satisfied with mediocrity. Remember, any picture you take that's accepted for publication in the yearbook will be preserved for a lifetime.

FIGURE 3.43. "Gazing in the brightness of a campus light, an actor rehearses in the tense moments before a performance," is this outstanding picture's caption. →

FIGURE 3.42. Reverence is portrayed in this dramatic scene from a popular play at Kansas State University.

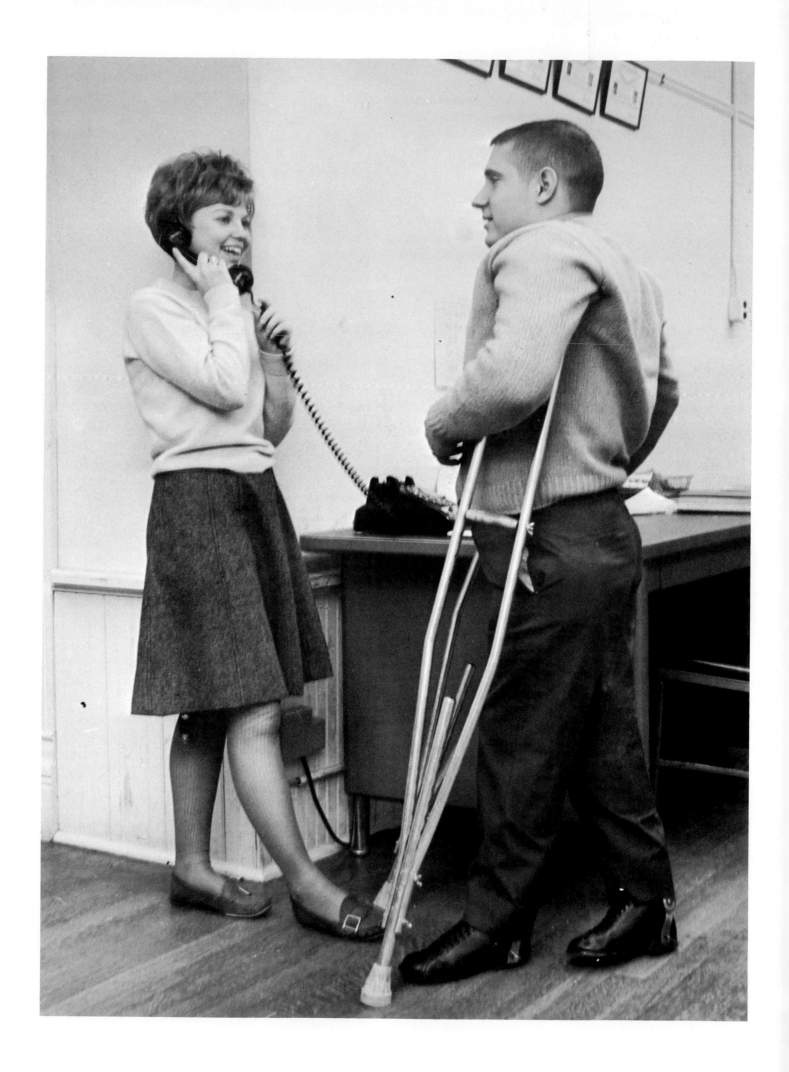

Judicious use of the telephone can save staff members many hours of time in preparing copy for the annual. You often can reach instantly, by phone, the most important news sources and get needed information from them in preparing accurate yearbook copy.

Chapter 4

Writing and Editing Copy

WELL-WRITTEN COPY is the one aspect of yearbook production that can be accomplished at no extra expense—except in hard work. It costs no more to print a page of good copy than a dull, inaccurate, or trite one. No part of your education is more important than learning to express yourself clearly, effectively, and precisely. Writing for your yearbook offers you an unparalleled opportunity to learn to write. It's not easy but, once mastered and properly used, the art of writing clearly can be one of the greatest accomplishments of your entire educational experience.

In spite of this golden opportunity, one of the most frequently neglected phases of yearbook production is writing effective, interesting copy. Adequate copy, well written and carefully edited, is an essential element of the school annual. Though yearbook authorities do not all agree on the quantity of copy necessary, they generally agree that a yearbook that fails in its treatment of copy does not successfully fulfill its obligations to the reader.

Adequate Copy Helps To Tell the Story

Adequate copy in the yearbook is a relative term. At one extreme are the advocates of much copy, including essays, short stories, poems, and other literary efforts. At the other extreme are those who say, "Let the pictures tell the story with a little copy here and there to fill in the holes."

As is generally the case in most controversies, the truth can be found midway between the extremes. An examination of yearbooks with top ratings shows liberal use of both copy and illustrations. Pictures alone cannot tell the complete story. Photos fail to answer the reader's questions about who participated, when and where the event took place, and the interesting sidelights. Similarly, copy alone does not tell the story so vividly and effectively as does a combination of pictures and type.

With interest in picture magazines and candid cameras at an all-time high, some editors experimented with having practically no yearbook copy. However, they discovered that by eliminating copy, they also were eliminating much of the yearbook's effectiveness. With photographs alone, they were able to present only a sample of the activities of the school year and to raise questions that were unanswered.

Once the editor realizes the importance of effectively handling copy in the yearbook, he must consider the different types of copy needed and determine a style for each. Before any copy is written, the editor should develop a style sheet for uniformity in capitalization, punctuation, and usage.

Five Different Types of Copy

All material written for publication is referred to as copy. To discuss yearbook copy, let us use five categories:

1. Body or Text Copy
2. Headlines
3. Cutlines or Captions
4. Identifications
5. Mood Copy

Each kind of copy has a function to perform. Often one or more of the five kinds of copy is not needed to complete a page. However, it is the editor's responsibility to make each page interesting and easily readable.

Body copy may be defined as the actual text of the book. It is the copy spread throughout the book recording the events of the school year. It is the story of school organizations, scholastic, sports, and social activities, and other events that take place during the year. It is body copy that leaves a lasting impression with the reader and communicates information vital to his complete understanding of the subject being presented.

Styles of body copy vary with different yearbooks, but in all cases the basic rules of good writing apply. Body copy therefore ought to be interesting and informative. It should be lively, colorful, well organized, and contain specific details. The copy is successful if a disinterested observer can pick up the annual, look at the pictures, read the copy, and get a clear picture of all the school's activities.

Headlines also are important. Their value in giving the yearbook personality and individuality cannot be overemphasized. The primary function of the headline is to attract the reader and motivate him to read the body copy and look at the pictures. The yearbook page can be compared to a store, with the headline serving as the show window advertising the contents of the page. Secondary functions of the headings are to complete the page layout and to aid in making the book more attractive.

Cutlines or captions, which are the lines of copy appearing above, below, or alongside pictures and illustrations, serve a dual purpose. They interpret the action in a photograph, and often they name persons whose identities would be otherwise lost. In too many cases, yearbook editors neglect to write lively, informative cutlines. A trite, meaningless caption or cutline can all too easily spoil the effectiveness of an excellent illustration and weaken a book.

Identifications of group photographs and panels are an essential part of the yearbook. Their function is simple—to identify accurately and completely every person appearing in the pictures. Their importance is greater than many editors realize. The yearbook may be of "All-American" quality to most readers, but to the person whose name is omitted or spelled incorrectly in the picture identification, the book is a failure.

Most annuals have, scattered throughout, copy that is difficult to classify. It's used to establish a mood or feeling—endow the book with a soul. Sometimes it takes the form of fine writing and, in special cases, even poetry. Writing of this type may be used in a dedication or in telling the story of an outstanding accomplishment. It often is important for the mood of copy, headlines, and captions to match the mood of the event they record. The mood of copy about a teacher retiring, for example, would differ from the mood expressed by cheerleaders or a pep band. Mood, besides being a separate category, often is an ingredient of other categories.

To Write Interestingly, Get the Facts

The more you know about the subject you cover for the annual, the more likely you are to produce an accurate, interesting story. Therefore, writers who are to record the activities of music groups, dramatics, clubs, fraternities, dormitories, sports, features, in fact everything that is to have space in the book should be appointed early in the year.

Thus, if it's your job to cover the band, try to go to any important band concert. Get a copy of the program; it may be useful to you later. Go with the photographer when he takes the group picture. Get the identification of each individual in the group as suggested in the chapter on photography. Watch the band's activities at football games, parades, and contests, and perhaps suggest to the photo editor a shot or two that will properly depict its activities and accomplishments. Try to capture the spirit and enthusiasm of the group in copy and pictures. Do the same for all activities you have to cover.

Information Forms Often Used

If you have a large number of activities to write about, it will not be possible to cover all of them in person. A printed or mimeographed sheet can be sent to the president of each organization that has space in the annual, requesting

Please fill out this questionnaire for use in the Royal Purple and return to Kedzie 103 not later than _____. If more space is needed, you may use the back of this sheet.

1. Correct name of organization:

2. Purpose and motto of organization:

3. Number of members; increase over last year:

4. Requirements for membership:

5. Faculty sponsor:

6. Officers:

7. Organization history:

8. Organization projects and activities of the year:

FIGURE 4.1. This questionnaire is designed to get needed information from general organizations and clubs. You may want to change it to meet your specific needs. Leave plenty of space at the bottom of sheet.

specific information that may be used in preparing the copy. Figure 4.1 and Figure 4.2 are two examples of forms used, with some slight variations, in a number of schools. Even if you do not plan to use a form of this kind, it will be worthwhile to study each one carefully because they point out information needed to give uniform coverage to similar organizations and activities.

Take a Look at the Dummy

At this point it's a good idea to take a careful look at the dummy to find out the exact space available for text copy and also to determine if you need to get information for cutlines, identifications, or other copy needed to complete the page.

Editor Makes Specific Assignments

In most cases the editor or copy editor will give specific instructions to each writer when making assignments regarding the number of lines of copy and the number of characters or strokes per line needed for text copy and cutlines. The character count method of estimating the copy required to fit a given space is discussed in detail in the chapter on layout.

```
                    ROYAL PURPLE
                  ORGANIZED HOUSE
              INFORMATION QUESTIONNAIRE

        Please fill out this questionnaire as accurately and completely
   as possible and return to the Royal Purple, Kedzie 103, not later
   than _____.  Be sure this information is correct.  The
   information will be used in the Royal Purple.  (Type or print clearly.)

    1.  Name of organization:

    2.  Name of housemother (or sponsor):

    3.  Officers:
        President previous spring semester:
        President fall semester:
        V-President:
        Secretary:
        Treasurer:
        IPC representative:
        IFC representative:
        Panhellenic representative:

    4.  Number of members: _____.  Increase over last year _____.

    5.  Outstanding student members:  (Queens, FMOC, etc.)



    6.  Special projects of the group this year:



    7.  Social activities: (Include planned spring activities)



    8.  Intramural record: (sports participated in and honors won)



    9.  Brief history:
        a. Where and when founded _____
        b. Established at K-State in _____
        c. Number of chapters _____

   10.  Additional remarks of interest: (Special awards, honors, etc.)
```

FIGURE 4.2 A special questionnaire often is sent to fraternities, dormitories, and other housing groups requesting specific information applicable to all such organizations. Design a form to meet your needs.

Interview Often Needed

In a good many instances you will probably want to interview the adviser, the president, or some of the leading members of the organization to get further needed information. Be careful to select the best source for accuracy. Keep in mind that you are writing a history of the organization or activity for the entire year and not just getting a news story for the school paper that covers only one event. Quite often the individual you are interviewing does not realize this fact. You ought to cover the obvious and important events of the year.

For best results, all the methods of getting information discussed may be used, plus any other sources available. All names, titles, and facts used in the story ought to be checked. Use the school directory, city directory, school catalog, and, if possible, get IBM cards for each student from the registrar for detailed information about the class, curriculum, hometown, and other useful information. In case of doubt use the telephone and get someone from the organization to come to the yearbook office to check identifications against the picture that is to be used. Use the telephone often. It will save you hours of time and energy. You can often reach the most important people immediately by telephone, and get information you need instantly.

Clear Thinking Precedes Clear Writing

After you have gathered the information needed, you must give careful thought on how best to present it to your readers. Humorist Will Rogers in a famous quip once said, "In Hollywood the woods are full of people that learned to write, but evidently can't read. If they could read their stuff, they'd stop writing."

In a recent talk to Kansas scientists and extension staff members, Dr. Lowell Brandner, professor of journalism, Kansas State University, expressed similar feelings.

Before you can consider communicating an idea, you have to have one to communicate. If the idea is hazy in your mind, words cannot clear it up. Clarity is more a result of thought than of style or any editorial technique. Words often get blamed for muddying up ideas. Too often it was a muddy idea to start with, and words can improve an idea only by the rarest of accidents. Write clearly is a wasted plea to anyone who does not, will not, or cannot think clearly. A better admonition would be THINK CLEARLY.

Write a Rough Draft

First write a rough draft covering all the important facts you feel need to go into the story. You may have to rearrange the facts to get the most important and interesting one in the lead. You may have to cut some facts out entirely to make the story fit.

Lean back in your chair and read what you have written. Does it answer the questions *who, what, when, where, why,* and *how?* All these questions don't have to be answered in the lead, as is sometimes advocated in newspaper reporting. However, they should be answered by the pictures, cutlines, identifications, and text copy presented in the finished book. Polish the story. Use short words, short sentences, and short paragraphs, but don't make the paragraphs too short. The annual is a book and will look more like one if most paragraphs are at least four or five lines long. When you are satisfied with what you have written, read it aloud to a person not acquainted with the subject. If he understands, type it carefully to fit the specifications and give it to the editor.

Get Copy to Editor Early

Writers should start getting their assignments to the editorial desk as early as possible in the production schedule. Remember that deadlines are the latest time to submit copy. Beat the deadline as far as you can. Such a procedure allows time for careful editorial handling of all copy and provides an opportunity for you or others to rewrite the material if necessary. The editor and copy writer should have a meeting of minds at the completion of the first assignment. It is important to have a clear understanding between the editor and writer before additional copy assignments are made. If the yearbook is to have a uniform style, the editor must adopt a "style book" and follow it carefully. This is a good time to insist that all writers follow the style adopted.

Copy that is handed to the editor early can be meticulously checked for accuracy of facts and figures. Accuracy in the annual needs strong emphasis. The fact that the yearbook is meant to be a lasting record of the school year makes accuracy doubly important. Facts in copy should be checked with the best authority, then double-checked. An individual enjoys seeing his name in print, if it's spelled correctly, but he dislikes errors in his title, school, or class. Some style rules appear in the Appendix of this book and can be used if your school does not have its own.

Copyreading Marks

One of the routine tasks of the editorial staff

Ag School Compiles Research Information

Co-ordination of 10 departments and 105 county extension agencies is a task of Harold E. Jones, extension director.

Robert Bohannon, assistant to the dean and the extension director, confers with Frank R. Carpenter, assistant dean.

Compiling factual information, the School of Agriculture conducted a variety of research projects. Studies in dairy science and biochemistry, measuring quantities of material in food, air and body tissues by microanalysis, led to a research grant from the National Aeronautical and Space Administration. Co-operative studies by the Schools of Agriculture, Veterinary Medicine, Home Economics and Arts and Sciences showed the degree to which economical factors of meat palatability could be inherited in various breeds of livestock.

The new Director of Resident Instruction, Duane Acker, told Kansas rural youth about opportunities in agriculture, explaining that the agricultural image was one of process and distribution as well as production. C. Peairs Wilson, former dean of academic instruction, became director of the experiment station.

Agriculture School Department Heads—*Top Row*: Thomas B. Avery, Poultry Husbandry; Rufus F. Cox, Animal Husbandry; Robert P. Ealy, Horticulture. *Second Row*: Herbert Knutson, Entomology; Howard L. Mitchell, Biochemistry; John A. Nordin, Agricultural Economics. *Bottom Row*: Charles L. Norton, Dairy Science; Raymond V. Olson, Agronomy; John A. Shellenberger, Flour and Feed Milling Industries.

of the annual is marking corrections on copy. The conventional copyreading marks should be applied, for they are a universal language used by both printer and journalist.

Shown in the Appendix of this book are the copyreading or editing marks and their applications. A severely marked piece of copy such as the example shown should not be sent to the printer, but ought to be retyped to eliminate confusion from overlapping marks.

Of course if the typing is to be reproduced by the offset process, the final copy must be typed exactly as it is to be printed. Copyreading marks cannot be made on final copy that is to be photographed and reproduced in the yearbook.

Proofreading Marks

When proofs of the copy are returned to the editorial desk by the printer, they must be checked carefully for typesetting errors. As in the case of copyreading marks, the conventional proofreading marks should be used. Proofs are marked with the symbols shown in the Appendix of this book, then are returned to the printer for corrections.

One rule the staff should keep in mind is that proofreading is not the place to make changes in the copy. Proofreading is intended to correct errors made when the type was set. Changes in copy should be made before it is sent to the printer. Most printers charge extra for changes made in the copy after the type has been set.

Have Page of Copy Set Early

The importance of having a clear understanding between the printer and the staff on how the book is to be printed cannot be overemphasized. Perhaps the best way to get an understanding is to prepare early in the season at least one page of copy that will be used in your yearbook and have the printer set it in type and send you page proofs. You should select a page that will use as many as possible of the type faces and type sizes that are to appear in the finished yearbook.

The sample page should show at least one large group picture, or a panel containing a large number of faces. This will give you an idea of the amount of space that will be required to set the names of the individuals shown in the composite

←

FIGURE 4.3. A proof of one page of the annual set early in the year will afford writers information on how copy should be typed. It also provides information on how much copy is needed to fit the space.

picture. Figure 4.3 is a page the *Royal Purple* staff had set early and used as a sample. Several proofs were pulled and posted in the yearbook office so that all writers could study it and type all copy as nearly like the finished page as possible.

Yearbook staffs using cold type composition, instead of regular type, will also profit from having a representative page of the annual prepared and proofed to be used the same way. Figure 4.4 is a good example of a page using cold type composition that shows the different styles and sizes of finished composition that are available.

If an actual page from your annual is not set and proofed in advance of copy typing, a clear and definite understanding must be had between the staff and the printer if copy is to be prepared so it will fit the space left for it on each page.

Examples of Organization Write-ups

Here are some examples of interesting write-ups from award-winning annuals that will give you an idea of the kind of copy being used by leading yearbooks.

The *Centennial Sunflower*, Topeka (Kansas) High School, had an interesting story to tell about its band's activities. The copy, from the headline to the last sentence, holds the reader's attention.

Sounds of Music Lift Trojans to New Levels

IN MID-FEBRUARY, Troy's band and directors literally took a bow as they inaugurated another "first." The occasion was the receipt of the manuscript of Dr. Benjamin Dunford's composition, *People of the South Wind*, a Centennial Suite. It was written especially for the group, after the well-known composer had studied recordings and the recommendations of music critics. "The first time a major composer has been commissioned to write for a high school concert band," was Director Neaderhiser's proud comment.

Long hours of practice as a marching band at fall athletic events built the confidence and spirit which grew through the winter months into concert stature, equal to the mature performance of the Centennial Suite at the annual spring concert.

For the second year Mr. Don Jacoby, trumpet virtuoso, was guest conductor for Troy's colorful musical group, following a clinic of several hundred students from Eastern Kansas schools. His enthusiasm both inspired practice and gave added vigor to the "Sound of Music" on the Trojan stage.

The write-up of the Civitan Club, published in the 1962 *Boone Legend*, William R. Boone High School, Orlando, Florida, gives a good picture of the year's activities.

Hi-Tri officers for 1959-1960—**Front Row:** Finch, Drompp, Gibson, Shafer, Hight, Smith, Klise, Carruthers, Hammon-tree, Gerni. **Back Row:** Dealter, Clark, Simpson, Walker, Harvey, Hodge, Carr, Deck, Greensfelder, Martin, Rohrbaugh.

Hi-Tri goals prepare girls for tomorrow's leadership

To kick off the annual membership drive, Mrs. Meinzer, the executive director of Y.W.C.A., approves the presentation of a Hi-Tri pin to Mr. Mertz by Diane Gibson and Carolyn Lowe.

Hi-Tri members strove diligently to attain three goals. The first was acceptance of responsibility. Each girl was expected to earn three service credits; she acquired some points by grading teachers' papers, selling potato chips, and packing Thanksgiving baskets for the needy. Two leadership sessions were held during the year: the Northern Mid-Winter Conference at Fort Wayne and a State Y-Teen Conference at Lake Wawasee. Through service and attendance, girls learned "To grow as a person."

Since all enjoyed singing, music ranging from a crazy version of "Old MacDonald" to the "Y-Teen Hymn" preceded meetings. After business had been concluded, skits, talks, or panel discussions were presented. Preparations for a dance extended fellowship outside the Y-annex as members turned the armory into an enchanted island of "Bali Ha'i." Through group participation, girls learned "To grow in fellowship with people of all races, religions, nationalities."

Each member considered the third and final goal of utmost importance. All meetings were opened with devotions, and most serious programs were presented by candle light. Through prayer and devotion, girls learned "To grow in the knowledge of God."

FIGURE 4.4 Yearbooks using cold-type composition can be pleasing if carefully planned in advance and copy typed to fit. Courtesy of the *Tattler*, Logansport High School, Logansport, Indiana.

CIVITAN

Earns Money for Primrose
By Vending Fruitcake

There's a lot of crumbs in 1,600 pounds of fruitcake! This tasty delicacy, provided by the Civitan Club of Orlando, was sold by Boone's Junior Civitans as one means of raising the money necessary for the accomplishment of their many projects. Twenty per cent of the net gains made by the sale was donated by the J.C.'s to the Primrose School for Mentally Retarded Children. With these funds the school was able to buy specialized equipment which it always needs.

Collaborating with the annual March Cancer Drive, Junior Civitans made a door-to-door canvass for donations. In doing this the boys fulfilled their obligation to serve the community.

As a contrast to a year dominated by altruistic activity, the annual Inaugural Ball, held in the spring for the first time this year, provided festive, holiday-like fun and frolic.

Projects and activities formed the background against which members grew in stature to become better citizens both today and in the future.

The work of the student council is well told in the following copy from the 1964 *Indian,* Anderson High School, Anderson, Indiana.

Student leadership develops in council

Leadership, citizenship and sportsmanship were the bywords of a hard working Student Council. Leadership came in the American Field Service program as council members assumed the task of raising money in hopes of sponsoring two foreign exchange students next year. They sold 1,900 shares of AFS stock at $1 a share to AHS students. Members represented the student body in citizenship and demonstrated sportsmanship by decorating the football field and serving in the Homecoming event.

Student Council provided social recreation and entertainment for classmates by sponsoring the Fall Wind-Up and Twirp Week dances. With a nightclub atmosphere, the Twirp Week dance sported the theme "Boys' Night Out" and Mr. Debonair, the ladies' choice.

Penny Postman service was once again provided for the thrifty-minded teenagers of AHS at Christmas. Much of the proceeds from the project was spent for food for the needy.

Near the end of the year, council members with three or more semesters of service were honored at the Awards Day Program and the successful year was concluded with a Spring Banquet.

It often is difficult to find something interesting to write about general and departmental clubs; the 1962 *Cornhusker,* University of Nebraska, Lincoln, demonstrates that it can be done:

Pi Tau Sigma:

DOWNTOWN DISPLAY PLACES FIRST

Through intricate design and clever planning, Pi Tau Sigma's downtown E-Week window display won first prize for the Mechanical Engineering department. The apparatus consisted of two characters from the "Peanuts" comic strip rolling a metal ball down a ramp, thereby lighting up the individual letters in the words, "Mechanical Engineering."

Pi Tau Sigma, the Mechanical Engineering honorary, sponsored two smokers honoring the upper one fourth of the sophomore ME class. As a highlight of the sophomore recognition, the honorary awarded Arvis Grindulis an Engineering Handbook for having the highest class average in the department.

"But She Won't Be Lonely Very Long," headline from the 1964 *Yucca,* North Texas State University, Denton, compels you to read what follows, and it's worth it:

Upperclassmen swarmed past the forlorn freshman as she hurried toward the Union Building. She glanced at her watch: nearly 8 a.m. "Surely someone in here can tell me," she thought to herself.

She walked into the Union Building, saw the crowds of students and quickly retreated. "Too many people. I'd be too embarrassed to ask." She turned toward the Administration Building. "They'll tell me." But the lines inside that building were too long, too menacing to her.

A few minutes before 9 a.m. she saw a girl wearing a bright green jacket in front of the Music Building. A printed card on the girl's blouse read, "Ask Me."

With an attempt at nonchalance the freshman asked the girl, "Oh, say, could you by any chance tell me where I'm supposed to register? I'm sort of new here."

Much later that day the weary freshman trudged slowly back to her dormitory.

After supper she wrote a letter home. ". . . . It's really interesting here and everybody has been just great. I can't get over how friendly all the kids are. My roommate and I get along just fine. We both bought beanies today but we don't have to wear them if we don't want to. They say the rest is easy if you can make it through registration and I did—finally. So far I'm having a swell time. Wish you were here. . . ."

Copy About the Work of the School

Copy about the work of the school and its teachers and administrators depends on accurate facts. Information needed to write about each department or the number of students in each class, or personal information about a faculty member can be obtained from the proper administrator. The copy can be checked with the same source after it is written.

Although the administration section should contain numbers, dates, and other factual information, the copy still can be interesting. With a little thought, such facts can be skillfully woven into the story.

The contributions of the school's administrators are clearly set forth in the 1963 *Riparian,* Broad Ripple High School, Indianapolis, Indiana. Note the use of first names and proper titles. This important information is often omitted in high school annuals.

Administrators lead pupils along road to future

Helping to maintain Ripple's standing as one of the top schools in the nation, administrators and faculty members strive for higher academic standards and better pupil-teacher relationships.

Principal J. Fred Murphy supervises and plans all classroom work and curriculum study. He confers with teachers and pupils on personal problems and serves as the final disciplinary officer of the school, in addition to administering the guidance and counseling program.

Vice-principals Harold K. Harding and Roger Riley serve as treasurer of extra-curricular funds and general supervisor of co-curricular activities, respectively. They work jointly as supervisors of teaching personnel, and with problems relative to curricular revision and expansion.

Showing pupils the way to a better college and career choice after graduation and a wise high school program plan at Ripple is the job of the class counselors. Seniors receive advice from Mr. Albert Mahin and Miss Melba Schumacher. Mr. Dale Hamner and Mr. Arnold Pahmeier administer guidance to juniors, and sophomores get a boost from Mrs. Maenell Newsome and Mr. Edward O'Nan. Helping freshmen carry on Ripple's academic reputation are Miss Marie Sullivan and Miss Barbara Vargo. Mr. Robert J. Bryant, guidance counselor, aids pupils on immediate plans for college.

Settling pupils' problems concerning social and classroom relations is the responsibility of Mr. Warren K. Jackson, dean of boys, and Mrs. Rosalind Ewing, dean of girls.

A wonderful job of recording the scholastic accomplishments of the students at Central High School, Davenport, Iowa, is done by the 1964 *Blackhawk*. Too often scholastic achievement and scholarship awards are not covered.

Two Seniors Reach Finals in Merit Test; 17 Scholars Win Letter of Commendation

Two Central seniors—Anita Nagel and Craig Shumate—achieved finalist standings in the National Merit Scholarship Qualifying Test. They, along with students from 16,500 schools across the nation, took the test in March, 1963.

Seventeen students received Letters of Commendation for their achievement on this test. They are: Tom Altermatt, Kent Anderson, Dave Brown, Kathy Brown, Judy Cohen, Bill Curnan, Dale Denklau, Mike Devine, Larry Duncan, Francie Fries, Herman Goellnitz, Bill Hintze, Richard Ives, Bruce Judd, Marilyn Metcalf, Bob Phelps, and John Swander.

The 32,000 commended students, together with semi-finalists, make up two per cent of all high school seniors in the United States. In comparison, Central's group makes up three and one-half per cent of the senior class.

To increase the opportunity of financial assistance, the NMSC sent names, addresses, and test scores of commended students to two colleges or universities of their choice, making them eligible for scholarships offered by other corporations.

This year's ninth annual Merit program was concluded in late April when Merit Scholars were named. One of Central's finalists, Craig Shumate, was awarded an NMSC scholarship to Iowa State University.

Also doing outstanding scholastic work were Central's four number-one students according to class rank—Francie Fries, Sue Hoover, Joan Robers, and Craig Shumate.

A good example of how to tell the community and students the value to be derived from the study of modern languages is exemplified in the 1963 *Tabulae*, Lyons Township High School, LaGrange, and Western Springs, Illinois.

Language Classes Investigate Customs, Culture of Foreign Countries

Due to the increasing awareness of maintaining good foreign relations and promoting world understanding, new stress is being placed on mastering foreign languages. As one result of this emphasis, the Language Department introduced new methods of teaching which included hearing-repeating techniques. Tapes, records, and the South Campus language laboratory aid the teacher in his foreign language instruction. Magazines and newspapers provided another supplementary area of learning. Besides learning a foreign tongue, the students also gained a knowledge of the culture from which the language developed.

Sometimes the yearbook ought to tell the people of the community and the state about some outstanding feature of its school. It helps to build the prestige of the institution.

Here is the story about the medical school, from the 1963 *Razorback,* University of Arkansas, Fayetteville:

The multi-million dollar University Medical Center at Little Rock is regarded as one of the most modern in the nation. It is one of the outstanding features of the University of Arkansas. Here the latest equipment is utilized in serving both medical students and patients.

Dedicated in 1957, the Medical Center was constructed at a cost of more than fourteen million dollars. In 1961, the T. H. Barton Institute for Medical Research was completed and occupied. One of the finest medical research facilities in America, the Institute should prove to be a factor in attracting and holding qualified teachers and research personnel.

Students receive not only detailed classroom instruction in their prospective fields but also a great deal of experience in the application of this knowledge, because many people come to the Center for medical attention.

The University of Arkansas Schools of Pharmacy and Nursing are housed in the Education Building at the Medical Center, together with the School of Medicine.

At least once every four years the yearbook can render a real service to its readers by discussing the advantages to be derived from the study of the various courses and curriculums offered. The 1964 *Dome,* University of Notre Dame, South Bend, Indiana, does an excellent job in the following write-up.

HISTORY AND ECONOMICS

It surely must be a temptation for the freshman to

judge every study by his first course in that area; the errors of such a conclusion are particularly evident in the subjects portrayed here. History, of necessity, is built on fact, just as economics rests largely on lifeless numbers; the elementary courses in these areas stress their basic foundations. But the primary concern of each of these studies is life itself, making them two of the most exciting and essential areas of a liberal education. The dividing line between the two is, in fact, often hard to distinguish. Historical events commonly admit of economic interpretations and economic developments, in turn, very often are triggered by historical landmarks. Then, too, both subjects are the basis of progress in political science, or sociology, or for that matter, in any understanding of the world of men.

Writing Effective Sports Copy

If you are writing sports, you must select from the diversity of events and thousands of words written about the school's teams during the year information for a compact summary of the season. In a few paragraphs, you have to present a resume along with interesting highlights and sidelights typical of sports news. For each sport, you must have the season's record, the team's accomplishments, something about the coaches, and perhaps a one- or two-sentence summary of each game. More important than most yearbook sports editors realize is a record of the scores of all games. As the years go by, it often turns out that the school annual is the only reliable record of past contests. You want your section of the "book of reference" to be complete and accurate. The season's record can be presented effectively in summary form, listing scores of each game and naming the schools involved. Be sure to arrange the scoreboard in a manner that permits the reader to tell easily which scores refer to the home team and which refer to opponents. The following examples illustrate how this may be done.

The 1962 *Tower,* Wheaton College, Wheaton, Illinois, uses a popular method to present wrestling scores.

Summary

Wheaton		Opponents
13	Northern Illinois Univ.	15
15	Central Michigan Univ.	13
36	Carroll College	0
11	Franklin & Marshall	14
9	Westchester	21
6	University of Wisconsin	20
14	Superior State	12
8	Purdue	17
19	Indiana Central	9
27	Washington University	5
19	Wabash	9
19	Notre Dame	8

Augustana Quadrangular	—Second Place
Great Lakes Tournament	—First Place
Wheaton Invitational	—First Place
NCAA Regional Tournament	—Second Place

Another easily read style is shown by the 1963 *Provi,* Proviso East High School, Maywood, Illinois.

Sophomore Football Record

	Opponents	East
*Aurora East	19	7
Niles East	7	6
New Trier	7	38
Waukegan	19	40
Evanston	12	13
Morton East	13	19
Highland Park	0	7
Oak Park	0	19

* Non-Conference

Be sure the facts are accurate. Newspaper files of the period when the contests were held are one source of information. It is wise to confirm this material and get added subject matter from the coach of the team. Remember, in sports coverage, that write-ups age more gracefully and are better appreciated in later years if they are unbiased, fair-minded, and sportsmanlike in character.

Here is an example from the 1964 *Shield,* Highland High School, Highland, Indiana, showing the type of sports copy acceptable in school annuals:

Trojans Captured Trophy
In Whiting Holiday Tournament

Highland's Trojans of '64 ripped off four successive victories over Hammond Tech, Hammond Gavit, Merrillville, and Gary Wirt. After losing a heartbreaker to Calumet (65–63), the team downed Rensselaer, but then was beaten by Lebanon.

The Trojans bounced back in the Whiting Holiday Tourney to defeat the hosts as Harry Withrow set a school record, scoring 35 points. The team went on to tip Bishop Noll in overtime to capture the trophy.

Highland suffered another heartbreaking loss to Gary Edison (65–63). The team again strung four victories together over Culver Military Academy, Griffith, Portage, and Chesterton before losing to Hammond Morton. Rounding out the season, Highland won at Lowell, fell to Crown Point and East Gary, then finished with victories over Dyer Central and Thornton Fractional North.

In the new Hammond sectional, rated one of the toughest in the state, the Trojans fell before Gary Tolleston in the first game, 72–75.

The *Shield* also printed a detailed schedule showing the scores of all games.

One paragraph is devoted to each football game in the 1964 *Cornhusker,* University of Nebraska, Lincoln. A lead-in label head is used effectively at the beginning of each paragraph.

Colorado: Homecoming fans saw Nebraska smash Colorado in a 41–6 victory, the third consecutive conference win for the Scarlet gridders. The Golden Buffs, sparked by quarterback Frank Cesarek, marked up the first six points early in the game. Favored NU then gained a 14–6 halftime advantage with two touchdown thrusts. The Husker drive riddled the Buffalo line during an explosive second half, as Bob Hohn circled the left end for a 35-yard touchdown run. The final score came as NU sophomore Henry Woods completed a 43-yard flip to Preston Love. Scarlet and Cream defense checked Colorado attempts after a Husker fumble gave visitors a chance to score.

Missouri: Chalking up the first NU victory over Missouri in five years, Cornhuskers squeaked past the Tigers to a 13-12 win. The Scarlet and Cream took the opening kickoff and marched 76 yards in 11 plays to light up the scoreboard. With 8:30 left in the half, Mizzou crossed the goal line for a six-pointer but failed on the PAT attempt. A second half fumble put the pigskin in Nebraska's hands for the Scarlet's second tally. Missouri fought back with a successful 35-yard pass to put the Tigers within winning distance. An attempted two-point conversion on a pass from touted QB Gary Lane was broken up in the end zone by Husker defensive back Bruce Smith.

The story of the track team often is neglected because the meets are held late in the spring. The *Indian*, Shawnee-Mission High School, Merriam, Kansas, did not let this handicap stop them:

COMBINING depth and spirit, head coach Bob Karnes fielded a squad of talent-laden Indian thinclads. As the season progressed S-M was recognized as having one of the finest track teams in the state.

By a display of versatility, the Redmen ran over the Trojans of Topeka by a 86–46 score in the first meet of the campaign. Although this was the initial contest, the Indians turned in a seasoned performance.

Wyandotte was next to fall under the churning feet of the Tribe as they lost 91 to 39. Shawnee-Mission, with Larry Youngblood capturing the 100- and 220-yard dashes and also the broad jump, won twelve of the sixteen events.

The Ottawa Relays gave the cindermen an early chance to meet state-wide opposition. But this did not hinder the tracksters as they swept their second straight class AA title, defeating second-place Wichita East by 18 points. Jim McHenry turned in a top-notch performance for the Warriors as he ran a near record-breaking mile. Also Tom Jones placed first in the discus and javelin.

Record Accomplishments of Seniors

In some annuals, senior write-ups consist of nothing more than a presumably humorous comment about each person. A book done in this style fails to record really important material. It is wise to consider that, in later years, a concise record of the accomplishments of each senior is far more valuable than a quip that soon loses its meaning. In many cases, too, it is difficult to write something humorous and completely fair. A record of the activities of each senior ought to be compiled and presented in an efficient and effective manner. Perhaps the best way to gather the information is to see that each senior turns in a record of his accomplishments on cards provided for the purpose.

Here are a number of ways in which the material can be presented:

RANK, JACK M. . . . . Kansas City
MECHANICAL ENGINEERING
Delta Sigma Phi; Alpha Phi Omega; A.S.M.E.; K-State Players; Intramurals.

RAMSEY, HAROLD A. . . . . Uniontown
Dairy Production
Farm House; Alpha Zeta; Ag Association, pres. 4; Dairy Club; Collegiate 4-H; Westminster Foundation; Ag. Council; Freshman Phi Kappa Phi Recognition.

George Addy
Student Council; Torch Club; Honor Society; Classical Club; DCT; Wheel Club, Vice President; AVA-Library.

WOLF, JOHN DAVID
Basketball; Football; Hi-Y, Vice President; Homeroom Vice President; Track; Varsity Club.

LASCH, RICHARD E.: Miami Shores, Fla.; B.S. in Zoology.

Top Row
SUSAN J. CONRAD—Booster Club 1-4; Drama Club 3,4; FBLA 2-4; GAA 1,2; Y-Teens 1-4; Monitor 4. MIKAEL COOK—Letterman's Club 3,4; Monitor 4; Baseball 1-4; Football 1-4; Intramurals 1-3; Track 1; Wrestling 2-4. WILLIAM A. COOK—Letterman's Club 2-4; Football 1,3; Track 1; Wrestling 2-4. LAURA M. CUCULIC—Booster Club 2-4; Drama Club 4; FTA 1-4; Student Court 4, Recorder 4; Trojanal 1-4; Shield 2-4.

MILLER, EUGENE F.—*Mechanical Engineering*: Kappa Mu Epsilon. MILLER, ROBERT B.—Eureka, *Veterinary Medicine*: Acacia Pres.; Jr. AVMA; Young Republicans; Intramurals. MISAK, DALE E.—Freeport, *Physical Education*: Tau Kappa Epsilon; Phi Epsilon Kappa; Varsity Gymnastics; FTA; Intramurals.

The last two examples illustrate how all the students appearing in the same row of a panel can be presented in one paragraph. This plan usually results in a pleasing typographical display and enables the reader to locate easily the write-up for the particular individual desired.

Headlines Attract Readers

Too many pages of an annual are not read because the reader's interest is not stimulated. With emphasis today on rapid and competitive reading, uninteresting headlines are an invitation to look elsewhere for something brighter and faster moving. Headlines occupy a position of importance. Their value in giving the yearbook personality and individuality should not be overlooked.

Although it is difficult to establish classifications for all headlines, four types are in common use in yearbooks. They include:

1. Feature or Magazine Headlines
2. News Headlines
3. Label Headlines
4. Combination Headlines.

The feature or magazine headline is used widely and is recommended by many yearbook authorities. It offers an opportunity for originality, cleverness, and the use of catchy phrases. Good examples are to be found in many of the leading national magazines.

Here are some features headlines selected from both high school and college annuals:

Winter Weather Wearies Students

Nothing matches homecoming excitement
Tanksters Plunge Forward

Behind the Footlights at the Ring

Four In A Row Less 37 Seconds

Exchange Students Bring Good Will, Charm

Cold, Wet, Numb

Weekend: cheers, cotillion, coaches

Beaches, Babes, and Bikes

The news style of yearbook headlines is merely an adaptation of the newspaper headline one sees everyday. In the yearbook the news head is more general in nature and does not refer to events of immediate or spot importance. Many annuals use news heads exclusively. Examples of news headlines used in current yearbooks follow:

Rainy Homecoming Greets First Queen

Close Finish Reflects Successful Campaign

Indians falter in late season slump
North Scholars In Televised Contest

Thrill rides and booths contributed to the excitement of the Carni-Gras

Fall Registration Sets Enrollment Records

The label headline is easiest to write and is the least effective, for it simply tags or labels the page. However, it is not necessary to ban label heads from the annual. In cases where pages are crowded, a label consisting of the organization's name is possibly justified. Attractive display will offset some of the ineffectiveness of label heads, but with too many labels, the book loses personality—or develops dreariness. Here are a few examples of label headlines:

Marching Band
Botany Club
Cheerleaders
Indoor Track
Commencement
Administration

Combination headlines merely combine two of the three types of headlines mentioned. They may involve the use of a label head and a news head or a label head and a feature head. News heads and feature heads are seldom used together.

The first line or "kicker" should be set in type about one-half the point-size of the main head. It is often set in all caps if the main headline is set in caps and lower case. You need plenty of white space for a combination headline. If you are going to have a lot of different elements on the page, perhaps you should select a less complicated headline style. Shown below are several different examples of combination headlines:

SOCIAL STUDIES
Students See Problems In Light of Obligations

Vacation Ends
Enrolling, Meeting Friends Fill First Day of School

Elements in Combination

"South Pacific"

True Love, Happy Talk
Recall Island's Charm

Hurts and helps
Injuries, skill balance scale

SENIORS: Tul-Wat
Graduates Face Tomorrow
With Challenging Hopes

Headlines Should Summarize

It is generally agreed that headlines should be drawn from the copy and that they ought to tell the reader something about what follows. Words that appear in the lead of the story generally are not used again in the headline. Instead of an exact repetition, synonyms or phrases that basically contain the same meaning will convey the idea more satisfactorily. Headline writing is an art learned by practice, not by just knowing the rules or by reading about it. Imagination is perhaps the most important factor in headline writing. It is good experience for the copy writer to compose the headline for every story. When the editor proofreads the copy and headline, he may find it necessary to rewrite the headline, because it is too similar to others already sent to the printer. Many yearbook staffs follow the practice of keeping a list of all headlines already used in their book. Thus, popular verbs and common nouns are not overused.

Writing headlines for the annual is often confusing because you are writing them about things that happened several weeks ago. How can you make them interesting to the reader? Here are some tips that may be useful:

1. Use the historical present tense.
2. Use strong active verbs.
3. Drop a, the, and other short words. Substitute a comma for and.
4. Build the headline around what follows in the write-up.
5. Most newspaper headlines are two- or three-line heads. Reading surveys show that three-word lines are the most effective. Of course, it's impossible to write every head with three words to a line, and if this were done, its effectiveness would be lost.

Short Headlines Are Effective

A three- or four-word head, written and displayed so that it packs a punch, is probably among the most effective that can be produced. However, in many cases space is a limiting factor, and the character count of the headline must be carefully checked. Heads are better too short than too long because white space is an effective means of drawing attention to type. Then, too, if the headline is too long to fit the space, the printer will have to return it to you for rewriting, thus losing valuable production time and increasing costs.

Unit Count Needed for Headlines

In the chapter on layout the character count method of estimating the amount of copy needed to fit a given space is discussed. The method of character count for headlines must be given more careful consideration if they are to exactly fit the space left for them in the layout. Because of the limited number of characters, letters, and spaces that appear in a headline, it is necessary to adopt a method that allows more space for a wide letter such as m and w and less space for such letters as l and f. This is called the *unit count* system.

Here is a unit count schedule often used in writing headlines:

1. All lower case letters count 1, except l,i,f,t which count $\frac{1}{2}$ and m and w which count $1\frac{1}{2}$.
2. All capital letters count $1\frac{1}{2}$, except I which counts 1 and M and W which count 2.
3. Space between words counts 1.

To see how this plan works, take the headline used on the sample page, Figure 5.3:

A g S c h o o l C o m p i l e s
$1\frac{1}{2}$ 1 1 $1\frac{1}{2}$ 1 1 1 1 $\frac{1}{2}$ 1 $1\frac{1}{2}$ 1 $1\frac{1}{2}$ 1 $\frac{1}{2}$ $\frac{1}{2}$ 1 1 = $18\frac{1}{2}$

R e s e a r c h I n f o r m a t i o n
$1\frac{1}{2}$ 1 1 1 1 1 1 1 1 1 1 $\frac{1}{2}$ 1 1 $1\frac{1}{2}$ 1 $\frac{1}{2}$ $\frac{1}{2}$ 1 1 = $19\frac{1}{2}$

Thus, if all the headlines in the *Royal Purple* were set in this family of type and this point-size, the unit count for one-column heads would probably be set at a minimum count of 17 and a maximum count of $19\frac{1}{2}$. It's difficult to write a meaningful headline with a rigid unit count so it is necessary to establish a maximum and minimum count that can be used. If the same type were used for a head extending across the entire width of the type page, a unit count of 32 to 38 probably would be used.

Study Magazine and Newspaper Heads

The headline writer, usually the editor of the yearbook, cannot depend entirely upon his own ingenuity for new ideas. He should study other publications to see the way they write headlines. Magazines and newspapers offer excellent source material for examples of good headlines. It's advisable to keep a file of headline ideas, rather than to depend on memory to recall something seen a long time ago. With a backlog of material for reference, much of the drudgery of headline writing will be avoided, and more effective headlines will result.

In most cases, the annual will be more attractive if the same type face is used in all headlines throughout the book. Sometimes it may be advisable to select a different type face for one or two sections of the book. The same style of headline, whether news, feature, label, or combination, should be uniform for each section or chapter of the annual.

Breakers or subheads will best serve their function if they are carefully written in a style similar to that used by good magazines and newspapers. In short, they should be written from the copy, and they should tell the reader something. Labels are no better as subheads than they are in top headlines.

Generally, the breaker is set in a blacker and sometimes slightly larger type face than the body copy and is surrounded by white space for emphasis. To accomplish this, the breaker must be short so that it can be indented on either end.

Breakers are not needed unless there is a lot of copy. If the copy is not long enough to warrant at least two breakers, there probably should be none.

Writing Cutlines

In many yearbooks, editors have adopted a sort of halfhearted attitude toward writing cutlines. This is a mistake, for the cutline is as essential in the book as the cover or the pictures. A look into any of the successful picture magazines of today reveals the importance attached to captions and cutlines. Each is carefully written and edited to exact specifications.

For most purposes, cutlines should be brief, accurate, captivating, and informative. Silly meaningless phrases such as "Oh you kid" or "Up in the Air" are better omitted. In their place, specific identifying cutlines can be written.

Observing a few standard rules will help provide good cutlines for the yearbook:

1. The cutline must be written to fill an allotted space.
2. It must be placed near the cut.
3. It should be in uniform style of writing and type.
4. One should accompany each picture.
5. Cutlines can often blend names and identifications into an interesting statement.
6. Cutlines should be in type smaller than that used for the body copy.

The cutline should help the picture tell the story. It ought to add something of interest that is not apparent by looking at the picture. Its effectiveness is increased if it tells something that is not covered in the text copy. How do you get the information to accomplish these objectives?

It's suggested in the chapter on photography that each photographer taking pictures for the annual be required to turn in a suggested cutline with every picture submitted for the book. He is in a better position than anyone else to know why the picture was taken and what is significant about it. Perhaps it's the free throw that won the game. You may need to get additional information from someone who is shown in the picture, or should know about it because of his position as coach or adviser, or his close association with the activity pictured. Study the picture carefully; often the number on the jersey of an athlete will enable you to identify him. It's just as important to get information for writing a cutline as it is for writing text copy.

Examples of a few well-written cutlines set in typical styles are shown below:

Snatching a rebound, Ron Salatich gives Ripple possession of the ball during the Washington game. The Rocket victory broke the Continentals' thirteen-game winning streak.

COACH BILL LUFLER has a record of 90 victories contrasted to one defeat and a tie at UM. He calls this year's tennis squad his best.

MUSCLES TIGHTEN along the firing line as 'Cats and Sooners wait tensely while Alan Langton lofts a charity shot goalward.

VICTORS AND VANQUISHED head for the showers after Central win over Phillips. Although the contest was a preseason game, "Crackerbox" Nichols Gymnasium was filled to the rafters.

HUSTLING Bill Jones (8) demonstrates why he was unanimous choice for the all-star team as he leaps high to tip one in for the Wildcats.

They might not have to sing for their dinner, but the Alpha Chi's sang for the second-place sorority trophy that songleader Ida True holds.

As supervisor of the School of Arts and Sciences, Dean Rodney W. Babcock spends much time co-ordinating the work of the 22 departments, to better prepare students for their careers. He retires this year after being dean for 25 years.

Easy To Follow Identifications

A routine but essential phase of copy writing for the yearbook is assembling picture identifications. Although identifications are among the most important elements of the annual, many editors resort to a haphazard manner of handling them. The fact that writing identifications requires a minimum of writing skill offers little incentive to the good writer and often results in neglect of this important task.

In compiling identifications for group pictures, it is well to use both first and last names wherever possible. When groups are unusually large, first names may be eliminated to cut down on the size of the identification. By all means, make certain that names are correctly spelled and under no circumstances let John Jones' name appear under Bill Brown's picture. To do an accurate job of compiling and correcting identifications, work should be started early in the year. Material should be taken from identification sheets, typed, and carefully checked.

Readers will be aided in finding people in group pictures if a careful and consistent job of arranging the identification is done. Name the rows within a group picture to prevent confusion. For example, it is better to say top row, instead of row one. Individuals in group pictures are always identified from left to right, so it is unnecessary in most cases to include "from left to right" in the cutline.

Begin the identification of a group with the name of the organization (SKYWOOD HALL — Top row:) as it is often hard for the reader to identify the group unless this is done. This is especially true if more than one group appears on the same page.

A few examples of writing and displaying identifications are shown below:
A group picture with three rows:

SKYWOOD HALL—Top row: Mrs. Neil Swanson, Beverly Briles, Virginia Briles, Helen Cazier. Second row: Reeva Hansen, Freda Tuback, Helen McDonall, Lola Bush. Bottom row: Joyce Haselwood, Laura Shelor, Doris Cline, Louise Barnes.

GERMAN CLUB—Bottom Row: JoAnne Walsh, Martha Kastner, Mary Elizabeth Taylor, Wanda Wright. **Second Row:** Mrs. Suzanna Underwood, sponsor; Rose Baier, Danny Retz, Theodore Slack, Kaye Noble. **Top Row:** Mary Bruder, Nancy McCormack, Ronald Lacey, William Klopp, Marilyn Hawkins.

A panel of individual photographs:
BLUE KEY—*Top Row:* Kenneth Bell, Arthur Cotts, Jim Davis, Jack Dean, Norville Gish, Dick Gorman, Jim Gretzinger. *Bottom Row:* Ward Haylett, Robert Heline, Jack Roth, Ralph Salisbury, Dean Schowengerdt, John Woolsey.

GRADUATE WOMEN'S HOUSE—TOP ROW: Mrs. Lillian B. Fuller, Marion E. Barnes, Grace M. Cables. **SECOND ROW:** Joan E. Carroll, Mary J. Freeburg, Lorraine E. Galle. **BOTTOM ROW:** Mary F. Hodgson, Hazel E. Parry, Margaret J. Watkins.

A group gathered around a table:

WHO'S WHOOT STAFF—Enid Keiswetter, special features; Laberta Kugler, county page editor; Tennyson Collins, photographer; Don Jacobson, business manager; Dale Johnson, sales manager; Marlys Waln, assistant editor; Maridell Byler, artist; Dale Apel, editor-in-chief; Stanley Wood, collegiate 4-H editor.

SENIOR CLASS OFFICERS—Robert Tointon, president; Betty Brammell, secretary; Jerry Friesen, treasurer; Howard Hill, Jr., vice-president.

Identification of a single person in a photograph:
TIRELESS EDITOR Ralph Salisbury was never long separated from his copy- and picture-cluttered desk in the Orange and Black office. Supervising the tedious job of assembling the 448-page annual, besides taking many of the pictures and editing copy, took most of Ralph's time.

A familiar face to all intramural participants is that of director Frank Myers, who has been at Central High 29 years.

Mood Copy Adds Impact

In addition to the mine-run copy that gives a clear and factual report of the year's activities, there is a place in yearbooks for mood copy: writing of a semi-literary nature to give emphasis to an important happening. Writing that stirs the emotions of the reader can be used effectively in the opening section, the chapter beginnings, or to emphasize some accomplishment of unusual importance to the school. It should be used sparingly, however, or it will lose its effectiveness.

Writing of this type may be likened to the climax of a play. The audience must be prepared step by step for the high comedy, tragedy, or heroics in order to appreciate them. In the examples to follow, an effort is made to set the scene for the reader.

The Centennial Wolverine, Michigan State University, East Lansing, does a superb job of telling the history of 100 years at its school. One of the high points is a color painting of Beaumont Tower, captioned—
MSC: On the eminence where State's College Hall was built a century ago to open a new era in education, Beaumont Tower stands in 1955 as a symbol of the will and ideals of the men who brough higher education to the common man.

On the next page appears a picture of former President Robert Sidey Shaw and the following headline and copy:

From the past: Principles
For the future: Vision

Beaumont Tower rose on the hill in the heart of Michigan State's circle in 1928, significant of the past in marking the site of old College Hall, significant of the future in reminding that the ideals of the College would not be forgotten.

Enrollment had risen to 3,800 and the campus had spread across the Red Cedar, but greater days were yet to come as State evolved into one of the world's great universities under the influence of two events of world importance—the 1929-37 depression and its public works programs, and the 1939-45 World War II with is tremendous utilization of Land Grant college resources and attendant upsurge in enrollment.

Two great figures stood at the head of Michigan State in this period: Robert Sidey Shaw and John Alfred Hannah.

The mortar was still wet in Kedzie Chemistry, the Library, and Demonstration Hall when Shaw ascended to the presidency in 1928. The world was in the grip of inflation and everybody was prosperous—except the farmer.

The economic collapse of 1929 plunged Shaw and State into circumstances almost no one had foreseen. But if people couldn't work—there were no jobs—they could study.

Sometimes the editor of a yearbook may want to emphasize the outstanding record of a student or faculty member. The person to be honored must have made an important contribution that is recognized by almost everyone at the school. The yearbook is usually dedicated to the individual selected, but it can be done in other ways.

The *Royal Purple* demonstrates one of the methods. The school had been in the football doldrums for 15 years, when a young athlete, unheralded and unsung, came to Kansas State. He was from a high school so small that he had played only six-man football. It was a steep hill to climb, but during his senior year, he contributed more than any other man to help record six wins, three losses, and one tie, the best season in 19 years.

The editor prepared the copy about his hero with care. No special page was reserved, but on the seventh page of the football section the athlete's picture appears along with three other lettermen and an action picture of a football game. The action picture is captioned: "It was a high spiraling kick—Joe caught on the twenty, cut out for 80 yards, and scored his second TD against CU."

Then, in dramatic fashion, the editor used the space reserved for text copy to print the following eulogy about a man who put a school back in the football headlines:

JOE MAKES GOOD

Veryl (Joe) Switzer ended his senior season at Kansas State by doing just about everything a football player can do.

He led the Big Seven conference in punt returns and was third in the nation in that department. Joe also tied for second-place scoring honors in the conference.

The AP and UP selected Joe for their first all-conference teams. The midwest chapter of the Football Writers Association of America elected him the Outstanding Back of the Midwest.

Climaxing his collegiate career, Joe crashed over for two touchdowns and led the West all-stars to a 31-7 victory in the Shrine game.

Sometimes the editor wants to interpret the moods, hopes, and aspirations of the students at his school. The *Ibis*, University of Miami, presents several pages of pictures of students studying, playing, and preparing themselves for competition and contests of many kinds. One page of dramatic interest has only two large pictures and a small amount of copy. The picture at the top of the page shows a young lady practicing at the piano, with hundreds of empty seats in the background, and only one seat occupied by a man. At the left side of the page is a picture of the entwined hands of two young lovers. The only copy on the page is:

Only a lonely echo and a single admirer, but that's how it usually is at the beginning . . . only determination and a hope of greatness . . . only a dream and the courage to wait for its realization. Time will, perhaps, bring the crowds and the applause. Now there is only work, and waiting for tomorrow.

There are other dreams just as important. You find them in the shadows when night approaches. The pressure of academics is muted by a gentle touch and a faint whisper. Sometimes the touch is enough and has a tender eloquence that tells the story of young love.

Write With Feeling

Don't be afraid to put feeling in your writing. Give it your best effort. It could be the beginning of a writing career for you. Perhaps you may make a lasting contribution to literature. Is it presumptuous that man aspire to the immortality of Shakespeare, Mark Twain, or Walt Whitman? Who shall say what man may dream!

Remember the yearbook is the family album of your school. Record in affectionate terms its fine accomplishments. Write the story as you would tell it to your sweetheart, with a kiss now and then.

Chapter 5

Two heads are better than one in determining if a picture will "make size." Sometimes it's necessary to change a carefully planned layout to properly display the photograph selected for use.

Designing Yearbook Layouts

PREPARING EFFECTIVE and interesting page layouts is one of the most difficult problems facing a yearbook staff. It is also one of the most important aspects, because the general appearance of the pages invites a reader to go through your annual.

Need for Layout and Design

Before discussing in detail the proper arrangement of pictures, drawings, and other printed material, it is well to consider the function of page layout. Primarily it *is to help achieve clear presentation and immediate comprehension of the printed message.* Arrangement of the material should make it easy for the reader to "read on the run."

America is fast becoming a viewing instead of a reading nation. Television and "picture" magazines make it easy to grasp messages presented without effort.

As editor of a yearbook, you are competing for a part of every reader's attention. To get it, you must make it easy for him to follow and understand the material presented. If you confuse or slow him down with cluttered or crowded pages, you lose him. To hold him, you must arrange all pages orderly, logically, and attractively.

Logical Arrangement a Help

A logical arrangement of material on the page of an annual leads the reader down the same well-trod visual path he has traveled ever since he learned to read books, newspapers, and magazines. Too often editors of yearbooks, in a sincere effort to produce an outstanding book, decide their annuals must be arranged differently from all other books. They forget that they cannot change the reading habits of all who come in contact with "their book." Don't irritate readers by trying to change their reading habits.

Careful study of pages reproduced from award-winning annuals in this book will give you a clear understanding of what is meant by an orderly and logical presentation of material. Headlines lead the eye directly into the text copy, as an invitation to read the story presented. Pictures are carefully cropped (uninteresting parts eliminated when making printing plates) to bring out their most important features. Often the pictures used have been enlarged from a small part of the original negatives. Cutlines are always placed near pictures they identify.

Allocating Space Important

The first step in planning layouts for your annual is assigning the material to be presented to definite pages. A simple and almost universal method used in allocating space is shown in the following table:

Foreword	2	1	Title Page
Contents	4	3	Dedication
Division, "The School"	6	5	View of building
Superintendent,	8	7	Division, "The School"
Board of Education		9	Principal, Office staff
English faculty	10	11	Mathematics faculty
and classroom picture			and classroom picture
Science faculty and	12	13	Social Studies faculty
laboratory picture			and classroom picture
Home Economics faculty	14	15	Modern Language faculty
and laboratory picture			and laboratory picture
Music faculty	16	17	
and classroom picture			

A preliminary outline of the whole finished book can be made by this method. The table above shows only the first 16 pages of a theoretical book. You will need several sheets of ordinary typing paper with a line drawn through the center of each from top to bottom. All pages to bear odd numbers should appear on the right-hand side of the line, and pages to bear even numbers on the left-hand side. Using this method, you can tell at a glance which pages will face each other in the finished book. You can arrange related subject matter on facing pages. For example, if two pages are devoted to school plays, a more effective layout can be made by planning a two-page spread, that is, two pages facing each other.

Allocating space in this way enables you to switch pages from one section to another without having to replace several preliminary page layouts. Then, too, an outline of this kind shows the number of pages proposed for the entire annual. This enables you to determine whether it will be necessary to add to or eliminate pages to keep the annual within the number of pages contracted.

Advantages of Page-by-page Dummy

As soon as a fair allocation of space has been

FIGURE 5.1. A double-page spread from a dummy, reproduced in miniature, shows how illustrations, text copy, headlines, and cutlines are usually portrayed. The dummy indicates the pictures needed.

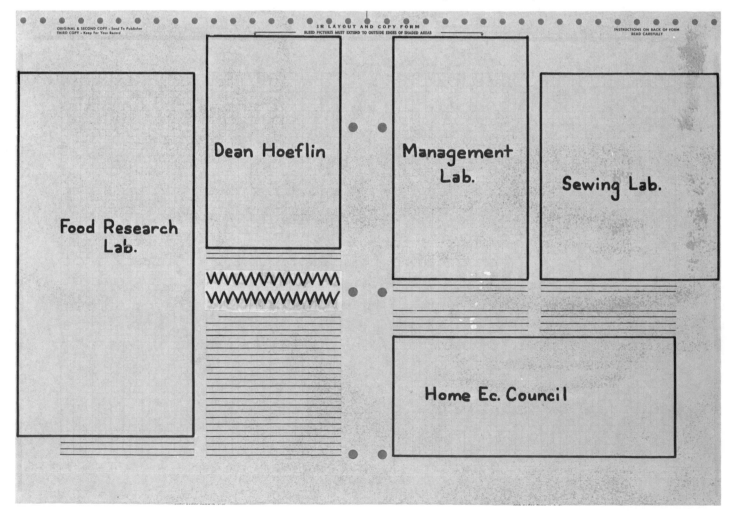

made, it is wise to make a fairly detailed dummy of the plan you have outlined.

A loose-leaf dummy with sheets the exact size of the pages in your annual is most satisfactory. Ordinary white paper can be used but paper with cross-hatch lines, similar to that shown in Figure 5.1, makes it easier to sketch in the areas representing illustrations and type masses. Dummy sheets are often furnished by the printing company, or they can be purchased at your local book store. It is helpful to indicate on the dummy whether the pictures are to be studio portraits or informal shots. Results achieved in final layouts depend to a large extent upon the pictures that are planned and taken. The dummy pages should not be allowed to become a strait jacket on your effort, however, for you can often improve original layouts when all the pictures to go on a page are before you.

Establishing Uniform Page Margins

The elements you usually have to work with in making a layout for a page in any annual are: white space, illustrations, headlines, text copy, and cutlines.

White space can be used effectively to give emphasis to headlines, illustrations, and cutlines. It can also be used to establish standard type margins for each page and thus add to the beauty and effectiveness of the annual. Figure 5.2, a left-hand page from the *Royal Purple,* shows a method of establishing effective type margins as used in most well-printed books. Inside margins (the margin at the gutter or center of the book) should be the narrowest. In this case, 6/8 of an inch. Here the top margin is 7/8 of an inch. The outside margin is 1 inch and the bottom margin, widest of all, is 1⅛ inches.

There are many other satisfactory combinations of margin widths for an annual. The important point to remember is that the inside margin should be the narrowest, the top slightly wider, the outside margin slightly wider than the top margin, and the bottom margin the widest of all. Keep in mind that one-half of the pages must be designed for left-hand (the even numbered) pages and the other half for right-hand (the odd numbered) pages. In planning a right-hand page, for example, the narrow margin is the left margin (the one next to the gutter of the book) and margin widths are increased clockwise. Left-hand pages have the narrow margin on the right and margin widths increase counterclockwise.

Containing Type Within Margins

You will note that all type is contained within the margins thus established. However, the reproductions of the pictures used are allowed to "bleed" off the page (run through the margin off the pages) in some cases. Most authorities on layout feel that the illustrations either should be bled off the page or be kept within the type margins. Allowing a picture to extend into the margin (and not bleed) produces a ragged effect.

Further examination of Figure 5.2 reveals that all type material and the nonbleeding illustrations are printed flush to the type margins on both the left and right sides of the page. Normally type also should be positioned flush with the type margins at the top and bottom of the page. This arrangement of all elements in line with the type margins eliminates ragged effects, and adds to orderliness, readability, and clear-cut appearance of each page.

Not all book designers and typographers insist that all copy blocks be printed flush to the right- and left-hand margins. Some feel that satisfactory results are obtained when, for instance, the cutlines (lines of copy near pictures that interpret or identify) are moved in a few picas from the margins at both the left-and right-hand sides. Or that perhaps the same treatment might be followed regarding headlines or text copy. Excellent results can also be achieved by using this plan *but it must be used consistently* throughout the book.

Handling Illustrations

After definite page margins have been established for the annual, the next step in making the layout is to decide where to place the illustrations, always keeping in mind that you must leave space for cutlines and, in most cases, for a headline and text copy. Soon after action or event pictures are taken, it is a good plan to get contact prints (photographic prints the same size as the negatives) from the photographer to study carefully and to select those to be used. Check the preliminary layout in your dummy and see if you can improve it now that you have the actual pictures that are to be used. You may need to make several miniature layouts of the proposed page to find the most effective arrangement. Figure 5.3 illustrates how this is done. An hour's time often is required to arrive at an effective and orderly arrangement of the several elements to appear on the page. Do not give up until you are satisfied.

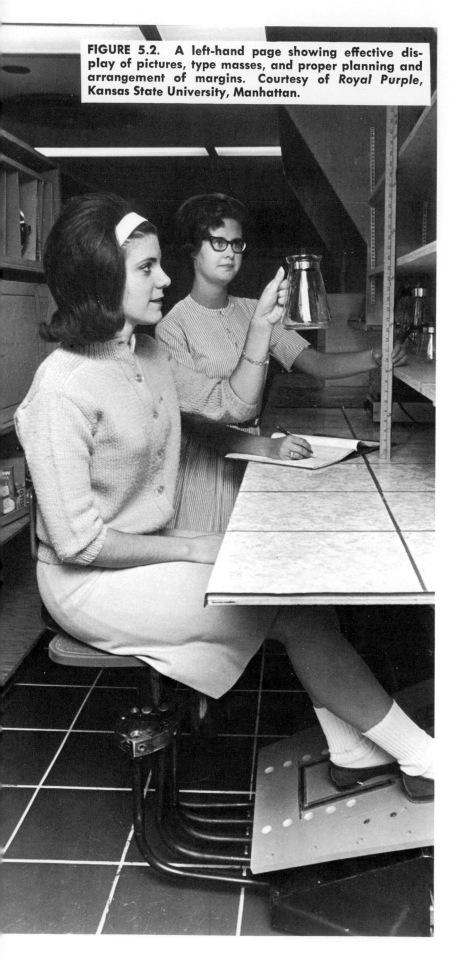

FIGURE 5.2. A left-hand page showing effective display of pictures, type masses, and proper planning and arrangement of margins. Courtesy of *Royal Purple*, Kansas State University, Manhattan.

Coeds conduct research for development of a specially designed food preparation center for handicapped women.

At Merrill Palmer Institute in Detroit, Mich., Dean Ruth Hoeflin continues with her second semester post doctoral studies.

Research plays top role in home ec curriculums

Research played an integral part in the six curriculums of the College of Home Economics. Foods and nutrition research focused on dietary habits of underprivileged, preschool children in Riley County. The department also conducted a National Livestock and Meat Board test about pork cookery.

A family economics project utilized a kitchen with a motorized chair designed to help semi-invalids manage homes.

In testing resistance of fabric to weathering and light, clothing and textiles used a weatherometer. The research machine simulated humidity, temperature and rainfall conditions. Another device, a scott tester, studied chemical and physical effects of radiation exposure to cotton fabric.

When you have finally decided on the layout to be used, mark the contact prints for the photographer, indicating the part of the print you plan to use, and tell him to make an enlargement of the area to be used. He should be instructed to make the enlargement at least as large or larger than it is to appear in the annual. Many engravers and printers like the print to be at least 1½ times as large as the proposed reproduction. Reducing the print when the plate is made tends to minimize or eliminate any scratches or minor blemishes in the photographic copy. It also gives the photographer a chance to bring out detail in certain areas of the picture that may be important to the story the picture portrays.

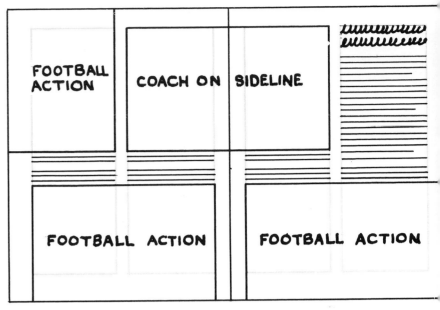

FIGURE 5.3. Miniature sketches can be used to visualize how the finished pages in the annual will look.

Using White Space for Emphasis

Examining Figure 5.2 again, you will note that the pictures have been cropped as closely as possible and still show the important features the editor wants to emphasize. White space around the picture tends to emphasize it. The ¼-inch white space left between pictures eliminates any confusion that might result from "pushing" them together on the page. You must determine the amount of white space left between pictures, then use that amount throughout the book or at least throughout any given section.

In assigning any particular picture to a position on the page, make certain the people or individuals pictured are not looking off the page. This directs the eye of the reader off the page. The picture on the left-hand side of the page in Figure 5.2 would not give a pleasing effect if moved to the right-hand side of a right-hand page. Be sure you examine each page several times to avoid such an error.

Selecting Pictures To Bleed

Bleeding pictures off the page should be given careful consideration. It must be remembered that most annuals are printed in signatures of 8, 16, or 32 pages. The large sheet of paper that forms the printed signature is folded to page size by a folding machine. The folding machine sometimes does not fold the sheet at the exact spot desired, perhaps missing by as much as 1/16 to 1/8 inch. After the folded signatures are assembled and sewed at the binding edge, the entire book is trimmed on a cutter. These operations may result in cutting away more of the picture that bleeds off the page than had been planned when the layout was made. Therefore, it is best to bleed only

pictures that will not be seriously affected if slightly more or less is trimmed away. Class panels should not be bled at the top or outside of a page. The picture of each individual in the panel is often less than one square inch in area, and parts of heads may be trimmed away. The possible "over-trimming," of course, spoils the appearance of the book and disappoints, if not angers, students whose pictures are mutilated.

Do not bleed too many pictures in the annual. When the bleed is used occasionally or in two or three sections of the book, it emphasizes the pictures and affords a change of pace. Bleed pictures probably can be used with best effect in the feature section, sports section, and, in some instances, in the opening and division pages of the annual. The class and organization sections can then be planned without bleed photographs or with only an occasional use of bleed for emphasis and variety. Never use any layout device to the point of making it offensively noticeable.

Balancing Facing Pages

Another matter that requires consideration when photographs are bled off pages is the layout of the facing page in the annual. Most layout men feel that the mass weight (the darkness or tone) of the two pages should be equal or almost equal. This principle applies whether the pictures bleed or not, but it becomes more acute when bleed is used, as the page area covered by pictures then becomes much larger. Remember that *the proper presentation of the interesting and vital part of a*

JOYCE FRASER

Joyce . . . anticipates attending Northern Illinois U. . . . would like to become a history teacher . . . considers Girls' Club favorite activity . . . for two years was employed as a switchboard operator.
Girls' Club Bd. 2; Council 3; Student Council Com. 3; Class Bd. 2; Girls' P.E. Leader 3,4; Aide 1,2,4.

LAURIE LOUISE FROST

Will study teaching at JC . . . found Spanish to be her favorite subject . . . will look back on the fun of going to the Corral and dances.

FREDERICK MICHAEL FREELAND

Mickey . . . will study business at U. of Illinois . . . enjoyed tennis, bowling, and basketball . . . chooses French as favorite subject . . . likes to play bridge. South Junior H.S. Pittsfield, Mass. 1; Basketball 1; Tennis 2,3,4; Bowling 2.

JOHN GORDON GALATY

Will attend Trinity College and make English his major field of study . . . especially liked American History . . . will never forget the thrill of playing varsity basketball.
Football 1,2,3,4; Basketball 1,2,3,4; Intramural Baseball 3,4; Rep. Assem. 2; Boys' Club Bd. 1,2, Treas. 4; German Club 3,4; Corral Show 4.

JEAN CLAIRE GALLAS

Jeanie . . . plans to study law at Colorado Women's College . . . liked School Spirit Committee and horseback riding . . . thought bringing Jr. class float to school was hysterical . . . did volunteer work at a hospital.
Student Council Com. 4.

ROBERT JAMES GAMBLE

Red . . . will attend either Northwest or Central Montana State College . . . liked intramural basketball and softball . . . spends free time working on cars and welding . . . terms algebra as favorite subject . . . was employed as a welder.
Intramural Basketball 1,2,4; Intramural Softball 1,2,4.

ARTHUR ALAN GARZONIO

Gar . . . will pursue studies in mechanics with General Motors . . . enjoyed working on his car . . . will always remember working in a gas station.

PATRICIA JEAN GATINS

Pat . . . intends to study teaching at Marquette U. . . . preferred ice skating to other activities . . . recalls basketball games . . . enjoyed working for the Sear's Roebuck Company.
St. Francis Xavier H.S., Fort Myers, Florida 1; St. Gertrude H.S., Richmond, Virginia 2.

Pep assembly, dance, prize-winning float   provide Homecoming memories for seniors

ELIZABETH ANN FREY

Beth . . . is undecided about future vocation . . . still laughs about distilled water being sprayed throughout the chemistry lab . . . will long remember the donation of a doll to the physics lab.
Thornton Fractional H.S. 1,2; Terrapin Club 1,2; Latin Club 1,2; Library Club 1,2; Pep Club 1,2; German Club 3,4; Home Ec Club 3,4; Jr. Red Cross Council 3.

VICTORIA LOUENE FREYMAN

Treens . . . hopes to become interior decorator or airline hostess after study at Lindenwood . . . rates basketball and football games high . . . considered history favorite subject.
Dramatics 1,2,3,4; GAA 1,2,3; Pep Club 1,2.

LAURA LEE FRIHART

Intends to study teaching at Northern Illinois U. . . . enjoyed basketball games and the Corral . . . likes reading and American history . . . will never forget Sophomore guidance classes and Senior Homecoming.
Pep Club 1,2.

BRUCE LEE FRISBIE

Has decided on police work as his career . . . interested in photography . . . liked basketball and football games . . . regards American History and physical education as favorite subjects . . . was a stock boy.

Long hours of hard work is reflected in the senior class float, second place winner in the blue division.

GAIL VIRGINIA GEISER

Geez . . . plans to study teaching at Purdue . . . enjoyed Friday nights at the Corral . . . will always remember the '62 Homecoming.
GAA 1,2; Home Ec Club 2,3; Spanish Club 3,4; Pep Club 2; Honor Study Hall Sup. 3.

KATHLEEN RUTH GERKEN

Gerk . . . will make psychiatry major field of study at Valparaiso U. . . . preferred water skiing to other activities . . . will always remember painting Corral office when she was a freshman.
Pom-Pon Squad 3,4; Senior Discussion Leader; Student Council Com. 1,2,3; German Club 3,4; Corral Show 3; Aide 1,2; Pep Club 1,2; GAA 1,2,3.

CHRISTINE ANNETTE GIANACAKOS

Chris . . . plans to enter Moser Secretarial School after graduation . . . enjoyed working on homecoming floats . . . preferred Sociology to other subjects . . . will never forget interviewing faculty members for a psychology panel.
Business Club 4; Jr. Red Cross Council 4; GAA 1.

JERRY HOLMES GILBERT

Anticipates studying law at the U. of Illinois . . . preferred chemistry to other subjects . . . will always remember falling at the finish of a hurdle race in the state meet at Champaign.
Football 1,2,3,4; Intramural Basketball 1,2,3,4; Track 1,2,3,4; German Club 2,3.

FIGURE 5.4. Formal, or symmetrical balance, is achieved by placing elements of exactly the same size and tone value equidistant from the vertical axis. *Tabulae*, Lyons Township High School, La Grange, Ill.

picture is more important than slavishly following any theory of layout. Good judgment often helps more than iron-clad rules in presenting arrangements that add to the variety and interest of finished pages. However, you should use your ingenuity to get some semblance of eye balance on facing pages.

In preparing the dummy, care should be taken to arrange the different elements on facing pages so the two pages are in equilibrium. This is called balance, or balanced layout. Balance can be visualized as perfectly balanced scales, on which have been placed two objects of equal weight, equally distant from the fulcrum. The fulcrum or vertical axis of a two-page spread is the line where the two pages meet at the backbone (often called the gutter) of the book. The two general types of balance are called formal balance and informal balance.

Achieving Formal Balance

Formal or symmetrical balance is achieved by placing elements of almost exactly the same size or tone value at equal distances from the vertical axis, as shown in Figure 5.4. Formal balance can also be obtained on both the vertical and the horizontal axis as shown in Figure 5.5.

Layouts using the principle of formal balance are the simplest and easiest for the beginner. Many of the pages of your yearbook may be arranged in this manner, especially when the impression desired is one of formality., However, the material that must be used on facing pages often makes it impossible to achieve a formal or balanced layout. Then, too, for the sake of variety, it is often desirable to break away from formal balance on some pages of your book.

Planning Informal Balance

Informal or asymmetrical balance uses the same principle as formal balance. Again using scales to illustrate, informal balance comes when the heavy object or objects are moved closer to the fulcrum and the lighter object is moved farther away, thus bringing the scales into balance again. Figure 5.6 illustrates the principle of informal balance. Informal balance may also be accomplished by keeping all illustrations within the type page.

Pleasing informal balance is more difficult to achieve than formal balance. Informal balance is sometimes called eye balance. It is often necessary to make several preliminary sketches using all the elements that must be placed on facing pages before a satisfactory layout is achieved. The beginner in layout-making often falls into the error of believing that informal balance licenses him to cast aside the principles of good layout that have been achieved during the more than 500 years of the printing industry. Such is not the case.

Deciding on Picture Shapes

Judging from yearbooks being produced, opinions vary widely on the exact shape to which pictures should be cropped when planning layouts. The conservatives in yearbook design believe all pictures should appear in rectangular shapes as shown in Figure 5.2. At the other extreme are those who feel that it is satisfactory to cut pictures to form stars, triangles, letters of the alphabet, footballs, odd "cookie-cutter shapes," or almost any shape other than rectangular.

As is usually the case, the truth is found somewhere between the two extremes. While it is almost impossible to find a picture cropped in any shape other than rectangular in the news or editorial sections of *Life* or *Look,* perhaps the yearbook staff should be allowed more license in this matter because yearbook pictures are often taken by amateurs. For instance, the back of a head in the foreground or some object in the background may distract from the effectiveness of the photograph, but this part of the picture can be eliminated by trimming the part to be used in an oval, circular, or octagonal shape. If adequate funds are available, as is usually the case with commercial magazines, the objectionable part of the picture would be eliminated by retouching, or perhaps the photographer could eliminate it by making an enlargement and holding back that part of the picture by the "dodging" method.

Make Shape of Pictures Functional

The important thing to remember is that the shape of the picture must be functional. The shape bears a harmonious relation to the photograph used and it must fit in with the layout. Pages from award-winning annuals presented in this book will show other than rectangular pictures that have been used effectively.

Nevertheless, indiscriminate cutting of photographs in odd shapes is very likely to result in bad layout. It often distracts from the interest of the photograph, also. Freak shapes usually do not harmonize with symmetrical type blocks that appear on the same page. Whether the pictures are to be reproduced as rectangles, ovals, circles, or other shapes, they should be absolutely symmetrical. An amateur seldom can trim photographs symmetrically. It is safer for you to send uncropped pictures to the engraver or printer who is producing the yearbook with crop marks on the photographs indicating only where and how they are to be cropped. Figure 5.9 illustrates the proper way to make crop marks on a photograph.

Angling or Tilting Photographs

The matter of tilted or angled photographs needs to be given thoughtful consideration when preparing page layouts. A few years ago, when the angled photograph became popular in yearbooks, it was considered an attention-compelling device. When new, it probably did attract much attention. However, since then some books have gone to the extreme of angling many pictures in the book, and the good effect has been lost. An occasional angled picture may increase the reader's interest, but judgment must be used to see that tilting the photograph does not reduce its effectiveness by making it appear that a building is falling over, or that a football player is running uphill. If a picture is angled, the reader must tilt his head to one side or shift the position of the book to observe it properly. This is particularly true if the cutline also is angled.

Consequently, when you tilt a photograph, have a good reason. Tilt it only slightly, not more than 20 degrees, and be sure it adds to the effectiveness of both the picture and your page layout.

Use of Headlines

When planning the tentative layout, space must be left for the printed copy that is to appear on the page with the photographs. Space allotted for headline and text copy usually can be reserved in one block or area, as the headline should be placed so it will lead the eye directly into the story. Space reserved for this purpose on the page in Figure 5.2 is a rectangular area 3¼ inches wide by 1½ inches high.

The headline has been set in 24-point type. The basic measurement for all typographic purposes is the *point,* which is 1/72 of an inch. The height of type is always expressed in points. Thus, 24-point type is ⅓ of an inch high. Plenty of white space has been allowed both above and below the headline. Small headlines with plenty of "air" or white space are more effective than large black headlines that crowd the page. And you will note that small headlines do not distract from the illustrations and other copy on the page, and allow room for more words in the headline. The headline has been set in capital and lower case letters. Tests have shown that copy set in this manner is more readable than if set in all capital letters. This is particularly true of long lines.

Making the Headline Functional

Opinion is widely divided as to the function of the headline in a yearbook, its placement on the page, length of line to be used, and size of type to be employed. Also you have the question: Should each page have a headline?

FIGURE 5.5. How formal balance on both the vertical and horizontal axis is accomplished is shown in this spread from the *Shield,* High School, Highland, Ind.

Science Club Built Greenhouse Addition to Biology Room

To further the cause of science and to promote interest in the field are the goals of the 20 members of the Science Club. Anyone in grades ten through twelve who is truly interested in science and is taking a science course may apply for membership. One of the great achievements by the club was its acceptance into the Junior Academy of Science, in 1961.

A major project for the Science Club this year was to raise funds for the construction of a greenhouse on the biology room. To do this, they sponsored soc-hops and other fund raising events.

In working toward their goal as a club, the group visited various spots of scientific interest and sent club representatives to the meeting of the Junior Academy of Science.

SCIENTIFIC APPARATUS ENABLES Science Club members to pursue their interests. Members in the club such as James Evans, Bob Rezny, and Chuck Williams, shown here with their sponsor, Mr. Jon Hendrix, find modern equipment in Highland High's science department.

62 SCIENCE CLUB—*Bottom Row:* R. Rezney, treasurer; Mr. J. Hendrix, sponsor; J. Evans, president; C. Williams, secretary. *Second Row:* D. Kletzing, B. Dove, K. Rich, S. Wozniak, T. Lukas, R. Roades, R. Lorton. *Top Row:* V. Waltz, J. Minter, E. Luetzelschwab, J. Yuhasz, H. Marsh, D. Evansin, T. Humphrey, V. Hodges, J. King.

GERMAN CLUB—*Bottom Row:* M. Boyd, secretary-treasurer; Mrs. H. Beretz, sponsor; A. Bohanon, president; T. Hertwig, vice president. *Second Row:* K. Pudell, K. Nicksic, R. Boston, F. Antonovitz, P. Angell, M. McGee, C. Daville, J. Petrukitas. *Third Row:* M. Pecsek, K. Markward, J. Cady, B. Dove, J. Evans, J. Ashton, J. Beade, S. Eidner. *Top Row:* M. Hendrickson, B. Gregory, E. Luetzelschwab, S. Decker, C. Dorschel, D. Eaton, E. Antone, J. Minter, H. Soudriette.

Newly Innovated German Club Plans Fund-Raising Projects

Christmas caroling and dinner at German restaurant were the most important projects this year for the German Club. A new arrival on the scene, it is open to sophomores, juniors, and seniors, who are taking German. Officially known as Der Deutshe Verdin, their purpose is the study of the civilization, culture, and people of Germany. In the late fall they displayed items of handicraft in the showcase opposite the German room.

Although the club was formed only last fall and many of its long-range projects are still in the planning stages, it still had several events this year. The club tried to observe the German holidays, especially Christmas. Songfests with the songs sung in German, and the playing of traditional German games were also a part of the club's activities.

Later, after more experience is gained in the language, the club hoped to put on German plays. With these and other activities the club planned to provide entertainment for the members.

DECORATING THE SHOWCASE with traditional German novelties and souvenirs, Kathy Pudell awaits the approval of fellow German club members, Al Bohanon and Kathy Markward. Mrs. Helen Beretz, sponsor, brought the items from Germany last summer.

Before the advent of lavish illustrations in newspapers and magazines, headlines were used to arouse the interest of the reader and lead him to read what followed. The headline has been well compared to the show window of a store as a device to catch the eye of the passer-by and get him interested. But the headline as an attention-getting device often must take a "back seat" on yearbook pages filled with large pictures that have more impact on the reader.

However, there are many pages in the annual where headlines have the important role of obtaining and directing the attention of the reader. A glance at a well-written and properly displayed headline on pages devoted to clubs, organizations, activities, sports, administration, etc. not only helps the reader find the material in which he is interested but also invites him to read other pages in which he does not have much personal interest. Whether the headline should assume its historic role as the dominant attention-getting device of the page will be determined by the illustrations and other material of interest presented. The editor must carefully consider all these things in determining whether to use a headline.

The position of the headline on the page decides to a large extent the force it will exert on the reader. The headline should be placed so it will direct the reader easily into the story (the text copy). Headlines that are placed directly above large pictures or illustrations lose some of their effectiveness. The picture tends to block the natural path of the eye to the rest of the page and the copy you have prepared for the reader.

Proper Headline Length

The longer the line of type, the more difficult it is for the reader to take it in at one glance. Sometimes, if it extends across two pages, the lines on facing pages do not appear as a straight line. Because of folding and binding operations previously discussed, the part of the headline on one page may be slightly higher or lower than that on the facing page. Your reader is also forced to jump the margins at the gutter of the book and is often confused and does not read the entire headline. A short headline properly worded and displayed is usually the most effective and can more easily be placed to direct the reader into the copy. However, headlines extending across two facing pages in the annual are sometimes useful to tie the two pages together and to form a double-page spread.

Yearbook staffs often are inclined to use head-line type too big and black for best results. The theory that big headlines lend emphasis and gain interest probably can be traced to their use by newspapers, and admittedly they do have the effect of carrying the reader to a particular story. This practice has come down from the time when most newspapers were sold on the street by newsboys, or displayed and sold at newsstands. The big black, red, or other colored headlines could be read at a distance by prospective purchasers. Even today, when most newspapers are delivered to homes or offices, except in a few cities such as New York, the tradition of large, lurid headlines remains.

But your problem of getting readership and interest in the annual is quite different. Most readers of your yearbook are students and others whose pictures are in the book, or parents, friends, or other individuals with a strong interest in the school. The problem is not to sell them a copy of the annual for five or ten cents because of their curiosity about a big headline, as with a newspaper.

The reader of a yearbook holds the page about 14 inches from his eyes and can read medium-sized headlines more easily than large ones. And don't forget that smaller headlines in the annual leave more room on the page for pictures and copy vitally necessary for telling the complete story.

Omitting Headlines

The idea that "every page in the yearbook should have a headline" seems to have gained widespread acceptance, probably because books and magazines devoted to the publication of annuals emphasize the need for so-called good headlines. Also, some staffs have obtained this idea from speakers at yearbook conventions and from yearbook judges who have criticized certain pages of annuals for omitting needed headlines.

While it is true that most pages will be better and more interesting if they have a well-written and properly displayed headline, it is equally true that some pages are less interesting and effective because of unneeded headlines. The nature of the material that goes into making a yearbook requires that the editor give uniform treatment, even to headlines, in certain sections of the book. A case in point could be the organization pages. If you use a headline on the page showing the glee club, a headline should be provided for the band page. The same rule applies to fraternities and all organizations in a given section.

On the other hand, perhaps for the sake of variety, the sports section might be planned with fewer headlines. You can do this by having only one headline on the first page of the football section and subheads on the following pages to tell of each game.

Selecting Type for Copy and Cutlines

The text copy in Figure 5.2 is set in 12-point type with 2-point leading (pronounced ledding) between the lines of type. This may be done either by inserting thin strips between the lines after they have been cast or by casting a shoulder on the slug itself. If done in the latter manner, the type would be referred to as set *12 on 14*. If type matter is set without any extra space between the lines, it is referred to as *set solid*. The larger the type, the more leading needed to make it read able. Six-point type is often set solid. Usually 10- or 12-point type is used for the text copy of an annual and leaded from 2 to 3 points depending on the type face used and length of line.

Lines of type that are set too long are difficult to read. Reading tests indicate that they should be between 26 and 52 characters in length, with approximately 40 letters to the line as ideal. To arrive at the number of characters in a line, you count all the letters, spaces between words, and punctuation marks used in the line. The text copy in Figure 5.2 has been set 21 picas wide and the character count of the line is 44. If the layout is to be effective, copy must be written to fit exactly the space provided.

FIGURE 5.6. Two facing pages illustrate the pleasing use of informal balance. The mass weights of the pages are approximately equal. Courtesy of the *Tower*, Wheaton College, Wheaton, Illinois.

Placing Cutlines on Page

Cutlines are placed directly below the pictures shown in Figure 5.2. It is a good plan to place identification cutlines in an annual above bottom-of-the-page pictures instead of below them because of the large number of group pictures of organizations that require identification of each individual. When the names of large groups are set in type, they often do not result in a symmetrical block of type, and when placed above the photograph instead of flush to the bottom margin, the lack of symmetry is not so obvious. Of course, you can write news cutlines to fit the space and run them below the pictures at the bottom of the page if the pictures do not bleed, but it seems more logical to follow a definite and consistent policy in this matter.

It will be noted that the cutlines are set in 9-point type, smaller than the text copy. This is common practice and makes it easy for the reader to spot material he wants to read. The copy has been written to fit the space and plenty of white space is allowed each cutline for emphasis and clarity. The first two or three words of each cutline are set in boldface type to invite the reader's attention. Often this feature is omitted. Instead of boldface, the first two or three words can be set in ALL CAPITAL letters or in SMALL CAPITALS. Any style you adopt should be used throughout the book.

Major Classifications of Type

While this chapter is primarily devoted to layout, some elementary knowledge of type classifications and type families is necessary to understand the discussions that follow. This knowledge also will be useful to you in working with the printer of your annual. In all cases, the printer should be consulted and relied upon to help and advise in the selection of type.

It is almost impossible to find two type-experts who use exactly the same names for major classifications of type. To complicate the matter further, one writer may classify type in four categories while another will list as many as twelve.

The five major classifications of type discussed here are: Text, Roman, Sans Serif, Square Serif, and Script. The last four are those most commonly used in printing yearbooks. Text is discussed first because of its historic significance and to give you an insight into at least one of the factors that influence type-design.

This is Shaw Text, a Text type, 18 point.

Text resembles the old Germanic handwriting that was in use when Gutenberg and other printers started designing movable type. It was familiar to all who could read. Hence, what more logical alphabet could be used to introduce the public to the newly discovered method of printing books? It is not often used today except for religious purposes and for social printing, such as wedding invitations.

This is Bodoni Bold, a Modern Roman type, 18 point.

Roman type is used extensively in all forms of modern printing. Practically all books, magazines, and newspapers use it for text matter. Readers are therefore conditioned to reading Roman type from the first grade throughout their lives. You can rely on it to be read rapidly and with little effort.

The Roman types are characterized by serifs. A serif is a hair line—a light line or stroke crossing or projecting from the end of a main line or stroke in a letter. Note the fine serif, or crossline, at the base of the m, n, p, and h, also at the top and bottom of the letters i and l in the headline above. The serifs vary in weight and thickness with different type families.

Roman types are subdivided into Modern Roman and Old Style Roman. In fact, they are often listed separately in the major classification of type, and are referred to simply as Modern and Old Style.

This is Garamont Light, an Old Style Roman type, 18 point.

The wedge-shaped serif and the graceful curve from the body of the letter to the serif, as in the Garamont shown above, distinguish Old Style from Modern. You should note that this characteristic is more pronounced in lower case letters than in capitals. Don't let the term "Old Style" prejudice you against the use of types thus classified. The term does not have the same meaning when used in classifying type as it does when used to describe a hat, dress, or coat. Old Styles such as Garamont, Caslon, Cloister, and many others often are used in the finest of book printing. Old Style faces are being designed and cut every year. Roman types probably are used more than any other classification in text matter as well as headlines and cutlines of annuals. However, in recent years they have been used extensively in combination with other types, such as Sans Serif and others.

This is Tempo Bold, a Sans Serif type, 18 point.

Sans Serif is a class of type that is becoming extremely popular for headlines in yearbooks. It is also often used for cutlines, and sometimes for text copy. The Sans Serif letters are distinguished by their extreme simplicity. The letters have no serifs and this gives the type its name, Sans Serif, i.e., without serifs. In text matter, it is wise to set Sans Serif type faces in short paragraphs with plenty of leading between lines. Sans Serif faces are probably most effective when used in headlines or cutlines and with the text matter set in a Roman face.

This is Stymie Bold, a Square Serif type, 18 point.

The Square Serif letters are similar in design to Sans Serif letters except for the addition of thick square serifs. The Sans Serif and the Square Serif type are so similar in design, except for the serifs themselves, that some typographers place them in one general classification and call them Gothic. The Square Serif types are sometimes used effectively for headlines in yearbooks, and are quite effective if set in medium-size type with plenty of white space.

This is Stylescript, a Script type, 18 point.

Scripts are types designed to look like modern handwriting. In the case of Kaufman and Brush, the finishing stroke of each letter joins with the opening stroke of the next letter, except for capi-

tals. Scripts are sometimes used as headlines in yearbooks, but it is difficult to write headlines to fit the space, for scripts should not be letter-spaced. A line of type or a word is "letter-spaced" when more than the normal white space is left between the letters and words to make the whole line of type fit a specified length or measure.

Some of the Script types, such as Raleigh and Bernhard Cursive, are so designed that the letters do not join together. They are often referred to as "Cursives."

This is Garamond Bold Italic, 18 point.

Italic types are not truly a classification in themselves but are slanting variants of Romans and some of the Sans Serif faces. The Sans Serif Italics are properly referred to as *Obliques*. Italics are sometimes used for cutlines and less often for headlines in yearbooks, but they are not particularly effective. They are excellent for a line or two, or perhaps better still, for one word in the body copy to give emphasis and contrast. They are not good for large bodies of type and are especially hard to read when set in all caps.

The names by which type is commonly known, such as Bodoni, Garamond, Century, and Caslon, are family names. A complete family of type consists of one particular design of type in all its sizes, weights, widths and variants.

Lithotyped Composition

Some of the smaller yearbooks produced by the offset process of printing do not use machine-set type for the text copy, cutlines, or, in rare cases, even headlines. Instead, the written material is copied on an electric typewriter and then reproduced by the photolithographic process. This method does not permit a wide selection of type to be used in the annual and is often called *lithotyped composition*. However, some electric typewriters now have letters closely resembling actual type faces and in more than one size. While this method does not approximate the beauty and symmetry of a well-designed page set in type, it is often used because the annual must operate on a limited budget. Of course, many of the excellent books produced by photolithography use the finest of machine-set type. Most concerns printing yearbooks, however, encourage the staff to use regular typography whenever finances will permit.

Instructions for the Printer

One of the commonest complaints made by yearbook staffs is: "The printer did not arrange the material on the page the way we wanted it." If the printer is to arrange the reproductions of the pictures, the cutlines, the headline, and the text copy exactly as you planned it in the layout, you must give him complete and detailed instructions.

Your first step is to make a layout sheet for the printer. Figure 5.7 shows the layout sheet that was prepared for the printer, giving detailed instructions for the arrangement of the page reproduced in Figure 5.2. The exact space to be occupied by picture reproductions, cutlines, headline, and the text copy has been clearly indicated on the sheet. It should be noted, in the interest of clarity, that the layout sheet used in Figure 5.7 has been reproduced actual size. This necessitated trimming away the original margins of the layout sheet. The margins are useful in indicating to the printer the name of the annual, the page number, and where the cuts are to bleed.

The second step in preparing copy for the printer is to mark the pictures so the reproductions or halftones can be made to fit the layout. Spaces reserved for illustrations on the layout usually are indicated by numbers. As mentioned earlier, you should select the pictures to be used and get enlargements of the interesting area of each picture when making the orginal layout of the page. It is also necessary at that time to determine whether the picture will "make size," that is, whether it will reduce or enlarge so the plate will fit the area provided.

Determining Whether Picture Will Make Size

There are several common methods to determine if a photograph will make size. Perhaps the quickest and easiest method is to use a proportion rule, one type of which is shown in Figure 5.8. This scale is made of two pieces of circular cardboard, the smaller fitting over the larger, and fastened together in the center with a metal rivet in such a manner that the inside or smaller circle of cardboard can be turned to the right or left to bring any number shown on the margin of the inside circle in direct alignment with any number shown on the outside or larger circle. A scale of this kind, or one working on the same mathematical principle, often is loaned by the printer or sold at a nominal price to yearbook staffs.

How To Use the Proportion Scale

To illustrate how the scale is used to determine if copy will make size, a 7½ x 9½ inch picture is shown actual size in Figure 5.9. Assume that the finished illustration should be 3½ x 4½ inches. First, rotate the inside circle on the scale so the numeral 3½ is in direct alignment with the numeral 4½ on the outside circle. This represents the size of the desired cut . Second, hold the scale in this exact position and look at the photograph Figure 5.9. It is evident that you need to eliminate parts of the photograph so that the important point of interest can be reproduced as large as possible. There is quite a lot of area at both the top and bottom of the picture that can be eliminated and perhaps improve the final result. Thus the critical measurement is the width to be used. Place a ruler on the photograph and you will find that the ideal width to use is 5½ or 6 inches. Now locate 5½ on the inside scale. It is opposite 7 on the outside scale. This indicates that you must use 7 inches in height. Applying the ruler to the photograph again you find the exact area you want to use for best results.

Make Crop Marks on Photograph

Indicate with a grease pencil on the margin of the photograph, as illustrated in Figure 5.9, approximately where the printer is to trim the finished negative after he has photographed the copy. These marks are called "trim marks." It is a much safer method than actually trimming the photograph to this size, because an error made in the calculation will show up on the ground glass of the engraver's camera when he is making the cut. Trim marks allow him to take in a little more of the photograph than is necessary to make size. If too much of the photograph is actually trimmed away he cannot make size and will have to request a new photograph and thus delay the work and cause extra expense for a new print.

A grease pencil is most convenient for making trim marks because any mark made in the wrong place can easily be removed without damaging the photograph. Some prefer to use a light blue pencil because the marks made in light blue do not rephotograph when a black-and-white halftone is made. However, the marks are not easily removed without damaging the photograph, and, in case of error, it is sometimes desirable to change the trim marks on a photograph before sending it to the printer. All prints for reproduction should be made with a white margin all the way around so crop marks can be made on the margins.

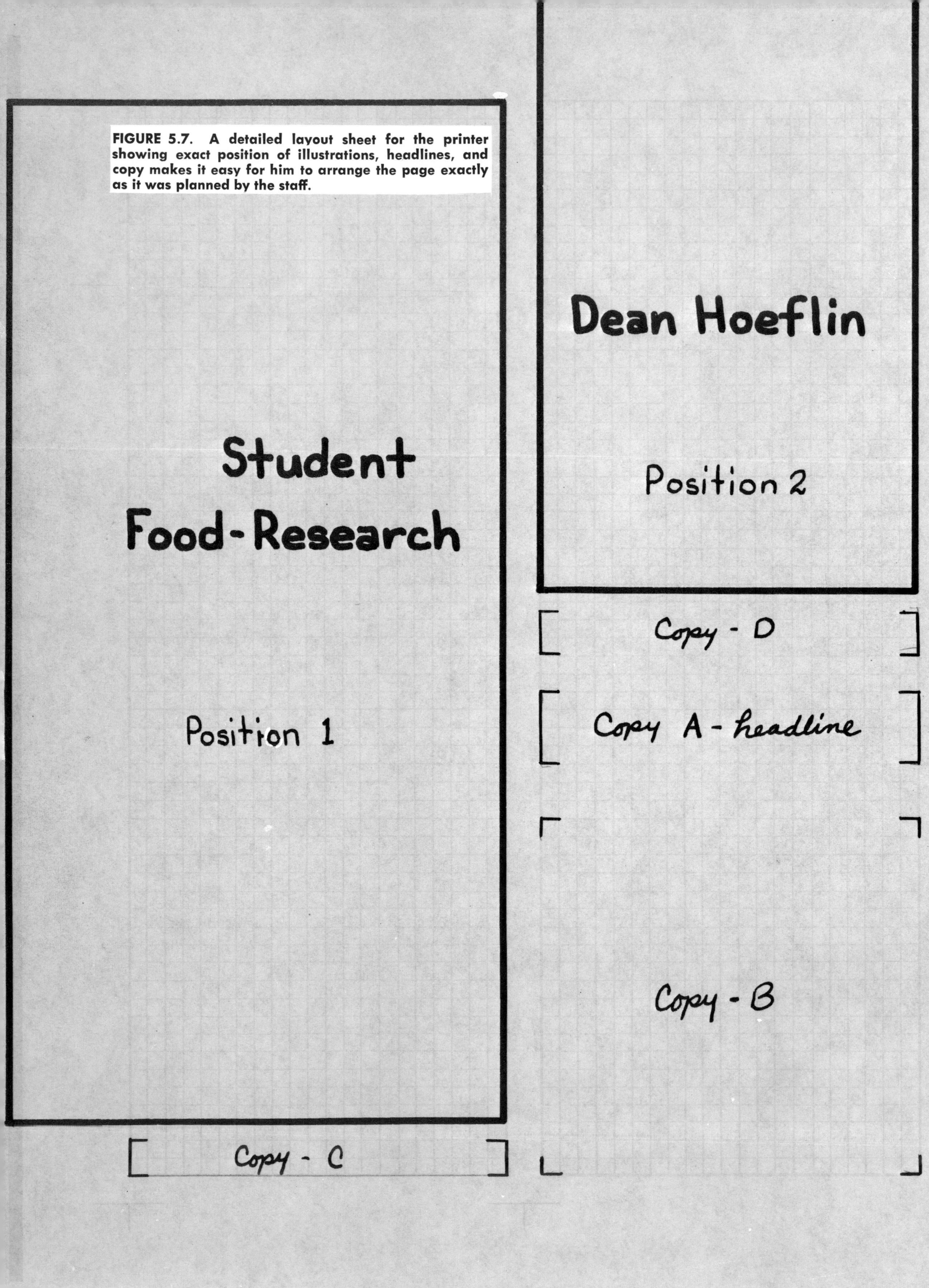

FIGURE 5.7. A detailed layout sheet for the printer showing exact position of illustrations, headlines, and copy makes it easy for him to arrange the page exactly as it was planned by the staff.

Dean Hoeflin

Position 2

Student
Food-Research

Position 1

Copy - D

Copy A - headline

Copy - B

Copy - C

Estimating Size of Cut by Formula

If a proportion scale is not available when ordering cuts, you can determine if pictures will make size by solving a problem in simple proportion. The width of the cut is to the height of the cut as the width of the picture is to the height of the picture.

The problem would be expressed as follows: $3\frac{1}{2}:4\frac{1}{2}::5\frac{1}{2}:X$. To find the unknown (X) divide the product of the extremes (in this case, 3.5X) into the product of the means (in this problem, 4.5 x 5.5 or 24.75) or $24.75 \div 3.5 = 7.07$ inches. As can be seen by using the two methods, the results are the same. However, the use of the proportion scale is quicker because the figures often are in fractions of an inch and cannot always be reduced easily to decimal points. Also, the proportion scale results in fewer errors. Get one if you possibly can and use it always.

Giving Engraver Complete Instructions

In addition to the trim marks on the front of the picture, it is important to give the engraver complete instructions as to the size of cut wanted, if your book is done by letterpress. On the particular cut being discussed, it would be necessary to inform the engraver that the top edge of the cut is to bleed off the page. Some engravers furnish stickers on which this information can be written and pasted to the back of photographs. If stickers are not available, the information can be written on the back of the photograph. If this is done, a pencil with soft lead must be used, and care taken not to press down when writing. If you fail to observe this precaution, the writing may show through on the front of the photograph and a new print will have to be obtained before a cut can be made.

Estimating Copy for Given Space

If the finished page in the book is to be effective and in accord with the layout provided, it is important to furnish the exact amount of copy needed to fill the space. Space provided for text copy in the layout prepared for the printer in Figure 5.7 is marked copy "B." The height of the copy is $3\frac{1}{2}$ inches. Copy in this case is set in 12-point type with 2-point leading. This means that each line of copy for this area would occupy a space 14 points in height. To determine the number of lines of copy that can be printed in an area one inch high, divide 14 into 72. (Remember,

there are 72 points per inch.) By dividing 14 into 72, you find that it will require 5 1/7 lines of type to fill an area 1 inch high. To find the number of lines required, multiply 5 lines (the 1/7 of a line is ignored) by the height of the area, which is $3\frac{1}{2}$ inches. The answer is $17\frac{1}{2}$ lines, so 17 lines are written.

One more factor must be known to determine the amount of copy needed to fill a space. You need to know the family of type to be used. In this particular case, it is 12-point Palatino. By measuring the length of the line, it is found that each line is 21 picas wide (a pica is $\frac{1}{6}$ of an inch). The set width (the average number of characters of a type that can be set in a line measuring one pica in width) of 12-point Palatino is 2.09. By multiplying the measure of the line (its width in picas) by the set width, the character count of the line is found. Thus, in a line 21 picas wide with a set width of 2.09 there is room for 44 characters.

Preparing Copy for Printer

To type copy B in Figure 5.7, the typewriter would be set to type 43 characters per line. The reason for this is that yearbook copy usually contains more than the average number of capital letters, which are wider than one normal character space. Then, too, the area to be covered by the type is usually limited in the yearbook. If a full page of type were being set with no illustrations on the page, it would be satisfactory to use the 44 character count.

All copy should be typewritten and double-spaced with wide margins. The space in the margin is used by the printer for instructions to the typesetter. In this case, the instruction would be to set the type 21 picas wide in 12-point Palatino, 2-points leaded. He would use abbreviations that are easily understood by the printer. In rare cases, the staff marks the copy before it is sent to the printer.

Double-spacing makes it possible to edit copy without retyping. If only a few errors are made on a page, it is a waste of time to retype the whole page, when simple editing marks can be used that are clear to the typesetter. If a number of corrections are made, it is better to retype the page than to send in "dirty" copy.

The name of the book and the page number are typed in the upper right-hand corner of each sheet of copy. Above the copy at the left-hand margin, the copy is keyed to the layout. In this instance, the following would be written: "Copy B," and a circle drawn around it with a pencil. The circle indicates to the printer that the words are not to be set in type but are instructions indicating where the copy goes on the layout.

Estimating Copy for Cutlines

To estimate the amount of copy for cutlines, the same method would be used as just explained. The first two or three words of the cutline are set in boldface, and require more space than the rest of the words in the cutline. Allowances would have to be made in figuring the character count of the first line of each of the cutlines. In most instances, the two cutlines would be typed on the same sheet of copy paper, but a different sheet would be used for the text copy. The reason for this is that the cutline copy might be given to a different linotype operator from the one setting the text copy.

Typing Copy on Layout Sheet

Some printers of yearbooks issue instructions to type the copy single-spaced on the layout sheet instead of on a separate sheet as has just been discussed. If this plan is followed, it is sometimes difficult to indicate the exact space to be occupied by the different copy blocks. Also, the space is often too crowded for editing corrections when copy is single-spaced. If a large amount of copy is used on the page, it is impossible to type it on the layout sheet because space is not available. Under such circumstances, it will be necessary for you to work out the method you are to use if copy cannot be typed in the area provided on the layout sheet.

Don't Puzzle the Reader

The editor's job is to make the yearbook interesting. Readers don't want to be puzzled by crowded and cluttered pages they cannot easily understand.

The situation has been well stated by Bradbury Thompson, art director of *Mademoiselle* magazine. He said:

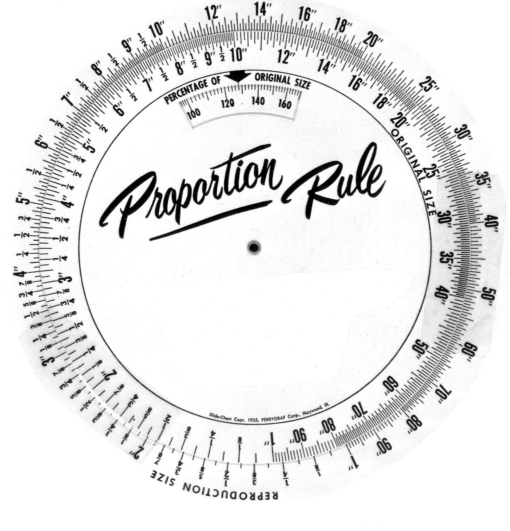

FIGURE 5.8. A Logarithmic Scale of Proportions, often called a proportion rule, can be used to determine if a photograph will make size.

→

FIGURE 5.9. This photograph, reproduced actual size, shows crop marks that are used to guide the printer in the selection of the portion of the picture to be included in the finished plate.

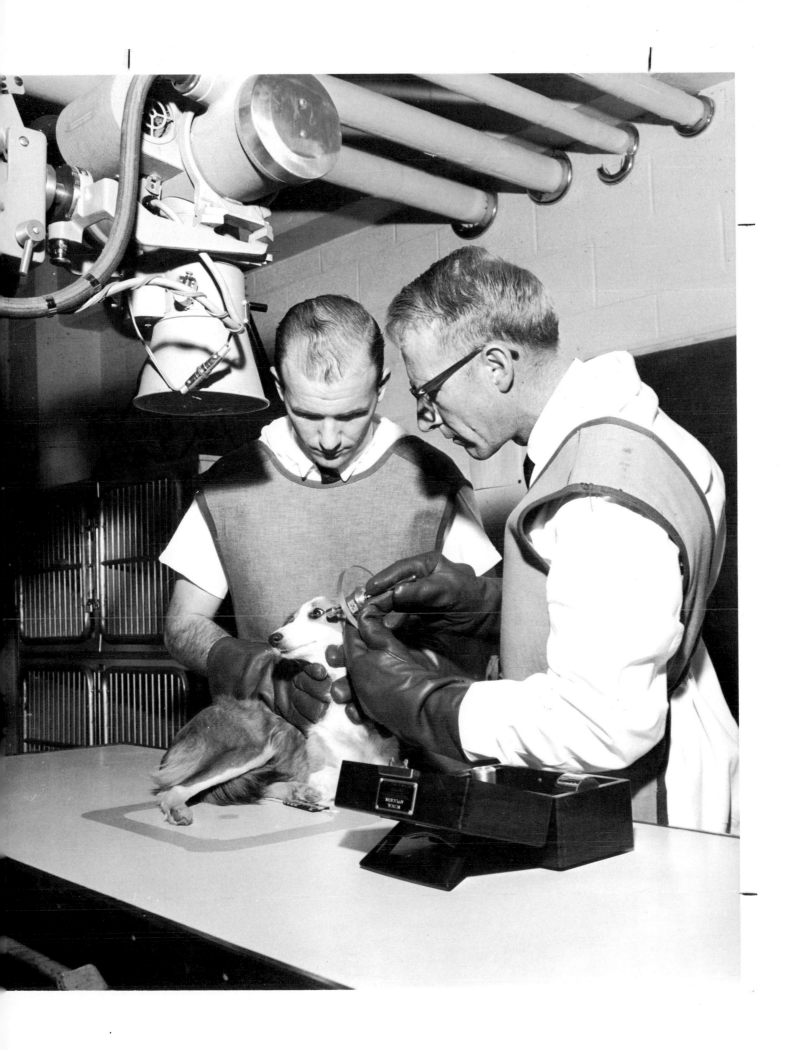

To be different is a very desirable thing. To be understandable, very necessary. If the art director can be different, understandable, and at the same time, have a logical reason for being so, he has had one of his better and more fortunate days.

While it may be true that the editorial art director has greater creative freedom than many of his colleagues in the more commercial market places, it is equally true that he has many more critics—thousands more. At *Mademoiselle*, we have 523,000 of them. Each of them feels her purchase of the book is her license to criticize. These readers want to be amused and intrigued, but they rebel at being puzzled. So, even the much envied editorial freedom is restrained by public acceptance.

Simplicity Aids Effectiveness

Usually the simpler the design of the page, the more effective it will be. Good results can be achieved by organizing the material into as few elements as possible.

Douglas C. McMurtrie, a leading authority on printing and book design, has compared printing to modern engineering design and construction. He said:

The twentieth-century concept of design is based on the principles of the engineer, who learned early in his work the apparently simple axiom that *form should follow function*. Asking first the purpose for which the object of structure was intended, and analyzing the possibilities and limitations of the materials to be used, the engineer proceeded in a businesslike and unromantic way to design his product so that it would serve most efficiently its intended use. When design had been so determined, the engineer stopped, superadding on furbelows to the simple elementary plan.

Examples of sound modern engineering design are to be seen in recently erected skyscrapers, in the cradle telephone, in present-day airplanes, and in thousands of objects of everyday use, where intelligent planning has replaced the old rule of "doing it that way because grandfather did it that way." Perhaps the most graphic symbol of modern design is the streamlined railroad train.

All these products of modern engineering design, when viewed through twentieth-century eyes, are seen to have a beauty of form so elementary and fundamental that scant training in art is essential to its appreciation. The most important feature of modern design is simplicity. Rococo ornament, furbelows and "gingerbread" are taboo. We have learned a new respect for the beauty of pure form, without benefit of decoration.

When the engineering principles of design were applied to typography, they brought about important changes, particularly in advertising and commercial printing. An analysis of the purposes which printed advertising was to serve brought about a realization of the steadily decreasing time the average citizen has free for reading, in the face of numerous recently developed attractions competing for his attention. The typographers concluded, therefore, that the prospect must be able to "read as he runs" if the selling story was to bring results.

This realization brought about a new respect for legibility, for type large enough to be read with comfort, for headings set in capitals and small letters (upper and lower case to printers) rather than in capitals only, which are far less easy to read. It was also found that dynamic or unbalanced arrangements were more likely to arrest the eyes of hurried readers than the static, balanced layouts favored by tradition. Display types were simplified in design and reduced to their most elementary form, and serifs, which accented and finished off the main strokes of letters, went into the discard. Simplicity in layout led to arrangements of illustrations and type areas in geometrical forms.[1]

In Defense of Good Looks

In an editorial entitled "In Defense of Good Looks," Kathleen K. Leabo, editor of the *Scholastic Editor* (November, 1963) emphasizes the importance of good printing for all publications.

The other night we happend to see what must be one of the grayest newspapers ever put into print. In heads, layout, type and pictures, it was a monotone, from the top of Page One to the last column on the back page.

And when we saw it, we were reminded of the eternal argument of content vs. good looks and the sheer absurdity of such an argument. As if they are mutually exclusive . . . or even begin to trespass upon each other's territory.

Frequently we hear the question: "What difference do good looks make if a publication has good content?"

Our answer is usually another question: "Do you want anyone to read it?"

First, one point must be made clear: No matter how handsome a publication may be, it is hollow and weak if it does not have good content—in copy and pictures. We have all seen the beautiful girl with the personality of an oyster. She doesn't wear well after first glance. Without good content, neither will the beautiful paper.

But content alone won't insure success either. Idealistically, we might hope that readers will plow through gray pages to get at gems hidden in the fog. But, if we look at the situation realistically, we know that they won't.

Why should they?

The simple fact is that printed material doesn't have a captive audience. And even if it did, a captive audience can simply shut out a presentation which lacks appeal and interest. Even the best of content has to be sold to the fickle attention of the reader.

A newspaper or a yearbook is, in a way, much like a speaker. He may have an enormous amount of information of great value to pass on, but if he tries to feed it to his audience in a flat, dead monotone, in mumbling enunciation devoid of inflection or life, he is talking to the wind.

Good looks—i.e. appealing makeup, attractive typography, interesting layout—are the enunciation and the inflection of the publication. Good looks are simply effective presentation of what you have to say.

If you have nothing to say, then good looks become only an abstract exercise in the graphic arts.

But if you have something meaningful and interesting to communicate, an appealing appearance can make the difference between getting through to your reader and being buried quickly in wastebasket or back bookshelf.

[1] From *The Book* by Douglas C. McMurtrie. Copyright 1943 by Douglas C. McMurtrie. Used by permission of Oxford University Press, Inc.

A publication is a means of communication. And communication by definition requires someone to get the message. If you fail to make a reader want to read your publication, there is no communication. Your content is wasted.

Thus we hold that good looks are not only helpful but essential. Unless maybe you have found some way to get a reader down and make him read your material. Since not many of us can use a club on our readers, we had better try the gentle but effective persuasion of good looks.

Summarizing Layout Steps

Making the layouts for your annual can be an interesting and rewarding experience if you start early and do each job promptly and efficiently. Remember the important steps you must take to insure attractive and easy-to-follow layouts for your annual:

1. Prepare page layouts so they display material in an orderly and simple manner that allows the reader to follow his normal reading habits.

2. Plan ahead and get pictures that will tell the story of the event covered. Crop pictures to bring out the important feature you want to show. If you are tempted to angle, bleed, or crop a picture in an odd shape, be sure that it will improve both the layout and the picture before you put the plan into effect. Leaving a uniform amount of white space between pictures will help to give your annual character.

3. Select type faces for headlines and copy that are easy to read. Adopt a typographic plan for use throughout the book. Use type of uniform sizes for headlines, text copy, and cutlines. Give each headline and type mass uniform display in regard to white space and type margins. This, too, will give personality to your book.

4. Prepare a detailed layout sheet for the printer for each page in your yearbook, showing where illustrations, headlines, text copy, and cutlines are to go. Write all headlines and other copy to fit the space provided in the layout. Be sure the pictures you send to the engraver or printer (in some cases pictures are sent directly to the printer if he has his own plate-making department) will "make size." Remember that carefully made layout can be a complete failure if you fail to provide pictures, headlines, and copy that fit spaces. Also, the all-over design and pattern for your entire annual is weakened if the printer is forced to crowd the material on the page because of too much copy. The same thing is true if he is forced to leave "gaping holes" because there is not enough copy to fill the space.

Views of the school can often be used effectively in the opening and division pages of an annual. Here is a fine example of the kind of pictures needed from the Debris, Purdue University, West Lafayette, Indiana.

Chapter 6

Planning Harmonious Opening and Division Pages

SOON AFTER THE STAFF has been selected and before work is started on the page-by-page dummy, careful consideration should be given to the theme to be used. The theme is the central idea used for atmosphere—a uniformity of treatment that carries through the book and keeps it from being just a collection of pages. The theme is the basic plan or design of the yearbook.

The Theme Can Be Simple

The theme can be as simple a thing as the format, the architecture, the pattern, or the general makeup of the book. In this sense all well-printed and planned books can be said to have a theme. Webster's *Collegiate Dictionary* has a definite pattern or theme. The cover has a simple design with an ornate "W" enclosed in a laurel wreath stamped in the lower right-hand corner. The same family of type is used on the cover and title page. The copyright, contents, and preface pages are harmonious in type face and treatment.

A definite orderliness is followed on all the pages of the book. The format of the pages is uniform throughout, each page being divided into two columns, and the words arranged in alphabetical order. Each word to be defined is set in boldface type, followed by the standard pronunciation, definitions, and other information—always in the same order and with the same treatment in type.

Thus even a dictionary has a theme or pattern that anyone familiar with reading and books can readily follow.

Themes have been more highly developed in certain types of books because the material they contain lends itself to elaborate treatment. Some novels, children's books, and annuals have gone to great lengths in developing themes to give certain atmosphere or to enhance the beauty of the books. Overemphasis of yearbook themes, however, places too much importance on a single phase of the book. Again it is important to remember that the chief functions of an annual are (1) to print pictures of all students and (2) to tell of the students' accomplishments and activities. If the theme contributes to this end and adds to the beauty of the book, it has made a worthwhile contribution and more than justifies its cost.

Developing the Theme

The theme that reflects the individuality, atmosphere, or spirit of the particular school for which the annual is produced is much more effective than a theme that could be used in any of a hundred different schools. Care should be given to selecting a theme that will tie in with the school and one that can be easily and effectively worked out with the talent and resources available.

The theme is to the book what landscaping is to a home. It should not be overdone. It should be introduced strongly in the opening pages of the book, used on the division pages and perhaps also on the cover and end sheets. In most cases it should not be used on other pages of the book except as it may influence the layout or general format of the book. In general, the pages of a yearbook are made less interesting and less attractive if they are cluttered with special borders and designs that are repeated page after page.

The chief aims of the book must ever be kept in mind and the theme subordinated to those ends. A home should not be obscured by too much landscaping; likewise, students and their accomplishments should never be overshadowed by too much emphasis on theme development.

Plan Opening and Division Pages Carefully

Opening pages of an annual should present the information a reader expects to find in any well-printed and carefully written book. The division pages correspond to chapter headings or main divisions. They subdivide the subject matter in an orderly and logical manner. Yearbook staffs sometimes get the erroneous idea that there is something peculiar about the opening pages of an annual so they need not follow a definite style or order in presenting this important and informative material.

Common practice, ordinary reading habits, and good sense dictate that the opening pages should give the name of the book, where, when, and by whom it is published. Front pages usually contain a foreword or preface and sometimes a copyright notice and a dedication. They should have a table of contents listing the several chapters or divisions of the book, giving page numbers of the beginning of each chapter or division.

Arrange Opening Pages in Proper Order

A small yearbook of 100 pages or fewer probably would not require more than four opening pages—title page, dedication, foreword, and contents. Large yearbooks often have seven or more introductory pages: page 1, subtitle; pages 2 and 3, title; pages 4 and 5, dedication; page 6, foreword; and page 7, contents. There are many variations that may be made in such pages.

If a book is copyrighted, the notice of copyright must appear either on the face or the reverse side of the title page. The sequence in which the opening or early pages should appear is definitely established by custom and by the styles used by leading book publishing companies. Therefore, the reader expects to find them in the following order: the subtitle, title page, dedication (if used), foreword and/or preface, and the table of contents.

You should plan the opening section of your annual so the contents page (the one listing chapters or divisions of the book) will appear within the first eight to twelve pages and be easy for the reader to find. There is a tendency by some staffs to run several pages of views, a prologue, or perhaps several feature pages before presenting the table of contents. This slows down and confuses the reader. The list of chapters is the material he wants to see first and refers to oftenest.

Introduce Theme Strongly

As you will note from sample pages that follow, some yearbooks use a uniform pattern, format, or central theme throughout the opening and division pages of the book. Good editors often extend the same treatment to the cover and end sheets of the annual, thus adding to the harmony of the entire production.

Copy Helps Clarify the Theme

Most themes will be more effective and better understood if supported by good copy. Copy telling the reader about the basic plan should be introduced strongly in the opening section, perhaps on the foreword or preface page. Also some copy supporting and clarifying the theme can be used on the division pages, but should be kept to a minimum in most cases.

The Mood of Miami

Here is some outstanding copy used to introduce the theme of the *Ibis*, University of Miami, Coral Gables, Florida.

The University of Miami
is a complex institution of higher learning
humanized by personal striving,
integrity and love.
A university
that enriches the individual,
instead of merely processing him,
remains worthy of our devotion.
Guest photographer
Paul Barton, '63,
took the pictures on the following pages.
They are a testament to
both the truthfulness of his vision
and the specific elements
that compose the unique
MOOD
OF
MIAMI
These photographs
state that Miami's beauty
is more than the sum of her architecture
and climate.
Its ultimate source
is the insight,
imagination
and disciplined skills of her people.

Use Uniform Typography

The typographical treatment of the opening and division pages of the annual must be in harmony too, whether the treatment is simple printed material or calls for art work and pictures. A careful selection of one distinctive type face for the major heading on each of the opening and division pages will do much to establish a definite pattern or typographical theme for your annual. The name of the book on the cover and the title page and such headings as dedication, foreword, and contents should be displayed in the same type face.

Titles for the different chapters or divisions should be set in the same type. Minor copy blocks on these several pages can be printed in a different type face from the headings . However, you should enlist the help of the best printer available in selecting the type you use. The character of the book is largely decided by what is done in this respect. A wisely chosen typographical style used for title and content pages does much to establish a feeling of quality for the entire annual.

Lean heavily on the plans and advice given you by artists and typographers. They usually know their jobs. Do not make hasty or careless decisions that will affect the beauty and readability of your book. Just because you have authority to make decisions does not make you infallible.

Establish Pattern by Repetition

Occasional repetition throughout opening and division pages of an illustration of some object, such as the mascot or seal of the school, will help to establish a pattern or theme and make the reader aware that the pages so illustrated have special importance and significance. As you will note from the samples shown in this chapter, such objects as letters of the alphabet, keys, and school seals have been used to help carry the theme throughout the introductory and division pages.

Unity of treatment often is achieved for front and chapter pages by printing a different line or verse from the school song on each of the several pages. The same result can be accomplished by using slogans, verses of poetry, or inscriptions from college buildings.

Don't Overdo Design or Illustration

Any device, such as an object or phrase repeated, to tie special pages together and establish a pattern or theme should not be overdone. Use such a device sparingly and try to present it each time in an interesting and slightly different way. Remember that the most important thing about the title page, for instance, is the name of the annual, the school, and the address. The typography should make these things clear at a glance. They must not be overshadowed by any design, picture, or other copy. The same is true of the table of contents and division pages. Carefully arranged white space is also of the greatest value in this part of the annual.

Reflect Individuality With Pictures

Pictures are used oftener than any other device to embellish opening and division pages of a yearbook. If you decide to use them, be sure you get pictures that add individuality and interest to the book. Pictures used for this purpose must be of the highest technical quality and must command attention of the reader. Plan carefully in advance the pictures to be used and see that they are taken as early in the year as possible.

If you plan to use a dramatic action picture from the homecoming football game for the sports division page, for instance, don't wait until the homecoming game to start taking such a picture. You may get one that can be substituted most beneficially for the one you originally planned and find impossible, or very inconvenient, to get. Too often, nothing dramatic happens at the homecoming game or the photographer fails to be in the right place at the right moment. Then, too, it may rain or snow, the camera may be out of order, or the film may be ruined in processing. Similar situations can arise if you are planning to use a picture of cheerleaders, the cheering section, the marching band, the team rushing onto the field, or some other big football moment. Don't wait until the last performance to shoot the picture. Start early and have a substitute that can be used. If the substitute is not used on a division page, it can be printed elsewhere in the book.

Art Work Lends Variety

Art work produced by a commercial artist or by someone highly skilled in your school often can be used advantageously to enhance the beauty and harmony of the introductory and division pages. You must be careful about selecting art work. Be sure you have someone who not only can develop the idea you have in mind but who can produce something of high merit as well. Poor art and design can detract from the beauty and effectiveness of any annual. Good art work can often be used to present historical themes and other ideas for which pictures cannot be taken. It adds variety and relief from the large number of pictures that of necessity must be included.

A uniform art technique (usually developed by one person) should be used throughout the special pages under discussion. Be particularly careful about using hand lettering for the headings and copy that appear on these pages. Hand lettering by amateurs is nearly always bad. The safest plan is to select a type face the printer has in stock. Most standard type faces are artistically beautiful and many of them represent the lifework of an eminent type designer. They have stood the test of time and if used properly will add distinction, clarity, and beauty to your layouts.

Color Used in Good Taste Adds Beauty

Color printing is probably used more extensively in the front and division pages of the annual than in any other type of book. The use of color has done much to standardize the practice of limiting the opening pages to four or eight pages and the division pages to multiples of four. This plan is made necessary for economy and production reasons. Color pages usually are printed in signatures of 4, 8, 16 or 32 pages, and in the case of division pages, are cut apart and tipped in by hand at the proper place in the book. Discuss the matter of color printing in detail with your printer before making final plans. He will be able to work out production methods that will save both time and money.

FIGURE 6.1. The cover of the *Sunflower* is of black material. The name in white and the year and block "T" in gold are embossed giving a two-color effect. Both colors used contrast well with base material.

FIGURE 6.2. The subtitle (sometimes called half title) is printed in black only, but gives a two-color effect because the gray bar above and below, as well as the outline of the T, were photographed through a screen when the plate was made.

FIGURE 6.3. A two-page title page presents all the information needed as well as outstanding views of the school. The pattern of the book is emphasized by use of the block T in a different manner than previously.

FIGURE 6.4. The theme is explained with excellent copy and outstanding pictures of the school's towers. The table of contents lists each chapter or division of the book and the page on which it begins.

TOWERS are made for memories. Their architects are the builders of dreams, the molders of spirit, the creators of beauty in lasting stone. To all Topeka, Troy's Tower has symbolized aspirations, perfection, and strength...on grey days and fair... against Summer's brilliant skies...faintly through the mists of Autumn...in Winter's buffeting winds and blanketing snows... and framed in the blush of Spring's blossoms. Towers are the poignant symbols of life...the reaching of youth toward adulthood...the fingers of Earth pointing to the Eternal. Towers are made for memories.

SPRING . . .

AUTUMN . . .

WINTER . . .

Table of Contents

FIGURE 6.5. This two-page spread about the Bellamy Flag Award further emphasizes the theme and also "points with pride" to the fact that Topeka High School is one of only a few schools to win this coveted award.

FIGURE 6.6 A division spread furthers both the theme and established pattern of the book by using the T design, appropriate copy, significant picture, and general layout. Copy of the kind used here aids the reader.

Color used in good taste in the opening and division pages of an annual can do much to add beauty and harmony. Select the colors to be used with the same care you use in selecting the clothing you wear or the decoration scheme you use in your home. It is usually best to get help from someone experienced in the use of color printing. Colors used should, of course, harmonize throughout the entire book and should always include the cover and the end sheets.

Display Basic Information Prominently

There are other devices to establish a pattern or theme throughout the opening and division pages of the annual, but most of them defy classification. The most important consideration in preparing layouts of the opening and division pages is to present them in a clear, orderly, and logical manner. The information presented on such pages is of basic importance. It needs to be presented in an easily readable type and pages must not be cluttered or crowded with too many pictures or illustrations. In planning your layouts, provide ample white space to give the type a good chance.

Because of the high cost involved, it is impossible to reproduce opening and division pages in color in this book. However, effective arrangement of material, typographical dress, and devices used to produce harmonious opening and division pages should be apparent.

Natural Color Pictures Often Used

More and more pictures in full natural color are being used each year in both high school and college annuals. If the yearbook can afford to use only a few color shots, they are often placed in the opening section of the book. If finances permit, color pictures are also used for division pages. To encourage the use of natural color, several concerns specializing in printing annuals offer to print, free of charge, the end sheets or perhaps one page in the opening section of the book in four-color process, provided certain conditions regarding early copy are met by the staff.

However, remember that pictures taken in color must have fine technical quality and impact on the reader if they are to make a worthwhile contribution to the theme of your annual.

The Theme Should Wear Well

In selecting the theme the staff must bear in mind that the annual has a life expectancy of many years. The plan should not be one that will be outdated in a short time or look silly to the reader or editorial staff a few years after publication. Photographs, art work, or lettering used in the opening and division pages should be outstanding in quality, or they will repel the owner of the book instead of adding to his pleasure of ownership. A book that has used a beautiful and simple type display on the opening and division pages will wear much better with the owner than a more elaborate one that has used conflicting colors, poor photographs, inferior art work, or crude lettering.

The theme should be in harmony with the character of the school. A book produced in the form of a diary would not be appropriate for a boys' school (most boys do not keep diaries). And by the same rule, a book using football as a theme would not be in character for a girls' school.

The theme must be studied carefully by the staff, and an outline of how it is to be used must be made. The theme should neither dominate the book nor distract the reader from the important purpose of the annual.

Theme of Sunflower Outstanding

The theme of the 1965 *Sunflower,* Topeka High School, Topeka, Kansas, shown in Figures 6.1 to 6.6 inclusive, is an excellent example of what a theme should be. First, the opening pages are arranged in the proper order and give all the information the reader expects to find in a well-designed book. Second, the pages are economical to produce—printed in one color. Third, the theme reflects the individuality of the school and establishes a basic pattern followed throughout the book.

Several devices are used to establish the pattern or theme of the *Sunflower.* The same family of type is used for important headings on opening and division pages. The especially designed "T" is repeated often enough to unify the pages. The copy used on the special pages clarifies and emphasizes the theme.

Name of Yearbook Used as Theme

The catchy phrase, "Under Morton's Hat" is used as a unifying idea in the 1963 *Top Hat,* Oliver P. Morton High School, Hammond, Indiana. Figures 6.7 to 6.11 inclusive illustrate how the theme is developed. The same family of type is used on the cover and on the opening and division pages. The clever drawing of the top hat, cane, gloves, and the intertwined letters are repeated just often enough to lend emphasis. The copy and pictures used are excellent.

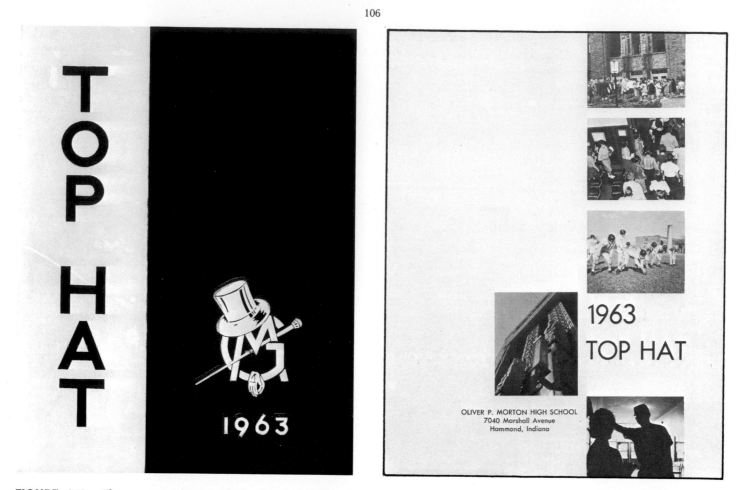

FIGURE 6.7. The cover material of *Top Hat* is red and white. The name of the book is debossed in red on the white area, while the design and date are embossed in white on the red portion of the cover to lend contrast.

FIGURE 6.8. The title page has the needed information, and the activity pictures add interest. The picture of the school building is printed in natural color (reproduced here in black) and adds a pleasing effect.

FIGURE 6.9. The table of contents spread is made effective by good activity pictures and the list of chapters with page numbers. White space is used effectively to emphasize the importance of these pages.

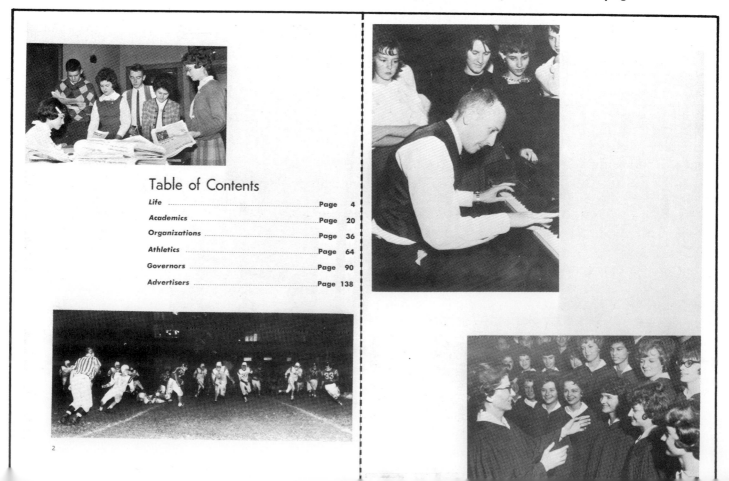

FIGURE 6.10 "Under Morton's Hat" explains the theme and tells of the many fine accomplishments of the school. This is the kind of copy needed to encourage students to do their best and have pride in their school.

FIGURE 6.11. This is one of the excellent division spreads in the *Top Hat*. The layout, the copy, and the photographs are outstanding.

Key Used As Central Idea

The *Tucsonian* of Tucson High School, Tucson, Arizona, used the idea that, "each student began forging the key that would open the door to his future," as the central idea in this annual. The method in which the theme is developed illustrates perfectly how a theme that has been used many times before can be interpreted in your own individual way. You can approach it in a new way with new illustrations, pictures, and copy. It's like writing a story about a football game—give it your own personal touch.

The staff evidently decided to save money on the printing of the opening and division pages and spend it on the cover and end sheets of their annual. They achieved excellent results as shown in Figures 6.12 to 6.16 inclusive.

Theme Inspired by Poem

A poem entitled, "more brightly must our spirit shine," written by Carol Bruzdziak, a member of the senior class, provided the idea for the theme of the 1964 *Galaxy*, Henry Ford High School, Detroit, Michigan. The spirit represented as a flame is reproduced on the cover, opening pages, and elsewhere in the book as shown in Figures 6.17 to 6.22 inclusive. In addition to the poem and the drawing of a flame, a color is used as a device to establish and emphasize the theme. The opening and division pages printed in black and a golden yellow (but reproduced here in one

FIGURE 6.12 Four colors—white, black, blue, and gold are used effectively on the cover of the *Tucsonian*.

FIGURE 6.14   The title page is the first right-hand page in the *Tucsonian* and gives all information needed.

FIGURE 6.13   The end sheets of the *Tucsonian* are printed in black and gray form an interesting pattern and continue the theme.

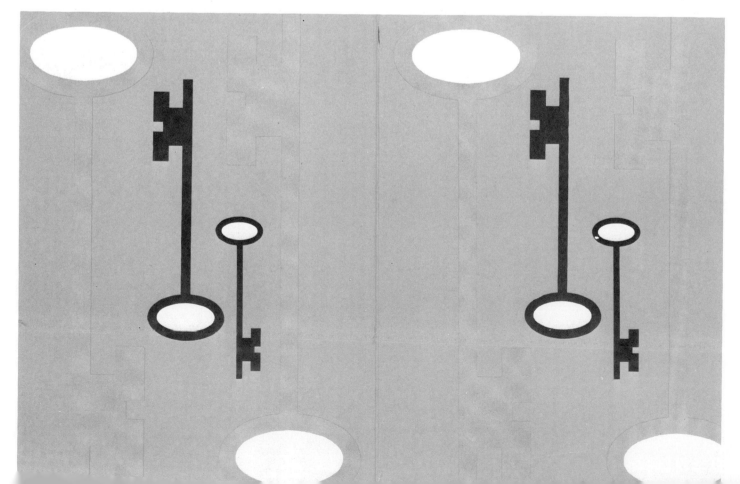

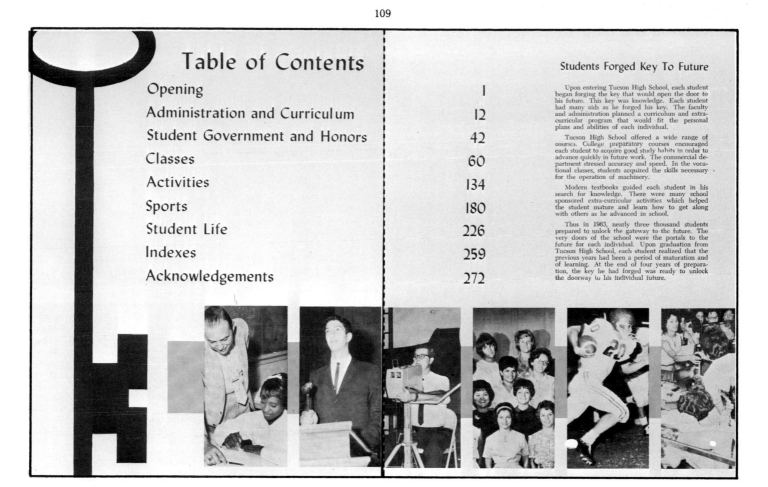

Table of Contents

Students Forged Key To Future

Upon entering Tucson High School, each student began forging the key that would open the door to his future. This key was knowledge. Each student had many aids as he forged his key. The faculty and administration planned a curriculum and extra-curricular program that would fit the personal plans and abilities of each individual.

Tucson High School offered a wide range of courses. College preparatory courses encouraged each student to acquire good study habits in order to advance quickly in future work. The commercial department stressed accuracy and speed. In the vocational classes, students acquired the skills necessary for the operation of machinery.

Modern textbooks guided each student in his search for knowledge. There were many school sponsored extra-curricular activities which helped the student mature and learn how to get along with others as he advanced in school.

Thus in 1963, nearly three thousand students prepared to unlock the gateway to the future. The very doors of the school were the portals to the future for each individual. Upon graduation from Tucson High School, each student realized that the previous years had been a period of maturation and of learning. At the end of four years of preparation, the key he had forged was ready to unlock the doorway to his individual future.

FIGURE 6.15 The table of contents and theme copy are combined on this double-page spread. The pleasing use of white space adds emphasis to each element portrayed. Repetition of key helps to develop theme.

FIGURE 6.16 Two-page divisions are featured in the *Tucsonian*. The student art work lends variety from the photographs on other pages of the book. The key and reverse lettering continue to carry forward the theme.

Activities

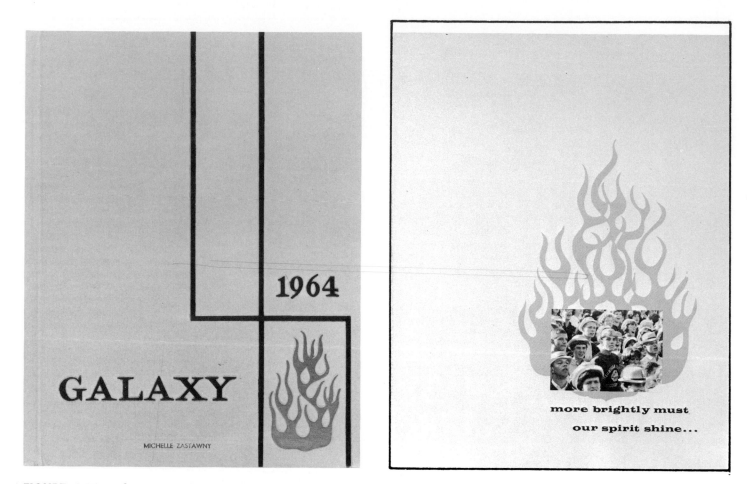

FIGURE 6.17. The cover of the *Galaxy* introduces the theme by using an embossed design of a flame in gold.

FIGURE 6.18. Page one, usually reserved for the subtitle, further develops the theme.

FIGURE 6.19. A double-page spread (pages 2 and 3) is used for the title page and a listing of staff members.

It is printed in two shades of yellow and black. Use of the same type as used on the cover is effective.

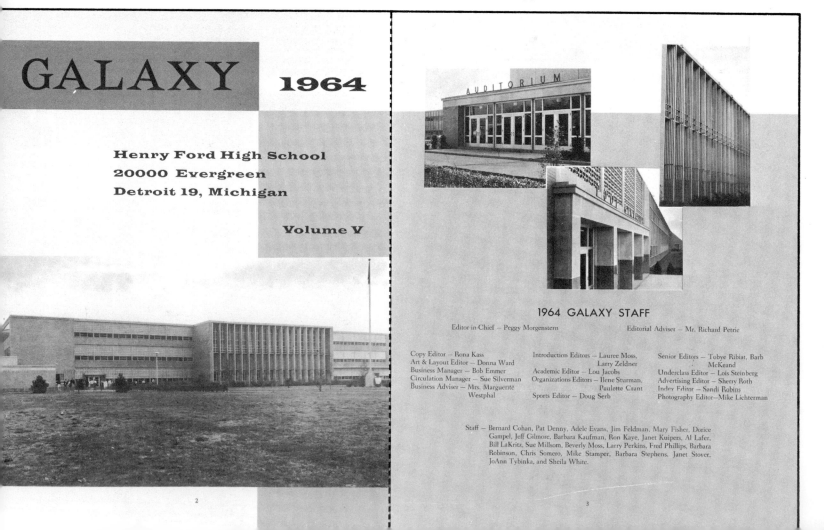

GALAXY 1964

Henry Ford High School
20000 Evergreen
Detroit 19, Michigan

Volume V

1964 GALAXY STAFF

Editor-in-Chief — Peggy Morgenstern   Editorial Adviser — Mr. Richard Petrie

Copy Editor — Rona Kass
Art & Layout Editor — Donna Ward
Business Manager — Bob Emmer
Circulation Manager — Sue Silverman
Business Adviser — Mrs. Marguerite Westphal

Introduction Editors — Lauree Moss, Larry Zeldner
Academic Editor — Lou Jacobs
Organizations Editors — Ilene Sturman, Paulette Crant
Sports Editor — Doug Serb

Senior Editors — Tobye Ribiat, Barb McKeand
Underclass Editor — Lois Steinberg
Advertising Editor — Sherry Roth
Index Editor — Sandi Robins
Photography Editor—Mike Lichterman

Staff — Bernard Cohan, Pat Denny, Adele Evans, Jim Feldman, Mary Fisher, Dorice Gampel, Jeff Gilmore, Barbara Kaufman, Ron Kaye, Janet Kuipers, Al Lafer, Bill LaKritz, Sue Millsom, Beverly Moss, Larry Perkins, Fred Phillips, Barbara Robinson, Chris Somero, Mike Stamper, Barbara Stephens, Janet Stover, JoAnn Tybinka, and Sheila White.

more brightly must our spirit shine . . .

As we live on from day to day,
And watch the sunsets fade away,
And see the stars come out at night,
    We wonder.

We think of all that we have done,
The places seen, the races won,
The lessons learned, the tables turned,
    And we perceive.

There is an ember burning low
Within each heart that wants its glow,
And from this quiet flame is shed
    A light.

This light is love and as it grows
Its flame consumes our hearts, and shows
Throughout our minds and eyes and souls
    A spirit.

This spirit makes the world go round,
For friendship, faith, and hope abound
Within the circle of its warmth
    And we are happy.

Its sunlit golden gleams would spill
Around about us and instill
An encompassing essence of
    Good will.

Then those of us who have a spark
Must make our spirits burn the dark
And grow to circle all of man
    Together.

— Carol Bruzdziak

5

FIGURE 6.20. The poem that inspired the theme of the *Galaxy* is printed in full on the right-hand page of this interesting two-page spread.

FIGURE 6.21 Two pages are devoted to presenting the table of contents in the *Galaxy*. The carefully made layout, together with the dramatic full-page picture, adds interest.

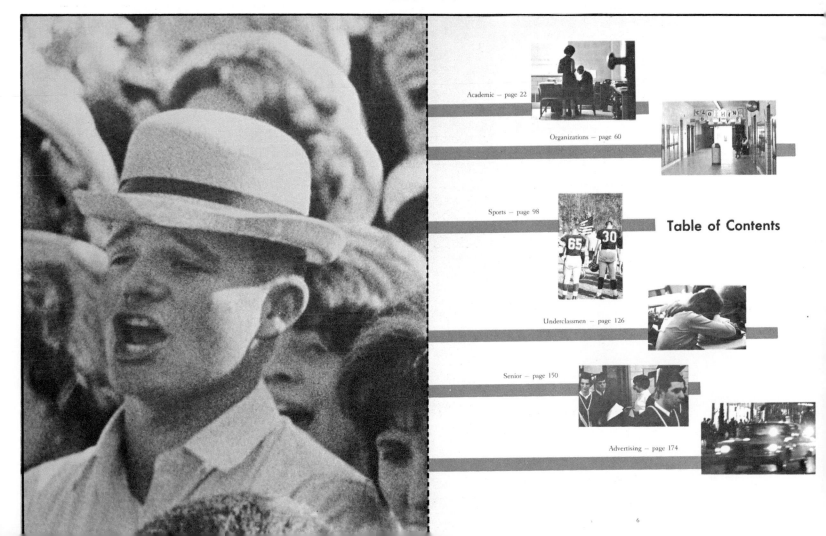

Academic — page 22

Organizations — page 60

Sports — page 98

Table of Contents

Underclassmen — page 126

Senior — page 150

Advertising — page 174

6

FIGURE 6.22. The division pages of the *Galaxy* are particularly pleasing because of the interesting and dramatic pictures effectively displayed.

UNDERCLASSMEN . . .

When the halls echo the last melancholy voices of the June graduates, the Ford underclassmen return in September to once again sustain the traditional school spirit. Theirs is a difficult task, for it is their duty to provide the school with the unity that is the Henry Ford heritage; a heritage which is a part of every student and teacher, and one that implants into every heart the spirit of pride and sportsmanship which go hand in hand with learning.

FIGURE 6.23. The name "Milestone" (in special lettering) and the date are embossed in gold on a gray base material to produce an outstanding cover.

FIGURE 6.24. Page one of the *Milestone* serves as the title page giving needed information. The seal and special lettering add individuality to the book.

FIGURE 6.25. This two-page spread is made interesting by the proper use of white space. Opening and division pages can almost always be made more effective by using white space generously.

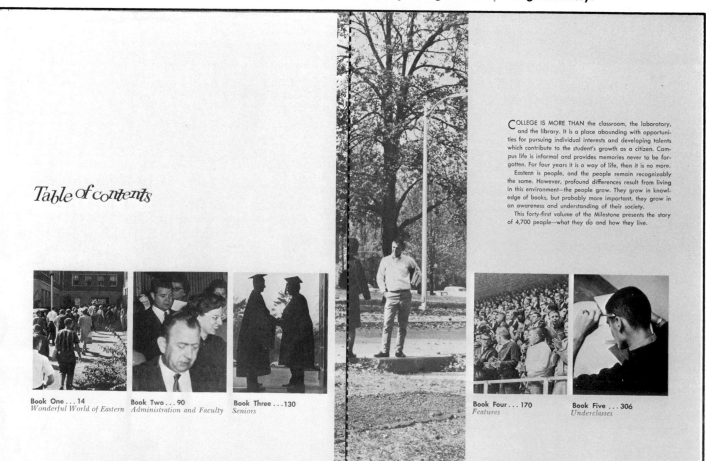

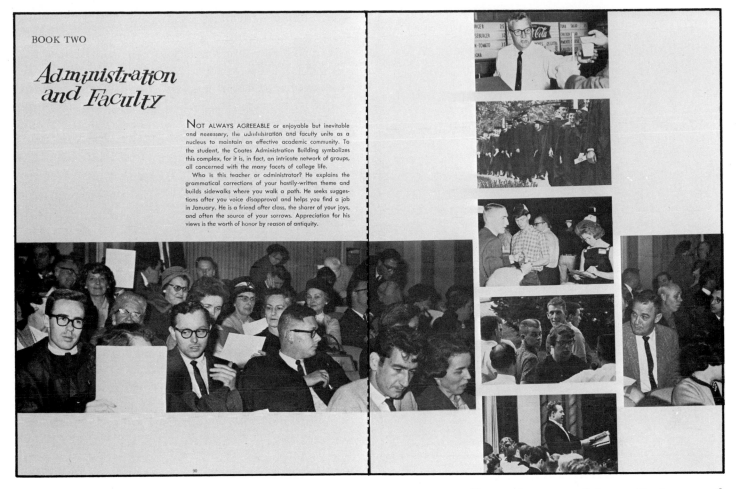

BOOK TWO

Administration and Faculty

NOT ALWAYS AGREEABLE or enjoyable but inevitable and necessary, the administration and faculty unite as a nucleus to maintain an effective academic community. To the student, the Coates Administration Building symbolizes this complex, for it is, in fact, an intricate network of groups, all concerned with the many facets of college life.

Who is this teacher or administrator? He explains the grammatical corrections of your hastily-written theme and builds sidewalks where you walk a path. He seeks suggestions after you voice disapproval and helps you find a job in January. He is a friend after class, the sharer of your joys, and often the source of your sorrows. Appreciation for his views is the worth of honor by reason of antiquity.

FIGURE 6.26. The two-page division pages in the *Milestone* **are printed in only one color. The special** lettering, significant pictures, and the continuing use of the distinctive layout pattern emphasize the theme.

color) illustrate how effective a tint color can be in carrying out the theme of an annual. The use of tint colors, or tint blocks as they are called, can add emphasis to certain portions of a page.

Hand Lettering Aids Theme

The *Milestone* of Eastern Kentucky State College at Richmond used a special hand-lettered type for the headings on the cover and on the opening and division pages to establish its pattern. The lettering is well done and readable, which is highly important. Often hand lettering by amateurs is not good and ruins the very effect it is striving to accomplish.

Significant pictures, effectively displayed, add to the impact of the pages and do much to establish a format or pattern carefully followed in the rest of the book. How the theme of the *Milestone* is developed is shown in Figures 6.23 to 6.26 inclusive.

Type Used To Establish Uniformity

The 1965 *Chanticleer,* published by Duke

FIGURE 6.27. A red-grained material is used for the cover of the *Chanticleer* **and the title and date are deeply embossed. The seal of the university embossed in silver lends effective contrast.**

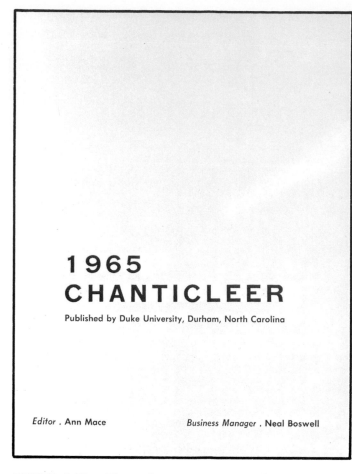

1965 CHANTICLEER

Published by Duke University, Durham, North Carolina

Editor . Ann Mace   *Business Manager . Neal Boswell*

FIGURE 6.28. The title page is printed in red and black, "1965 Chanticleer" is in red, the remainder of the copy is printed in black, providing pleasing contrast.

University, Durham, North Carolina, depends heavily on a distinctive type face and liberal use of white space to establish a pattern for opening and division pages. Large university yearbooks in many instances do less than high schools to develop distinctive themes. However, most college yearbook themes are carefully designed to produce a harmonious effect and present the important copy needed on introductory and division pages. Figures 6.27 to 6.33 inclusive demonstrate how the *Chanticleer* handled this problem.

Alma Mater Used as Theme

The staff of the 1965 *Gopher,* University of Minnesota, Minneapolis, used their Alma Mater Song in a restrained manner for their central theme. Magnificent pictures in full color are used in the opening section and division pages. They are reproduced here in one color only but demonstrate the type of pictures needed for the opening and division pages of a yearbook.

Excellent use is made of white space to emphasize the headings, copy, and photographs. They used a Roman or serif type for headings which is a relief from the Sans Serif type so often used. How the theme is developed is shown in Figure 6.34 to 6.37 inclusive.

Stock Covers and Division Pages

Often staffs in small schools, because of lack

FIGURE 6.29. A two-page spread is devoted to contents. Here again type and white space are dominant, however the excellent drawings on the left-hand page provide individuality for the yearbook.

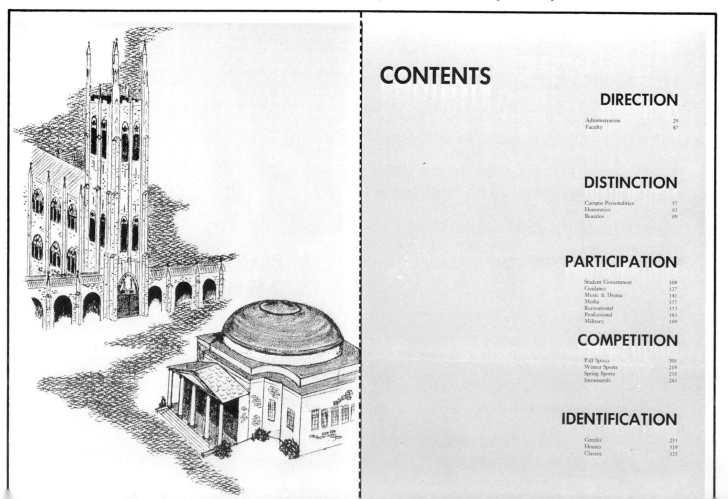

CONTENTS

DIRECTION

DISTINCTION

PARTICIPATION

COMPETITION

IDENTIFICATION

of funds or talent to produce an original theme, use stock covers and division pages prepared by their printer. Figure 6.38 shows a stock or standard cover that the staff may use at no charge for embossing dyes. Figure 6.39 is a two-page spread from a portfolio of stock division pages. The staff may select as many of the excellent still-life photographs as they wish for division pages at no extra charge. Of course, each page so used must be counted as one of the pages called for in the contract.

Theme Developed With Stock Designs

Even when a stock cover and stock division pages are selected, you still have an opportunity to develop a basic plan or theme of sorts, if you use your ingenuity. Suppose you decide to select the stock cover and division pages shown in Figures 6.38 and 6.39. They both present geometric designs. The same family of type could be used on the cover, division pages, and on opening pages. The opening pages you must produce yourself and you can thus continue the theme typographically. Perhaps you can go further and redraw the design on the cover in black ink. Use this design for page one. Place the name and date of your annual in the space now reserved for the title and use the space now occupied by "66" to print the needed information about the publisher, name of your

COMPETITION

FIGURE 6.30. This is the first page of a four-page section divider that is printed on a pebbled stock.

FIGURE 6.31. The second and third pages of each division in the *Chanticleer* are printed in color (shown here in only one color). The left-hand page is a two-color drawing while the right-hand page is in full color.

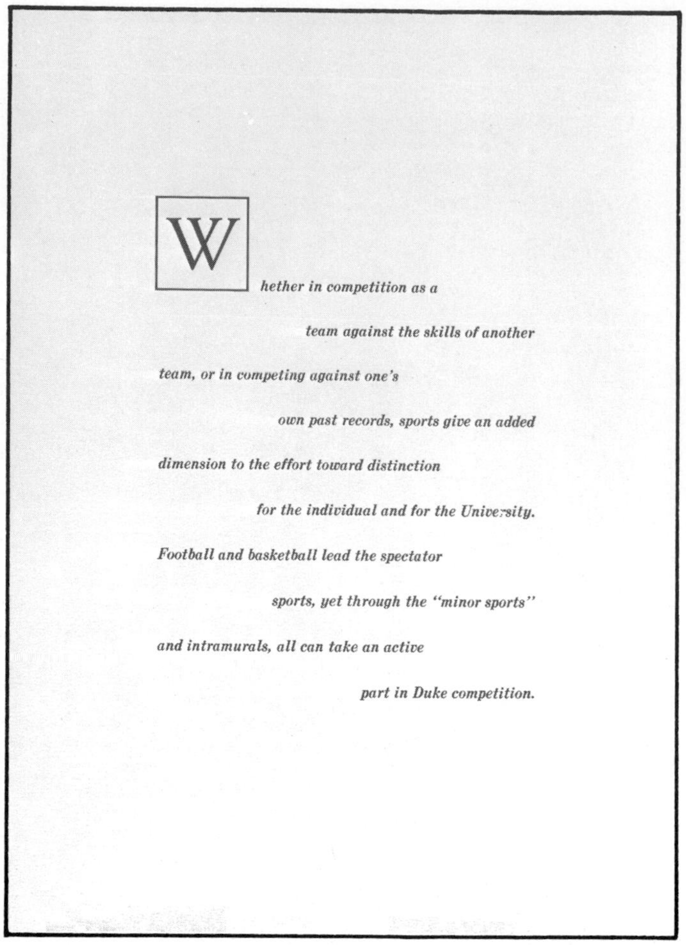

FIGURE 6.32. Page four of the division reverts to the use of type again with some significant copy. An initial boxed "W" in red lends a touch of color.

W hether in competition as a

team against the skills of another

team, or in competing against one's

own past records, sports give an added

dimension to the effort toward distinction

for the individual and for the University.

Football and basketball lead the spectator

sports, yet through the "minor sports"

and intramurals, all can take an active

part in Duke competition.

WINTER SPORTS

FIGURE 6.33 This is one of the many subdivision pages used in the *Chanticleer* to subdivide the chapters.

FIGURE 6.34. The cover of the *Gopher* is a rich brown material with name, date, and design embossed in gold.

FIGURE 6.35. The title page of the *Gopher* is printed in gold and black. The simplicity of the design is emphasized by generous use of white space.

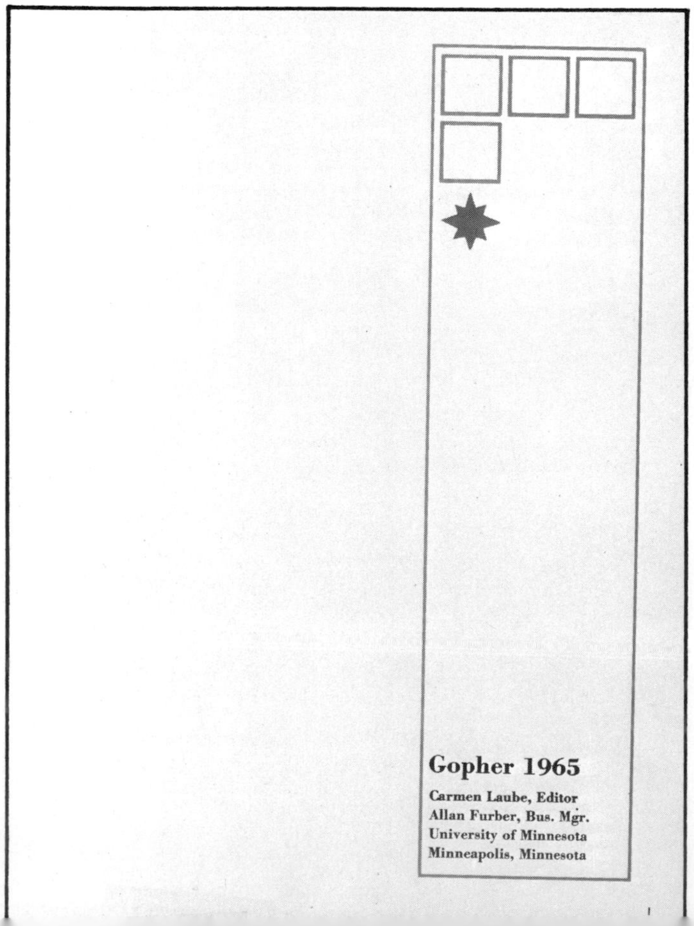

1965 Gopher

Gopher 1965

Carmen Laube, Editor
Allan Furber, Bus. Mgr.
University of Minnesota
Minneapolis, Minnesota

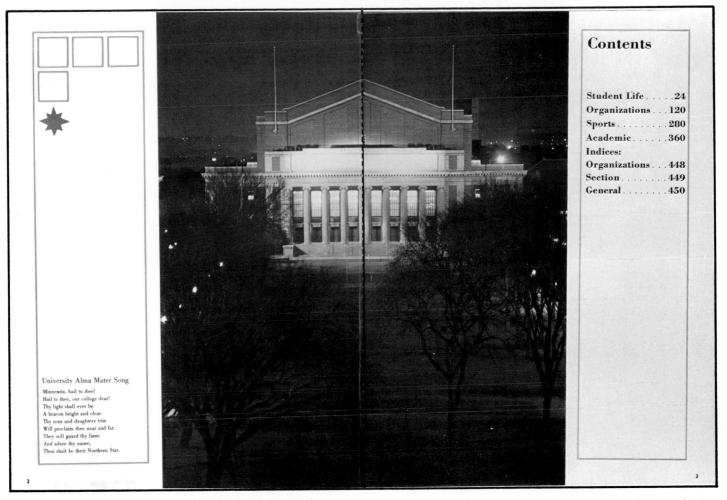

University Alma Mater Song

Minnesota, hail to thee!
Hail to thee, our college dear!
Thy light shall ever be
A beacon bright and clear.
Thy sons and daughters true
Will proclaim thee near and far.
They will guard thy fame
And adore thy name;
Thou shalt be their Northern Star.

Contents

2   3

FIGURE 6.36. Pages 2 and 3 are devoted to the Alma Mater song and table of contents. The beautiful color picture is taken at night. Showing the lights of the city in the background provides the proper mood.

FIGURE 6.37 The same simple design and type used in the opening section are continued on the division pages of the *Gopher*. The color pictures of high technical quality and carrying impact are outstanding.

Student Life

Minnesota, hail to thee!
Hail to thee, our college dear!

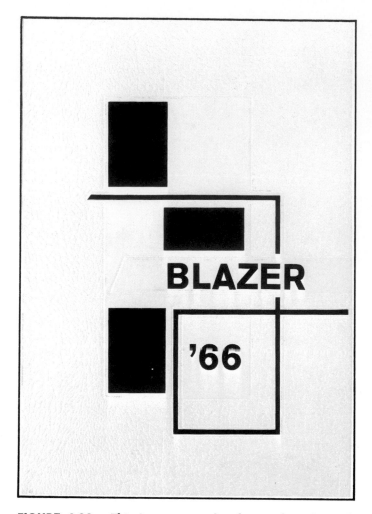

FIGURE 6.38. This is an example of a stock embossed cover. The design is embossed with silk-screen color on title, date, and design.

FIGURE 6.39. A double-page spread from a portfolio of stock division pages show illustrations that may be selected by the yearbook staff free of charge.

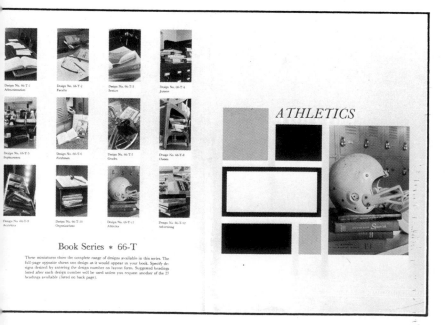

school, town, and state. On page two you could use a picture of your school building and page three could be a table of contents using either of the geometric designs, with the heading "contents" set in the same type as used for cover and division pages. The list of chapters with beginning page number of each chapter can be included.

Theme Possibilities

It would be an almost endless task to classify and describe the hundreds of themes that have been used by annual staffs. A list of themes used in yearbooks entered in the National Scholastic Press Association's Critical Service has been arranged and discussed under 24 plausible headings, by Fred L. Kildow, director of the association.

Here is a condensed and partial list of some of the more popular themes reported in that survey:

1. Themes based on the *school* and its activities are probably the most universally used.
   A. Photographic themes using pictures of the school and its activities are easily developed and understood by the readers.
   B. Plans and themes developed from traditions; seals or mottoes of the school; the school song, cheer or mascot; a significant art piece, painting, sculpture in the school or on the campus are used effectively.
   C. Schools named for famous men suggest innumerable theme opportunities: for example schools named for Edison, Washington, Lincoln, Roosevelt, etc. can use illustrations depicting the lives of these men.
   D. The school's important anniversaries—twenty-fifth, fiftieth, etc.—are occasions that the staff should exploit in planning the annual.
   E. Special events in the life of the school can be used as a theme for the annual. Erection of new buildings, abandoning of an old school, a fire, a flood—all offer once-in-a-lifetime opportunities.
   F. Outstanding success in school activities: education, religion, athletics, music, forensics, dramatics, publications, etc.—afford excellent opportunities for logical themes.
   G. Student life, depicting what students do, has been used in hundreds of books.
2. Themes based on *the community, the town, the state,* and *the nation* offer many interesting and worthwhile plans for school annuals. Theme possibilities could be listed under the same outline but applied to the community instead of the school.
   A. For example, a photographic theme of the city could be developed in much the same manner as if the school or campus were used.
   B. Other possibilities are the industries, location, special events, special accomplishments in government or civic activities, anniversaries, history, name, important citizens, etc.
   C. Large universities and colleges that draw students from the entire state can develop themes based on the history of the state, its industries, special

events, accomplishments in different fields of endeavor, location, state song, state flower, great men, anniversaries, etc.

    D. Schools such as the military and naval academies could base their themes on the armed services, loyalty, preparedness, or on the nation as a whole. A high school could use the nation as a theme if it happened to have the proper tie-up with nationally prominent men or events.

3. *Miscellaneous themes.* Many of the themes listed by Mr. Kildow defy classification in an outline as brief as this one, but a few of the more interesting possibilities are mentioned under this category.

    A. Timely tie-ups, occasioned by contemporary events such as the presidential elections, World's Fair, anniversary of printing, or the Byrd expedition. World War II was responsible for many patriotic and military themes.

    B. Modern inventions, the movies, television, tanks, airplanes, atomic bombs, and space travel have been much used.

    C. Characters from mythology, lives of great men, time, "catch phrases," hobbies, keys, magnets, rhymes, progress, and travel offer possibilities.

Themes Used in 1964 Annuals

A recent survey of themes used in 1964 yearbooks is reported by Mrs. Lucille Kildow, associate editor of *Scholastic Editor.* In the April, 1965, issue of "Yearbook Helps" she says:

School Centered Themes

There are many ways to make your school the central idea in theme selection. Consider the following possibilities, all ideas used in 1964 All-American yearbooks:

Tour Through School. Tour of that year 1964 . . . Through these Halls . . . Through these Doors . . . Tour of the Year

School as a Community. It's Our World . . . World within a World . . . This is the City in which We Live and Work and Play . . . This is our World

Pride or Spirit. We Are Proud . . . We Proudly Present . . . We Point with Pride . . . We Are All for You, Marion High . . . CHS Spirit . . . That's the Lancer Spirit

Viewpoint. Catalina Vistas . . . Kaleidoscope . . . Through the Keyhole . . . Viewpoint . . . Profile of a Year . . . Impressions of 1964 . . . Panorama . . . As Others See Us . . . Being Ourselves

Catch Phrase. More, More, More in 1964 . . . Our Red Letter Year . . . This, We Remember . . . Trumpet Summons to the New Frontiers . . . Precious Moments . . . Teens are Typical . . . Time of Our Life . . . Beginning of a Beginning

Not all excellent themes can be school centered. There comes a time when staffs must look to other sources for theme ideas. However, all good themes should be related to the school. Otherwise they cannot be good themes for their books.

Theme Suggestions From '64 AA Books

To start your own theme thinking, check the following list of some of the theme ideas on which 1964 All Americans were planned. You may find just the one that clicks for you:

Abstractions of Hickory High . . . Anticipation . . . Art of Living . . . Creation . . . Creativity . . . Days of Washington-Lee . . . Directions . . . Faces of Ben Davis . . . The Focus is on People . . . Formulas . . . Friendship . . . Individualism . . . Light . . . Measure of a Man . . . Mobility . . . Moods . . . People, People Everywhere, the More the Merrier . . . Progress . . . Quicksilver . . . Road of Life . . . Roads . . . Sounds that Typify Murphy High . . . Stage . . . Steps . . . Stock Market (graphs) . . . Sword (King Arthur) . . . Time . . . Year of Challenge . . . Zodiac.

Development of Theme Often Neglected

Too often the staff selects a theme and during "brain-storming" sessions plans how it shall be accomplished, then does practically nothing about its actual production until it's too late to do a good job. The material needed for these pages can be rather intangible and nebulous so you tend to put it aside for more easily solved problems. It tends to become a staff project with no one individual responsible for getting the word done.

During planning sessions it's easy to say, "get dramatic pictures that will portray the theme, write mood copy that will help develop it." However, it's quite another matter to do it. Sometimes the entire production is held up because one or two appropriate pictures were not taken. The fine mood copy will not write itself, and even making the significant layouts often seems impossible.

Delegate Responsibility for Theme

If the theme is to be properly developed, the editor or adviser must appoint one of the most capable members of the staff to do this important work. Even after this is done, continued help and supervision are needed to see that satisfactory progress is being made.

At each planning session detailed notes should be made on just how the theme is to be accomplished. Both the editor and person in charge of theme production ought to keep notes, because notes have a way of "getting lost" or becoming incoherent. Try to have a session with the service man from the company that is to print your annual. He can give you useful information on type faces to use, the most economical method of printing special sections, and many other details.

Producing a satisfactory basic plan for your yearbook need not be a difficult job if you start early, select a workable plan, and place the responsibility for its execution in the hands of one capable individual.

Pictures and copy telling about student experiments in school arouse the interest of readers and direct their attention to the academic activities, the primary function of schools. In this picture the student and the equipment she is using are arranged to tell an interesting story.

Chapter 7

Showing Academic Activities

APPLYING the principles of layout discussed in a previous chapter will improve the interest and readability of your yearbook. However, excellent pictures and clear writing are major factors in getting and holding readers' interest.

Getting Pictures To Aid Layout

By studying the layout techniques used in the pages presented from leading annuals, you will see how outstanding results were achieved in getting the right pictures to tell the story. The "story-telling" feature of the picture, its impact, its beauty, its composition, and its technical quality all contribute to the success or failure of the page layout and must be carefully considered in any discussion of yearbook production.

Headlines Can Aid Impact

Study the excellent headlines, cutlines, and body copy shown on the following pages. They demonstrate the attention-getting power of a well-written headline and its contribution to good lay-

out. The same is true, to a slightly lesser degree, of text copy and cutlines.

Emphasizing the Work of the School

The public goes to entertainment activities of a school, and newspapers know people are interested in such entertainment as school athletics, plays, pep bands, queens, and musicals. They keep school interesting and are important "teaching" devices that help students learn in association with others. However, the primary function of schools is academic, so a yearbook that omits or slights academic activities will not portray the school year well. All good yearbooks now have sections devoted to academic activities. Much of the credit for this development can be attributed to yearbook-judging services, and to writers and speakers who have advocated developing the actual business of the school in the annual as good public relations. They feel that the annual affords a good opportunity to inform patrons and taxpayers about the serious educational contributions of the school.

Don't crowd out the school's most important function by devoting all the space to extracurricular activities.

Excellent progress has been made toward including administrators, faculty, and academic activities in most leading annuals. In fact, a few of the annuals have devoted so much space to the operation of the school that they have crowded out many of the features that made the yearbook a treasured record of the fun and entertainment activities of school days. It is possible to overdo a good thing! A sensible balance between academic and extracurricular activities in the school annual is essential. The annual is published primarily by the students and should not be turned into a glorified catalog. It should continue to serve its traditional purpose as a student publication.

Displaying Curricular Activities

It is worth noting in the pages which follow that some schools concentrate all of the pages about the work of the school in one section of the book. Others, particularly the large university books, place the material about the deans and academic matters at the beginning of the section showing pictures of graduates. When the pages about the academic activities of the school are concentrated in one section, more emphasis is probably given this material. On the other hand, scattering strictly scholastic material at strategic spots throughout the annual results in emphasis through repetition. Then, too, placing this matter in the class section helps to break up the monotony of too many pages of class panels. The manner in which you plan to display the academic activities in your yearbook should be decided before too many of the pictures have been taken.

The following pages in this chapter show reproductions of pages from award-winning annuals, with a brief discussion of some of their effective results. Yearbook pages shown have been reproduced directly from the printed pages, and naturally, some detail has been lost, particularly in the photographs. Thus, the pictures illustrate composition, storytelling ability, beauty, and impact, more than photographic quality.

Granite Presents Its Principal in Style

The academic section of most yearbooks starts

FIGURE 7.1. This double-page spread from the *Granitanian* is an excellent example of good layout. The pictures are carefully cropped and excess white space is thrown to the outside of the pages.

Principal Reho F. Thorum

With the aid of Marie Christenson, office secretary, Granite's principal, Mr. Reho Thorum, explains to Karen Johnson, a junior, the new IBM numbering system. Each of the six buildings on campus now displays a number instead of the traditional lettering.

Vice Principal Leland Bird

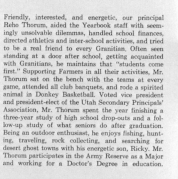

PRINCIPAL VOTED PRESIDENT-ELECT
of Secondary School Principals' Association

Friendly, interested, and energetic, our principal Reho Thorum, aided the Yearbook staff with seemingly unsolvable dilemmas, handled school finances, directed athletics and inter-school activities, and tried to be a real friend to every Granitian. Often seen standing at a door after school, getting acquainted with Granitians, he maintains that "students come first." Supporting Farmers in all their activities, Mr. Thorum sat on the bench with the teams at every game, attended all club banquets, and rode a spirited animal in Donkey Basketball. Voted vice president and president-elect of the Utah Secondary Principals' Association, Mr. Thorum spent the year finishing a three-year study of high school drop-outs and a follow-up study of what seniors do after graduation. Being an outdoor enthusiast, he enjoys fishing, hunting, traveling, rock collecting, and searching for desert ghost towns with his energetic son, Ricky. Mr. Thorum participates in the Army Reserve as a Major and working for a Doctor's Degree in education.

At his side, and in charge of student activities, registration, IBM procedure, and text book rentals, was our dedicated Vice Principal Mr. Bird. His friendly "Good morning students" echoed through the school to tell us about tryouts for Pep Club, outstanding honors received by fellow Granitians, and faculty meetings for teachers on Tuesdays. With a family of six children, four girls and two boys, at home, Mr. Bird and his wife attended every dance held at Granite this year and maintained membership in a dance club. He oriented new teachers to school regulations and procedures, arranged and rearranged the school calendar to fit the students needs, and retained his membership in such organizations as the Phi Delta Kappa fraternity, UEA, NEA, and the PTA. A stereo fan, our efficient vice principal particularly enjoys outdoor work such as gardening and landscaping.

Busing an exhausting day, Vice Principal Leland R. Bird, chairman of student activities, schedules the Study Hall for the Yearbook initiation banquet held during March.

by presenting top officials of the school. Here the staff has a chance to set the tone and style for the following pages. The 1965 *Granitanian,* Granite High School, Salt Lake City, Utah, gets off to a good start as shown in Figure 7.1.

The layout of the two-page spread is excellent. Pleasing page margins are established and plenty of white space is left around each element presented to lend emphasis. Excess white space is thrown to the outside of the pages. The text copy gives an interesting account of the principal's association with students, his activities in the community, and his high standing with his associates in the state.

The copy about the vice-principal also is interesting. A teacher with six children who takes his wife to every school dance during the year is unusual. This is the kind of reporting needed to give life and sparkle to a yearbook. The headline is both interest compelling and effective typographically. Incidentally, the same style of headline is used throughout the book.

Semi-posed Pictures of Teachers

Excellent semi-posed pictures of teachers at

Salina (Kansas) High School are presented in the 1964 *Trail,* as shown in Figure 7.2. The combination headlines tag the pages as well as arousing the interest of the prospective reader. Such headlines can be used satisfactorily on large pages (9 by 12 inches in this case) but tend to be confusing on small crowded pages.

The copy reports what is new and significant in each department of the school. Several pages in this section are devoted to interesting shots in laboratories and classrooms. It requires a lot of planning and photographic ability to get such excellence in individual pictures but it is certainly worth the effort.

Pleasing and Readable Type

An interesting aspect of education is emphasized in the 1965 *Riparian,* Broad Ripple High School, Indianapolis, as illustrated in Figure 7.3. The pictures and copy tell the story about actual class work and how this knowledge can be developed "through hobbies, service, vocations."

The pictures are carefully planned and of excellent quality. The typography is attractive and readable. Cutlines are well written and properly

FIGURE 7.2. This carefully prepared spread from the *Trail* is simple and functional. The piano keyboard adds just the right atmosphere and variety. Headlines and copy fit the space provided for them.

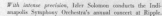

Realistic chalk textures and highlights challenge Art II pupil Anne Walton to sketch still life with detailed accuracy.

Music theory pupils Kim Hauseman, Patty Graus, and Carolyn Ward build triads and chords on model keyboards.

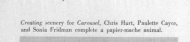

Guided by their emotions, tastes, and abilities, inspired art pupils transfer ideas to the material mediums of poster board, chalk, and paint during advanced art class.

Fine arts develop skills through hobby, service, vocations

With intense precision, Izler Solomon conducts the Indianapolis Symphony Orchestra's annual concert at Ripple.

Filling Ripple's halls with the sound of golden lyrics and the sight of artistic designing, pupils in the fine arts departments contribute to school cultural growth and achievement.

The Music Department offers opportunities f o r singers and instrumentalists alike. Vocal music training begins with a general course in Chorus I and continues upon merit of ability and talent to specialized studies in Golden Singers and Madrigals. Theory classes study the basic principles of musical composition in classical and modern pieces. Instrumental music courses offer instruction at all levels for a wide range of instruments. Advanced pupils have the opportunity to play in Ripple's Orchestra or Band.

Through the wanderings of a pencil, the carvings of a knife, or the stroke of a brush, art pupils utilize the opportunity to express themselves in sketches, sculpture, and paintings. A full eight semesters of possible art courses give pupils a chance to mix principles of color, design, and texture with their own personal tastes. In Ceramics and Craft Art pupils develop the ability to transform such common mediums as clay, paper, and leather into creative beauty of practical application.

Creating scenery for Carousel, Chris Hurt, Paulette Cayce, and Sonia Fridman complete a papier-mache animal.

Rehearsing her part in Ripple's annual Christmas music festival, harpist Patti Graus works on a medley of carols.

29

FIGURE 7.3. How pages can be tied together by a headline and appear as a single unit is shown in this layout from the *Riparian*. It is called page linkage.

FIGURE 7.4. This two-page spread from the *Whirligig* is linked together by the headline. Despite small pages, plenty of white space is provided for proper display of each element on the two pages.

BOARD OF EDUCATION — *Seated:* Mr. Richard M. Wilson, Mrs. Lessie E. Hoyle, Mr. Richard K. Hunter, chairman; Mr. James E. Perrin. *Standing:* Superintendent Philip J. Weaver, Dr. W. J. House, Dr. George H. Evans, Mr. Robert F. Moseley, Attorney. *Absent:* Mr. L. P. McLendon, Attorney, and Mr. George E. Norman.

PTSA OFFICERS, *left to right,* are, Mrs. H. Clements, president Mrs. E. Lashley, and Mr. T. McLean. *Absent:* Mrs. Bernard Cantrell.

Members of school board and PTSA work toward

SUPERINTENDENT P. J. Weaver greets students at annual faculty tea for seniors.

As the 1962-63 school year began, the school board, superintendent, and other administrators were faced with many problems. One which concerned GHS most was the great increase in tenth grade enrollment. To help in solving the Grimsley overcrowding an early schedule was devised, bringing three dozen of the 100 teachers to work at 7:30, with their first class at 7:45. Thus classrooms were available more periods a day. As a more permanent solution they began construction of the new Ben L. Smith High School in southwest Greensboro.

The administration accepted the opportunity for GHS to be among the pioneer schools in the United States to try out a two-hours-per-day composition laboratory devised and supervised by the NEA in Washington. The board arranged for lay readers to help the three participating teachers at GHS.

advancing our school

The PTSA board, in their meetings this year, planned programs to bring about a clearer understanding among parents, teachers, and students.

PTSA COUNCIL. — *Around left table:* Mrs. Roy M. Smith, Mr. Garland B. Murray, S. Welch, M. Rountree, M. Earle, Mr. John R. Green, Jr., Mrs. John R. Green, Jr., A. Phillips, D. Newman, B. James, B. Lambeth, I. Pearce. *Around second table:* Miss Jean Wood, Mrs. Mary Alice Moody, Mr. J. Trevor McLean, Mr. P. G. Cobb, Mrs. W. P. Byrd.

The first meeting was a reception at which the parents and teachers became better acquainted. Further understanding resulted from visits to classrooms, following the schedule of their son or daughter and there hearing something of the teacher's plans for the year.

Mrs. W. C. Singletary, Mrs. C. L. Earl, Mrs. Fred C. Rich, Mrs. J. I. Jessup, Jr., Mrs. J. D. Long, Mrs. Paul Main, Mrs. W. D. Okerson, Mr. J. H. Barnes, Mrs. J. H. Barnes. *Standing:* Mrs. Harry Clements, Mr. A. P. Routh, Mrs. Eugene M. Lashley, and Mrs. Harry D. Kellett. The board met at regular luncheons to plan programs.

FRONT ROW: Walter W. Hansen, Glen R. Durrell, Julius A. Pattillo, A. E. Darlow, Doyle Chambers, James S. Plaxico, Randall J. Jones. ROW 2: D. E. Howell, Lynn L. Gee, Fred LeCrone, John W. West, Frank P. Gardner, S. D. Musgrave, Roger E. Koeppe, W. Raymond Kays.

College Of Agriculture

Recognized for national leadership in many areas, the College of Agriculture at Oklahoma State University is ranked among the top seven universities in the nation in enrollment.

To be able to tackle the duty of supplying food and fiber for our rapidly expanding nation is the major objective of the qualified and capable graduate students in this field. Keeping pace with demands of a dynamic agriculture, many departments in agriculture have developed a very strong graduate program.

Offered as major options in the 15 departments listing courses in the college are agri-business, science and production. The revised curriculum provides training for a vast area that touches at least one-third of all jobs in the United States.

Outstanding success achieved by agricultural graduates in many fields of endeavor has built a strong reputation for the University in many sections of the world.

Recent changes in the College of Agriculture provide for greater attention to counseling and advisement of students and placement of graduates in challenging jobs of the present and the future.

DR. A. E. DARLOW
Dean of the College of Agriculture

FIGURE 7.5. Outstanding pictures are effectively combined with pleasing typography and good layout to complete this spread from the *Redskin.* It is an effective introduction to the Ag. College.

placed. The teachers are shown in panels of good studio pictures, just before the senior class section.

Whirligig Makes Good Layout on Small Page

The work of the board of education, superintendent, and Parent-Teacher-Student Association should be covered in all but the very largest high schools. How this can be done effectively is shown in Figure 7.4.

The *Whirligig,* Grimsley High School, Greensboro, North Carolina, is printed on a small-size (7½ x 10½ inch) page but demonstrates how excellent layouts can be made even under this handicap. It's easier to make attractive layouts on larger pages and that is one reason why many annuals and pictorial magazines use larger pages.

Full-page Picture Lends Emphasis

The staff of the 1964 *Redskin,* Oklahoma State University, Stillwater, used a full-page picture, symbolic of the work carried on, to introduce each college in the university. The two-page spread used to open the section about the college

of agriculture, shown in Figure 7.5, is an outstanding example of what can be accomplished if interesting pictures are taken and printed large enough to give proper impact.

Most yearbooks need to use more full-page pictures that stop the reader and invite him to read what has been written. Because of the need to conserve space the staff too often reduces the book to a collection of small dreary pictures. You ought to have some points of high interest in your annual just as other publications do.

Science and Engineering Featured

How the Institute of Technology covers every aspect of science and engineering is shown in Figure 7.6 taken from the 1965 *Gopher,* University of Minnesota, Minneapolis. Copy and pictures of this kind present important information that is interesting to students and all citizens of the state.

The editor of a yearbook in a large university or college should try to cover a few such featured examples in addition to the usual material about administrators, colleges, etc. If a new phase of the

FIGURE 7.6. Pictures, headline, and layout present a compelling story and invite anyone turning the pages of the 1965 *Gopher* to stop and read.

Graduate students in IT operate such complex instruments as this large mass spectrometer for precise measurement of atomic masses.

Scientists Fill Need in Today's Complex Society

Science is everywhere. It affects everyone every day. Science and technology influence our government policy. They are an integral part of our industry and the economic structure of the world. There is a great demand for qualified scientists and engineers to meet the needs of an increasingly scientific society. The Institute of Technology is striving to meet this need. With 3,400 students, the Institute of Technology is the second largest unit within the University. Course work in the Institute of Technology covers every aspect of science and engineering.

Mathematics is the language of science. It is essential in every field of scientific work and in many other areas. Accounting, insurance, medicine and pharmacy are some of the professions which require a math background.

Chemical engineering has grown by leaps and bounds since the end of World War II, as shown by advances in the uses and varieties of plastics for home and industry. Chemical engineering at the University is continually on the move.

Electrical Engineering is another fast-growing field. Electronics have produced today what seemed impossible only ten years ago. World-wide communication by satellite and the miniaturization of products through the use of transistors are results of electronic developments.

The Institute of Technology takes in an impressive number of specialized areas. Aerospace engineering, geology, geophysics, agricultural engineering, civil engineering, mechanical, metallurgical and mineral engineering, and physics and astronomy are all part of the curriculum.

university's educational or research program is presented each year, eventually almost complete coverage is attained.

Research Professors Cited

Fifteen leading research projects and the professors who conducted them are cited in the 1964 *Cornhusker*, University of Nebraska, Lincoln. Two pages from this section are presented in Figure 7.7.

A project of this kind, done carefully and honestly, adds much to the prestige of the university and at the same time gives credit to the individuals who are making worthwhile contributions to research and the school. Perhaps the following year the staff might want to recognize outstanding teachers or authors who have written significant

books. The possibilities are almost limitless.

Interesting Pictures of Department Heads

In a large university it's almost impossible to print pictures of all faculty members in the annual, but pictures of department heads often are printed. The 1965 *Cincinnatian*, University of Cincinnati, did a splendid job of presenting the dean of each college together with pictures of each department head.

One of the interesting features of the spread, shown in Figure 7.8, is the method of grouping two or three department heads in one picture. This is a departure from the usual plan of getting separate pictures of each individual. The plan used by the *Cincinnatian* staff allowed more leeway in making interesting and effective layouts.

FIGURE 7.7. Significant pictures, and outstanding typography are combined to produce this interesting spread from the 1964 *Cornhusker*. Note the lead-in names set in boldface at the beginning of each paragraph.

NU Professors Conduct Vital Research Projects

In the research section, the 1964 CORNHUSKER hoped to show the significance of professors' contributions to their respective fields and to the University. In addition to preparing for daily classroom activities, these outstanding men contributed many hours working on projects to aid the dynamics of progress. The staff also wished to indicate the wide scope of activities present at the University.

With assistance from both NU and national institutes, researchers conducted extensive studies in a variety of fields, including music, chemical engineering, philosophy, medicine and veterinary science. To choose the outstanding researchers, the staff contacted college deans and department chairmen in the fall and asked for recommendations. From over 50 replies, the staff selected 15 research projects on the basis of productivity, pertinence to the fields and importance within the colleges.

George Young, Veterinary Science

George Young, the 1960 Veterinarian of the Year, is working on a project to develop pathogen free swine. In one phase of the research, he has observed virus activity in culture tissues collected from swine with enteric diseases. To supplement state funds for the disease research, Professor Young was presented $102,000 in outside grants. In 1961 he received Distinguished Service Awards from the Animal Health Institute and Gamma Sigma Delta. He is also a diplomat of the American Board of Microbiology.

Thomas Thorson is studying the distribution of water in the blood and tissue cells of marine animals as a part of his specialization in the field of water ecology of vertebrate animals. He is also studying the fresh water sharks of Nicaragua and Guatemala, testing their ability to survive in salt and fresh water. Dr. Thorson spent two summers in Guatemala in connection with the projects. His work has been supported by the National Science Foundation for eight years and by the U.S. Public Health Service.

Thomas Thorson, Zoology

Robert Koehl is completing the first study of the Nazi SS Officers Corps based on their personnel records. His research on the organization has disclosed that the majority of the officers possessed a lower middle class background and that both ambition and talent were revealed in their records. Aid from the Woods Foundation and the Rockefeller Foundation enabled Dr. Koehl to work at the Berlin Document Center during 1960-61. He also used the World War II Records Division of National Archives in Virginia.

Robert Hurlbutt has surveyed the influence of Isaac Newton's science on theology and philosophy. Compiling his information in book form, Professor Hurlbutt wrote HUME, NEWTON AND THE DESIGN OF ARGUMENT. The book covers Newtonian physics and how it is used in formulating arguments for the properties of God. The work also contains Hume's critique of the Newtonian theology. After working on the book for seven years, he received a NU grant in 1963 which enabled him to complete the work.

M. J. Carver, of the Nebraska Psychiatric Institute, has been concerned with the free amino acids of the central nervous system. He investigated the distribution of the amino acids in phenylketonuria, an inborn error of human metabolism. This condition is characterized by a severe degree of mental retardation. Professor Carver is also developing the chemical counterpart of phenylketonuria in laboratory animals so that further biochemical studies can be made on tissues not readily accessible in humans.

Robert Hurlbutt, Philosophy

Robert Koehl, History

M. J. Carver, Medicine

132

133

Candid Shots Add Personal Touch

An interesting and novel way of presenting the teachers of history and economics is shown in Figure 7.9, reproduced from the 1964 *Dome,* University of Notre Dame, South Bend, Indiana. The candid shots of teachers as they lecture to their students shows personality and informality.

The other pictures on the spread lend variety. The copy is interesting and enlightening. The pictures taken of each department are handled in a slightly different manner and this contributes variety to the section.

Copy Tie-in With Picture

An unusual and significant picture, shown in Figure 7.10, is used by the *Ibis,* University of

Miami, Coral Gables, Florida, to help tell of the progress made by their school of law. A visiting professor from Yale is effectively photographed in front of the law school office directory. The copy is excellent and is tied in with the photograph.

What Is Adequate Coverage?

What is adequate coverage of the faculty and academic activities of my school? This is a question each staff must answer. The sooner a definite decision is made, the better job you will be able to do.

The size of the school and the size of the annual will have a lot to do with the treatment of this section. The number of pages that can be devoted to pictures and copy about administrators, teachers, classroom and laboratory work, as well as other phases suggested by the sample pages shown, ought to be determined as soon as possible.

FIGURE 7.8. Judicious use of white space and careful cropping lends emphasis to these two pages from the 1965 *Cincinnatian.* **The content of the written material as well as the typography is excellent.**

Academic Coverage in High School Annuals

Most high school annuals picture every faculty member either in group pictures, *recent* portraits, or with organizations they sponsor. In some of the very largest high schools, not all teachers' pictures are included, but an effort should be made to do so.

The principal, vice-principal, and other administrators are always included. The board of education and superintendent are sometimes omitted if they have several high schools under their administration and do not come in close contact with students at a particular school. In small schools, and in some large ones, pictures of secretaries and cafeteria and custodial employees are often included in the annual. Those who often contact or visit students earn space in the yearbook.

Picture Students in Class

Significant pictures of students in classrooms and laboratories should be a must for every annual. Close-up pictures of students using laboratory equipment, demonstrating before the class, or concentrating on the project at hand will improve the morale of the school and the community. Any new equipment or additions to the school should be covered.

Interesting and informative copy and headlines add to the effectiveness of the section. A lot of time should be given to collecting and writing information about new courses, field trips, and any new developments at the school.

Covering Academics in College Annuals

Small- and medium-size colleges usually print pictures of all faculty members and administrators. Large universities are often forced to settle for a few pages about each college and top administrators of the university. They get pictures of deans and assistant deans and, generally, run pictures of department heads. Pictures of buildings and classroom and laboratory scenes are also a must for college annuals.

As you have observed from study of special pages from yearbooks shown in this chapter, there are many areas that ought to be covered. Select one that is important and previously has been neglected and develop it in your annual.

FIGURE 7.9. The candid pictures of teachers contribute a lot to the interest of this spread from the 1964 *Dome*.

The layout pattern is distinctive and the use of white space effective.

HISTORY AND ECONOMICS

It surely must be a temptation for the freshman to judge every study by his first course in that area; the errors of such a conclusion are particularly evident in the subjects portrayed here. History, of necessity, is built on fact, just as economics rests largely on lifeless numbers; the elementary courses in these areas stress their basic foundations. But the primary concern of each of these studies is life itself, making them two of the most exciting and essential areas of a liberal education. The dividing line between the two is, in fact, often hard to distinguish. Historical events commonly admit of economic interpretations and economic developments, in turn, very often are triggered by historical landmarks. Then, too, both subjects are the basis of progress in political science, or sociology, or for that matter, in any understanding of the world of men.

(Top) Mr. Gray, and (top right) Mr. Norling, History. (Above) Mr. Sheehan, and (right) Mr. Montavon, Economics.

(Top) Fr. Engleton, History. (Above) Mr. Howett, curator of Art Gallery, lectures on Rennaissance Painting to a cultural History course.

The need for interesting and significant copy in college annuals is even greater than for high school annuals. Many of the academic activities of colleges and universities are not clearly understood by students, alumni, or citizens of the state. Some of the activities are looked upon with a jaundiced eye by certain critics of the school and ought to be explained in detail.

Readers of yearbooks expect better writing from college students than from high school staffs. Then, too, you have a chance to learn how to write for publication while preparing copy for your college annual.

Plan Academic Section Early

The academic section of your annual should be planned early. The spring before actual publication is not too soon. These are pages you will want to check carefully with administrators and department heads, to be certain that pictures of everyone who should be included are taken. This is at least one section in the annual where you should ask the person in authority to check the finished copy before it is sent to the printer. Too often unnecessary mistakes are made on these pages of an annual when it is done in a hurry.

Take Pictures During Summer

Another important reason for starting early to produce the pages about the academic activities at your school is that it is one of the few sections you can prepare to meet early printing deadlines. Many high school and college annual staffs work hard to get pictures of administrators, department heads, and faculty members taken during the summer before their annual is produced. This becomes more urgent if any of these pictures are to be reproduced in natural color. The cooperation you may get in this from administrators may surprise you, especially if you explain the importance of expediting the picture-taking and if you present your plans for improving coverage.

Quite often it is possible to take pictures of new buildings or new facilities at the school during summer. Some staffs even take classroom and laboratory pictures during the previous spring.

VISITING PROFESSOR, FOWLER V. HARPER OF YALE LAW SCHOOL, AT ENTRANCE TO UNIVERSITY OF MIAMI SCHOOL OF LAW

School of Law

Fowler V. Harper, visiting professor from Yale Law School, stands as a symbol of the University of Miami Law School's strides towards academic and professorial leadership. In a period of flux and tremendous growth the Law School has spent the past year expanding its programs and developing new teaching techniques that have been appreciated by both the faculty and the student body. Under the leadership of Acting Dean M. Massey, law students have continued a campaign for larger scholarship funds, started an expansion of our *Law Review* distribution, continued the student instructor program and have seen the introduction of a new practical lecture series. The student body itself has taken its place in the expansion program with its continuation of the Wesley A. Sturges Memorial Scholarship Fund and the operation of the new "Equity Playhouse," the proceeds of which are applied to the scholarship fund for operating expenses. Student participation and leadership are qualities in which the University of Miami Law School are strong. For the second year in a row the student body has collectively contributed to the Sturges Fund to benefit future law students.

67

FIGURE 7:10. This page from the *Ibis* shows how a simple layout is made effective by a significant picture.

However, this must be carefully planned so that seniors and teachers who are not returning the following year will not be included. If the yearbook is well planned, pictures of this kind can usually be taken early in the fall semester. If you plan to include some new or special feature about academic work at your school it is important that you start to work on that section as soon as you can.

The use of an interesting picture to introduce the class section orients the reader and thus performs a functional purpose. The antics of the senior cheerleaders are used as a sub-division page in the **Royal Purple, Kansas State University, Manhattan.**

Chapter 8

Making Class Layouts Functional

LESS THOUGHT and care are often given to planning page content and layout for the class section of the annual than to any other part of the book. Yet the class pages are the most important ones in the entire book. They are the real reason for the annual's existence.

Review of Requirements for Class Section

Before beginning to allocate space and to make tentative page layouts for the class section, it is well to review briefly the important matters discussed in previous chapters that will have a direct bearing on the kind of pictures you will have to work with and just how you need to display them to accomplish the best results.

Here is a summary of some of the important points discussed regarding the class section:

1. The function of the class section is to give *identity* to every student in school by printing his picture with his name in the annual. Class sections are the backbone of the school annual and have more universal appeal to students, parents, and friends than any other section in the book. Class pictures, often of seniors only, were the original reason for class books, which preceded and were developed into modern school yearbooks.

2. Class pictures should be of the finest quality obtainable. Don't be so concerned about cost that you contract for inferior pictures—remember they are the ones that will be viewed by the owner of the book for an entire lifetime. All portraits used should have uniform backgrounds and head sizes. The practice in many schools of referring to class portraits as "mug shots" does nothing to encourage quality pictures. Mug shots are the pictures taken of criminals, or at best, for identification of an individual on a passport or driver's license. For the class section get the finest portraits you can to record the accomplishments of students in your school. Don't accept mug shots!

3. The importance of significant summaries of seniors' activities has been discussed, as has

Figure 8.1 caption area:

SeniorTheater Snares Promising Talent; Tea House Profit Establishes Precedent

Courtney Thomas Camp: JV Wrestling 11; Varsity Wrestling 12; Intramurals 11, 12

Jack Campbell: JV Football 10, 11; Varsity Football 12; Varsity Club 12; Intramurals 10, 11, 12; Hi-Y 10; French Club 10

Jacqueline Ann Candela: Windup 11, business editor 12; National Honor Society 11, 12; Quill and Scroll 11, president 12; Class Council 12; Welfare 12; Hospitality 12; Publications Alternate 10, 11, 12

Richard Leslie Capek: Earth Science Club 12; Teahouse of the August Moon 12; Maryland, My Heritage 11; Dance Club 12; Woodwind Ensemble 10; Hoot-Jam 12; Variety Show 12

Francis Elliott Carlson: Art Club 11, 12; Intramurals 11, 12

Lane Easton Carlson: Music Man 11; Concert Chorus 11, 12; Football manager 11; Hoot-Jam 12; Folk Sing 10, 11; Folk-Singing Club 12; Maryland, My Heritage 12

Robert Alden Carlson: Key Club 12; Varsity Wrestling 11, 12; JV Wrestling 10, 11; Cross Country 11, 12; JV Football 10

Vivien Lynne Carothers: Concert Chorus 12; Music Man 11; Coordinating Council 12; Tri-Hi-Y 10, 11, 12; GSA 10, 11, 12; Hockey Honor Team 11, 12; Volleyball Honor Team 11; Ski Club 12; Senior Class Publicity

Ralph Carter: Key Club 11, 12; Varsity Football 11, co-captain 12; Varsity Club 11, treasurer 12; Publications Representative 10, 11, 12; Varsity Wrestling 12

Teresa Kay Carter: Pitch 12; Publicity 11; FTA 11, 12; Tri-Hi-Y 10; FHA 10

Aldo John Cavallo: King and I 12; Maryland, My Heritage 11; Teahouse of the August Moon 12; Audio-Visual 11, 12; Marching Band 10, 11, 12

Joan Anna Cavin: FBLA 12; School Store 11

Patricia Athena Chaconas: Drama Club 10; FBLA corresponding secretary 12

Diane Chaddock: Ski Club 12

Dianne Thomas Changaris: National Honor Society 11, 12; SCA Alternate 12; Drama Club 12; Library Assistant 12; Girls' Ensemble 12

Brian David Chase: Intramurals 10, 11, 12; Biology Club 10; Chess Club 10

Ronald Chasen: Band 10, 11, 12; Bridge Club 11, president 12; Intramurals 10, 11; Hi-Y 10

David Lee Christeller: Honor Society 11, 12; Hi-Y 12

Gary Joseph Coates: National Honor Society 11, 12; SCA Representative 10, 11, 12; Honor 12; Varsity Baseball 12; Lab Assistant 12

Kaye Ruth Coates: National Honor Society 12; Tri-Hi-Y 12; Earth Science Club secretary 12; Chorus 11, 12; Class Council Alternate 12

Distracted Captain Fishby, alias Paul Davids, reluctantly succumbs to comfort, Okinawa style. Indoctrinated by Geisha girl Linda Sentman, his "present" from a friendly villager, he soon appreciates cricket cages, kimonos, and Japanese customs. Complete with a Japanese fan dance, a spirited performance of "She'll be Coming 'Round the Mountain," and a real goat, this Senior Class play, Tea House of the August Moon, entranced audiences and rang up $140 for the Senior Class, excluding Budget card money.

John Leonard Cobb: National Honor Society 12; Wheel Club 10, 11, treasurer 12; Special Services chairman 11; SCA president 12; Concert Chorus 11, 12

William Cochran: Hi-Y 12; Track Team 10, 11; Ski Club 11, 12; Lab Assistant 12; Fantasia 10; Cross Country 11; Intramurals 10, 11

Sharon Ruth Cohen: National Honor Society 12; Pitch page four editor 12; Quill and Scroll 11, 12; Correspondent Suburban Record 11; Yearbook Club 10; GSA 10

Cheryl Cole: Out-of-School Publicity chairman 12; SCA Corresponding secretary 12; Cheerleader 12; Sophomore Class liaison 12; Dorians 10, 11, 12; FTA 11

Charles Edward Collinge: Football manager 11, head manager 12; Hi-Y 10, 11, 12; Varsity Club 12

Elizabeth Comee: Dorians 10, 11, vice-president 12; Gymkana 11, 12; Pom pons 12; Volleyball Honor Team 11; Powder Puff Basketball 11; Opera Workshop 11, 12; GSA 10

Eddie Compton: Key Club 11, sergeant-at-arms 12; Varsity Club 11, vice-president 12; Varsity Baseball 10, 11, 12; Varsity Basketball 11, 12; JV Basketball 10

Philip Mattes Corddry: Varsity Baseball 10, 11, 12; JV Basketball 10; Varsity Basketball 11, 12; Varsity Club 11, 12

42 Seniors

Seniors 43

FIGURE 8.1 A good headline and an interesting picture invites the reader to stop and read the 1965 *Windup*. Pictures of seniors and their write-ups are arranged so it's easy to find the information wanted.

correct identification of each student by his first name, middle initial, and last name. Careful planning with your photographer is required to assure correct identification of each portrait. Most staffs have accepted this responsibility. They have discontinued printing class wills, prophecies, cute sayings, and other short-lived trivia in this section.

Allocating Space for Class Sections

In allocating space you must decide whether all seniors are to be presented in one section, followed by underclassmen arranged in alphabetical order without regard to class, or if another plan is to be used. That is perhaps the simplest way to arrange individual pictures so they can be located easily by the reader. However, it may be traditional in your school to allocate space for each class, or in case of a large university, to print class pictures from each college in separate sections. If a definite plan has been established, it is well to consider it carefully because that is the plan most readers will expect to find in the book. They are accustomed to the system.

Preparing Functional Class Layouts

Preparing functional and interesting layouts for the class pages of the yearbook is one of the most difficult tasks in producing an annual. Class sections have many elements to be integrated into double-page spreads: individual pictures, headlines, identifications, summaries, and perhaps an activity shot. Doing it well requires a lot of time and care—and provides the right amount of space for each of the elements. The photographs ought to be as large as space will permit and be artistically cropped to give the most pleasing results. At the same time adequate space must be left for the headline, summaries, and identifications to be properly displayed without crowding. It's a job requiring a lot of technical knowledge as well as unlimited patience. Get your printing serviceman or adviser to help you if you are uncertain about the class layouts.

Variety in Layout Adds Interest

Some variety in layout is needed in the class section. If you have a large number of class pages, it is a good plan to make several different layouts and rotate them throughout the section. While variety in layout improves the class pages, the general pattern should be the same for the entire section, to make it easy for the reader to find what he wants.

The use of significant action pictures spotted throughout the class pages adds variety and interest. The activity pictures should be of good quality and preferably of class activities—award winners, jams in hallways between classes, etc. Proper display of the pictures and well-written cutlines explaining them are a must. No section of the yearbook, and particularly not the class section, should be a catch-all for poor pictures left over from other sections.

List Abbreviations To Be Used in Summary

To save space, abbreviations for activities

FIGURE 8.2. The two pages in this spread from the *Clarion* are effectively tied together by the layout and made to appear larger than they are. This is accomplished despite small-sized pages (7½ x 10½ inches).

often are used in the senior summaries. The abbreviations may be meaningless, even to students in the school, unless they are defined in the annual. Here is one paragraph from the first page of the senior class section as printed in the 1965 *Royal Purple*:

> *Abbreviations for Activities:* ACS—American Chemical Society; Act.—Activities; Adm.—Administration; Ad. —Advertising; Ag.—Agriculture; Ag. Mag.—Agricultural Magazine; AFROTC—Air Force Reserve Officers Training Corps; A.G.O.—American Guild of Organists; AHEA—American Home Economics Association; AIA— American Institute of Architects; AIAA—American Institute of Aeronautics and Astronautics; AIChE—American Institute of Chemical Engineers; A.I.I.D.—American Institute of Interior Designers; AIIE—American Institute of Industrial Engineers; AIP—American Institute of Physics; Am.—American; ANS—American Nuclear Society; ASA—American Society of Agronomy; ASAE— American Society of Civil Engineers; ASLA—American Society of Landscape Architects; ASME—American Society of Mechanical Engineers; A&S—Arts and Sciences; Asst.—Assistant; Assn.—Association; Assoc.—Associated; AVA—American Vocational Association; AVMA— Student Chapter of American Veterinary Medical Association; AWS—Associated Women Students; Aux.—Auxiliary.

Pages from award winning annuals illustrating a variety of layouts and methods of presenting class pictures are shown in this chapter. They may aid in planning the class section of your book.

Functional Headline Adds Interest

A functional and interesting presentation of seniors is shown on the double-page spread, Figure 8.1, from the 1965 *Windup*, Walter Johnson Senior High School, Bethesda, Maryland. Excellent use of white space provides proper margins and effectively presents the pictures, copy, and headline.

The headline arouses the interest of the reader and invites him to read about "Teahouse of the August Moon" sponsored by the seniors and pictured on the opposite page. This kind of headline is much more functional than one that skips from page to page without calling attention to what's interesting about the particular page or pages where it's printed. Action pictures of the type shown, together with an informative cutline like this one, add variety to the class section.

Unusual and Orderly Layout

An unusual and orderly arrangement of seniors is shown on this two-page layout from the 1963 *Clarion*, Senior High School, Appleton, Wis-

FIGURE 8.3. It's difficult to make a layout that presents as many elements as shown in this spread from the *Camelback*. Purpose of this one, presentation of advisers and class officers, justifies the layout.

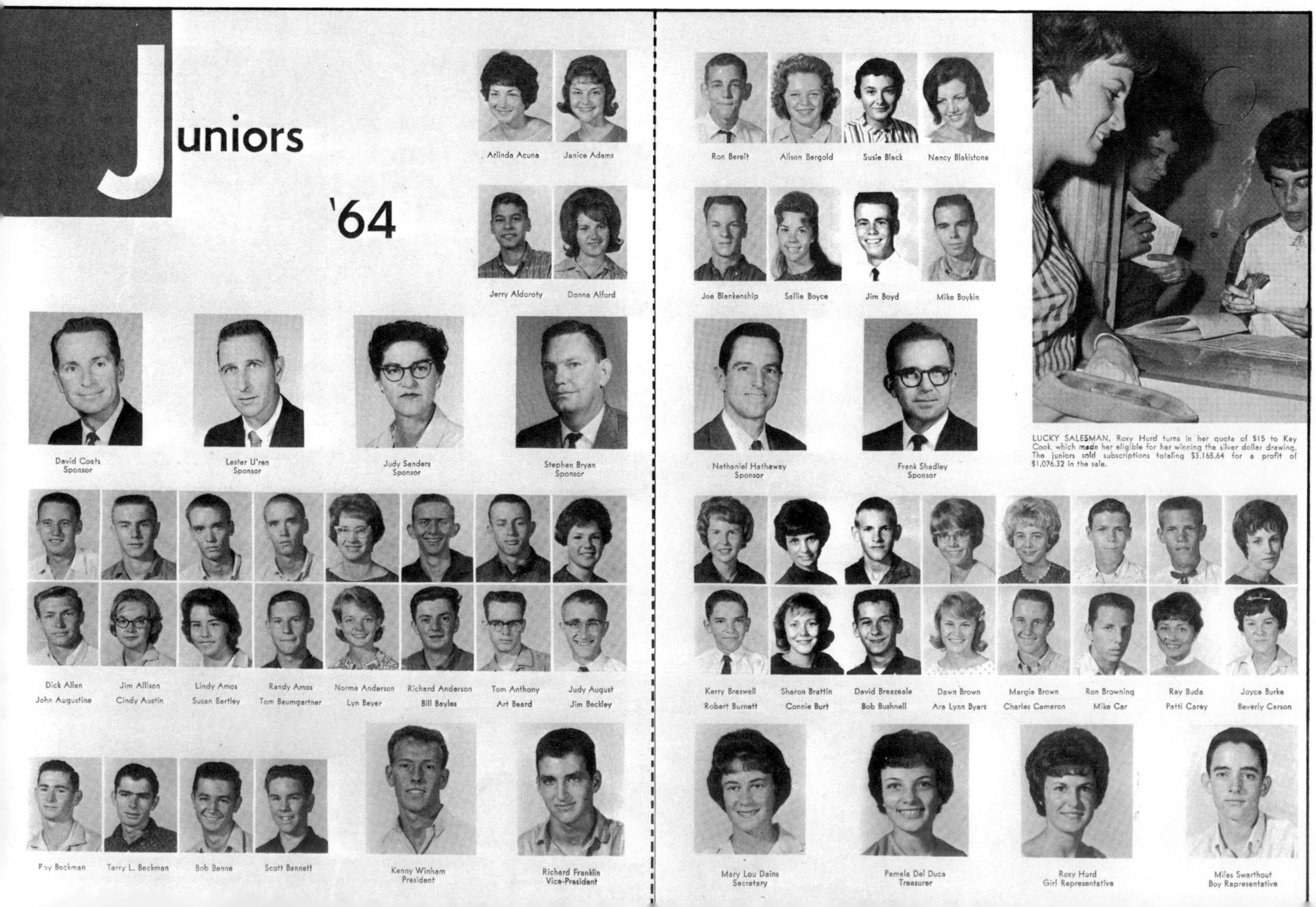

consin, Figure 8.2. The method of identification used makes it easy to locate instantly each student pictured. Printing the name and information of all individuals in each row in one paragraph gives a pleasing typographical effect.

The pictures are of excellent technical quality with uniform background and head sizes. The name of each student is printed in bold face in the summaries and helps the reader find the write-up he wants.

Advisers and Officers Featured

The advisers and class officers are featured in the carefully planned spread, Figure 8.3, from the *Camelback*, Scottsdale High School, Scottsdale, Arizona. Such a layout requires careful planning to achieve pleasing results.

The especially designed label head lends variety to the pages. The activity picture is appropriate and well posed, and the caption tells an interesting story. The individual pictures are carefully posed and well lighted. The method of identification is simple and effective.

Group Picture of Absentees Insures Coverage

In an effort to get a picture of every student in school in the yearbook, the staff of the *Indian*, Shawnee Mission North High School, Shawnee Mission, Kansas, takes group pictures of homerooms of all sophomores and juniors. In addition, a group picture of all students who were absent when original sittings were made is taken at a later date, as shown in Figure 8.4.

The group pictures are of good quality, carefully arranged to show each student's face, and each student is properly identified. Individual pictures are used in the senior section.

Excellent Pictures Command Attention

Outstanding pictures of class officers are used in the 1964 *Debris*, Purdue University, West Lafayette, Indiana, to open the class section, as shown in Figure 8.5. The variety of poses used and the excellence of the pictures demand attention of anyone turning the pages of this annual.

The layout is distinctive and follows the pattern and format of other pages in the *Debris*. Showing pictures of class officers of all four classes on one page is unusual; thus, it provides variety and arouses the interest of viewers.

FIGURE 8.4. Thirty group pictures, one for each homeroom, of the junior class are printed in the 1965 *Indian*.

This layout presents the final spread showing picture of absentees taken to assure 100 per cent coverage.

SWANSON. **Back:** Linda Uhlman, Don Walker, Alex Turner, Eric Van-Denthasen, Bruce Warkentine, Richard Waller, Mary Tudor. **Second:** Connie Wade, Susie Vincent, Cam Vinz, Pat Tucker, Becky Wallower, Richard Vanschoelandt. **Front:** Linda Vandeputte, Martha Tucker, Steve Twaddell, Shirley Walkup, Laurie Turrell, D. J. Walters, Mary Lou Wade.

Mournful expressions expose the feelings of these students during the AFS basketball game as the Senior All-Stars are defeated at the hands of the Faculty Heroes.

Sam Sparks contemplates becoming a world traveler during study hall period profitably spent in the library.

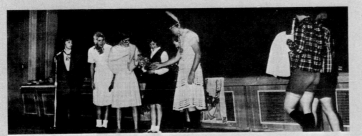

Petite Princess Jurgemeyer enviously paws at the bouquet held by a surprised Janet Selders, newly-crowned queen of the the pep skit.

WEAVER. **Back:** Sonny Woronick, Linda Zillhart, Mike Wurm, Terry Williams, John Wohlgemuth, Mark Wootton, Paul Yonally. **Third:** Gretchen Woodward, Kris Wilson, Rick Wiser, George Wombolt, Tom Wilson, Jane Zeller. **Second:** Laurie Zaugg, Nancy Wilson, Sue Wyrick, Larry Zawicki, Linda Woody. **Front:** Bruce Young, Beth Wilson, Linda Zimmer, Tyea Wisor.

to produce a memorable evening in an Oriental garden—

Prom—1965 . . . a sample of achievements to come . . .

TASCHETTA. **Back:** Paul Weimer, Jim Westerfield, Bob Wellman, Scott Williams, Ken White, Kathy Weathers, Joe Welch. **Third:** Regina Wheeler, Kris Wattenberg, Harry Wheeler, John Williams, Tim Wheat, Jon White. **Second:** Annette Westermann, Barbara Wenzel, Karen Whitton, Marilyn Whitesell, Barbara Wiglesworth. **Front:** Brenda Warkentine, Linda Weidemier, Linda Whalen, Janet Wever.

200

JUNIOR ABSENTEES. **Back:** John White, Bob McDaniels, Gerald Fowler, Mike Hopkins, Jim Suman, Alicia Krechmar. **Second:** Mike McDaniels, Jan Scoggins, Sharon McGuire, Alberta Ray, Rita Bower, Pam Dennis. **Front:** Sally Eshnaur, Jackie Garrett, Karen Kittrell, Judy Payne, Maureen Vanlerberg.

201

FIGURE 8.5. Well-posed pictures and a distinctive layout are combined in this interesting two-page spread from the 1964 *Debris*. Generous use of white space is used effectively for emphasis.

FIGURE 8.6. Careful use of white space accentuates each element shown on this spread from the 1965 *Royal Purple*. It's easy for the reader to locate the picture, identification, and summary for each individual.

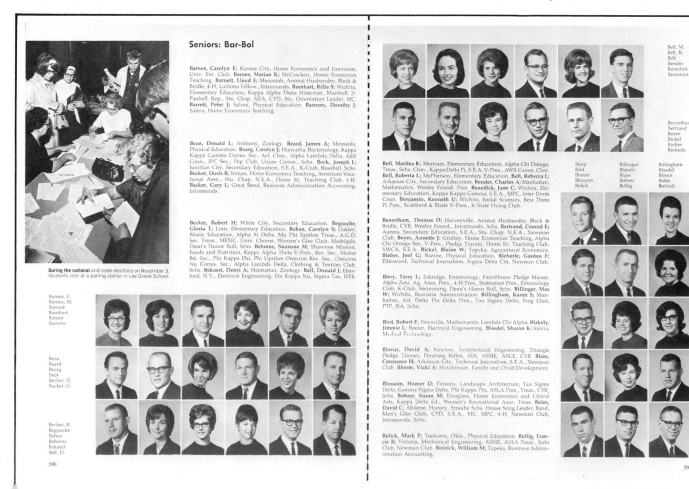

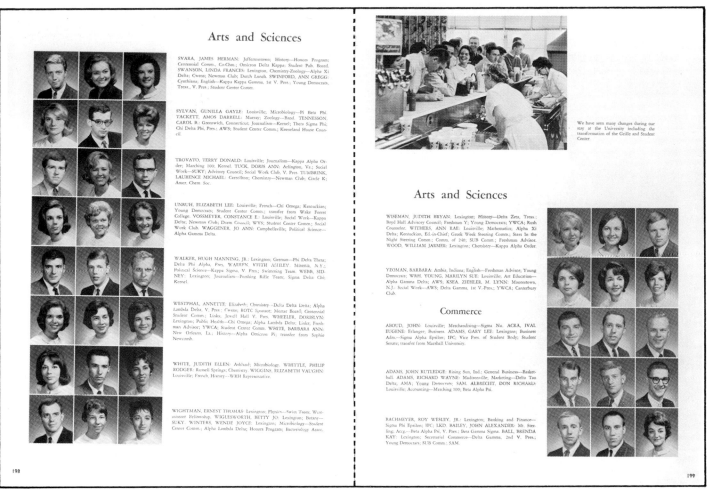

FIGURE 8.7 Excellent use of white space and careful arrangement of summaries are combined in this pleasing spread from the 1965 *Kentuckian*. The type selected is readable and effectively displayed.

FIGURE 8.8 Throwing white space to outside of each page make the two pages meet the eye as a single unit in this layout from the 1965 *Tower*. Cropping of pictures and excellent typography contribute to the effect.

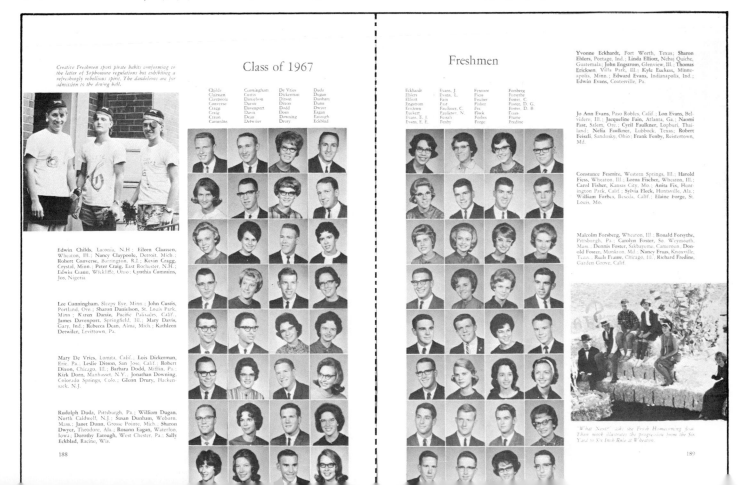

ANDERSON, J.G., — Swift Current
B.A.; P.R.O.; PRO, MASA, V. Pres. St. Andrew's; Social Comm. for Q'Hall.
BAYNTON, G.W., — Lloydminster
B.A., L.L.B.; U. of S. U'Grad., Mackenzie (2), Caswell Co. Schols.; IBM, Engineered Homes Bursaries; Debating, Curling, Judo.
CHASSE, W., — Toronto
FERGUSON, T.H., — Saskatoon
Law Sports' Rep. M.A.B.; IM Sports, Leader Campus Conservatives.
GILLILAND, J.J.B., — Regina
B.A.

GRAHOLM, L, — Haney
B.A.Sc.; Bridge, Debating, Golf, ISC.
HENGEN, P.C., — Regina
B.A.; Sheaf Rep.; Law; MIAB, Football.
KUCEY, R.J., — Saskatoon
B.A.; COTC.
MacBEAN, F.A., — Regina Beach
B.A.; MAB Board; MIAB Sports.
MacLEAN, D.A.K., — Saskatoon
B.A., St. Andrew's Schol.; Athletic Award--Law; Pups B'ball, IM Football, B'ball, V'ball, Hockey.

MacPHERSON, J.A., — Grenfell
B.A.
NORMAN, K.E., — Saskatoon
B.A., U. of S. U'Grad., P.E. McKenzie Schols.; Canada Law Book Prize; Social Dir.; IM Sports--Football.
NOTTINGHAM, S.J., — Saskatoon
B.A.
PHENIX, M.A., — Saskatoon
Law Soc. Exec.-NFCUS; Greystone Rep.
PRESTON, W.D., — Rosetown
B.A.

RATUSHNY, E.J., — Kamsack
B.A.; Carswell Prize (1st Yr); McLean Prize (Constitutional Law) Law President; IM Sports; Varsity Band; "Glorious Leader"--Intensely Vigorous College "9."
SHABBITS, S.J., — Yorkton
B.A.
SKELTON, D.R., — Harris
B.A.; Student Editor--Sask. Bar Review.
THAUBERGER, J.J., — Regina
B.A.; Univ. Ent. Schol.; Newman Club; IM Sports; Student Editor, Sask. Bar Review.
WALDBILLIG, F.L., — Cudworth
B.A.; V'ball, Hockey, Curling.

WILSON, G.T., — Saskatoon
B.Comm.

Andreychuk, A.R. Saskatoon	Barker, D.G. Weyburn	Carey, B.P. Rosetown	Caron, P.J. Calgary	Carson, G. Snowden	Carson, I.B. Snowden	Dell, D.W. Swift Current	Dobrowney, O.O. Saskatoon	Egleston, D.J. Regina	Evans, R.L. Regina	Gibson, J.L. Saskatoon
Gibson, W.G. Saskatoon	Henderson, M.W. Saskatoon	Lueck, A.R. Indian Head	Lutter, R.M. Goodsoil	Magnuson, K.M. Spiritwood	Maher, R.D. North Battleford	McCallum, I.P. Estevan	McTavish, I.R. Kapuskasing	Nimegeers, C.M. Weyburn	Ozirny, M. Maple Creek	Pinel, L.F. Moose Jaw
Pilzel, R.P. Moree	Roszel, L.A. Saskatoon	Sali, L.M. Qu'Appelle	Sihvon, A.M. Regina	Sinclair, G.B. Saskatoon	Stevenson, W.W. Richlea	Thompson, R.W. Battleford	Truwick, A.H. Regina	Watson, K.G. Calgary	Webster, D.W. Hearre	Woods, M.S. Regina

Functional Arrangement Aids Reader

The orderly and functional arrangement of pictures, headlines, identifications, and summaries makes it easy for the reader to locate the information he wants in the senior section of the 1965 *Royal Purple,* Kansas State University, Manhattan, as illustrated in Figure 8.6.

The page margins in this section are narrower than in the rest of the annual, to provide space for larger pictures and adequate summaries. This plan often is used for the class section of annuals having a large number of class pictures to present. However, unity of margin treatment should be observed and the narrow margins should be used throughout the entire section.

The headline is simple and functional. It indicates to the reader that all members of the senior class whose last names begin with the letters "Bar" to and including "Bol" are to be found on these two facing pages. This is the same method used in a dictionary to expedite its use.

Seniors Arranged by Colleges

The staff of the 1965 *Kentuckian,* University of Kentucky, Lexington, arranged seniors according to the college in which they were enrolled. This is a common practice in large universities. The results are seen in Figure 8.7. The portraits are excellent and the uniform head size and background contribute to the pleasing results obtained. Pictures of historical significance were used on many of the pages in the class section to help carry out the centennial theme of the *Kentuckian.*

Individual Pictures of Freshmen Included

Individual pictures of all students, including freshmen, are printed in the *Tower,* Wheaton College, Wheaton, Illinois. The college collects a fee at enrollment to cover the cost of each student's picture and a subscription to the annual. This plan provides a photograph of every student in school for the class section.

The pictures are excellent as can be seen in Figure 8.8. The panels bleed at the bottom of the page, the safest place to bleed panels showing small faces. If a little more is trimmed away than was planned in trimming the pages, it does not make a significant difference in the final results.

Unusual Presentation of Class Pictures

An interesting and perhaps unusual method of presenting class pictures is shown in Figure 8.9, from the 1965 *Greystone,* University of Saskatchewan, Saskatoon, Canada. Seniors' pictures from each college in the university are printed in a pleasing size and are followed immediately by underclassmen often on the same page but shown much smaller. This plan saves space and presents class pictures from each college in one section of the annual.

Take Class Pictures Early

An early start and careful planning make it possible to get at least some of the class pages to the printer to meet early deadlines. As has been mentioned, many high school staffs send seniors to the photographer during summer for portraits. In some cases, pictures of underclassmen are also taken at the same time. Pictures for class pages need not be delayed until after enrollment.

More colleges and universities each year are collecting an activity fee during registration to cover a subscription to the annual and the photographic fee. If this plan is followed, the photographer can start taking pictures immediately after school starts in the fall and can usually deliver prints to the yearbook well before Christmas. With such a plan, second semester seniors should be permitted to have pictures taken soon after they enroll. Their pictures may be printed at the end of the regular senior section.

←

FIGURE 8.9. This space-saving arrangement of seniors and underclassmen on the same page is from the 1965 *Greystone.* Careful cropping of pictures and arrangement of copy are combined to produce a functional layout.

Dramatic scenes from plays properly photographed provide the annual staff a great opportunity to get interest and impact into the organization and activity section of their annual. This scene from the Stanford Players' production "Time Remembered" is reproduced full-page size in the 1965 Stanford Quad, Stanford University, Stanford, California.

Chapter 9

Treating Organizations and Activities Uniformly

THE EDITOR of the yearbook faces an especially difficult problem in making effective layouts for the organization and activity section of the annual. This problem is created because space in the annual often is sold to organizations, and the memberships of two organizations to be pictured on facing pages sometimes vary greatly. Then, too, members of some organizations may feel they should determine just what is to appear on "their" page in the yearbook. Even if organizations are not required to pay for space in the annual, they frequently want to "help" plan their pages.

Plan Organization Pages in Advance

If the organization section in the annual is to be orderly, interesting, and fair to each organization presented, the editor and staff must determine the kinds of pictures needed for each organization and activity to be presented. To insure getting pictures of good quality and uniform coverage for all organizations and activities, it is best to establish a plan that will permit you to supervise and control the photographer taking the pictures.

This can be done by requiring the organization to pay the photography fee directly to the annual. You can then see that the photographer gets the type of picture you need to carry out your plans. The photography fee is sometimes included in the amount charged for space in the annual. In a few cases, the charge for space, photography fee, and subscription to the yearbook is covered in a compulsory activity fee paid by each student when he enrolls. All of the above methods insure that money for photographs will be controlled by the annual staff.

Strive for Uniform Treatment

It is not easy to get uniform coverage of organizations and at the same time provide variety in layout. Some large university annuals picture more than 200 organizations, and a large high school often has half that many. If all the organizations in a large book are shown in formal group pictures, the effect is likely to be monotonous. Then, too, not much variety in layout is possible.

A plan frequently used is to present the fra-

Columbians fill year with service projects

The Columbian Literary Society is an organization devoted to promoting service projects for both the school and the community.

After the initiation of the new members at a formal candlelight ceremony, the 63-'64 club year began with the traditional "Get Acquainted Week," when the girls make name tags for all the students to wear so they can learn to know each other. During the first two weeks of school an information booth was set up in the library foyer to help sophomores and newcomers.

Other activities during the year were varied. Mums were sold at homecoming time and a float was made with the help of the "Columbian Fathers." On Valentine Day "Hummingbird Columbians" delivered "suitable" greeting to both students and teachers, for a price. This project, more commonly known as the "Singing Valentines," is a favorite and grows more popular each year. One of the service projects for the year was collecting clothing and food baskets for needy families.

Columbian officers—Linda Weaver, Joanne Mailer, Sherry Holloway and Dottie Dunlap—talk to Miss Pauline Poynor about the Great Books that her class received from Columbians last year.

FIGURE 9.1. Effectively posed pictures showing everyone in a happy mood contribute much to this well-balanced spread from the 1964 Bruin. Individuals are well arranged in the group and properly identified.

Columbian members '63-'64—*Top row*: Sharon Hunt, Irene Phillips, Karen Hunt, Carol Ed Allen, Judy Smoot, Becky McNeill, Glenn Ann Blakemore, Dede Bethell, Carolyn Plunkett, Nancy Hinton, Almetha LaBorde. *Second row*: Susan Hennig, Lou Ann Fultner, Joyce Littlejohn, Marsha Crane, Connie Goswick, Linda Carol Wegner, Patty Ball, Pam Cravens, Becky Vaughan, Jane Jeffery. *Third row*: Sharon Johnson, Patricia Strang, Charlotte Strang, Ellen Orsburn, Dee Whitcomb, Diana Claybaugh, Martha Owensby, Gwynne Robbins, Susan Turner, Judy Tamm. *Bottom row*: Susie Heard, Sherry Holloway, Joanne Mailer, Mrs. Katherine Lemley, sponsor, Donna Standiford, Dottie Dunlap, Terry Kirkpatrick, Mary Leigh Easton.

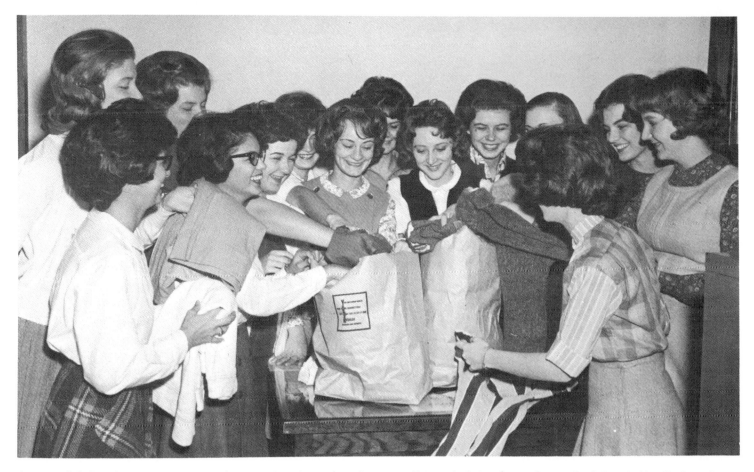

As one of their civic projects, the Columbians conducted a clothing drive to collect used clothes for needy people of Fort Smith. Charlotte Strang, Dee Whitcomb, Dianna Claybaugh, Patricia Strang, Susie Heard, Sharon Johnson, Jane Jeffery, Sharon McFarlin, Connie Goswick, Almetha LaBorde, Nancy Hinton, Judy Robinson, Judy Smoot and Karen Wear pack collections in paper bags before distributing them to various families

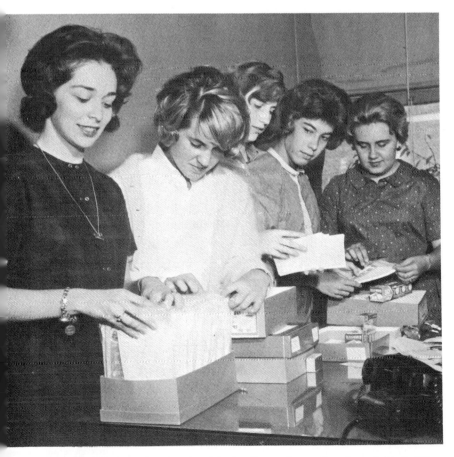

Vickey Manchaca, Becky Vaughn, Marsha Crane, Susan Hennig and Linda Weaver package Northside stationery as one of their money-making projects.

Here they are, the "Singing Valentines." The "Hummingbird Columbians" present their Valentine Day special.

ternities, sororities, and dormitories in panels composed of individual pictures. The other large organizations can then be pictured in formal groups and perhaps the small organizations and committees can be shown in informal groups. A plan of this kind will provide variety from section to section and yet give uniform treatment to fra-ternities, honoraries, clubs, etc.

Picture All Members of Organizations

Each organization with space in the annual should have a picture showing *all* its members, correctly and clearly identified. A large organization, such as a pep club, may require several group pictures to show all its members properly.

After the tentative layouts are made, it's a good idea to review carefully the instructions given in previous chapters on exactly how to arrange large groups and how to get identifications of each person in the group. Don't fail to photograph one of the groups early to be sure the photographer is getting the kind of pictures you

have planned.

News pictures showing the principal activities of each organization add interest to the annual and ought to be included if space and finances will permit. Some staffs, instead of trying to get an activity picture of each organization, feature some activity participated in by several organizations—such as engineer's open house, since it is a joint effort of all engineering organizations. This permits you to print larger and more effective news pictures. The same plan can be used for religious groups, fraternities, dormitories, and departmental clubs. If space is provided in layouts for activity pictures, be sure to get significant ones when the news is being made, and not be forced to use posed pictures of someone raiding the ice box or something equally unimportant.

Present Extracurricular Activities

College and high school yearbooks often present such extracurricular activities as dramatics, forensics, publications, music, and judging teams in the same section with organizations. This plan provides an opportunity to introduce more interest and variety in layout in the section. It is not

FIGURE 9.2. This spread from the *Blackhawk* is tied tied together by both the group picture and headline. The headline leads eye of reader into the text copy.

A Cappella. FRONT ROW: Joy Fisher, Jolayne Liddy, Mary Jane Aye, Jill Reed, Jan Jurgens, Kay Davidson, Sylvia Eichhorn, Carol Haley, Eileen Keller, Sue Metcalf, Joanne Kuehl, Lynne Levien, Vicki Russell, Connie Frien, Wenonah Allen, Kathy Bonwell, Grace Dipple, Barb Classon, Mimzi Haut, Sue Kretschmar, Cindy Newport, Tewanta Dover. SECOND ROW: Jacquie Schlembeck, Lynnell Kahler, Sharon Litscher, LaVene Getting, Marcia Longenecker, Linda Siegel, Jane Alter, Pat Freeman, Myrl Thornbrugh, Stepie Carlson, Sue Thede, Kathy Hertsgaard, Betty Carlson, Sally Thode, Shirley Rietemeyer, Merry Alford, Sue Zimmerman, La Voona Kreva, Kathy Meyer, Pam Shreck, Sue Keenan, Jonell Stroehle.

THIRD ROW: Rick Baker, Neil Easterbrook, Steve Kruse, Dave Leidenfrost, Dana Harris, Mike Hollen, Jim Berry, Jim Porter, Doug Hanson, Hank Neuman, Jeff Nordeen, Mike Liljequist, Charles Shreves, Jim Robertson, Mike Thomas, John Ivanoff, John Dougherty, Eugene Merrell, Carl Cartwright, Tom Doty. FOURTH ROW: John Smiley, Ray Hardesty, Steve DeReus, Byron Kohrs, Richard Golinghorst, Bob Wilbur, Louis Wolf, Bill Carlson, Steve Klindt, Jim Nelson, Bill Ray, Paul Doyle, Richard Norcross, Gary Sissel, Fred Hinton, Bill Fritzsche, Jerry LoRang, Gary Vallem, Tim Haut, Eduardo Frischtak, Harold Babb, Vernet Goering, Jim Wold.

Many Activities Highlight Year for Central : a Cappella Members

As student teacher Miss Rose Mary Klingbiel watches the rehearsal, Mr. Anderson asks the basses for more volume.

Sharon Litscher and Sue Thede join the a Cappella in rehearsing a number for the Variety Show.

Among the activities which kept this year's a Cappella busy were the All-State Festival, the Pops Concert, the "Messiah," and the Variety Show.

This year Central was the host of the Tri-City Music Festival. Because of physical arrangements, the festival was held in the West High School Gymnasium. A local television station broadcast the festival this year for the first time.

The Variety Show celebrated its twenty-fifth anniversary with "Hits Through the Years" as the theme. Some of the hits featured were "Love Is a Many Splendored Thing," "High Lili High Lo," "Standing on the Corner," and the "Desert Song."

"This year I have an excellent soprano section which adds color to the a Cappella," commented Mr. Milton Anderson, director. "It's difficult to compare groups because of the way I work in developing each group. Each has a distinct personality as a direct result of voices available."

The a Cappella wound up the year with a picnic at Club Mo-Kan.

Accompanying the a Cappella this year was the pleasant task handled by Mr. Paul Still.

Glee Club Entertains At Programs, Dance

Glee Club voices were heard all over Indianapolis this year as the girls performed at various civic functions. The Manual stage is also familiar to the club which sang in Christmas, Ivian, and Memorial Day auds. "Hoedown Charlie Brown" and a group of square-dancers were featured at the Band-Glee Club Concert. The only "outside" appearance this year was Homecoming. Joining with over 400 other girls, Manual's 65-member Glee Club presented an All-City Girls' Concert March 27.

A select group from the club, the Glee-ettes, went "on the road" to the Fletcher Place Community Center, Broad Ripple Christian Church, and Indianapolis Historical Society meeting, and a party for William H. Block Company staff members.

Fun increased at the Glee Club's Cherry Tree Hop, Christmas Banquet, and spring picnic at Brown County. Officers for the year were Conni Dorville, president; Martha Melton, vice-president; Linda Thomas, secretary; Joyce Stout, treasurer; and Janie Forester, historian.

"Martha" Carol Maier and "George" Phil Steele lead the royal dance after their coronation at the Cherry Tree Hop.

GLEE CLUB—FRONT ROW: Janette Baron, Kathy Francis, Martha Melton, Barbara Stellhorn, Bonnie Birt, Sue Woolsalse, Gali Thornbrough, Carol Maier, Janie Forester, Sandy Heard, Shirley Hillman, Jan Phelps, Conni Dorville, Linda Thomas, Monna Hines, Rosie Hines. SECOND ROW: Pat Lynam, Elizabeth Roberts, Rosemary Lemme, Nita Breeden, Dietra Boles, Jill Jenkins, JoAnn Moran, Joyce Stout, Linda Taylor, Priscilla Harbrow, Karen Bertels, Judy Hancock, Ruth Hamersley, June Cook, Pam Payne, Kathy Reynolds. THIRD ROW: Miss Freda Hart, director, Patty Sutt, Lynne Schmedel, Linda Stevens, Mary Louise Roch, Bev Boyd, Pat Roberts, Martha Taylor, Suzanne Barnes, Janet Horton, Suzanne Klein, Bonnie Jerrell, Darlene Ragsdale, Sherry Jacobs, Charlene Bartram, Beverly Porter, Robin Cain. FOURTH ROW: Sandra Roberts, Louise Short, Betty Parrett, Susy Hattabaugh, Becky Weidner, Linda Wilson, Barbara MacKinnon, Sandy Dwiggans, Alice Bone, Suzann Kern, Brenda Spreen, Nancy Horn, Susan Menges, Jessie Waynick, Jean Reuter, Penny Reed, Nancy Bentz, Judy Verhines, Linda Harkness.

42

'Y' Clubs, Red Cross Work for Others

Connie Goss, President Linda Wilson, and Sharon Wisler work on Y-Teen scrapbooks while Vickie Weaver, Emily Daly, Theresa Comer, Connie Goodin, Sally Olds, Sally Stephans, sponsor Miss Virginia Edington and YWCA sponsor Miss Felicia Smith offer suggestions for the project.

Service and friendship are the cornerstones of three Manual clubs. In the Indianapolis Model United Nations, April 24-27, Manual's Tri-Hi-Y represented Ghana, Yemen, Mali, and the Federation of Malaya. Miss Ellen Ramar sponsors the club which gave money for world service, school, and community projects from December candy sale profits.

The Y-Teens became active this year after a year's absence and provided a candle-squirt gun booth at the Pow Wow. After making tray placemats and centerpieces, and towel dolls for children in Riley Hospital, High School Red Cross visited the Indianapolis Red Cross Chapter House April 18, with their sponsor, Mrs. Betty Baker.

Tri-Hi-Y members Sharon Boyer, President Phyllis Roch, Judy Humphrey, Cathy Sparks, Elizabeth Roberts, and Sue Macewen inspect a poster announcing their Get-Acquainted Party.

Working on towel dolls for children in Riley Hospital are High School Red Cross members Micky Bush, president, Sheila Bush, Janice Coop, Darlene Jarvis, Sue Flike, and Wilma Cobb.

FIGURE 9.3. Satisfactory solution of a difficult problem is shown in this two-page spread from the 1963 *Ivian*. An effective layout is made in presenting four different clubs in a limited space.

FIGURE 9.4. How a good headline can add impact to a layout is shown in this spread from the 1965 *Riparian*. Careful cropping of pictures and pleasing use of white space also add to the impact.

News Bureau—LEFT: Paul Mannweiler, Gary Olin, Nancy Lyon, Linda Jamison, Jim Cooney, Sandi Servaas. RIGHT: Georgie Kerr, Nancy Wright, Sue Murchie, Paula Dintaman, Susan Engert.

Little Rip Editor Nancy Lyon receives latest *Riparian* staff news from Personnel Editor Jan Thompson, Ad Editor Bob Basler, and Exchange Editor Melinda Meyer.

Riparian photographers take top honors at first Press Day

Flashing cameras caught candid shots as the members of the *Riparian* photo staff worked together to add extra interest to Ripple's publications through photography. Under Miss Fran Lindley, sponsor, the amateur photographers developed and enlarged pictures for both the *Riparian* Newspaper and Yearbook. The staff received five top honors for pictures entered in the Arlington Press Day Photo Contests.

News Bureau staffers acted as correspondents from the *Riparian* to the local newspapers. They kept Indianapolis citizens informed of the achievements and activities of Broad Ripple pupils. Personnel, Newspaper Advertising, Exchange, Managing, and Copy Editing Department directly assisted in business duties of the newspaper staff for the production of the biweekly *Riparian* paper.

Outstanding journalists are elected to honorary membership in Quill and Scroll, sponsored by Mrs. Ruth Marie Griggs. A fall induction dinner at Dodd's Flagpole Townhouse, the Holiday Punch Party for former *Riparian* staff members, the Arlington Press Day conference, and the Spring Awards Banquet comprised this year's schedule.

Quill and Scroll—BACK ROW: Sara Compton, Jerry Johnson, Gary Olin, Tom Olvey, Scooter Engel, Don Baddenbroom, Jim Cooney, Marty Zohn, Mrs. Ruth Marie Griggs. SECOND ROW: Harriet Bickell, Judy Huehl, Barb Gavin, Peggy Ward, Lee Ann Fink, Andy Ogle, Jane Remley, Gracia Johnson. FRONT ROW: Debbie Dorman, Nancy Wright, Linda Scott, Georgie Kerr, Cindy New, Margo Eldridge, Sandi Servaas, Mary Cook, Susie Frakes.

Photo Staff—LEFT (bottom to top): Bill Schnackel, Steve Shepple, Jim Beuhi, George Angrick, Joe Refkin, Mike Walsh. RIGHT: Ken Ogle, Neil Gifford, Ron Hostetler, John Fulton, Phil Logan.

54

55

always possible to determine whether a certain group should be classified as an activity or an organization, and placing them all in the same section relieves the staff of the responsibility of making arbitrary classifications in this connection. Getting the pictures to present properly the extra-curricular activities mentioned above requires careful planning and a definite policy that provides fair and accurate presentation of all important activities.

As can easily be seen, the organization and activity section of the annual probably will require a more detailed dummy than any other section in the book. This is true because all pictures taken must fit the space sold or allocated to each organization. However, you should plan the dummy so each organization presented is given the amount of space justified by its importance.

Omit No Important Organizations

Some schools' yearbooks have lost the support of a large portion of the student body because unimportant organizations were allowed to purchase several pages in the annual, while important honoraries were omitted because they did not have money to pay for space in the book. Where a situation of this kind has been allowed to develop, the schools affected have been forced to change the method of financing space for organizations. Some schools have adopted an activity fee that covers the cost of space for all organizations as well as a subscription to the annual. Other financing methods also have been adopted. One of the greatest advantages of an all-inclusive activity fee is that it makes possible assigning space needed for each feature to be presented in the book without having to worry about collecting for the space allocated.

FIGURE 9.5. This two-page layout illustrates how orderliness eliminates undue crowding of the material presented. The *Whirligig* is printed on 7½ x 10½-inch pages and required care to prepare effective layouts.

Youth Council's enthusiasm sparks school spirit

The Youth Recreation Council displayed boundless energy and school spirit this year in planning and supporting open houses that provided wholesome fun and welcome relaxation for all. The council, headed by Sally Jo Welch, received encouraging response from the student body, and post-game dances were invariably crowded and gay.

In the fall the council distributed identification cards, necessary for student admission to the dances, as well as a set of conduct rules to be followed at YRC-sponsored activities. Games with Page High furnished opportunities for special joint open houses, some in our gym, some in the Page cafeteria.

YOUTH COUNCIL OFFICERS — *Clockwise:* McKenzie, Lane, Chairman Welch, Steed.

YOUTH RECREATION COUNCIL members are, *front row:* Johnson, Huckabee, Simmons, Wentworth, Flintom, McIntosh, Poer, Cantrell, Christiansen, Sauer, Bowman, and Bourne. *Second row:* Steed, V. Eldridge, Gibbons, Drake, Root, Spencer, Robinette, McKenzie, Jones, Singletary, Turner, and French. *Third row:* Davant, Welch, Barrier, Duncan, Jamieson, Norman, D. Eldridge, McGill, and Ratcliff.

TRAFFIC SQUAD — *Front row:* Clark, Furman, Sparrow, Taylor, Carter, Washam, Marsh, and Henderson. *Second row:* Burwell, Mike Andrew, Ephland, Irvin, Crothers, Williams, Banks, Strader, and Womble. *Third row:* Melvin, Pearce, Barnes, Goldberg, Parks, Faulkner, Marus, Brown, and Hamilton. *Fourth row:* Landsperger, Harville, Adams, Lund, Powell, Hedrick, Mickey Andrews, Lutz, Oakley, and Lambeth.

Thirty-five squad members overcome traffic chaos

TRAFFIC CHIEF Lambeth and assistant Melvin at least *appear* helpful.

Members of the traffic squad patrolled before and after classes to alleviate the confusion of the stampede created by students changing classes. Under the leadership of Chief Lambeth, the squad transformed GHS's chaos of motion into almost orderly processions. On rainy days their duties were compounded, but with whistles, signals, and numerous shouts the mobs were directed to their proper destinations. The boys, watching over 2,200 students at Senior, kept the passage between buildings free from traffic congestion. With the guidance of their advisor, Mr. Whittemore, the traffic squad channeled GHS's largest sophomore class, stubbornest junior class, and slowest senior class to their correct classrooms. By carefully guarding the "up" and "down" stairs and the "in" and "out" doors, the squad prevented stray scholars from being trampled by their hurrying classmates.

Judgment, rather than money, is the determining factor.

Get All Needed Copy

If the organization and activity pages are to be attractive, it is necessary to write copy to fit the space provided in the layout. It should, of course, be remembered that the primary function of copy is to tell an accurate and interesting story about the organization or activity being presented. However, writing the exact amount of copy has an important bearing on the success or failure of the layout you have planned.

How to write copy to fit the space provided has been discussed in detail. However, the exact amount of copy needed cannot be determined until the final layout that is to be used for a specific page has been completed.

Uniformity of treatment for organizations and activities includes the kind of headlines, copy, and identifications used. If a news headline is used for one honorary organization, the same style and perhaps the same sized type should be used for all honoraries. Uniformity of treatment also should be used for text copy and cutlines. This does not mean that the same amount of copy must be written for each group.

An effort is made in the following pages of this chapter to show pages from annuals that illustrate effective solutions of layout problems often encountered in planning organization and activity pages.

Significant Pictures Provide Impact

Significant pictures, carefully cropped and reproduced large enough to provide excellent im-

FIGURE 9.6. The head size of individuals in the clubs shown here is kept uniform by a carefully planned lay-out. White space is also effectively used in this spread from the *Royal Purple*, Kansas State University.

Kappa Delta Pi—Top Row: Kathleen D. Nelson, Carolyn A. Cotter, Joan E. Lyne, Janet L. Hendricks, Janet J. Bender. Second Row: Joe H. Loeb, Judith K. Allee, Ralph E. Stegner, Karen L. Hosley, Franco A. Hammel. Bottom Row: Joyce E. Bocock, Ellen E. Sheedy, Judith F. Werner, Doris M. Schierling, Karen J. Carey.

Tau Sigma Delta—Top Row: Darrell E. Beach, Roy T. Miyaji, Dorothy A. Kandle, Mary C. Miller, Karen S. Billingham, Douglas I. Denny, Jerry A. Ogburn, David N. Hollis. Second Row: Paul A. Friesen, Thomas D. Jacob, Harold D. Bock, James R. Calcara, Dennis B. Maercklein, Stephen B. Holloway, John C. Williams, John H. Thies-sen, Homer D. Blossom. Bottom Row: Kenneth L. Kallenbach, William B. Livingston, Robert A. Cochran, Thomas A. Thompson, Terry L. Patterson, Joe B. Hollingsworth, Thomas R. Gossen, James J. Adams.

Future educators hear about job interviewing

"Interviewing the Prospective Teacher" provided a lecture topic at one meeting of Kappa Delta Pi. C. Fred Colvin, from the Wichita school system, presented the talk on teaching interviews. For another guest educator, Kappa Delta Pi invited a professor to discuss teaching opportunities.

Kathleen Nelson acted as president of the education honorary. Joe Loeb was Kappa Delta Pi adviser. The 70 juniors and seniors ranked in the upper fifth of their classes.

Seminars ready students for architecture exams

Seminars were scheduled by Tau Sigma Delta to help architects prepare for state board examinations. Through the project, students readied themselves for the tests they would take to become licensed architects after three-year apprenticeships.

Camel-green blazers bearing the Tau Sigma Delta crest were worn by members. The honorary tapped students in architecture and the allied arts with 3.0 grade averages or in the upper 20 per cent of their classes.

78

Interning medical technologists from St. Joseph's Hospital in Wichita explain different phases of their on-the-job train-ing to Alpha Delta Theta members. The interns showed slides depicting a typical day of work at the hospital.

Dorms hire medical technologists to shine shoes

Shining shoes in the men's dormitories, members of Alpha Delta Theta earned money for the Carl Dorf Memorial Scholarship, a $100 scholarship given to a medical technol-ogy student. Speakers for the medical technol-ogy honorary included former students in the three-year curriculum now serving internship periods in area hospitals.

Alpha Delta Theta—Top Row: Sharon A. Llewellyn, Sharry R. Kraft, Mary E. Guthrie, Sharon K. Blasdel, Susan J. McCoy. Second Row: Judith L. Stumpff, Mary L. Esau, Jlinda A. Smith. Mary J. Pflughoeft, Claudette A. Lank. Third Row: Ruby K. Brower, Mary B. Stephens, Kathryn E. Urbianek, Lois A. Wiley, Linda K. Shambaugh. Bottom Row: Almira S. Snodgrass, Ingrid E. Nesmith, Judith A. Wolf, Mary Z. Furney, Carolyn S. Crall.

79

pact, are illustrated in Figure 9.1 from the 1964 *Bruin*, Northside High School, Fort Smith, Arkansas. The layout provides plenty of white space to display properly all elements shown on the two-page spread. The page margins are properly planned and copy and headline are interesting and written to fit space provided in the layout.

Large Group Effectively Displayed

A good example of how to pose a large group that is to extend across the gutter of the book is demonstrated in the 1965 *Blackhawk*, Central High School, Davenport, Iowa, shown in Figure 9.2. This plan is often used in posing pictures of the orchestra or band or other large groups. *Care must be taken to leave an open space in the middle of the picture* so that no one's face disappears in the gutter of the book.

Three Clubs Presented on One Page

Activities of four different clubs are presented on a two-page spread in the 1963 *Ivian*, Emmerich Manual High School, Indianapolis, Indiana, as shown in Figure 9.3. Group pictures of the membership of Y-Teen, Tri-Hi-Y, and Red Cross were omitted and shots of their activities were used instead. This plan is probably the only practical one to use since most of the girls in school probably belong to each organization. The activity pictures are significant, and copy and cutlines help tell the story.

Variety of Pictures Aids Layout

An outstanding example of how to present the story of several related activities on a double-page spread is shown in Figure 9.4. The staff of the 1965 *Riparian*, Broad Ripple High School, Indianapolis, Indiana, got a variety of outstanding pictures to help tell the story of student publications. The pictures are interesting and of excellent technical quality. Throwing excess white space to the outside of each page provides a pleasing effect.

Simple Layout Most Effective

A simple yet effective arrangement of pictures and copy is shown in Figure 9.5, from the *Whirligig*, Grimsley High School, Greensboro, North Carolina. Many small- and medium-size annuals

FIGURE 9.7. Excellent pictures properly displayed produced this pleasing two-page spread in the 1964 *Garnet and Black.* **Harmonious typography and effective use of white space also adds to the impact.**

Abercrombie, Sue
Alexander, Jerri
Bates, Sandy
Burns, Robin
Christmas, Bonnie

Cox, Frankie
Crosland, Ann
Derrick, Brenda
Derrick, Harriette
Dutton, Cathie
Edwards, Chris

Ellis, Peggy
Goodnight, Joyce
Green, Bertie
Haskell, Sherrie
Hayes, Betsy
Hicks, Connie

Hoefer, Lilla
Horton, Ellen
Houston, Ann
Howell, Lorrie
Johnson, Jean
Joyce, Carole

Zetas excitedly applaud as a surprised Robin Burns is tapped by AKG at Song Fest.

JANE WALTER, *President*

ZETA TAU ALPHA

OFFICERS	
JANE WALTER	President
SUSAN MATTHEWS	Vice-President
BRENDA DERRICK	Secretary
ELLEN HORTON	Treasurer

Knight, Patty
Lewis, Diane
Mack, Patsy
McCrary, Susan
McDowell, Judy
Meadows, June

Medlin, Sherrill
Metts, Carolyn
Murray, Lula
Oehmann, Margery
Perna, Anida
Preston, Elaine

Richards, Ellen
Robison, Lynne
Sanders, Linda Carol
Schriver, Linda
Smith, Emily
Sweatman, Jennie

Talbert, Lana
Taylor, Gwen
Ulmer, Margaret
Walter, Jane
Wheeler, Emily
Workman, Maralan

Hard work and enthusiasm captured first place for the Zetas in Sigma Chi Derby Day in the spring . . . Beth Stuckey received the award for the Sorority Woman of the Year at the Greek Week Banquet . . . Homecoming in the fall bestowed honors on the Zetas, who, working with the SAEs and SPEs, won first place for their float in the Homecoming parade . . . and the election of Susan Matthews as Maid of Honor in the Homecoming Court. The pledges and actives worked together to make the retreat at the Y Camp a unifying and spirited function . . . The Zetas were rewarded for the long hours of tedious practice with the second-place trophy in AKG's Song Fest.

Zetas find a campus-wide Christmas drop-in is a way to spread the season's cheer.

153

are printed on small-size pages (7½ x 10½ inches) to save money and also to produce a book with more pages than would be possible if larger pages were used.

To produce effective layouts on small pages it is necessary to limit the number of elements to be shown. Too many elements tend to crowd the page and confuse the reader.

Keep Face Size Uniform

When it becomes necessary to present more than one organization on the same page or on facing pages, an effort should be made to keep the faces of the individuals in the several organizations approximately the same size. This is accomplished in the *Royal Purple,* Figure 9.6, by reducing the width of small groups and bleeding the large group picture.

If space is available, each club should have a headline, unless the clubs presented are in the same department or participate in a common activity. The identification cutline for each group ought to start with the name of the organization so the reader will not be confused.

Good Pictures Aid Layout

Excellent portraits with easy-to-find identifications make it easy for the reader to find the information he wants in the functional layout. A good example is Figure 9.7, from the 1964 *Garnet and Black,* University of South Carolina. The activity shots are significant and well captioned. The text copy is interesting and newsworthy.

Daring Use of White Space

An unusual and daring layout of Supper Theater plays, Figure 9.8, from the 1964 *Yucca,* North Texas State University, Denton, commands attention. An occasional layout of this kind, if well done, adds variety to the annual. So much interest is packed into the excellent pictures, copy, and headline that the extravagant use of white space is justified for the sake of contrast.

FIGURE 9.8. This unusual layout from the 1964 *Yucca* is attention compelling. The pages are tied together by photographs and the use of white space contrasts effectively with the picture on the opposite page.

Unique Evening Offered By Collegiate Thespians

During the day the UB Coffee Shop is filled with light pouring in the windows and students chattering. By night it is dark. Four times during the past year, the Coffee Shop has had its share of lights and action, when Supper Theater sets up shop.

A unique institution, Supper Theater is one of the more cultural and collegiate offerings on campus. Begun in the late 1940's, the group first appeared off-campus in a downtown cafe. In 1952 the Theater moved to North Texas as part of the speech and drama department and was the first college supper theater group in the Southwest.

The group offers the players a chance to perform for a different type of audience. In most other drama or theater groups with which they work, the audience is mainly students. Supper Theater, however, plays to a more mature group of patrons. The productions attract people from off campus as well as faculty and students. The arena drama also puts the actors in closer touch with the audience.

Gilbert and Sullivan's satirical *Trial by Jury* and Samuel Beckett's searching *Endgame* were presented.

The theater also offered the work of a young student playwright. Sophomore English major Ransom Jeffrey's play, *Tenfold Laughs and a Few Tears,* was selected from entries in the original one-act play contest.

The fourth selection was Tennessee Williams' *Twenty-Seven Wagons Full of Cotton.*

Dr. E. Robert Black is Supper Theater faculty sponsor. Managing director is Tom Donahl.

LEFT: Rita Thomas rehearses for a moving Supper Theater production drama while other Theater participants *(RIGHT)* check the growing list of guests for the next performance. *BOTTOM:* Sharon Brady and Tom Donald appear in a play by an amateur which was winner of the one-act play contest sponsored by Supper Theater.

Camilla Carr and Mike Smith are not hamming it up, but rehearsing for their roles in *Endgame.* Note the habitat.

146

At least one or two sports pictures used in an annual
should preserve for history such sidelights as the crowd,
the fieldhouse, or other playing field. This action-packed
photo combines players, crowd, press box, and scoreboard for the complete story.

Chapter 10

Attaining Variety in Sports Section

MAJOR sports contests at your school are reported in detail by the newspapers. This makes your job of presenting the same material later in the year-book easier in some respects, more difficult in others.

You can easily check the highlights of each game, as well as the final result, by reading the newspaper story. News photographers usually will sell you action pictures of the games they have covered. Then, too, the director of sports publicity at most schools has pictures of indi-vidual players that are available free of charge. Thus, you could do a passable job without taking new pictures for your annual.

Get Exclusive Action Pictures

Perhaps too many yearbook staffs take this easy way out. But if sports pages are to be inter-esting to students who get the annual, you must present some variety from pictures and write-ups

they have seen in newspapers and sports pro-grams. The reprinting of a picture everyone has seen several times gives the reader an idea that the whole section on sports is "old stuff," even if the picture thus repeated shows the most out-standing play of the entire year.

You should have your own photographers on the sidelines getting action pictures to be used ex-clusively in your annual. If you must use pictures taken by news photographers, select, whenever possible, unpublished photographs. Pictures of individual stars given out for publicity ordi-narily have been used so often they are no longer of great interest. Try to get new photographs, or crop and arrange the pictures in a way that will give a new angle to their presentation. It is not always possible, because of the expense involved, to take all new pictures for the sports section. However, be sure to get enough new ones to arouse the interest of your readers.

FIGURE 10.1. How a squad picture and scoreboard of all games can be effectively displayed is shown in this layout from the *Tucsonian*. The game pictures are placed so action moves into, rather than off, pages.

FIGURE 10.2 Functional arrangement of all elements displayed on this two-page spread makes it easy for the reader to get the story of basketball as told in the 1964 *Shield*. Note the well written cutlines.

FIGURE 10.3. Proper use of white space for margins and for emphasizing each element displayed are combined to produce an interesting spread in the *Riparian*.

FIGURE 10.4. This excellent two-page spread from the 1965 *Granitanian* is well planned to tell the complete story of the wrestling season.

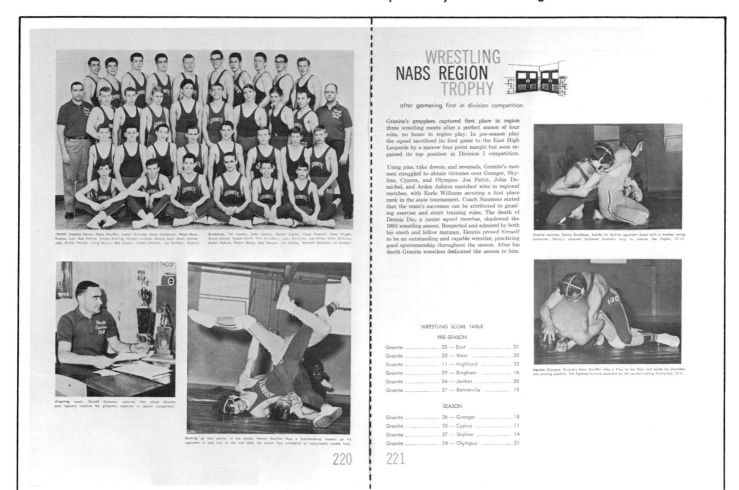

Tell Complete Story of Sports Program

The newspaper story of the sports program is presented day by day and, at best, covers only the highlights. You have an opportunity in the annual to tell the whole dramatic story from beginning to end—with a variety of pictures, interesting layouts, and a summary of all the important happenings. Then, too, remember you are presenting a story not only of the big stars but also of the substitutes who seldom get into the game. You should get coverage of the activities of the band, the cheerleaders, the rooters, and all other participants in the athletic program.

In planning the sports section, be sure you cover the program for one complete year. If the staff from the previous year did not include spring sports, you should start where they left off and carry through the next year. If the annual at your school is a fall delivery book, the previous staff probably covered the entire year.

Treat All Sports Uniformly

Page layouts in the sports section should provide for uniform treatment of all sports. A good group picture showing the entire squad in each sport will insure that every individual who took part is recognized. Formal arrangement of athletes in these groups usually is best because it makes possible easy identification of each individual. A summary arranged in tabular form showing the scores of each contest helps give complete coverage. With these two essentials taken care of, you can then present as many action shots of games, pictures of lettermen, and other features as space will allow, and still have room for copy and headlines.

The same principles of layout apply to the sports section of the annual as to the other sections discussed. Pages should be harmonious with the rest of the book in regard to margins, typography, and display of pictures. Sample pages from sports sections of leading annuals shown here have been selected to illustrate not only good layout but also to suggest how different sports can be covered effectively.

←

FIGURE 10.5. The scoreboard can sometimes be printed in reverse as on this page from the 1964 *Trail*. This saves space but you must select a dark area of the photograph so the printing can be read easily.

FIGURE 10.6. An unusual and convenient listing of results in all sports is presented on one page in the *Whirligig*, Grimsley High School, Greensboro, N.C.

1962 FOOTBALL SCORES

1962 BASEBALL SCORES

1962-63 BASKETBALL SCORES

TOURNAMENT SCORES

FINALS

1962 TENNIS SCORES

1962 TRACK SCORES

1962-63 WRESTLING SCORES

1962-63 SWIMMING SCORES

CROSS COUNTRY TEAM — *Front row:* Finch, Dalche, Snavely, Perkins, Wrenn, Robinson. *Back row:* Still, Boyte, Bell, Byrd, Baker, Souza, Coach Sawyer.

1962 GOLF TEAM — Sullivan, James, Jessup, Gardiner, Hudson, Permar, Howe, West, Williams, Hill.

Golf Team places well in all conference competition

VETERAN Howard Permar prepares to contribute to the success of the 1963 team.

In the past five years golf at GHS has been only a slightly regarded spring sport. A lack of interest among students has produced merely average teams, which have placed low in conference standings. The 1962 team was a vast improvement, however. The Whirlies competed against seven other conference teams in eight Central 4-A Conference matches and placed from second to fourth in each match. Throughout the season there was keen competition to gain the top six playing positions. Sherwood Jessup, the number one man, placed second in the state tournament with a 36-hole score of 144. He was also presented the Charles Baker Golf Trophy on Awards Day. Howard Permar, Bill James, Paul Gardiner, Dan Howe, and Spencer Sullivan completed the top six players. Coach Jamieson expects a further improved Whirlie golf team in 1963.

Football Squad Well Posed

A well-planned opening spread for the football section is shown in Figure 10.1, from the *Tucsonian,* Tucson High School, Tucson, Arizona. The football squad is carefully arranged and presented in a picture large enough so all individuals are easily identified.

Both the group picture and the headline tie the two pages together. The scoreboard showing results of all games and the general write-up present an interesting summary of the season. This plan allowed the staff to use the following pages in the section for action shots of games, and interesting activities connected with the football season.

Managers Pictured With Squad

The 1964 *Shield,* Highland High School, Highland, Indiana, gets off to a fine start in presenting the basketball story as shown in Figure 10.2. The varsity squad picture showing the four managers as well as the coach is excellent.

The varsity scoreboard is easy for the reader to understand, which is important though often neglected. The action pictures are carefully cropped and interestingly captioned. Technical quality of all the pictures is first class.

Presenting Sideline Activities

Coverage of sideline activities, a pep rally, and a dramatic action picture are all combined in the interesting two-page spread from the 1963 *Riparian,* Broad Ripple High School, Indianapolis, Indiana, Figure 10.3.

The pictures were taken at exactly the right moment to capture the excitement of the rooters and others involved. Often student photographers become so interested in the game action that they fail to get sideline shots at the right time.

Minor Sport Well Covered

Minor sports and intramurals are often neglected in the yearbook. Figure 10.4 from the 1965 *Granitanian,* Granite High School, Salt Lake City, Utah, illustrates how wrestling can be interestingly captioned. The scoreboard is easy to understand and gives a complete record for the season.

Dramatic Picture Introduces the Section

A dramatic feature picture of "the baseball diamond as seen through the eyes of the man in black—the umpire," is used to introduce the baseball section in the 1964 *Index,* Illinois State University, Normal, Figure 10.7. A good feature shot of this kind is often used as a sort of subdivision page to introduce each section. Significant pic-

FIGURE 10.7. This simple and attention-getting layout is from the 1964 *Index.* The excellent pictures and generous use of white space are combined to produce an interesting two-page spread.

The baseball diamond as seen through the eyes of the man in black—the umpire.

128

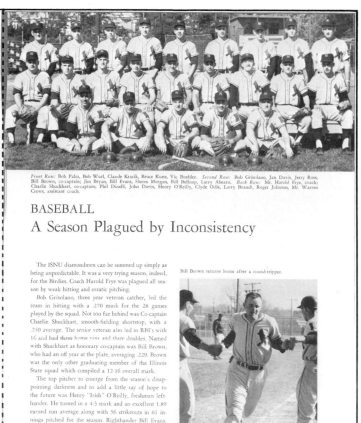

Front Row: Bob Palm, Bob Wurl, Claude Kracik, Bruce Kunz, Vic Buehler. *Second Row:* Bob Grisolano, Jan Davis, Jerry Ross, Bill Brown, co-captain; Jim Bryan, Bill Evans, Sherm Morgan, Bill Bellnap, Larry Ahearn. *Back Row:* Mr. Harold Frye, coach; Charlie Shuckhart, co-captain; Phil Diselli, John Darin, Henry O'Reilly, Clyde Odle, Larry Brandt, Roger Johnson, Mr. Warren Crews, assistant coach.

BASEBALL
A Season Plagued by Inconsistency

The ISNU diamondmen can be summed up simply as being unpredictable. It was a very trying season, indeed, for the Birdies. Coach Harold Frye was plagued all season by weak hitting and erratic pitching.

Bob Grisolano, three year veteran catcher, led the team in hitting with a .270 mark for the 28 games played by the squad. Not too far behind was Co-captain Charlie Shuckhart, smooth-fielding shortstop, with a .240 average. The senior veteran also led in RBI's with 16 and had three home runs and three doubles. Named with Shuckhart as honorary co-captain was Bill Brown, who had an off year at the plate, averaging .229. Brown was the only other graduating member of the Illinois State squad which compiled a 12-16 overall mark.

The top pitcher to emerge from the season's disappointing darkness and to add a little ray of hope to the future was Henry "Irish" O'Reilly, freshman lefthander. He turned in a 4-3 mark and an excellent 1.89 earned run average along with 56 strikeouts in 61 innings pitched for the season. Righthander Bill Evans, who pitched 59 innings, had a 4-5 record along with

Bill Brown returns home after a round-tripper.

129

tures are difficult to get and they must have both impact and excellent photographic quality if they are to do the job planned for them. Pictures similar to the one from the *Index* showing students from the school publishing the book, are among the most effective.

Page-size Action Shot

The effect achieved by printing a dramatic action picture of a football game full-page size is demonstrated in Figure 10.9, from the 1965 *Gopher,* University of Minnesota, Minneapolis. One large picture of this kind will do more to recall the elation and excitement of a football game than a dozen smaller ones.

Try to get at least one action-packed picture of each sport and print it big. The shot you are looking for may be only a small part of a negative that can be blown up to page size. You, of course, must have some small pictures to help tell the story and to provide contrast. Don't get the idea that your team is unimportant and that it does not produce its own heroes—sometimes even in defeat.

Lead-in Headlines Add Variety

An interesting summary of the football season together with excellent action pictures and an unusual studio picture of the squad are combined in the two-page spread from the 1964 *Cornhusker,* University of Nebraska, Lincoln, shown in Figure 10.8. The lead-in headings at the beginning of each paragraph on the right-hand page add variety and are inviting to the reader.

Intramural Sports Included

Intramural sports are an important part of the physical education program in most schools and the yearbook staff should make plans to cover them adequately. The 1964 *Royal Purple* presents the winners in five different sports, as shown in Figure 10.10. The pictures are carefully cropped and a lot of information is packed into the cutlines and identifications. The intramural section, if well done, adds interest for many students and their parents who may not be interested in varsity sports.

FIGURE 10.8 Good action pictures properly cropped and displayed arouse the interest of the prospective reader of the 1964 *Cornhusker*. The typographical plan contributes to the excellent results achieved.

FIGURE 10.10. Well-posed and carefully cropped pictures make possible this interesting spread from the 1964 *Royal Purple*. The action picture, together with two individual shots, provides variety.

FIGURE 10.9. This interesting layout from the *Gopher* is achieved by skillful use of good pictures, interesting headlines, and proper distribution of white space.

Long Pre-season Trip Results in 26-21 Win

Crockett obliges autograph seekers upon return to the Twin Cities.

After venturing to the West Coast, the players were glad to do a little sight-seeing shortly before sunset on the return flight from Pasadena.

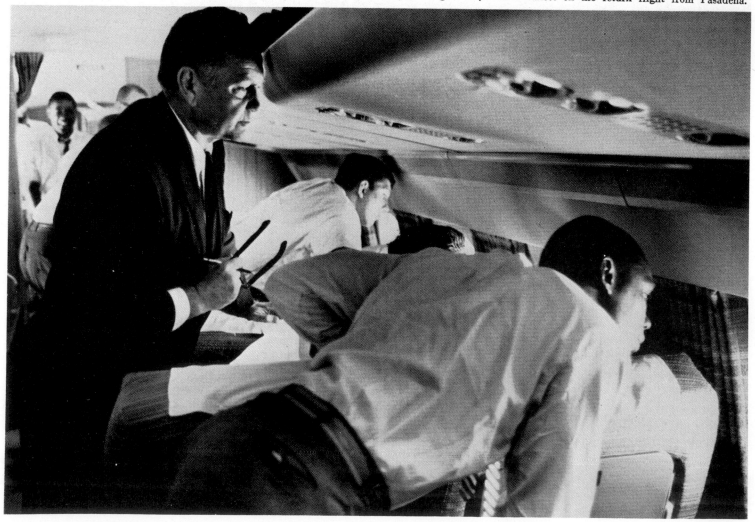

Gophers Rated Tenth, But Finish in Tie for Fourth

Often a picture taken in existing light conditions interprets the mood of the occasion more effectively than one lighted by electronic flash. This picture from the 1965 Cincinnatian, University of Cincinnati, illustrates the dramatic. results possible with existing light.

Chapter 11

Presenting Distinctive Feature Pages

THE MOST SIGNIFICANT recent change in yearbook content is the method used to present the highlights of the school year. Pages devoted to highlights in the annual are usually called the feature or school-life section, which is a direct outgrowth and refinement of the old snapshot pages that featured baby pictures of the seniors, friends of the editor, or almost any snapshot sent to the yearbook staff.

Feature Activities, Not Individuals

Leading yearbooks now present the big events of the school year in detail with "event" pictures, interesting headlines, news copy, and informative cutlines. The change from snapshots of individuals to pictures that feature activities has been made possible by modern cameras with flash attachments. This equipment enables the photographer to get pictures under almost any condition.

Then, too, the "picture" magazines have demonstrated how news events may be reported pictorially. The school press associations, yearbook photographers, engravers, and printers all have made worthwhile contributions to this new method of pictorially presenting the highlights of the year.

If you are to do an effective job of covering the highlights of the year at your school, you must go after news pictures that will help to tell the story. This requires careful planning when allocating space in the annual and by day-to-day vigilance to see that the pictures needed are taken. In most instances you will have to depend on your own photographer to get the pictures wanted, for newspaper photographers tend to cover entertainment functions only. Many of the pictures needed will be of academic or curricular activities.

Meet With Photographers Often

A weekly meeting with your photographers to plan in detail the pictures to be taken will assure that all events are covered and that the kind of pictures you have planned for in the dummy are secured. It's not enough to tell the photographer to cover a certain event. You should also discuss in detail the features you want pictured. It's a good plan to contact the person in charge of the event and find out what the outstanding features of the program are and when and where they will happen. That way, you will get his cooperation and your photographer will know when he should take the picture. Then, too, the photographer can look over the situation and decide where he should be to get an unobstructed view of the part of the event he is scheduled to take.

Remember that you usually have only one chance to get the pictures you need. Send, or better still go with, your best photographer and help him on the really big events—the ones you can't afford to miss. Be alert for any last-minute change in plans for staging the event, such as rain, that may postpone or drive the event indoors. You must be quick to change your plans to get pictures under unexpected conditions. Insist that your photographer develop exposed film promptly and make prints to see if he is getting the kind of picture you must have to produce a complete and interesting story of the highlights of the year.

Present Features Logically

A great variety in layout and page placement is used in different yearbooks to present the highlights of the year. The best plan is, of course, the one that makes these pages the most interesting to the reader.

The general style should be in harmony with the rest of the annual. It probably will lean more to the style of "magazine" layout because of the nature of the material being presented. Before you make your dummy, you need to decide whether to place all the feature pages in one section or to spot them at intervals throughout the annual.

Allocate Space for Feature Pages

If feature pages are placed in one section of the annual, the events shown are sometimes presented in chronological order. Therefore, the sec-

FIGURE 11.1 A well-written headline ties the two pages together and directs the reader to the text copy in this carefully planned layout from the 1964 *Shield*. The tall picture on the right-hand page adds variety.

WITH MOTHERLY DISGUST, Mrs. Antrobus, portrayed by Pam Ross, vents her anger on her son Henry, played by Jack Leach. Alexa Smith as Gladys, the Antrobus' daughter, looks on the scene with sisterly disconcern about the whole thing.

Students Combine Talent and Team Effort to Present Annual

HIGH-PRINCIPLED AND STUBBORN, Mr. Antrobus, played by senior Pete Tumbas, gives his family a stern lecture about their weak, yielding attitude toward the hardships of life.

LISTENING WITH APPROVAL, Dinosaur Sandi Barney hears the singing telegram which Pat Lowery brings the Antrobuses.

WITH CRITICAL EYES Mr. E. Colin Black, drama coach, keeps a close watch for rough spots during the final rehearsal.

Drama, Musical Productions

The curtain falls; a burst of applause. For the audience this is their way of expressing their satisfaction and approval of the student production which has just been presented to them. To the cast, the stage crew, and the many committee members, this is the perfect ending to their own production. The final product represents the long hours and hard, exhausting work put forth by ambitious and talented students. Each year the main endeavor of the Drama Club and the music department are the play and the operetta, respectively. Talented dramatists, vocalists and musicians spend time and effort to produce and present these two examples of student teamwork. Without the help of each and every one involved the presentation could easily become a "flop." This year the Drama Club presented Thornton Wilder's "The Skin of Our Teeth." The music department presented "Brigadoon," by Lerner and Loewe, as their operetta.

TRANSPOSING INTO THE character of Sabina, the maid, Diane Dickenson dons the appropriate costume and the "Isn't that ridiculous?" attitude necessary to give a realistic portrayal, even during a dress rehearsal.

tion might begin with enrollment activities, followed by each important highlight of the year in the order it occurred, and end with commencement.

On the other hand, several events of like nature are frequently displayed on one page or a double-page spread. A good example of this is grouping all parties, assemblies, sports features, etc. on certain pages with no attention to the time of the year the several events took place. When feature pages are spotted at several points throughout the book, an effort usually is made to present them in an orderly and logical manner. Thus, feature pages showing such highlights as homecoming decorations, parades, and half-time activities at games are shown in the sports section, while class plays, parties, and commencement might be placed in the class section of the annual. There are also other variations and methods of presenting the highlights of the year, as you can see by examining the pages that follow.

Consider Delivery Date

When allocating space for feature pages in the annual, you need to consider the delivery date of your yearbook. If the book is to be delivered to students in the late spring, you will be forced to omit late events and perhaps cover happenings from the previous year. If you plan to print a supplement, the pages covering these activities would not be allocated to the regular yearbook. Summer or fall delivery books usually can cover all important events for one complete school year.

Allocate Color Pages Carefully

More yearbook staffs each year are getting pictures of the big events of the year in full color. These color pictures are often scattered throughout several pages, along with black and white pictures, to add interest and variety. In allocating space for color pictures, be careful to plan to print them in the most economical way—you may need to check plans with your printer. A plan that provides for printing the color pictures in one signature, or better still, in one form (multiple) is more economical than scattering them indiscriminately over several pages.

The exact spot in the annual where feature pages appear is not so important as the actual layout of the individual pages. It is important not to

FIGURE 11.2 In years to come this probably will be one of the most enjoyed spreads in the 1964 *Triton*. Too often yearbook staffs fail to capture the fun and capers that made the year different from other years.

LEAPIN' TO THE LIVELY tune "Penetration," played by the new Rondels, Pete Coleman really catches the mood of the Leap Year Stomp sponsored by the seniors. Pete's partner, Gayna Williams, stomps with dignity.

"BUT I DON'T know how to dance the Watutsi!" bemoans Gail Ireland as Mike Fayles tries to teach her. "Don't worry," laughs Mike, "Just shake your top and your bottom and your middle a little and you've got it made!"

"SHAKE IT UP, BABY! Yeah, twist and shout," Nickie Denney and Bob Tannenbaum do a little hip-swingin' and foot-stompin' to the music of the Revelairs at the Key Club Stomp.

Sea Kings Caper At Pep Stomps

The Bird, the Bug, the Pony, the Mashed Potato, the Wobble and the Watutsi all appeared at P.V. as Sea Kings wiggled, twitched and stomped at a variety of informal dances.

To revive school spirit, the Boys' League sponsored a Back-to-School Stomp, September 13, featuring the rhythmic Revelairs. The stomp was highlighted by the first annual Battle of the Bands among the Coachmen, Del Mars and Chaparrals with the Coachmen winning.

The football victory over Gardena was celebrated at the Key Club Stomp, October 4. Enlivened by the music of the Revelairs, the stomp helped raise money for postage to send American magazines to foreign countries.

The rousing music of the new Rondels and their imitation of the Beatles highlighted the Leap Year Stomp, February 28. Sponsored by the Senior Class, the dance helped raise funds for the All-Night Party at Disneyland in June.

THE LAZY MOOD of summer still hangs on at the Boys' League Back-to-School Stomp in September as couples take a break from the fast twist tunes to do some cheek-to-cheeking to the music of the Revelairs. The stomp featured a Battle of the Bands.

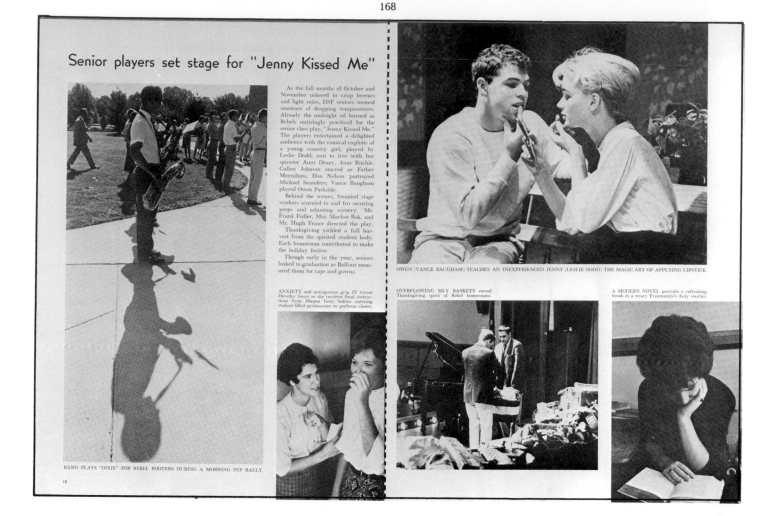

FIGURE 11.3. A change of pace from the rest of the pages in the 1963 *Historian* is established in the feature section by using narrower columns of text copy.

FIGURE 11.4. Several winter season events are well presented in this spread from the 1964 *Indian*. Besides being an unusual event of the year, the snow scene establishes the time better than a calendar would.

FIGURE 11.5. The horrors of Halloween are effectively presented in pictures and headlines in this interesting two-page spread from the 1965 *Windup*.

FIGURE 11.6 The effect achieved by throwing excess white space to the outside of the pages is demonstrated in this layout from the 1964 *Pine Needles*. One picture was selected to dominate the presentation.

It is time for the bids to come out. Leslie Covey (above) and Lois Mack (right) react expressively as they hopefully await the bid from Delta Gamma sorority. Anticipation and some anxiety are their emotions as they, at first hesitant, rip open the all-important envelope. A deep breath and then each is joyfully aware that the sorority of her choice has selected her to be one of its sisters.

Delta Gamma Sorority was selected as representative of sorority life at the University of Miami.

FIGURE 11.7. Close-up pictures, one of them "king-size," of happy girls produced this magnificent spread in the 1963 *Ibis*. Careful cropping of pictures and intelligent use of white space add much to the impact.

crowd the pictures and copy together. Leave some white space around each element on the page. Each picture shown should add something to the story and should be reproduced large enough in size so individuals and events are clearly shown. Good headlines and text copy can add much to the interest of the pages, and informative cutlines are essential.

Double-page Spreads for Feature Section

Big student productions of the drama club and music department are effectively portrayed on a double-page spread in Figure 11.1, courtesy of the 1964 *Shield*, Highland High School, Highland, Indiana.

A more effective layout can usually be produced by planning a double-page spread than a single page. Therefore, you need to devote two pages to a single event, or select related activities that can be treated in a manner similar to Figure 11.1.

Fun, Fads, and Fashions

Fun, fads, and fashions are all part of the year's activities and should be included in the yearbook—perhaps in the student-life section. The new dances that were the rage of the year are interestingly presented with good pictures and copy in the 1964 *Triton*, Palos Verdes High School, Palos Verdes Estates, California, Figure 11.2. The headline, text copy, and cutlines are written in exactly the right style to further the mood created by the pictures.

FIGURE 11.8. Pleasing use of an italic headline is combined with excellent pictures and a well-prepared layout to produce this effective spread in the 1965 *Bomb*. White space is well used on both pages.

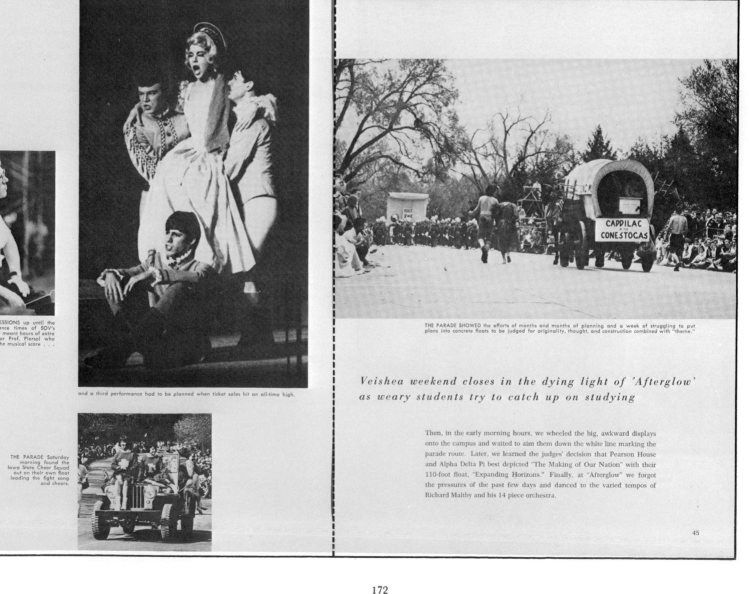

PRACTICE SESSIONS up until the performance times of SOV's "Kiss Me Kate" meant hours of extra work for Prof. Piersol who directed the musical score . . .

and a third performance had to be planned when ticket sales hit an all-time high.

THE PARADE Saturday morning found the Iowa State Cheer Squad out on their own float leading the fight song and cheers.

THE PARADE SHOWED the efforts of months and months of planning and a week of struggling to put plans into concrete floats to be judged for originality, thought, and construction combined with "theme."

Veishea weekend closes in the dying light of 'Afterglow' as weary students try to catch up on studying

Then, in the early morning hours, we wheeled the big, awkward displays onto the campus and waited to aim them down the white line marking the parade route. Later, we learned the judges' decision that Pearson House and Alpha Delta Pi best depicted "The Making of Our Nation" with their 110-foot float, "Expanding Horizons." Finally, at "Afterglow" we forgot the pressures of the past few days and danced to the varied tempos of Richard Maltby and his 14 piece orchestra.

44

45

Fall enrollment figures bulged with 3,346 freshmen. In the Men's Gymnasium Dr. James L. Rogers Jr. conducts the first hour of that group's orientation.

Look closely at those students with beanies or orientation packets. Some will be back in 1964. Others won't.

Freshman Tom Castillon of Fort Worth, like so many new students the first day at NTSU, pauses for a second wind and a puzzled survey of his surroundings.

"Would you mind helping me out just a little bit?" this new coed seems to be asking patient Green Jackets at the Information Booth on the campus.

But She Won't Be Lonely Very Long

Upperclassmen swarmed past the forlorn freshman as she hurried toward the Union Building. She glanced at her watch: nearly 8 a.m. "Surely someone in here can tell me," she thought to herself.

She walked into the Union Building, saw the crowds of students and quickly retreated. "Too many people. I'd be too embarrassed to ask." She turned toward the Administration Building. "They'll tell me." But the lines inside that building were too long, too menacing to her.

A few minutes before 9 a.m. she saw a girl wearing a bright green jacket in front of the Music Building. A printed card on the girl's blouse read, "Ask Me."

With an attempt at nonchalance the freshman asked the girl, "Oh, say, could you by any chance tell me where I'm supposed to register? I'm sort of new here."

Much later that day the weary freshman trudged slowly back to her dormitory.

After supper she wrote a letter home. "... It's really interesting here and everybody has been just great. I can't get over how friendly all the kids are. My roommate and I get along just fine. We both bought beanies today but we don't have to wear them if we don't want to. They say the rest is easy if you can make it through registration and I did—finally. So far I'm having a swell time. Wish you were here . . ."

36   37

FIGURE 11.9. Tall pictures positioned at the outside of each page demonstrate how shots of this kind add variety to the feature section, courtesy of the 1964 *Yucca.* Pictures are placed so individuals face into each page.

Several Events Covered by One Spread

Sometimes it's necessary to present several unrelated events on one two-page spread. The 1963 *Historian,* Douglas Southall Freeman High School, Richmond, Virginia, shows this can be accomplished, as in Figure 11.3. By featuring one event, "Jenny Kissed Me," in both the headline and a dominant picture, the two pages are effectively combined into one unit. The other events are covered in text copy, pictures, and informative cutlines.

Events Presented by Seasons

The staff of the 1964 *Indian,* Anderson High School, Anderson, Indiana, arranged the feature pages in chronological order by seasons, starting with autumn. Figure 11.4 is a two-page spread from the section devoted to winter activities.

A variety of events is presented with excellent pictures and cutlines. Many occasions not photographed are interestingly reported in text copy. The pictures are properly cropped, interestingly captioned, and effectively displayed with white space used well.

Two Pages for Each Month

A two-page spread was allocated for the big events of each month during the school year by the staff of the 1965 *Windup,* Walter Johnson Senior High School, Bethesda, Maryland. How the plan is developed is shown in Figure 11.5.

A combination headline tabs the month and arouses the interest of the prospective reader. The pictures are large enough to be effective and one is adroitly used to link the two pages together.

Portraying Everyday Happenings

Quite a few yearbook staffs in recent years have devoted space in their annuals to portraying the everyday activities and moods of students. Figure 11.6, a spread from the 1964 *Pine Needles,* University of North Carolina, Greensboro, is a pleasing example of how this can be accomplished.

The pictures taken for the two pages are carefully planned and of outstanding quality. The copy and cutlines contribute to portraying the mood of everyday living at the university.

"Atmosphere" Picture Sets the Scene

An excellent "atmosphere" picture showing the size and scope of Veishea weekend is combined with close-up shots, to produce an interesting spread in the 1965 *Bomb,* Iowa State University, Ames, as shown in Figure 11.8. White space is used generously to emphasize and lend contrast to the pictures, headline, and copy.

Happiness and Smiles Lend Impact

Close-up pictures of happy girls give more impact to pages of a yearbook than perhaps any other type of picture. Figure 11.7 from the 1963 *Ibis,* University of Miami, Coral Gables, Florida, is a magnificent demonstration of how to use smiles and laughter to present infectious happiness.

The pictures shown are the work of a dedicated photographer and have been selected from among many shots made of pledging activities. The editor who planned the layout contributed his part by selecting the right pictures and presenting them *big*—one page was too small for the outstanding picture.

Headline Arouses Interest

An interest-arousing headline combined with excellent pictures tells the story of enrollment at North Texas State University, Denton. Figure 11.9, from the 1964 *Yucca,* is an excellent spread, effectively tied together by two pictures. The headline, copy, and cutlines tell an interesting story that holds the reader's attention to the end.

→

FIGURE 11.10. Sometimes it's impossible to get a picture of an historical event because none is in existence. The 1964 *Sooner,* University of Oklahoma, illustrates the effectiveness of an artist's sketch showing "The Run of 1889" when Oklahoma territory was opened to settlers.

THE RUN OF 1889 opened the Unassigned Lands, here portrayed by the artist, Richter, an eyewitness, whose sketch is the only known reproduction of the actual event.

When Oklahoma celebrated its fiftieth year of statehood in 1957, the slogan was 'Teepees to Towers.' It was quite apropos. Oklahoma has vaulted not only from teepees to towers, but from towers to earth-circling astronauts. Leroy Gordon Cooper, born and reared in Shawnee, became the world's top astronaut at the time when he circled the globe 23 times in 34 hours, 20 minutes and 30 seconds on May 15 and 16, 1963.

Oil is probably the term most synonymous with Oklahoma. Tulsa is the Oil Capital of the World. Oklahoma ranks fourth nationally in oil production. Last year petroleum probers withdrew $775,873,000 worth of crude oil and natural gas from the Oklahoma earth. Expansion and development is prominent in the State. Natural resources are plentiful here. No space problems exist.

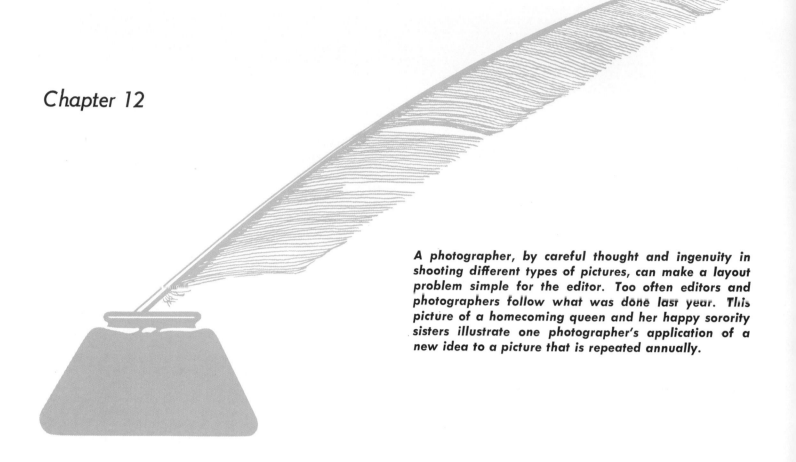

Chapter 12

A photographer, by careful thought and ingenuity in shooting different types of pictures, can make a layout problem simple for the editor. Too often editors and photographers follow what was done last year. This picture of a homecoming queen and her happy sorority sisters illustrate one photographer's application of a new idea to a picture that is repeated annually.

Handling Special Layout Problems

IN PREVIOUS CHAPTERS, the laying out of major sections of the annual has been discussed and illustrated in detail. However, in several other small areas of the yearbook, such as the advertising section, views of the school, photo essays, beauty queen pages, index, and perhaps a "final word" by the editor, good layout is needed also.

Too often no real thought is given to planning small sections or single pages of the annual. Don't quit making careful page layouts until the last page is sent to the printer. The good work you have done on the rest of your annual can be wrecked by jarring notes in the fringe areas. Follow the same general pattern of layout throughout the entire book.

Plan Ad Pages To Interest the Reader

A lot of thought and care should be given to planning the advertising pages of your yearbook. To be successful, advertising must sell something—either merchandise, service, or an idea.

Thus it is important that you design and plan the pages to get the interest of the reader. This cannot be accomplished by having advertisements that intrude on the reader in any obnoxious way. He should be led into reading the advertisements by the interesting way they are presented, and not because they are blocking orderly reading. Remember, the annual at your school should be published for the subscribers—not the advertisers.

Pictorial Advertising Lends Interest

One of the effective ways to interest readers in the advertising pages of your annual is to continue the same general style of layout and material used in the rest of the book. Make the advertising interesting by printing pictures of students and their activities on advertising pages. To do this, you must plan pictures carefully. Display and caption them in the same style you have used in the rest of your annual.

ity of pictures required for satisfactory reproduction in the annual. To obtain satisfactory results you must have the same high quality of typography, layout, and photography in this section of the book as in other sections.

The reproduction of pictures clipped from last year's annual, magazines, or newspapers will not print satisfactorily—you need the original picture or, better still, a new photographic print. Give the printer detailed instructions about the

The editorial staff should not be too dictatorial about the exact arrangement and layout of advertising pages. Advertisers pay for the space and sometimes have rather definite ideas about what they want. However, if a carefully thought-out plan that actually makes the advertising pages a continuation of the school's memory book is presented to advertisers, they usually are glad to co-operate.

Get Quality Photographs for Ad Pages

The advertising staff ought to be thoroughly informed about the kind of pictures and the qual-

type to be used and give him a carefully prepared layout.

Provide Space for Small Advertisers

You should be sure that the plan you finally adopt provides fair treatment for the small as well as the large space buyer. Sometimes, when pictorial advertising is used in an annual, the staff insists that each advertiser must buy a full or half page of space to be included in the book. This is unfair to the small businessman and a plan should be adopted that will allow him to purchase a small advertisement. In some of the advertising pages reproduced in this chapter you will note a plan that permits both large and small advertisements to be presented in an interesting manner.

Charges for Pictures Should Be Clear

If the advertiser is to be charged extra for pictures included in his advertisement, this must be included in the price quoted for the space when the advertising agreement is made. When pictures showing such regular school activities as

FIGURE 12.2. Good layout provides pleasing display of each advertisement shown on this page. Courtesy the *Indian*, Anderson High School, Anderson, Indiana.

FIGURE 12.1. Carefully planned pictures with well-written copy produced this interesting page in the *Riparian*, Broad Ripple High School, Indianapolis, Indiana.

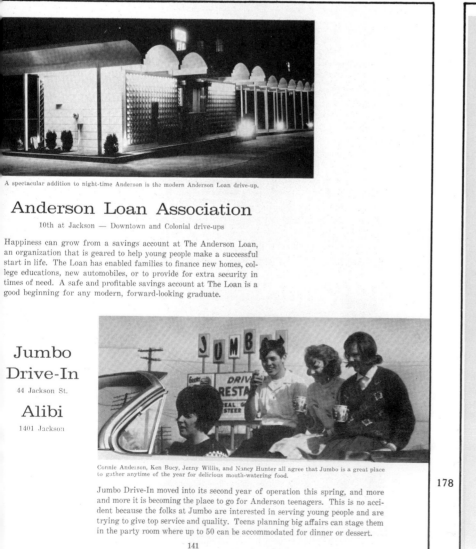

178

133

sports events, parties, etc. are scattered throughout the advertising section of the book, no charge is made for the pictures, as they help present the highlights of the school year. However, if pictures of students are taken in the establishment of the advertiser, he usually is charged for the cost of the photograph. If your annual is printed by offset, there will be no increase in cost of printing when pictures are used in the advertisements. However, if your book is printed by letterpress, you are usually required to pay extra for any new halftones ordered for the advertising section, and it is customary to charge this cost to the advertiser, especially for the reproductions of pictures taken in his place of business.

Student Pictures Add Interest

Interesting and well-posed pictures of students are used in the advertising section of the 1965 *Riparian*, Figure 12.1, to arouse the interest of the reader. The headline and copy "tie-in" the pictures with the product or service advertised. Identifying each person pictured adds interest and

FIGURE 12.3. A two-page spread of cooperative advertising by a shopping center may point the way for other staffs. Courtesy 1965 *Acorn*, Weber State College, Ogden, Utah.

helps make the advertising an interesting part of the yearbook.

Advertiser Selects Picture Wanted

An effective and distinctive page layout is achieved in the advertising section of the *Indian*, Figure 12.2. The advertiser is allowed some latitude in selecting the picture he wants to use. He can have a picture of his building, as shown in the advertisement at the top of the page, or students can be posed outside or inside his place of business if he wishes.

This plan is excellent, provided good pictures are taken. White space is effectively used to display each element on the page. Note the direct appeal to teenagers made in the copy. This is the kind of thinking and planning that makes yearbook advertising worth what it costs the merchant.

Shopping Center Buys Two-page Spread

The 1965 *Acorn*, Ogden, Utah, cashed in on one of the fast-growing shopping centers that are springing up all over the nation. Perhaps the two-page spread shown in Figure 12.3 will point the way to additional advertising for other yearbooks.

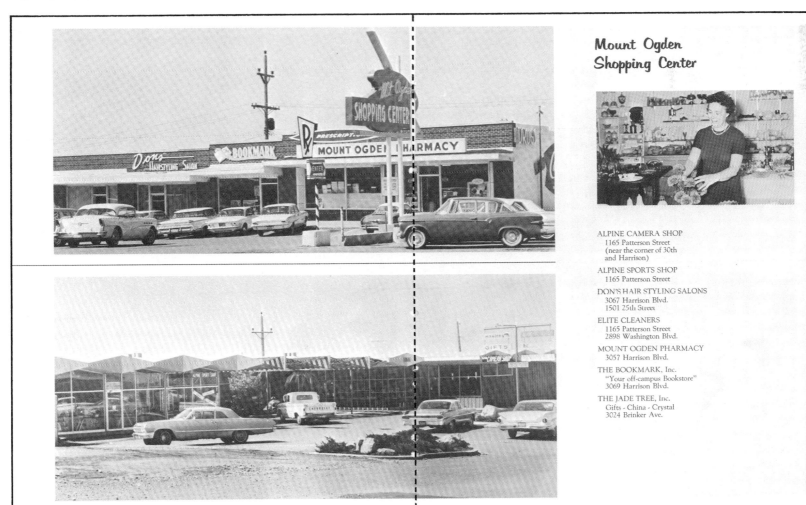

Mount Ogden
Shopping Center

ALPINE CAMERA SHOP
1165 Patterson Street
(near the corner of 30th
and Harrison)

ALPINE SPORTS SHOP
1165 Patterson Street

DON'S HAIR STYLING SALONS
3067 Harrison Blvd.
1501 25th Street

ELITE CLEANERS
1165 Patterson Street
2898 Washington Blvd.

MOUNT OGDEN PHARMACY
3057 Harrison Blvd.

THE BOOKMARK, Inc.
"Your off-campus Bookstore"
3069 Harrison Blvd.

THE JADE TREE, Inc.
Gifts - China - Crystal
3024 Brinker Ave.

The spread is well planned with excellent pictures and functional layout that ties the two pages together effectively.

Activity Pictures Used in Ad Section

Often, activity pictures taken at the school are used on the advertising pages to carry the interest of the reader through this section and to call his attention to specific advertisements. Figure 12.4 from the 1965 *Royal Purple* shows how this plan was used for a cooperative page of advertising from the lumber companies of Manhattan. White space is used judiciously and the cutline below the picture is written in the same style as other cutlines in the book, thus continuing the pattern previously established.

Ads Placed in Index Section

Some yearbooks scatter advertisements throughout the index of the book in an effort to increase readership. Annuals using conventional advertising are more likely to place advertisements in this manner and it is quite satisfactory, unless so many ads are allocated to this section that they make it difficult for the reader to use the index. It is well to remember that advertising that intrudes on an individual's usual reading habits does not accomplish its purpose. Perhaps one or two ads per page in the index is about all the staff should use. There are plenty of other ways to make yearbook advertising palatable to readers. Some yearbook staffs refuse to sell advertising space in the index section.

Sponsorship advertisements ought to be carefully planned and printed so all sponsors who contribute money are treated uniformly. Here again you must consider your readers as well as your advertisers.

Views Properly Displayed Set the Scene

The views (or in the case of large schools the view section) of the annual can do much to set the scene or establish the locale for the story of the school year. You can increase interest in the pictures used if you get students in the foreground. In most cases, you should get views taken while leaves are on the trees, and when lawns and shrubs show to best advantage. If funds are available for printing color pictures in the annual, probably the most judicious way to spend them is for good color views of your school.

Thoughtful planning of how and where the views are to be presented in the annual will help the photographer get the kind of pictures needed to do a good job. For example, if the view is to be printed across the end sheets of your annual, you will require a horizontal shot that can be enlarged to fit the area. If the view is to be only one page, you will probably want a vertical picture.

Each View Needs a Cutline

Detailed dummy pages showing sizes and shapes of views to be used are more important for these pages than for almost any other section of the book. Each view should have an adequate cutline, whether it is used on the end sheets, in the opening or division pages, or in a regular view section. The same typographical style as that used on other pages is usually best. Cutlines for pages that bleed at all margins can be printed either in reverse in some dark area of the picture or on a facing page. A small arrow can be used near the cutline pointing to the picture being described. Standard type margins used for other pages are generally used in the view section, for this aids in establishing the style of layout for the entire book.

FIGURE. 12.4. The picture of a basketball game interestingly captioned insures that this page from the *Royal Purple*, Kansas State University, will be read.

KANSAS LUMBER CO.
Phone PR 8-4411
431 S. 5th

HARDMAN LUMBER CO.
Phone PR 6-8846
West on K-18

RAMEY BROS. LBR. & COAL
Phone PR 8-3911
131 Houston

GRIFFITH COAL & LBR. CO.
Phone PR 8-4477
112 N. 2nd

Roy Smith (45) and Gary Williams (behind Smith) go high to tip a rebound to Jeff Simons (out of the picture to the right).

The Lumber Companies of Manhattan
Serving the People

578

Take Air-view Picture From Low Angle

A well-planned air view is used in the *Index*, Figure 12.5, to complete a pleasing two-page spread. The view was taken to show the entire campus and was shot from the proper angle to present sides as well as tops of buildings. Too often air views are taken from directly above buildings, and the results usually are both uninteresting and confusing.

The night picture on the left-hand page adds an interesting touch, and contrasts effectively with the close-up of the street sign. The copy and cutlines do their job well.

Dramatic Views Add Interest

"Clover Park is in a spacious land of towering peaks and thundering shores, flaming fields and brightly lit cities," reads part of the cutline for the two-page spread of dramatic scenes in the 1965 *Klahowya*, Figure 12.6. This spread, with the one that follows, sets the scene for the story

FIGURE 12.5. This two-page spread from the *Index*, Illinois State University, Normal, Illinois, effectively presents views of the campus. The layout is well planned and makes good use of white space.

about Clover Park High School more dramatically than a dozen pictures of the high school building could have done.

Look around you and see if you can introduce your school in a new and refreshing way. It is true that most schools cannot match the scenery and pictures shown in Figure 12.6, but often we overlook the interesting and significant things that lend individuality to our own school.

Night Views Are Significant

Pictures taken at night often can be used to show the campus as it is remembered best. The *Bomb,* Figure 12.7, demonstrates how this can be done effectively.

The same general typographical style is used in the view section that is used for other pages in the *Bomb*. The typeface used for headlines, cutlines, and body copy is uniform throughout the book. This uniformity of treatment maintains a pleasing pattern.

Quotation From Distinguished Alumnus

A variety of excellent pictures and a quotation from a distinguished alumnus are effec-

A ribbon of light wound around campus at the Big and Little Sisters' Flashlight Parade.

Running through the center of campus . . .

We have been speaking in generalities . . .
what you can find on campus
at any time.
But what happened this year?
What makes 1963-1964 memorable?
Of course, there was the name change,
and buildings being used for the first time.
There were new freshmen just beginning
and wise seniors attaining bachelor degrees.
Things were completed, things accomplished.
This year was important . . . let's reminisce.

S. UNIVERSITY

Expansion and change were the watchwords for the year as buildings filled the once empty area of West Campus.

FIGURE 12.6. This magnificent spread of dramatic pictures and equally dramatic copy should be an inspiration to all who see it. Courtesy 1965 *Klahowya*, Clover Park High School, Lakewood Center, Washington.

Clover Park is in a spacious land of towering peaks and thundering shores, flowering fields and brightly lit cities ⬧ It is a land of great beauty and considerable promise ⬧ Its people, its sports and fads are amidst scenic grandeur where some find life long friendships, some find opportunities, and all may touch majesty ⬧

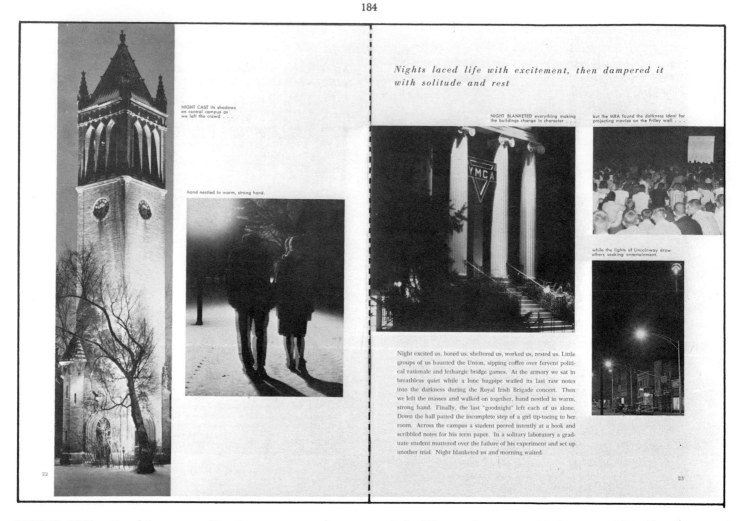

FIGURE 12.7. Good layout, well-written copy, and excellent pictures are combined to establish the mood of night life on the campus. Courtesy 1965 *Bomb*, Iowa State University, Ames, Iowa.

FIGURE 12.8. A quotation from an address by Herbert Hoover is used instead of specific cutlines to identify the views on this spread from the 1965 *Stanford Quad*, Stanford University, Stanford, California.

tively combined in the Stanford *Quad*, Figure 12.8. The generous use of white space is justified because it emphasizes the excellence of the picture used. The *Quad* used appropriate quotations from famous authors on several pages of the book.

Photo Essay Captures Flavor

Photo essays are being used by many editors in an effort to add perspective or to present the special flavor or atmosphere of their particular school year. Some pleasing results have been achieved by the proper use of pictures, copy, and white space.

The photo essay, if well done, can add a new and interesting feature to a yearbook. However, some of the results are downright confusing and ineffective. Then, too, there is a tendency to devote too many pages to this feature. If you forget that the function of a yearbook is to tell a history of the year, you are likely to devote too much space to interpreting or editorializing. Perhaps the literary magazine is a better place for long and controversial photo essays—at least it is less expensive, and provides an opportunity for individuals with different opinions to express their ideas in later issues. If editorial or interpretative matter makes readers want to express an opposite opinion, it probably should not be used in the annual. Americans expect to be able to state opposite views; yearbooks are not issued often enough for that.

In an effort to give prominence to the photo essay, it sometimes has been allowed to crowd out important introductory pages needed in all yearbooks. One such essay ran for more than 50 pages before the table of contents was printed, and in another annual the table of contents was entirely omitted.

A photo essay should be short, and used to add perspective or present some interesting development at the school.

Effective Use of Photo Essay

An excellent example of a photo essay used effectively is shown in Figure 12.9 from the 1965 *Cactus*. The pictures help to tell the story and have fine technical quality. The picture in the upper right-hand corner of the right-hand page was printed in full color in the *Cactus*, but is reproduced in one color only here. The copy is significant and well displayed.

FIGURE 12.9. Significant pictures, coherent copy, and pleasing use of white space are combined to present this excellent "photo essay." Courtesy of the 1965 *Cactus*, University of Texas, Austin.

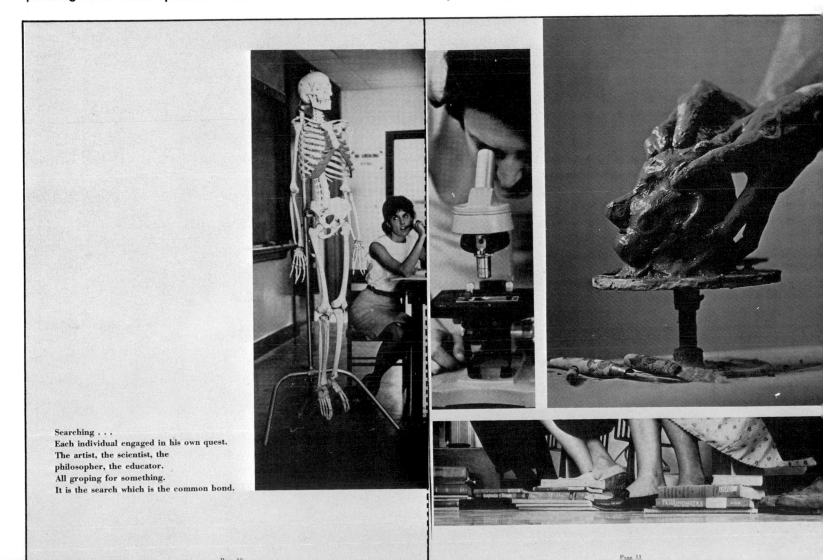

Searching . . .
Each individual engaged in his own quest.
The artist, the scientist, the
philosopher, the educator.
All groping for something.
It is the search which is the common bond.

Facial Expressions Tell Story

A variety of facial expressions is captured on this double-page spread from the 1963 *Shield,* Figure 12.10. Well-planned and carefully captioned pictures of this kind do much to recall special events that add interest and atmosphere to the annual for many years to come. They are examples of how pictures help tell the story. These well-cropped pictures are of excellent quality and are effectively displayed. The staff must be alert to select and photograph significant events and individuals if a feature of this kind is to be worth-while.

Essay on Division Pages

The 1964 *Sunflower* used each of its division pages to present a photo essay of sorts. Figure 12.11 shows the division pages introducing the school-life section. A well-written essay on the significance of student activities, pleasingly illustrated with good pictures, is a useful and effective way to present a photo essay.

The special typographical style with unjusti-

fied margins is used on all division pages. Appropriate pictures and generous use of white space add impact.

Planning Beauty and Popularity Pages

Planning page layouts for the beauty, popularity, and achievement section of an annual presents many problems that need careful attention. In most schools it is difficult for the editor to decide just how much space should be allocated to this particular feature, and just how many of the numerous "queens" and "kings" with their various attendants should be included in the book.

Yearbooks Start Beauty Contests

A few years ago almost every college and many high school yearbook staffs sponsored the election or selection of several queens who were presented in the glamour section. The practice of selecting beauty or popularity queens met with so much enthusiasm from the students that it was often used by the annual staff to promote the sale of the yearbook. For example, each student who subscribed for the book was allowed to vote for the candidate of his choice. Sometimes tickets for a special yearbook ball were sold, and only ticket

FIGURE 12.10. Interesting sidelights that are part of "that particular year" are well presented in this spread from the *Shield*, High School, Highland, Indiana.

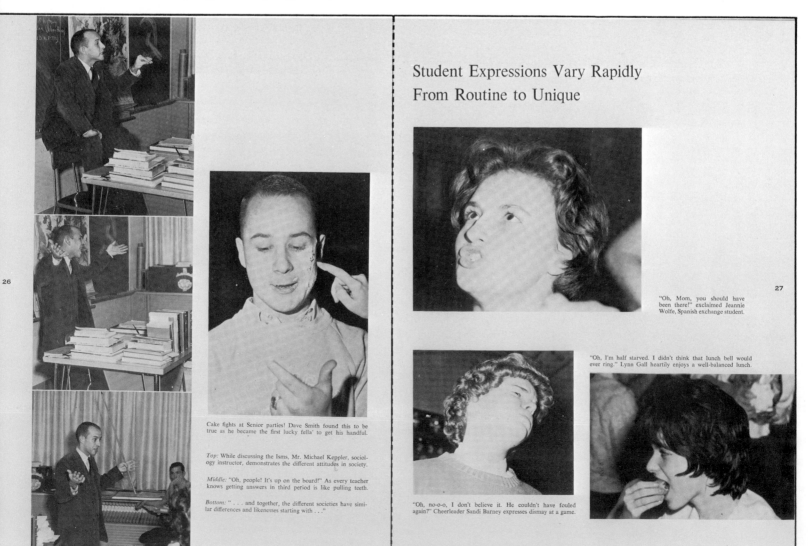

holders were permitted to vote for the annual's queens.

Often these contests were not properly supervised, and charges were made that the queens selected did not actually represent the whole student body but only those who had money to support the financial schemes of the yearbook staff. These charges caused some schools to discontinue the practice of electing yearbook queens or to revise the selection method so all students in the school were allowed to vote. In some instances, movie actors or other celebrities were asked to make the selections from pictures of the candidates.

Many Organizations Elect Queens

At the same time, many other school organizations saw the possibilities of arousing interest in their activities by electing their own queens to preside at homecoming, special dances, or almost any activity they wanted to promote. At first, some yearbook editors refused to include pictures of any queens except those selected as the annual's queens. However, it soon became apparent that this position was untenable and undesirable. After

all, the job of the yearbook is to present all the important highlights of the school year.

Treat All Queens Fairly

Because of such developments, it is apparent that the yearbook staff needs to exercise good judgment in how the school's beauty queens are presented. You should be sure that the plan you follow treats all queens fairly. The decision as to whether they are to be presented should be based on the number of readers of your annual who will be interested in their presentation. Thus, you probably would show the queens and attendants. sponsored by the yearbook, homecoming committee, ROTC dance committee, and all queens selected by any considerable portion of the student body. Minor queens elected by organizations to reign over a single dance are sometimes pictured on the organization's page.

Remember that the important thing is to give fair and uniform coverage to all queens of like importance. Do not devote too many pages of your annual to this particular activity. More important phases of school life must be omitted if you do so. Perhaps some of the pages of outstanding students reproduced from leading annuals will help you not only in layout problems but also

FIGURE 12.11. This spread from the *Sunflower*, Topeka High School, Topeka, Kansas, is an excellent example of how to use the photo essay in a functional way.

SCHOOL LIFE

WE BELIEVE that the life-giving substance of any school is echoed in its all-school efforts and in its material and intangible gains in the areas of government, international relations, publications, dramatics, music, assemblages, and the social and service areas—aspects that emphasize rounded growth. Dramatic productions drew attention to war-related incidents and high comedy and the annual operetta called forth praise for its unity of music, acting, dancing, and staging. Student Council dug deeply for ways to make itself more effective as a part of the American Way of Life, and a world community came into being with an active student exchange program involving many countries in its scope.

More Space for Scholarship

A definite, recent trend has been to limit the number of pages in an annual devoted to beauty and popularity contests. Sometimes this action has been instigated by school administrators or student councils, but oftener by yearbook staffs.

A good many staffs are now using several pages in their yearbook for students who make outstanding records in school and community activities and especially in scholarship. This trend is one that merits your careful consideration. Excellence deserves recognition.

Homecoming Court Honors Many

An interesting and comprehensive presentation of the homecoming queen and her court is presented in the 1965 *Echowan*, Figure 12.12. The two-page spread carefully identifies and pictures 34 different individuals including the queen and her attendants.

A plan of this kind records significant honors conferred on many students. It has much more

FIGURE 12.12. Pictures showing joy, sadness, enthusiasm, and other emotions are combined in this well-planned spread from the 1965 *Echowan*, St. Louis Park High School, St. Louis Park, Minnesota.

interest for subscribers and their friends than the same space devoted to only one or two individuals—it tells a more complete story too.

Scholarship Winners Presented

"Superior Scholarship Recognized, Lauded," states the headline for a two-page spread in the 1963 *Camelback,* Figure 12.13. This spread is part of a section devoted to honor students, homecoming king and queen, and "Miss Camelback," the yearbook queen. All the pages are treated uniformly in general layout plan and typography. The staff did an excellent job of recording all the significant information about each winner.

Two Pages for Yearbook Queen

A two-page spread is devoted to the yearbook queen in the 1964 *Pine Needles,* Figure 12.14. This is as it should be since the annual is published by the University of North Carolina at Greensboro, the state's university for women. The yearbook staff has only a limited number of activities to cover and devotes more space to the beauty section, classes, and curricular activities than is done in most coeducational colleges where more activities, particularly intercollegiate sports, demand space.

Mary Kleifgen

Cindy Pratt, Linda McKusick, Nancee Scholtec

1964 HOMECOMING COURT — BOTTOM ROW: Linda Joseph, Rollie Troup, Mary Kleifgen, Martha Hunkins, Holly Hovde, Nancee Scholtec, Cindy Pratt, Linda Zuel, Janet Ehrenberg, Linda McKusick. ROW 2: Ladies of the Court: Marit Fredheim, Carolyn Cheese, Nancy Wheelock, Janis Rude, Kathy King, Sue Knudson, Kathy McElyea, Joanne Youngren, Pat Aberle, Laura Carlberg, Bonnie Cameron, Mary Kennedy. ROW 3: Lords of the Court: Suresh Mahajan, Foreign Exchange; Tom Sipkins, Senior Class; Jack Spetz, Hockey Team; Dick Johnson, Golf Team; Walt Heustis, Ski Team; Randy Jones, Track Team; Bob Olson, Basketball Team; Paul Krause, Tennis Team; Dave Shapley, Swimming Team; Bill Posnick, Cross Country Team; Roger Lindquist, Baseball Team; Ira Rosen, Wrestling Team.

Elegance, Stateliness, Grace Combine in 1964 Homecoming Court

Holly Hovde

Rollie Troup

Linda Joseph

Martha Hunkins, Janet Ehrenberg

Linda Zuel

Superior Scholarship Recognized, Lauded

LEONORA COUVDOS

THE 1963 recipient of the Bausch Lomb Award was Dave Koval. This award from the Bausch Lomb Incorporation is a four-year science scholarship allocated on need to exceptional science students on faculty recommendation. Dave, also a National Merit Scholarship Finalist, received the Harvard Book Award as the highest boy academically in his junior year, and ranked in the top two per cent of his graduating class. He was active in Orchestra, Band and Orchestra Letterman's Club, Mu Alpha Theta, math honorary of which he served as president, and National Honor Society.

THROUGH CONSISTENT striving for scholastic excellence LEONORA COUVDOS has attained a grade average in the top five per cent of her class. She was a three-year member of National Honor Society, a member of Stellas and Beaver Builders. She intended to attend ASU and major in business.

WYNDLE HAESE, not pictured, was a National Merit Scholarship Finalist. His high grade average placed him in the top five per cent of the class of 1963. He held membership in National Honor Society and Speech Club and he received a speech award in Texas.

BETTY CROCKER Homemaker of Tomorrow was BARBARA BREWSTER. She attained the highest score in SHS which qualified her for the state award. She planned to attend St. Joseph's School of Nursing. Barbara was a member of Beaver Boosters and served on the *Camelback* staff during her senior year.

RODNEY LANDES was the president of the National Honor Society, veep of Scottsdale Singers, and of Key Club as well as being a member of Squires Hi-Y and Mu Alpha Theta. Moreover, Rod was in the fine arts production, "Damn Yankees", and was selected to attend N.C.C.J.

CONNIE NERRIE a member of Scottsdale Singers, and National Honor Society for two years, also performed in "Carousel", a summer fine arts production. Connie's scholastic achievements placed her in the top five per cent of the Class of 1963.

DAN JOHNSON, transfer from Michigan, ranked in the top five per cent of the Class of '63, and scored in the upper 10 per cent on the state math test. He was in J.V. tennis and baseball and varsity baseball. Dan belonged to National Honor Society, Mu Alpha Theta, Beaver Band, and Band and Orchestra Lettermen's.

SETTING A precedent, the class of 1963 named no valedictorian or salutatorian. In their place the top five and ten per cent were recognized. It was felt that such a system would better represent the achievements of the individuals. THOSE APPEARING elsewhere are Janet Reedy, Bill Yoder, and Bill Zar.

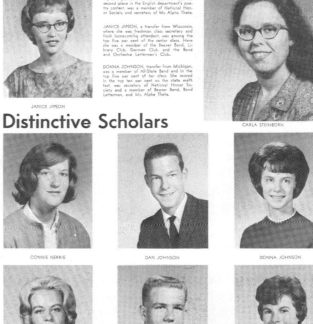

EXCELLING IN math and science enabled Carla Steinborn to attend a five-week summer math camp at ASC in 1962. Her high scholastic achievement placed her in the top five per cent of her class. she received second place in the English department's poetry contest, was a member of National Honor Society and secretary of Mu Alpha Theta.

JANICE JIPSON, a transfer from Wisconsin, where she was freshman class secretary and frosh homecoming attendant, was among the top five per cent of the junior class. Here she was a member of the Beaver Band, Library Club, German Club, and the Band and Orchestra Letterman's Club.

DONNA JOHNSON, transfer from Michigan, was a member of All-State Band and in the top five per cent of her class. She scored in the top ten per cent on the state math test, was secretary of National Honor Society and a member of Beaver Band, Band Lettermen, and Mu Alpha Theta.

JANICE JIPSON

CARLA STEINBORN

Distinctive Scholars

CONNIE NERRIE

DAN JOHNSON

DONNA JOHNSON

JUDY TEMPLETON was a transfer student from Washington, D.C. There she was active in the French Club, Pep Club, and Alliance Francaise. At Scottsdale Judy belonged to National Honor Society and ranked in the top five per cent of her class.

JAY OSBORN, in addition to his academic achievements, placing in the top five per cent, participated on the J.V. and varsity baseball teams. He was chaplain of Squires, a member of Mu Alpha Theta, National Honor Society, and Beaver Boosters, and attended NCCJ.

CONNIE WELLER, an active senior girl, was a member of National Honor Society for two years. Scottsdale Singers, Chansonettes, and Stellas. She was president of Beaver Builders and performed in the 1960 summer fine arts presentation "Carousel", in which she danced.

FIGURE 12.13. Outstanding scholars are presented effectively in this spread from the 1963 *Camelback*, Scottsdale High School, Scottsdale, Arizona.

FIGURE. 12.14. Excellent pictures are effectively presented in this well-planned spread. Courtesy the 1964 *Pine Needles*, University of North Carolina.

SENIOR MARSHALS — *(top to bottom)* — Sally Crumpler, Martha Rogers, Pat Smith, Marjorie Spangler, Lillian Dane, Joan Decker, Angela Blanton, Sandra Simmens, Ann Klutz, Jo Anne Allen, Barbara Wrenn, Judy Williams, Foy Clarke, Kaye Taylor, Libby Morrison, Margaret Inman; *(not pictured)* Sharon Beck, Marion Dotson, Rachel Spradley.

Jean Decker
Chief Marshal

Junior, Senior Marshals Serve University For Functions At Aycock

White gloves and sash
are the familiar trademarks
of a marshal.

Each year during the spring elections twelve junior and eight senior marshals are chosen by their respective classes on the basis of charm, poise, and leadership; the Chief Marshal is elected by the entire student body. These young women will represent the university and their class for all functions held in Aycock Auditorium and in various other capacities on campus; they are one of our many images to the Greensboro community of which the campus is so vitally a part.

JUNIOR MARSHALS — *(top to bottom)* Harriett Eiler, Barbara Davis, Sue Airey, Anne Starr Minton, Karen Ostdahl, Ann Sagar, Frances Sullivan, Carol Gaines, Lee Brinkley, Sara Robbins; *(not pictured)* Melinda Coleman and Sara Lou Thomas.

Page 120

Page 121

White Space Effectively Used

The staff of the 1964 *Yucca* made generous use of white space in presenting its beauty queens, shown in Figure 12.15. The layout follows the general pattern established on other pages of the annual. Simplicity of arrangement and good photographs are combined to produce this pleasing two-page spread.

Make the Index Usable

The index of your annual will be more usable if you arrange it in the accepted style followed by well-printed books. Too often yearbooks have separate indexes for faculty, seniors, underclassmen, advertisers, organizations, etc. In fact, an index to the indexes is needed in some cases. A general index listing everything in alphabetical order is easiest for the reader to use. Sometimes, names of organizations, advertisers, and general terms—such as superintendent, football, music, etc.—are set in all capital letters, boldface, or italics to make them stand out in the list of names in regular type.

How To Prepare an Index

Getting and organizing all the information needed for a detailed index of an annual requires a lot of work. Plans should be started as early in the year as possible. The first step is to prepare a

FIGURE 12.15. Leaving white space at the outside margins of both pages ties them together and provides an effective layout. Courtesy the 1964 *Yucca*, North Texas State University, Denton, Texas.

card file listing the name of each student whose picture will appear in the annual. In many large schools, a set of IBM cards giving the names of all students enrolled can be secured from the registrar's office. If IBM cards are not available at your school, you can use ordinary 3x5-inch cards and type the name of each student in the upper left-hand corner. The cards are then filed in alphabetical order.

Index Page Before Mailing to Printer

As soon as the first page is ready to send to the printer, enter the page number on the card of each individual whose picture and name appear on that particular page. For example, suppose you are sending in page 49 and John G. Smith's picture appears on the page. Look up his card in the file and write clearly "49." Then return the card to its proper place. If the name of someone who does not have a card appears on the page, prepare a card for him and file it alphabetically. Be sure the page number is not changed once it has been entered on the cards. If the number of the page is changed, all numbers entered on the cards must be corrected. Having a dummy that you follow exactly prevents such extra work.

Preparing General Index Cards

When all pages have been sent to the printer, you are ready to prepare the final cards and file them in order. Using the dummy or carbon copies of each page, prepare a "general index card." For example, if page 49 shows a picture of the

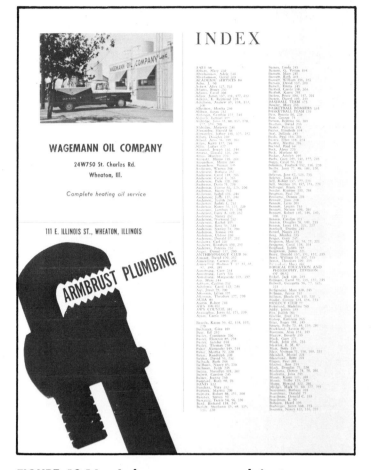

FIGURE 12.16. Index copy arranged in two narrow columns aids readability and makes economical use of all available space on this page from the 1965 *Tower*, Wheaton College, Wheaton, Illinois.

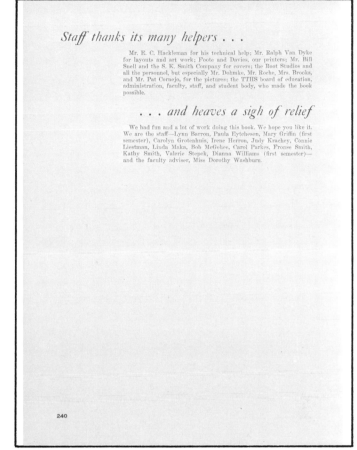

FIGURE 12.17. A simple and effective note of thanks to nonstaff helpers as well as a complete listing of all staff members is shown in the 1963 *Thorntonite*, Thornton Township High School, Harvey, Illinois.

band and orchestra, you will prepare two cards, one reading "band" and the other "orchestra," and write "49" on each, filing them in alphabetical order. The same plan is used for each page in the book. You can enter any material you want listed in the index, such as: name of each advertiser, football, principal, music organizations, etc. You may want to prepare two or three cards for some pages—this is called cross indexing. When all cards are completed, you are ready to type the index. Check copy carefully for errors before sending it to the printer.

General Index Aids Reader

A part of the first page of the general index from the 1965 *Tower* is shown in Figure 12.16. Note that such terms as ACADEMIC SERVICES, BASEBALL TEAM, and BASKETBALL BOMBERS are set in all capital letters, while names of individuals appear in regular type. Page numbers appearing after names are arranged in numerical order—the lowest page number first.

The *Tower* allocated the inside column of each index page to advertising. This orderly arrangement does not interfere with easy reading and at the same time provides excellent display of advertisements.

Planning the "Thank You" Page

Producing a yearbook is a big job and requires the cooperation and help of many individuals in addition to regular staff members. Appreciative editors like to devote the final page (or part of the final page) to "a last word," acknowledgments, or a "thank you" to people who helped produce the book. If you decide to do this, plan the layout and typography of this message so it will harmonize with the style of the rest of the annual.

If this page is to have real significance, it should thank certain individuals who made a real contribution, "above and beyond the call of duty," in the creation of a better annual. Give some thought to the content and writing of this special message—don't do it in a hurry. The "thank you" message can be brief, nostalgic, or elaborate, as shown in Figures 12.17, 12.18, or 12.19.

Spotlight on the Future

And so ends another school year.
For seniors, the high school career is over.
The HILLTOPPER staff finishes its work for the year,
and meets its last deadline.
But none of the deadlines could have been met
without the assistance of many people;
so the staff wishes to extend its sincere thanks to
Mr. Bob Cavanagh of American Yearbook Company,
Mr. Robert Merriman of Durand Manufacturing Company,
and Earl and Mike Loudermilk of Loudermilk Studios.
Mr. Frank Tout, Vice-Principal,
was always ready with a camera when he was needed.
Jerry Stanbrough and Doug Runciman spent time
in the darkroom each day developing pictures.
With this the spotlight dims for another year,
but not before it shines toward the future,
showing a never-ending parade of classes, sports,
activities, and people which make up Howe.
Now the challenge remains, spotlighting the future.

1963 HILLTOPPER STAFF

Editor-in-Chief	Sally Slater
Associate Editor	Ruth Ann McClure
Senior Editor	Ellen Bundchu
Senior Editor	Jodi Dobbs
Activities Editor	Roberta Sammis
Activities Editor	Jennie Bradley
Club Editor	Margo Garman
Club Editor	Susan Bowman
Sports Editor	Steve Sachs
Sports Editor	Tom Gilkison
Underclassman Editor	Sheila McBurnie
Underclassman Editor	Susan Campbell
Index Editor	Betty Cronau
Index Editor	Elaine Chavers
Copy Editor	Bob Vicars
Copy Editor	Mary Jane Freeman
Make-up	
Make-up	
Business	
Business	
Student Photographer	Peg Nation
Adviser	Mrs. Ellen Jenkins
Photography	Loudermilk Studios
Publisher	American Yearbook Co.
Covers	Durand Manufacturing Co.

FIGURE 12.18. The headline, pictures, and copy on this page impart a pleasing nostalgia for the "old school" in addition to doing the necessary job of thanking the right people. Courtesy 1963 *Hilltopper*, Thomas Carr Howe High School, Indianapolis, Indiana.

FIGURE 12.19. The editor of the 1963 *Bomb*, Iowa State University, Ames, did an outstanding job of presenting "a bouquet to the staff," acknowledgments, and photo credits on the final page of the book.

A yearbook is more than ink on paper. It is the life and breath of months of planning and work by a devoted staff. The cookies and cokes during the year are a small reward for an incomparable staff which saw the 1965 Bomb through major and minor crises. A yearbook is people. Thank you's are inadequate from an editor.

—cathy

a bouquet to the staff

Editor	CATHY LUNDON
Managing Editor—Copy	PAM HENRY
Managing Editor—Layout	BILL STRAND
Managing Editor—Photo	VIV VOELKER
Head Photographer	CONRAD KRASS
Academic Editor	SHIRLEY ROBINSON
Activities Editor	SUE FARMER
Art Editor	KEITH CRONN
Features Editor	LESLIE OSAM
Index Editor	DONNA RIPPER
Residence Editor	SUSAN FEAMSTER
Seniors Editor	MAURINE FOSTER
Sports Editor	BOB SPEERS
Bomb Beauties Chairmen	SUE SANDERS
	KAYE ROGERSON
Business Manager	GARY MURPHY
Assistant Business Manager	JIM TAIT
Sales Manager	GARY SHAFFER

Copywriters: Ron Anderson, Marti Beatty, Sally Boekleman, Bruce Borne, Charlie Brien, Jerald Fowlie, Danna Hageman, Jan Hille, Sandy Henry, Mary Beth Hertenstein, Nancy Houser, Jim Hufferd, Dee Jessen, Don Johnson, Kris Kasdorf, Lois Klitzhe, Patty Langford, Laura Lemon, Nancy Lettow, Ann Lowny, Gene Meyer, Jan Pies, Chuck Putzier, Bruce Rerick, Judy Reynolds, Suzanne Rice, George Ross, Gary Ruhser, Bob Savage, Theola Sorensen, Diane Swann, Craig Wells, Chuck Whitley.

Acknowledgements

Mr. Bob Johnson, advisor, who wanted to "advise."
Mr. John Thomas, business advisor, who helped spend money.
Mr. Wm. E. Holmes, Mr. Bob Schwartz, and the staff of the Iowa State University Press who readied the book for the press as well as correcting dangling modifiers and misspelled words.
Mr. Ed Hackleman, Mr. Ralph Van Dyke, and Miss Molly Flanders of Jahn and Ollier Engraving Company who made the book a reality by layouts and pictures.
Mr. Owen Heng who was unofficial consultant editor.

Mr. Wm. G. Snell of Smithcraft Covers who wanted us to have "just what you want."
Rappoport Studios of New York who spent weeks taking mountains of senior and group pictures.
Engravings by Jahn and Ollier Engraving Company, Chicago, Illinois.
Printing by Iowa State University Press, Ames, Iowa.
Cover by the S. K. Smith Company, Chicago, Illinois.
Binding by National Bookbinding Company, Stevens Point, Wis.

Photo Credits

Agriculturist: 71, 72, 73.
An Active: 400.
Applegate, Bill: 368, 396.
Behnke, Ed: 20, 121, 131, 152, 156, 177, 182, 196, 206, 207, 208, 209, 213, 262, 276, 298, 300, 339, 342, 349, 370, 373, 377, 384, 434.
Booth, Ed: 70, 184.
Buhr, D.: 10.
Burke, Judi: 342.
Burton, Richard: 101.
Buchanan, Nancy: 33.
Castro, José: 128, 404, 418.
Collins, Bob: 34, 35, 52, 53, 54, 132, 201, 239, 353, 365, 406, 407, 4333, 441.
Duffus, Jan: 258.
Dunn, Rick: 15, 28, 29, 31, 40, 44, 45, 105, 145, 195, 219, 222, 242, 243, 244, 247, 270, 306, 337, 371, 399, 417, 418, 421, 437.
Durbin, Ken: 11, 25, 64, 65, 212, 292, 318.
Erisman, Al: 55, 68, 69, 126, 184, 194, 215, 220, 222, 224, 225, 226, 229, 230, 231, 232, 233, 235, 246, 273, 321, 340, 352, 354, 355, 358, 367, 368, 375, 383, 390, 429, 433, 438, 440.
Fairchild, Larry: 337, 366.
Fay, Marty: 7, 55, 368, 48, 380.
Foster, Maurine: 92, 327, 329, 334.
Harmon, L.: 304.
Harcharik, Dave: 201, 204, 261.
Heiderstadt, Dick: 101, 123.
Hermann, Larry: 77, 83.
Hill's Studio: 42.
Hokenson, Sue: 23, 84, 241.
Holz, Helen: 340, 346, 347.
Homemaker: 79, 80, 81.
Howell: 88.
Information Service: 21, 66, 71, 74, 76, 82, 83, 84, 85, 86, 87, 89, 91, 93, 96, 97, 98, 99, 102, 103, 193, 195, 236, 243, 245.
Jones, Dorothy: 324.
Krass, Conrad: 2, 6, 14, 17, 18, 20, 25, 26, 27, 28, 29, 30, 32, 33, 35, 36, 39, 40, 41, 42, 43, 46, 47, 50, 51, 54, 56, 57, 67, 72, 79, 94, 95, 104, 106, 107, 123, 128, 134, 135, 151, 159, 172, 173, 174, 175, 176, 177, 180, 181, 182, 183, 186, 189, 191, 193, 194, 200, 202, 203, 208, 216, 218, 219, 234, 235, 236, 237, 238, 240, 244, 248, 251, 252, 254, 256, 257, 259, 261, 262, 264, 267, 268, 269, 275, 279, 280, 281, 284, 285, 290, 291, 293, 294, 296, 299, 303, 305, 309, 310, 344, 345, 363, 378, 380, 419, 426, 428, 437.
Latham, Suki: 14.
Lewellyn, Don: 14, 15, 19, 23, 68, 71, 75, 76, 77, 79, 80, 85, 88, 89, 90, 92, 98, 102, 201, 206, 209 240.
Lundon, Cathy: 7, 10, 11, 18, 32, 173, 247, 317, 322, 330, 441.
McTague, Joe: 241.
Me, Myself, and I: 2, 19, 47, 200, 258, 400, 413.
Mead, Bruce: 10, 128, 169.
Miller, Al: 32, 55, 100, 127, 131, 178, 179, 180, 187, 188, 189, 217, 225, 255, 256, 263, 271, 272, 274, 277, 278, 282, 283, 286, 287, 288, 289, 295, 301, 303, 307, 308, 395, 426, 429.
Montre, Larry: 439.
Mores, Steve: 366, 357.
Munsell, Don: 52, 124, 200, 207, 209, 226, 265, 311, 374, 424, 434.
Nelson, Russ: 76.
Newman Club: 205.
Osam, Leslie: 1, 37, 199.
Riessen, Gary: 100, 105, 129, 152.
Ritchie, Corwin: 17, 24, 30, 155, 242, 350, 351.
Rule, Ted: 130.
Sanderman, Ken: 366.
Schara, Ron: 438.
Sloe, Harold: 420.
Smith, Doug: 92.
Sommers, Gerry: 30, 157, 159, 164, 165, 166, 167, 198, 211, 244, 349, 355, 357, 360, 364, 387, 399, 410, 411, 415, 423, 424.
Steenhoek, Phyllis: 440.
Sunnquist, Roger: 253, 351, 235.
Sutcliff, Jaunita: 249.
Van Syoc, Lynn: 84.
Veterinarian: 185.
Wilhelm, Perry: 24, 25, 205, 361, 388, 403, 424.
Wilson, Jon: 435.

A complete page-by-page dummy of the proposed annual, together with a carefully planned production schedule, can help the staff to deliver its yearbook on time. Photographers, copy writers, assistant editors, and the editor all need an accurate dummy of the annual readily accessible if they are to do an intelligent job of carrying out their respective assignments.

Chapter 13

Producing the Book on Schedule

ALL PERIODICALS, like newspapers and magazines, which must be delivered to their readers on a specified date, follow a detailed production schedule that makes on-time delivery certain. The school yearbook, if it is to be delivered on a specified day, must follow a production schedule that will guide the staff and each craftsman concerned with the book so he completes his duties at the proper time.

When you remember that school yearbooks are prepared by students who often are inexperienced and who usually are carrying a full assignment of school work, a book appearing on schedule reflects credit to the staff, adviser, and the concern doing the work.

Special Discounts Offered

Many photographers, printers, and cover makers offer special inducements to get work done early. Concerns specializing in yearbooks require a steady flow of work into their plants if they are to operate economically. Yearbook photographers usually offer a special discount on all class pictures taken before November 1, so they can get the pictures finished and delivered to the staff before their regular Christmas business begins. Some printers offer a special reduction ranging from 50 cents to one dollar per page for all complete pages

received before November 1. Standard provisions in some contracts allow the staff to deduct as much as two per cent of the entire printing cost of the book if final copy is in by a certain date in January or February. Cash discounts of one or two per cent are granted for early advance payment, thus encouraging the business staff to sell subscriptions and advertising space early. Cover manufacturers commonly allow a discount from the quoted price for the yearbook cover if final specifications are received by January 1. These special discounts are offered to encourage the staff to establish a production schedule that will allow the book to be delivered on time. However, unrealistically early delivery precludes covering some important school events.

Establishing the Schedule

A schedule is defined by Webster's dictionary as: "A tabular statement of time of projected operations, recurring events, arriving and departing trains, etc., a timetable." To plan a timetable or production schedule that will make it possible to complete all work on the book by a given date, the staff must first decide on the date it wants the book delivered.

Establishing Major Deadlines

Assume that the delivery date is set for May 21. The staff must determine how much time the last concern working on the book (the printing and binding company) will require to do its part of the work.

Suppose the printing contract specifies that final copy must be in the hands of the printer seven weeks before delivery of the book. Checking a calendar establishes the final deadline for copy as April 1. With this information, other major copy deadlines can be worked out with the printer.

Detailed Production Schedule

With major deadlines established, members of the staff can work out a detailed production schedule that will enable them to complete their part of the work on time.

Here is a production schedule used for a large college yearbook done by the offset method. The book contained 600 pages and 7,500 copies were printed. If the annual is to be printed by letterpress, a production schedule for engraving must be established.

Production Schedule —

Dummy of book to be completed by Sept. 1.

Photographic Schedule —

1. All major college events occurring after April 1 last year (the date when the last pictures were taken for the previous book) to be covered.
2. Campus views, faculty, and classroom pictures to be completed by Oct. 1.
3. All group pictures of organizations to be taken before Nov. 22.
4. The fee for all individual class pictures paid for and pictures taken before Nov. 1 to be $1.25.
5. All individual class pictures of students in school first semester must be taken before Nov. 22. If taken after Nov. 1, the charge is $1.50.
6. Class pictures of second-semester students not in school first semester must be taken by Feb. 15.
7. Pictures of all committees, athletic teams, plays, entertainments, parties, all-school events to be taken at earliest possible opportunity.
8. Final pictures (not more than 10) to be taken by March 28.

Cover Schedule —

1. Cover contract to be let and design ap-

proved by Dec. 15.
2. Exact number of covers wanted to be ordered by Feb. 15.

Printing Schedule —

1. 10% of the book (60 pages) to the printer by Nov. 22.
2. 15% of the book (total of 150 pages) to the printer by Dec. 15.
3. 10% of the book (total of 210 pages) to the printer by Jan. 15.
4. 15% of the book (total of 300 pages) to the printer by Feb. 1.
5. 10% of the book (total of 360 pages) to the printer by Feb. 15.
6. 15% of the book (total of 450 pages) to the printer by March 1.
7. 10% of the book (total of 510 pages) to the printer by March 15.
8. 15% of the book (total of 600 pages) to the printer by April 1.

Printing Schedule (Color Printing) —

1. Opening section (8-page signature) to the printer by Dec. 15.
2. Two division pages in color including all color pages for each form or multiple by Jan. 15.
3. Two division pages in color including all pages for each form or multiple by Feb. 15.

Delivery Date —

Finished book to be delivered May 21.

Implementing the Production Schedule

The most carefully worked out yearbook production schedule is worthless unless adhered to by the staff. If the yearbook is to come out on time, each operation on the timetable must be completed on schedule. This requires cooperation of every staff member, every person whose picture is to appear in the book, and the aid of each concern helping to produce the annual.

Here is how the above production schedule was implemented:

The editor, faculty adviser, and student photographer met once each week (after March 28 when last pictures for previous book were taken and 14 months before delivery date) to schedule and plan pictures to be taken of outstanding school events. Such events as school plays, senior sneak, assemblies, interfraternity sing, and commencement were photographed. Baseball, track, golf, tennis, and intramural sports were covered. This included getting action pictures of the contest, squad photographs, and individual shots of coaches and outstanding players. The all-school events during summer school were covered in the same manner.

The editor, with the advice of the faculty adviser and help of assistant editors, planned a page-by-page dummy of the book during the summer months. Preliminary sketches were made of the opening and division pages.

With the opening of school in the fall, section editors and office workers were appointed, and the big drive to get pictures of 162 organizations and all individual class photographs was started.

It had been decided to have panel pictures of individuals in fraternities, sororities, dormitories, and certain all-school honorary groups. Group pictures were to be made of all other organizations. A special price of $1.25 was made for all individual pictures taken before Nov. 1. The price after Nov. 1 was $1.50 per sitting. A letter was sent to the presidents of each fraternity, sorority, and dormitory explaining the plan and assigning a day on which all of their members were to go to the studio for individual pictures. Two prints of each individual were made, one for the organization panel, and the other for the class section. All pictures of individuals in fraternities, sororities, and dormitories were completed by Oct. 15.

Stories in School Newspaper

In the meantime, stories in the school newspaper explained the saving to be made if class pictures were taken before Nov. 1. As the deadline approached, advertisements were inserted in the paper. This publicity caused students who were not members of organizations to arrange for their class pictures. A total of more than 6,000 pictures was taken before the Nov. 22 deadline.

Getting Group Pictures

All group pictures of general organizations were taken before Nov. 22 at the college studio. The individual pictures were taken at a commercial studio.

The president of each organization that was to have a group picture in the annual was informed by letter Oct. 1 of the plan and requested to come to the yearbook office within 10 days to discuss the matter. Each organization paid for its picture and received a photo receipt to give to the photographer when the group was photographed. If the president of the organization failed to come to the yearbook office within 10 days after the letters were mailed, a second letter was sent to the treasurer of the organization. If this letter failed to get a response, the president or faculty adviser was called by phone and informed that his organization would have to be omitted from the book if immediate action was not taken to get a group picture made before the Nov. 22 deadline. A total of 198 group pictures was taken before the deadline. Some large organizations required several group pictures to accommodate all their members.

Pictures by Student Photographers

Action pictures, candid shots, and all other photographs not made in one of the studios were taken by student or commercial photographers. The weekly meetings of the editor, faculty adviser, photographic editor, and staff photographers, started the previous spring, were continued. Definite plans were made each week to cover all activities wanted for the annual. Pictures of the campus, fraternity houses, classrooms, committees, etc. were scheduled so pictures would be ready for the printer at the proper time. More than 2,000 pictures were taken and processed by staff photographers during the year.

Covers Ordered on Schedule

Photographic prints of the art work to be used in the opening pages of the book were sent to cover manufacturers who wished to bid on this work. Bids and sketches were submitted Dec. 15, and the contract for the covers was let the next day. The exact number of covers was ordered Feb. 15. This date was 15 days after the beginning of the second semester. It allowed time to check the number of students who paid the activity fee. The subscription to the annual is included in the activity fee paid by each student when he enrolls.

Special Plan for Deadlines on Printing

The printing contract provided for only four major copy deadlines as follows: Twenty-five per cent of the pages to printers Dec. 15; 25%, Feb. 1; 25%, March 1; and the final 25%, April 1. However, to provide ample time for proper editing of copy, the staff set up eight deadlines for copy as shown in the production schedule. Care was taken to establish deadlines that did not conflict with vacation and examination periods.

With the photographic schedule operating as

planned (in most cases), it was possible to make the layouts ahead of time and assign copy writing well in advance of each printing deadline. The pages devoted to spring sports and to other spring and summer school activities were finished and mailed late in October. The eight opening pages in four-color process were also delivered to the printer in Otcober. The color pictures used on these pages were taken during late spring or soon after school opened in the fall.

The first printing deadline, calling for 60 pages of copy to be delivered to the printer by Nov. 22, was imposed on the staff by their own choice. The actual agreement with the printer required that 25 per cent of the pages be in his plant by Dec. 15. However, the meeting of the first deadline taught the staff members how difficult it is to prepare a complete page of copy properly for the yearbook. It conditioned them for the many deadlines ahead. It also gave the editor and assistant editors a good measure of the ability of each staff member and how much responsibility he could handle.

Gathering Information About Organizations

Information forms had been sent to each organization soon after the organization's photography appointment, asking for specific information about the organization's activities, number of members, purpose, names of officers, etc. A careful check was made to determine if the organization forms had been satisfactorily completed and returned to the yearbook office.

All seniors were given activity cards to fill out and return at the time their pictures were taken. A story and an advertisement in the school paper reminded them that all cards were to be returned before Nov. 15 so the list of their organizations and activities could be included in senior write-ups.

Cutlines Typed in Advance

The staff had learned from their work in meeting the first deadline that one of the most time-consuming jobs was typing name identifications for organizations. Identification slips giving the name of each individual in all group pictures were filled out at the time each picture was taken and were delivered with the photographs by the studio. The identifications were typed in the proper style (with two carbon copies) as soon as received. They were carefully copyread and filed for use when the page was ready for the printers. Cutlines for all activity pictures were also written

as soon as possible after the final prints were received. This work, done in advance of the final preparation of each page, lightened the load when each deadline had to be met.

Incentives Offered for Early Pictures

It should be noted that the photography schedule worked out by the staff provided that the charge for individual pictures was $1.25 each before Nov. 1 and $1.50 each after that. This opportunity to save money got excellent results when called to the attention of students through advertisements in the paper.

The women's dormitories had individual pictures taken for their pages in the annual. To encourage each dormitory to get pictures of members taken for the book, members were offered an extra 15 minutes late leave, on a night of their choice, if 95 per cent of them had pictures taken, and 30 minutes late leave if 98 per cent had pictures taken. This plan was approved by the dean of women and received enthusiastic support at all dormitories.

Each yearbook staff should plan appropriate incentives to get pictures taken early. Many high schools have individual class pictures taken during the summer vacation.

Early Deadline Aids Staff

Perhaps the most important thing accomplished by the production schedule was the establishment of eight separate copy deadlines. This allowed the editors ample time to check all copy carefully, write headlines, and even have unsatisfactory copy rewritten. Any yearbook, however small, will be improved if several deadlines are established. By meeting the first deadline the staff will learn a lot of things that will enable them to improve the quality of their work on subsequent copy.

Need Staff Meeting Each Week

During the busy season the editor should schedule a staff meeting at least once each week. It should be at a time when all staff members can attend. The agenda should be planned carefully so definite assignments can be made. All previous assignments that are due also are turned in at the staff meeting.

It is especially important to get contact prints from student photographers each week and order enlargements promptly so too much time does not elapse between taking pictures and preparing page layouts and writing copy. It is necessary to establish definite times when the studios working on the annual are to deliver finished group and individual pictures, so the pictures are available when needed to meet printing deadlines.

Progress Chart Visualizes Work

A chart that will visualize how work is progressing on each page of the annual is used by most staffs. Figures 13.1 and 13.2 illustrate one type of progress chart furnished to the staff by one of the large companies specializing in printing yearbooks.

If a satisfactory chart of this type is not provided by your printer, you can use the one shown here or prepare one on light-weight drawing board that will meet your needs. The chart can be as large or as small as the staff desires. The name of each section editor and the pages for which he is responsible may be shown on this chart. If the chart is posted in the yearbook office, it will stimulate competition among section editors and other staff members to complete their sections ahead of schedule. Then, too, the editor or adviser can see by looking at the chart where production is lagging and direct the efforts of staff members to the job most urgent at the moment. Sometimes the chart will reveal that only one picture is needed to finish a section, or that if copy is written for one or two pages, a printing form can be completed. Examination of the chart may show the editor or adviser that the section editors, photographers, or printer may not be doing the assignments on schedule and that drastic action is necessary to insure delivery of the book on the date wanted.

Separate Folder for Each Two-page Spread

A separate file folder, large enough to accommodate a layout sheet, should be made for each two-page spread in the annual as soon as the dummy is completed. The page numbers are indicated on the tabs, and the folders filed in numerical order. All the material pertaining to the pages is kept in the proper folder. As soon as finished pictures are received, they can be placed in the proper folder and kept until all pictures for the two pages are completed. Three copies of the identification or cutline can be typed and filed in the folder. It is a good plan to keep the orginal identification sheet so the copy readers can have it for reference.

As soon as all pictures for the two-page spread are received, a finished layout is made in triplicate and final copy, headlines, and identifications are completed. Two copies are sent to the printer and one is kept in the file.

It usually is satisfactory to file several photographs in the regular page folder. However, if a page contains a class panel or an organization panel composed of many photographs, it is better to file the photographs in a small 4" by 5" file so they can be kept in the proper order. Then, too, there is danger that some of the photographs may be bent or broken if placed in a large folder, especially if the photographs are large.

The plan of having a folder for each two-page spread in the book will save the editor many hours of needless searching for a particular photograph, identification sheet, or printer's proof. If the file is kept in proper order, the assistant editors or faculty adviser can carry on the work of producing the annual in the absence of the editor.

Work Out Efficient Distribution System

The business manager can save himself and the students a lot of time if he will work out a complete and detailed system for distributing the annuals. This involves considerable planning and cannot be done at the last minute. Early in the year some of the details of the book distribution plan must begin to take form. To prepare a record of each individual transaction, the plan must be put into operation early in the production schedule.

Any plan used to distribute the books should include a written record whereby the subscriber acknowledges receipt of his copy when it is delivered. If a file card has been kept for all subscribers, it is easy to have the individual sign his own file card as he receives his book. This plan helps avoid the confusion and difficulty of having each subscriber produce a book sales receipt. Many yearbook staffs get an IBM card from the registrar for each student enrolled and use them to record payments for the annual and for other information needed in producing the book.

Here is how the card-file system of distribution has been used successfully by one college. The system made it possible for the staff to distribute more than 4,000 copies of the book to subscribers in one day.

Early in the year a card was filled out for each subscriber. The card provided a place to show that the subscription price had been paid and a space for the signature of the person receiving the book. The cards were kept in an alphabetical file

Progress Chart

This chart can help you keep watch on the progress of your yearbook. You will also find it useful in planning economical placement of color printing.

Using the Chart for Planning Color

Each rectangle printed below represents a page in your book. Each row across shows the pages printed on a single press sheet. The tinted pages are printed on one side of the sheet; the white pages are printed on the reverse side. When the press sheet is folded it makes a 16-page signature. The pages printed on each side of the press sheet make a multiple of 8 pages.

In planning color it is economical to use pages within a single 8-page multiple since all 8 pages are printed on a single press run. For instance, it costs considerably more to print color on pages 1 and 2 (since they fall in different multiples) than it would cost to print color on pages 1 and 4 or pages 2 and 3.

The heavier color down the center of the chart denotes "natural spreads" where pages are run on the press as they appear in the book, that is, side by side. If you plan to run a picture, especially one in process color, across a spread, these heavier tints show you the best place to do it.

Using the Chart to Keep Track of Progress

The suggestions here provide a simple system for maintaining a complete, readily available record of yearbook assignments and progress. Once a complete ladder diagram is built, the chart can be used as follows:

1. Enter the initials of the person responsible for each page or two-page spread.
2. When the layout is complete, use a diagonal mark.
3. When pictures and artwork are complete, make a diagonal halfway.
4. When the copy is complete, finish the second diagonal.
5. When the page has been double-checked, make a vertical mark.
6. When the page has been shipped, make a horizontal mark.

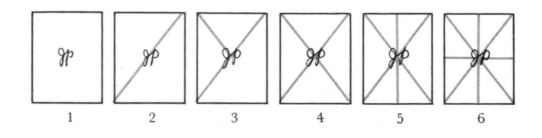

FIGURE 13.1. A progress chart kept up to date will show the editor at a glance the deadlines that must be met to assure delivery of the annual on schedule.

Our Job No. _____

Our Representative _____

Only by meeting copy due dates listed below can we be sure the publisher will ship our books on schedule, which is _____

	DEADLINE		DATE
1	Endsheet copy and specifications are also due on this date, along with a $2 deposit for each book ordered. After this date, we cannot change the number of books ordered, and changes in the number of pages are limited to plus or minus 8 pages.		
2	No changes in the number of pages in book can be made after this date.		
3			
FINAL	We must send a deposit of $2 per book with this shipment and return job stamp used to identify our copy. Red "Final Copy" sticker is to be attached to shipment.		

COLOR DUE DATES:

All color copy* for spring delivery books due: _____

All color copy* for summer delivery books due: _____

*Copy includes
PROCESS COLOR:
Transparencies, layouts, copy, photographs, and illustrations for a *complete 8-page multiple* where process color is used.

SPOT COLOR:
Layouts, copy, photographs, and illustrations for a *complete 8-page multiple* where spot color is used.

1	2	3	4	5	6	7	8	9	10	11	12	13	14	15	16
17	18	19	20	21	22	23	24	25	26	27	28	29	30	31	32
33	34	35	36	37	38	39	40	41	42	43	44	45	46	47	48
49	50	51	52	53	54	55	56	57	58	59	60	61	62	63	64
65	66	67	68	69	70	71	72	73	74	75	76	77	78	79	80
81	82	83	84	85	86	87	88	89	90	91	92	93	94	95	96
97	98	99	100	101	102	103	104	105	106	107	108	109	110	111	112
113	114	115	116	117	118	119	120	121	122	123	124	125	126	127	128
129	130	131	132	133	134	135	136	137	138	139	140	141	142	143	144
145	146	147	148	149	150	151	152	153	154	155	156	157	158	159	160
161	162	163	164	165	166	167	168	169	170	171	172	173	174	175	176
177	178	179	180	181	182	183	184	185	186	187	188	189	190	191	192
193	194	195	196	197	198	199	200	201	202	203	204	205	206	207	208
209	210	211	212	213	214	215	216	217	218	219	220	221	222	223	224
225	226	227	228	229	230	231	232	233	234	235	236	237	238	239	240
241	242	243	244	245	246	247	248	249	250	251	252	253	254	255	256
257	258	259	260	261	262	263	264	265	266	267	268	269	270	271	272
273	274	275	276	277	278	279	280	281	282	283	284	285	286	287	288
289	290	291	292	293	294	295	296	297	298	299	300	301	302	303	304
305	306	307	308	309	310	311	312	313	314	315	316	317	318	319	320
321	322	323	324	325	326	327	328	329	330	331	332	333	334	335	336
337	338	339	340	341	342	343	344	345	346	347	348	349	350	351	352
353	354	355	356	357	358	359	360	361	362	363	364	365	366	367	368
369	370	371	372	373	374	375	376	377	378	379	380	381	382	383	384
385	386	387	388	389	390	391	392	393	394	395	396	397	398	399	400

The numbers above represent the pages of a yearbook. All the numbers in each horizontal row make up one press sheet, or 16-page signature. The pages represented by numbers on tinted background are printed on one side of the sheet; those represented by numbers on plain background are printed on the other side. All the tinted or non-tinted numbers in a horizontal row make up one 8-page multiple.

Example: Pages 1, 4, 5, 8, 9, 12, 13, 16 print on one side of a press sheet and make up one 8-page multiple.

Facing pages are simply those which face one another in the book such as 2 and 3, 18 and 19, etc.

The best way to submit facing pages is in a sequence within a 16-page signature. For example, pages 2 and 3, pages 6 and 7, pages 10 and 11, and pages 14 and 15.

PROOFS require additional production time. They will not be submitted unless requested before first deadline.

DELAYS in submitting copy or returning proofs to the Company may cause delays in shipment of yearbook.

and divided into three groups so books could be delivered simultaneously from three separate points.

Be careful about allowing copies to be given out in advance. Staff members, naturally, will have an opportunity to look through the book before distribution begins, but it sometimes causes resentment if other persons obtain their copies in advance. Generally, it is best to make no advance copies available except to staff members, if for no other reason than that a person who sees the book elsewhere may delay several days in calling for his personal copy.

If proper publicity is given to the distribution plan and arrangements made so that students will not have to wait long, most of the books can be delivered in one day. Staff members will then be free to attend to details of closing the book's affairs.

Under the card-file plan, two staff members can work together in handling the mechanics of distribution. One worker looks up the card of the subscriber. The second person takes the file card, has the subscriber sign his name in the proper place, and then gives him a copy of the annual. Thus, the card-file plan provides a written record showing that the annual has been delivered to its owner.

Most Annuals Delivered in Spring

Most yearbooks are delivered to subscribers just before or during graduation week. This is the traditional time, and the distribution of the books becomes part of the commencement festivities. The chief drawback to this plan is that the staff cannot include all the activities for the current

FIGURE 13.2. This chart, posted in the office and kept up to date, shows each member of the staff the progress he is making on his section of the annual.

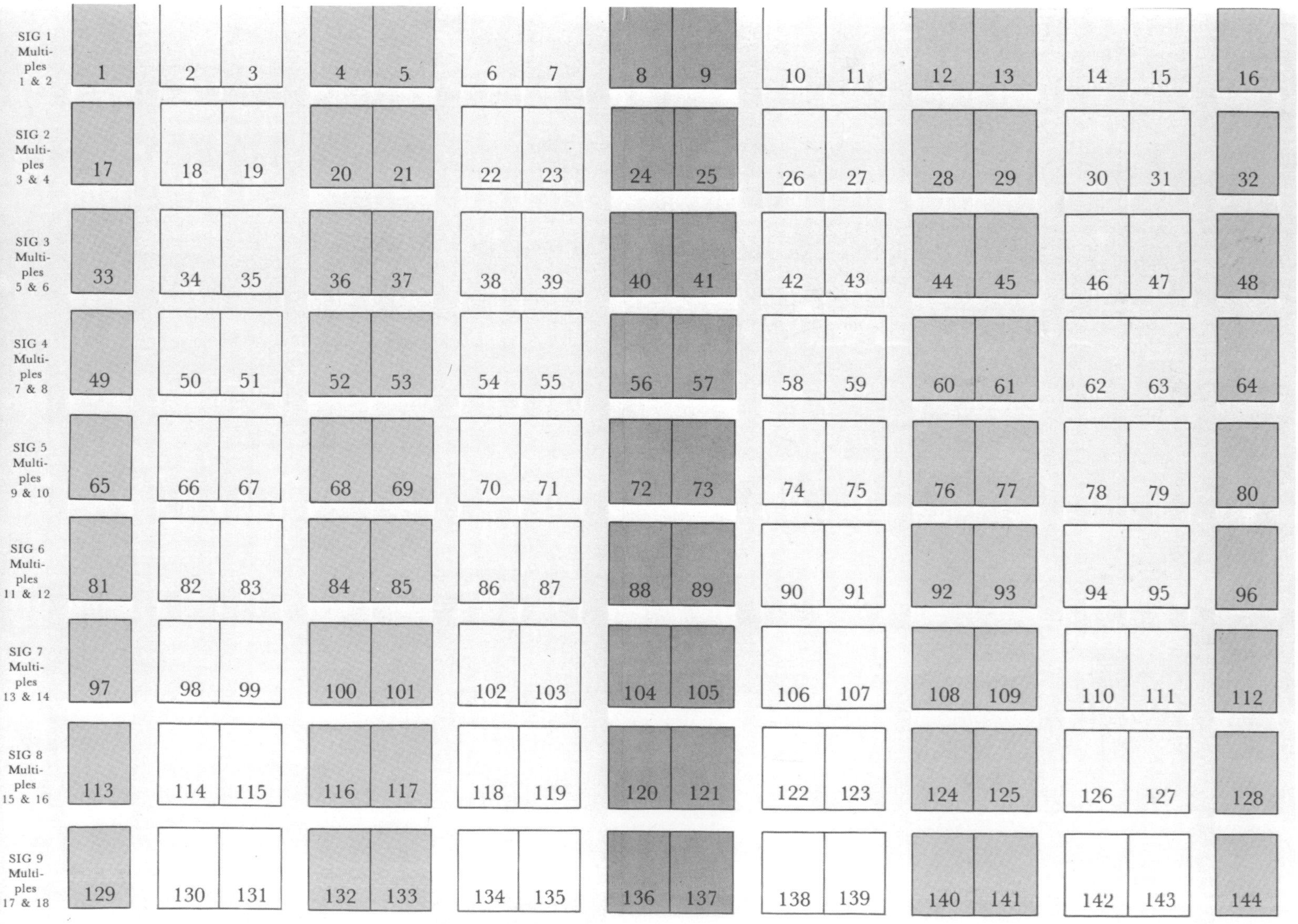

academic year. A few annual staffs have adopted a plan of printing one additional signature of 4, 8, 16, or 32 pages covering commencement and other late activities. These pages are printed after school is out and mailed to all subscribers during the summer. This section, of course, cannot be bound into the book, but in some instances a double-faced Scotch tape is used to fasten the supplement to the back page or end sheet. Activities covered in this manner do not appear in the proper sequence in the book. To illustrate: baseball, and other spring sports would not appear in the sports section. Most staffs, however, try to cover events from the time the previous annual ceased taking pictures until press time of their own book. Thus, one full year of school activities is represented.

Fall Delivery of Annuals

During recent years many schools have adopted the policy of delivering the annual to subscribers during the summer or at the opening of school in the fall. This plan has the advantage of permitting the staff to cover all the events for one academic year. Also, some printers have quoted lower prices for yearbook work done during summer months.

One of the chief disadvantages of fall delivery is the feeling of most students that the book should be delivered at the traditional commencement time. The book tells of students' accomplishments during the year at a time that seems more appropriate.

If late summer or fall delivery of the annual is planned, the staff will want to consider carefully the added cost for wrapping, addressing, and mailing books. This is a large item for a college or university annual. The plan would be less expensive for a high school as most students live in the community and can pick up their books at the school the day the books are distributed.

Another thing to consider is that the staff will have to be on the job part of the time during summer months to edit copy, read proof, collect for advertising and other outstanding accounts, and address, wrap, and mail books. This is a difficult assignment. Most staff members have summer jobs or feel they should have a vacation.

Outline Work for New Staff

One of the greatest contributions an outgoing annual staff can make to its successor is to leave a detailed production schedule. Each outgoing staff member, including the faculty adviser, ought to make an outline of the work his job entails and exactly when the work should begin, how it should be done, and when it must be completed to fit into the over-all production schedule.

Much emphasis has been placed on the importance of getting the work on the annual done as early in the year as possible. Perhaps a warning should be added here. It is possible to get the work done and to the printers so early that only one-third or one-half of the activities of the year are covered.

The staff must remember that its first obligation is to its readers and it should use all its ability and ingenuity to work out a production schedule that makes it possible for photographers, writers, printers, and others to finish work on schedule, but that, at the same time, provides an opportunity for each student to get his picture in the book and to receive an annual that tells as much of the story of the year as is humanly possible under the circumstances.

The production schedule printed in this chapter shows how pictures of second-semester students can be included in the annual. It also reveals the possibilities for getting pictures of late events and writing copy to help complete the story of the year.

An accurate and attainable budget, properly prepared and implemented, can do much to assure the financial success of an annual. It outlines the work for the business staff as well as pointing out the most important sources of income.

Chapter 14

Budgeting and Controlling Finances

BEFORE MANY PICTURES are taken or a line of copy is written for the annual, the first and most important step is to establish a complete and attainable budget. The financial success of the yearbook depends on how carefully and completely all items of income and expense are budgeted.

Definition of a Budget

In a broad sense, a budget includes all costs of operation as well as all sources of income. It takes into consideration how much money will be earned from all business ventures, such as sale of the books, advertising, sale of space to organizations, appropriations from the school, and various miscellaneous sources.

A budget also accounts for all items of expense, from the largest to the smallest, including the cost for covers, binding, printing, photography, and miscellaneous expenditures such as office supplies, postage, and freight.

When the budget is being drawn up, the business manager must work closely with the editor and the faculty adviser. After all, the editor's plans for the entire annual are based on the money taken in by the business staff. In short, the

business manager is the "earner," and the editor is the "spender." The two cannot be separated. The editor must plan the book to stay within the amount budgeted. The business manager is obligated to do his utmost to raise sufficient funds to cover the expenditures set up in the budget.

A conservative attitude should be taken in planning the cost. Every editor takes over the reins with high ambitions. He wants to give the students the best book in history. And that, of course, means more color work, more pages, and more campus scenes than ever before. But in cases where the income is limited, it is best to plan a book not too involved and expensive. It is much easier to add more pages or color work later in the year than to cut down on the size of the book at the last minute because disbursements have been higher than originally planned or income lower.

Where To Get Budget Information

The most reliable source for budget information should be available in your school if an annual has been published previously. Check the records carefully to find all sources of income for

the past three or four years. Also, all items of expense should be noted, as well as the total amount spent.

If such records are not available, or are incomplete, information from schools of comparable size should be obtained. High schools with membership in the National Scholastic Press Association can get information from the study it makes of budgets of annuals entered in its critical service. The Associated Collegiate Press makes a similar report on finances of college yearbooks entered in its critical service.

Studies of the finances of 1,031 high school annuals published in 1964 and 227 college yearbooks published in 1963 are reported here with permission of NSPA and ACP. Reference to these

two reports, Tables 14.1 to 14.7 inclusive, is made from time to time in this chapter. It should be remembered, however, that the costs of producing yearbooks, as well as methods of financing them, change from year to year and you should be alert to get the latest reliable information available.

Estimate for Income First

The first step in preparing a budget is to list all sources of income and the amount of money that can be expected from each source. A study of the two surveys mentioned above reveals that the primary sources of income, listed in order of importance, are:

1. Sale of yearbook subscriptions
2. Sale of advertising space

TABLE 14.1
HIGH SCHOOL YEARBOOK PRODUCTION COSTS*

Enrollment Group	No. Usable Reports	Cost Per Group				Cost Per Book		Cost Per Page		
		High	Low	Group Total	Average	High	Low	High	Low	Average
3000 plus	23	$18,700	$6,681	$ 258,555	$11,241	$ 7.77	$2.37	$69	$33	$47
3000–2401	38	13,600	3,521	245,981	9,104	8.02	3.11	64	32	39
2400–2201	33	14,000	5,506	289,926	8,785	9.98	3.18	70	20	35
2200–2001	33	14,892	4,872	286,346	8,677	10.00	3.81	55	19	35
Subtotal	127			$1,180,808	9,297					38
2000–1901	34	14,940	5,800	294,421	8,659	7.81	3.70	51	19	38
1900–1801	20	18,250	4,268	176,457	8,822	6.73	3.25	66	27	37
1800–1701	34	15,200	4,438	294,408	8,659	8.45	4.25	59	19	34
1700–1601	31	12,680	5,400	247,608	7,989	9.00	4.27	68	20	35
1600–1501	26	12,000	4,011	202,947	7,806	10.91	3.50	68	20	36
Subtotal	145			1,215,868	8,247					36
1500–1401	29	11,404	4,620	221,947	7,653	9.50	3.70	52	20	36
1400–1301	33	15,343	3,341	226,463	6,862	11.00	3.08	61	18	34
1300–1201	39	10,803	2,992	214,835	5,508	10.75	3.08	72	17	29
1200–1101	36	10,139	2,839	213,119	5,919	12.21	2.94	58	22	33
1100–1001	31	10,197	2,539	180,292	5,815	10.75	4.00	58	13	31
Subtotal	168			1,056,656	6,289					32
1000–901	31	10,289	2,893	160,525	5,178	11.80	3.72	46	16	29
900–801	41	12,300	2,520	202,565	4,940	11.18	3.49	50	21	31
800–701	46	7,855	2,135	229,659	4,992	11.32	3.16	43	19	32
700–601	44	7,059	1,725	172,528	3,921	10.40	3.90	44	15	27
600–501	54	9,421	2,250	216,555	4,010	11.30	4.02	40	19	27
Subtotal	216			981,832	4,545					26
500–401	55	9,400	1,694	213,658	3,884	15.05	3.62	35	17	27
400–301 (A & B)	47	9,485	1,384	169,847	3,613	17.20	4.32	34	14	26
300–201 (A & B)	51	7,000	818	137,531	2,696	15.75	3.18	32	12	23
200–101 (A & B)	53	5,204	675	117,287	2,212	18.40	3.72	42	11	21
100 less	8	3,691	878	15,807	1,975	22.94	5.74	35	11	19
Subtotal	214			654,130	3,076					24
Reg. C.S. TOTAL	870			$5,089,294	$ 5,849					$32
LATE ENTRIES All Enrollments										
All-American	12	10,500	1,871	68,095	5,974	11.08	3.70	43	• 15	31
First Class	57	14,678	1,395	271,616	4,765	10.80	4.09	54	12	22
Second Class	67	13,800	829	270,202	4,032	12.88	4.11	56	9	23
Third & Fourth Class	25	10,903	732	58,278	3,611	12.51	2.93	52	11	25
Subtotal	161			698,191	4,336					23
GRAND TOTAL	1,031			$5,787,485	$ 5,613					$31

*This survey report is based on a study of the information given on the entry blanks for 1,031 of the 1,078 high school yearbooks which were entered in the 1964 All-American Critical Service conducted by the National Scholastic Press Association, University of Minnesota, Minneapolis.

TABLE 14.2
HIGH SCHOOL YEARBOOK SIZE AND COST TO BUYER *

Enrollment Group	No. Usable Reports	No. Pages				Selling Price Per Book	
		High	Low	Group Total	Average	High	Low
3000 plus	23	352	144	5,489	238	$ 6.00	$3.25
3000–2401	38	352	132	8,758	230	7.50	3.00
2400–2201	33	352	168	8,381	254	6.00	3.00
2200–2001	33	456	152	7,994	242	6.00	3.00
Subtotal	127			30,622	241		
2000–1901	34	328	128	7,607	223	6.00	3.00
1900–1801	20	352	136	4,583	229	7.00	3.00
1800–1701	34	376	120	7,772	225	6.00	3.50
1700–1601	31	324	136	6,936	223	6.00	3.00
1600–1501	26	367	132	5,636	216	6.00	3.00
Subtotal	145			32,534	224		
1500–1401	29	392	128	6,123	211	6.00	3.25
1400–1301	33	384	128	6,661	201	7.00	3.00
1300–1201	39	328	128	7,557	188	6.50	3.00
1200–1101	36	246	100	6,404	177	7.50	3.00
1100–1001	31	256	96	5,684	183	6.00	3.00
Subtotal	168			32,229	191		
1000–901	31	352	108	5,501	174	6.50	3.00
900–801	41	245	92	6,453	157	6.00	2.75
800–701	46	272	80	7,117	154	6.00	3.00
700–601	44	219	80	6,324	143	6.00	3.00
600–501	54	208	84	8,005	148	8.50	3.50
Subtotal	216			33,400	156		
500–401	55	324	78	8,107	147	12.50	1.75
400–301 (A & B)	47	288	80	6,403	138	8.00	3.50
300–201 (A & B)	51	196	64	5,750	116	12.00	3.00
200–101 (A & B)	53	208	60	5,599	105	10.00	3.00
100 less	8	154	56	796	99	12.00	3.00
Subtotal	214			26,855	125		
Reg. C.S. TOTAL	870			155,640	178		
LATE ENTRIES All Enrollments							
All-American	12	296	96	2,279	189	6.00	2.75
First Class	57	384	76	12,336	216	15.00	3.00
Second Class	67	296	56	11,390	170	15.00	3.00
Third & Fourth Class	25	216	56	3,603	144	8.40	3.00
Subtotal	161			29,638	184		
GRAND TOTAL	1,031			185,278	179		

*This survey report is based on a study of the information given on the entry blanks for 1,031 of the 1,078 high school yearbooks which were entered in the 1964 All-American Critical Service conducted by the National Scholastic Press Association.

3. Sale of space to organizations
4. Sale of pictures to students
5. Miscellaneous.

In listing sources of income above, money received from activity fees is considered as subscription money. The survey of college yearbooks reveals that the activity fee is the largest source of income. However, most yearbook staffs treat this income as subscription money. In some cases the payment of the fees entitles the student to one copy of the annual at no further cost. The activity fee received by high school annuals is not very great—about 15 per cent according to Table 14.6.

Sale of Books Important

In considering the various business projects to undertake, the staff must carefully weigh each opportunity. For example, the sale of books, in most cases, is the biggest and most uncertain source of income. Here is the place to put forth the greatest effort, for financal success or failure is determined to a large extent by the number of books sold. Having the total price of the yearbook included in the activity fee docs away with that great uncertainty.

It is often difficult to estimate accurately the number of annuals that will be sold, but experiences of preceding staffs are excellent guides. The year-to-year size of the student body might be used as a yardstick in estimating the number of annuals to order, although this method is not always reliable. If the size of the school remains relatively the same, the staff should not expect much increase in sales over the previous year. Likewise, anticipated increase in enrollment does not always mean a greater demand for the book.

Another important factor to be considered is the price of the annual. Is the price of the book too high, thus limiting the number of students who can purchase yearbooks? On the other hand, is the price so low that it will not support a large share of the expenditures, or will necessitate an annual of poor quality? In establishing the price, the financial condition of the students must be taken into account. What are their reactions to the annual? Do they feel they are getting their

money's worth? These are only a few of the questions that should be asked by the yearbook staff in setting a fair price for the book. You can get useful information on the selling price for high school annuals, in schools with comparable enrollment, by studying Table 14.2.

Study Advertising Rate

Another item to be weighed carefully is the advertising rate. Is the rate too high, thus eliminating a number of advertisers who would buy space if they thought the rates were more reasonable? Or more likely, is the price charged for advertising too low, and, if so, can it be raised?

TABLE 14.3

High School Yearbook Income from Sales and Miscellaneous Sources*

| Enrollment Group | No. Usable Reports | Sales Income | | | | Miscellaneous Income | | | |
| | | Amount | | % Buyers | | No. Using | Amount | | |
		High	Low	High	Low		High	Low	Average
3000 plus	23	$13,754	$5,650	90	37	11	$2,400	$ 80	$1,236
3000–2401	38	13,000	1,800	94	30	21	2,750	56	708
2400–2201	33	10,200	1,233	89	15	18	2,557	110	718
2200–2001	33	14,000	4,972	98	33	23	1,803	150	591
Subtotal	127					73			754
2000–1901	34	10,507	4,724	97	49	24	1,450	51	761
1900–1801	20	10,139	4,616	87	65	10	1,120	46	240
1800–1701	34	10,611	4,298	95	38	21	1,483	25	666
1700–1601	31	7,575	3,231	95	50	18	1,178	151	735
1600–1501	26	9,000	3,000	92	52	12	3,200	100	828
Subtotal	145					85			680
1500–1401	29	8,200	2,216	95	50	19	1,014	50	461
1400–1301	33	9,110	3,258	95	54	20	4,493	50	884
1300–1201	39	7,472	2,800	99	50	19	5,982	40	713
1200–1101	36	6,425	2,000	95	31	17	680	22	284
1100–1001	31	7,026	1,732	95	25	16	4,389	43	760
Subtotal	168					91			615
1000–901	31	5,523	2,722	95	40	12	2,000	120	777
900–801	41	6,259	2,115	96	50	17	2,870	50	878
800–701	46	6,481	2,100	96	25	24	1,700	45	394
700–601	44	7,059	1,725	97	46	28	2,100	36	344
600–501	54	5,178	1,700	95	31	28	2,812	20	492
Subtotal	216					109			529
500–401	55	7,250	918	98	52	34	2,100	15	540
400–301 (A & B)	47	3,000	804	98	45	30	1,807	14	540
300–201 (A & B)	51	3,000	470	99	49	23	1,055	3	260
200–101 (A & B)	53	2,550	236	98	26	19	855	15	307
100 less	8	1,104	400	100	47	2	518	235	335
Subtotal	214					108			451
Reg. C.S. TOTAL	870					466			
LATE ENTRIES All Enrollments									
All-American	12	8,662	927	105	45	9	1,400	30	382
First Class	57	9,302	630	100	33	33	1,849	30	379
Second Class	67	7,500	562	100	33	34	2,625	30	570
Third & Fourth Class	25	13,526	735	100	30	12	1,078	25	355
Subtotal	161					88			427
GRAND TOTAL	1,031					554 (53%)			$ 570

*This survey report is based on a study of the information given on the entry blanks for 1,031 of the 1,078 high school yearbooks which were entered in the 1964 All-American Critical Service conducted by the National Scholastic Press Association.

Find out from the firm that will print the yearbook or from previous contracts how much it will cost to print a page—and sell the space at a good margin. It definitely is not worthwhile to sell advertising in the book if it is not profitable. For example, if it costs $30 to print one page, advertising revenue for that page should be at least $60. In other words, the money received from a page of advertising should pay for that page plus an additional one in the yearbook. Here again you can get needed information by examining Table 14.4.

However, the business staff must proceed cautiously when it considers raising rates. Too many businessmen consider yearbook advertising nothing but a donation and will refuse to pay any more than is absolutely necessary. The business staff can help the situation somewhat by staging advertising stunts throughout the year to convince the advertiser he is getting something worthwhile. This is discussed more fully in the next chapter.

A similar investigation should be conducted regarding the sale of space to organizations. How do they feel about paying for space in the yearbook? Is it possible to sell to organizations that have not purchased in the past? Can more space be sold to groups that buy a small space each year?

If the book is not already subsidized by the school board, it might be possible to charge the

TABLE 14.4

HIGH SCHOOL YEARBOOK INCOME FROM ADVERTISING*

Enrollment Group	No. Usable Reports	Advertising						Patron Plan		
		No. Using	Amount		Page Charge			No. Using	Amount	
			High	Low	High	Low	Average		High	Low
3000 plus	23	11	$2,590	$641	$100	$60	$52	1	$ 250	..
3000–2401	38	21	2,000	563	100	40	56	1	820	..
2400–2201	33	19	3,088	385	100	50	65	1	1,532	..
2200–2001	33	23	3,600	500	100	35†	62	3	764	$ 75
Subtotal	127	74					59	6		
2000–1901	34	25	7,150	180	100	30†	54	8	1,478	500
1900–1801	20	16	3,575	200	120	35†	63	3	275	20
1800–1701	34	25	4,085	250	100	30†	66	7	9,202	10
1700–1601	31	25	2,900	310	120	30	54	7	900	39
1600–1501	26	17	2,801	200	210	30†	57	5	966	48
Subtotal	145	108					58	30		
1500–1401	29	17	3,084	144	100	27†	55	6	940	30
1400–1301	33	25	4,383	372	100	40†	53	12	875	50
1300–1201	39	27	2,890	365	100	40†	48	9	3,200	150
1200–1101	36	22	5,195	450	100	40	51	11	7,000	86
1100–1001	31	21	2,800	650	100	35	54	7	7,100	176
Subtotal	168	112					51	45		
1000–901	31	24	4,000	90	200	25	55	15	3,000	69
900–801	41	30	5,132	184	100	30	41	19	2,940	70
800–701	46	37	4,761	100	120	30	45	13	6,481	15
700–601	44	30	2,395	300	200	30	40	28	2,150	18
600–501	54	51	3,000	100	100	30	41	24	4,200	18
Subtotal	216	172					43	99		
500–401	55	43	4,000	600	200	30	43	26	6,400	60
400–301 (A & B)	47	40	8,200	400	100	25	44	23	6,000	30
300–201 (A & B)	51	44	4,500	400	160	30	42	26	3,588	30
200–101 (A & B)	53	47	8,000	124	100	20	36	36	6,059	30
100 less	8	8	3,052	501	100	30	53	4	400	294
Subtotal	214	182					43	115		
Reg. C.S. TOTAL	870	648						295		
LATE ENTRIES All Enrollments										
All-American	12	10	3,668	693	100	37	64	5	1,115	73
First Class	57	36	4,000	783	125	25	58	18	1,850	90
Second Class	67	60	1,300	180	100	25	46	34	2,210	50
Third & Fourth Class	25	21	1,840	290	120	25	55	11	1,500	27
Subtotal	161	127					50	68		
GRAND TOTAL	1,031	775 (75%)					$47	363 (35%)		

*This survey report is based on a study of the information given on the entry blanks for 1,031 of the 1,078 high school yearbooks which were entered in the 1964 All-American Critical Service conducted by the National Scholastic Press Association.
†These rates lower than the production cost per page in respective books.

TABLE 14.5

HIGH SCHOOL YEARBOOK INCOME FROM ORGANIZATIONS AND INDIVIDUAL PICTURES*

Enrollment Group	No. Usable Reports	Organizations					Individual Pictures		
		No. Using	Amount		Page Charge		No. Using	Amount	
			High	Low	High	Low		High	Low
3000 plus	23	12	$1,660	$500	$25	$20	11	$4,062	$ 80
3000–2401	38	17	1,030	160	50	10	18	1,542	50
2400–2201	33	15	1,599	185	25	10	16	2,000	25
2200–2001	33	20	1,930	50	25	10	11	2,017	10
Subtotal	127	64					56		
2000–1901	34	18	2,240	100	30	2.50	19	2,236	120
1900–1801	20	8	1,136	107	40	12	7	2,058	272
1800–1701	34	18	2,525	47	25	13	17	4,065	40
1700–1601	31	16	2,653	300	30	8	14	2,196	151
1600–1501	26	12	1,900	300	40	12	12	2,481	182
Subtotal	145	72					69		
1500–1401	29	13	2,485	183	40	10	17	2,503	100
1400–1301	33	14	5,000	130	40	13	17	1,192	100
1300–1201	39	14	1,200	60	45	10	21	5,782	40
1200–1101	36	17	1,245	116	30	10	11	2,523	50
1100–1001	31	7	1,140	70	45	7	6	1,330	220
Subtotal	168	65					72		
1000–901	31	11	1,000	50	50	5	13	3,261	15
900–801	41	17	1,100	38	45	13	9	1,500	50
800–701	46	18	1,145	115	20	8	21	2,100	45
700–601	44	15	1,405	200	25	5	13	2,444	35
600–501	54	21	1,295	50	20	2.50	26	1,704	80
Subtotal	216	82					82		
500–401	58	15	608	30	25	7.50	18	636	60
400–301 (A & B)	47	11	1,000	94	15	12	8	714	25
300–201 (A & B)	51	9	580	120	25	8.75	14	400	13
200–101 (A & B)	53	6	1,049	50	15	10	7	387	20
100 less	8	0	..	..	..	..	0	..	..
Subtotal	214	41					47		
Reg. C.S. TOTAL	870	324					326		
LATE ENTRIES All Enrollments									
All-American	12	5	1,000	77	20	8	5	1,101	128
First Class	57	17	1,176	75	25	10	21	2,250	10
Second Class	67	19	2,000	250	28	15	23	7,143	10
Third & Fourth Class	25	4	513	50	25	10	11	980	10
Subtotal	161	45					60		
GRAND TOTAL	1,031	369 (35%)					386 (37%)		

*This survey report is based on a study of the information given on the entry blanks for 1,031 of the 1,078 high school yearbooks which were entered in the 1964 All-American Critical Service conducted by the National Scholastic Press Association.

board for the pages devoted to work of the school. A large number of pages is devoted in every annual to the athletic department. Should they pay for this space? There is little limitation to the possible sources of income, and all such potential sources should be canvassed carefully.

Estimating Expenditures

As in the case of estimating income, the school records will prove invaluable in figuring the expense side of the budget. Extreme caution should be used in allocating the anticipated income. It is easy to spend money, but spending it wisely is something else. The old saying, "A fool and his money are soon parted," holds especially true in publishing a yearbook.

Get Estimate of Printing Cost

An accurate estimate of the printing costs can be obtained by giving the printer a complete set of specifications as outlined in a previous chapter. If only the printing and binding are to be done by the concern, then the covers will have to be figured separately. If the annual is to be printed by letterpress, you will also need to get a bid for making the engravings.

In addition, have the printer calculate the cost for additional pages and more books. Deductions for fewer pages and fewer books also should be obtained. If the printing concern is in another city, an expense item must be set up in the budget for mailing copy and proofs and freight charges for shipping the books.

Cost of Pictures Important Item

Since the yearbook is essentially a "picture book," the cost for taking photographs, developing negatives, and printing finished pictures is an important expenditure. The trend in all yearbooks has been toward more complete pictorial coverage, thus, costs of this item have increased greatly.

Photographs and feature pictures to be paid for from yearbook funds should be accounted for in the budget. These usually include views, classroom and laboratory pictures, news or action pictures of all big school events, and action pictures of all sports, plays, and rallies. In some high schools, many good "candid" shots of activities and students will be donated to the yearbook staff by camera owners. This helps cut down expenses, but the main objection is that these photographs are usually made by amateurs and the quality of the pictures is often poor. Pictures that detract from the book should not be used. The cost of getting good color pictures should not be forgotten.

Individual and group pictures, if paid for directly to the yearbook by the person or organization having the picture taken, are figured on both sides of the budget. Money received for these pictures should be entered as income and, at the same time, the cost for taking the photographs, developing, and printing them should be entered as an item of expense.

TABLE 14.6

HIGH SCHOOL YEARBOOK INCOME FROM ACTIVITY FEES*

Enrollment Group	No. Usable Reports	Total No. Using	Voluntary							Compulsory				
			No. Books	Amount High	Amount Low	Card Cost High	Card Cost Low	% Buyers High	% Buyers Low	No. Books	Amount High	Amount Low	Card Cost High	Card Cost Low
3000 plus	23	6	4	$15,000	$1,500	$ 6.00	$4.00	95	58	2	$12,840	$1,500	$ 50.00	$ 9.75
3000–2401	38	8	6	13,725	3,900	10.00	7.00	95	80	2	10,692	3,969	14.00	12.75
2400–2201	33	7	7	9,470	1,409	10.00	6.00	94	71	0	..	..	..	..
2200–2001	33	4	3	7,570	3,500	10.00	5.00	75	47	1	9,225	..	9.75	..
Subtotal	127	25	20							5				
2000–1901	34	9	7	8,762	1,910	10.00	5.00	92	50	2	9,417	5,925	18.00	8.00
1900–1801	20	6	6	9,330	200	10.00	5.00	80	54	0				
1800–1701	34	7	7	8,484	793	10.00	5.00	90	38	0				
1700–1601	31	5	5	4,000	1,930	7.50	3.75	94	70	0				
1600–1501	26	6	5	5,140	250	13.00	5.00	75	65	1	10,750	..	5.00	..
Subtotal	145	33	30							3				
1500–1401	29	4	4	7,250	225	12.00	3.00	92	75	0				
1400–1301	33	1	1	3,195	..	7.00	..	80	..	0	..	..	..	..
1300–1201	39	2	2	2,110	1,601	7.00	6.60	83	82	0	..	..	..	..
1200–1101	36	10	5	2,937	364	9.00	5.00	80	42	5	10,954	5,124	30.00	5.00
1100–1001	31	7	6	3,150	572	9.00	3.00	95	60	1	10.00 per student			
Subtotal	168	24	18							6				
1000–901	31	5	5	6,783	232	8.00	4.00	95	25	0				
900–801	41	6	2	2,128	1,000	7.00	4.50	82	77	4	5,700	3,380	20.00	10.00
800–701	46	5	3	3,650	2,137	10.00	3.00	95	70	2	9,000	5,250	25.00	..
700–601	44	4	3	3,236	800	25.00	8.00	91	88	1	4,450	..	..	..
600–501	54	7	4	2,726	1,888	8.00	7.00	89	75	3	2,727	2,000	15.00	5.00
Subtotal	216	27	17							10				
500–401	58	3	1	3,000	..	12.00	..	83	..	2	..	600	12.00	10.00
400–301 (A & B)	47	11	5	1,080	670	10.00	3.00	93	73	6	6,762	1,530	30.00	4.00
300–201 (A & B)	51	9	2	1,800	165	15.00	5.00	95	90	7	3,000	900	100.00	7.00
200–101 (A & B)	53	7	1	1,356	..	35.00	..	47	..	6	3,200	860	40.00	4.00
100 less	8	2	0	..	..	..	..	..		2	1,900	298	..	..
Subtotal	214	32	9							23				
Reg. C.S. TOTAL	870	141	94							47				
LATE ENTRIES All Enrollments														
All-American	12	0												
First Class	57	10	7	8,422	1,775	12.50	6.50	85	74	3	4,800	3,265	10.00	7.00
Second Class	67	12	5	8,910	1,038	18.00	5.00	100	80	7	8,500	900	25.00	8.00
Third & Fourth Class	25	0	0											
Subtotal	161	22	12							10				
GRAND TOTAL	1,031	163 (15%)	106							57				

*This survey is based on a study of the information given on the entry blanks for 1,031 of the 1,078 high school yearbooks which were entered in the 1964 All-American Critical Service conducted by the National Scholastic Press Association.

TABLE 14.7

TYPICAL BUDGETS FOR COLLEGE YEARBOOKS

School Enrollment	Income							Expenditures						
	Book Sales	Ads	Activity Fees	Organizations	Photos	Misc.	Total	Printing and Paper	Covers	Engraving	Art Work	Photos	Office	Total
10,000 plus High: $58,752	$25,030			$11,700	$4,060	$ 90	$40,880	$21,714	$2,261	$8,663		$2,330	$5,375	$40,343
Low: $7,706 Average: $40,000		$1,500	$37,341	3,500			42,341	30,000	4,500			1,500		40,000
10,000–7001 High: $58,846	17,658	2,756		9,170	6,449		36,033	19,756	1,606	2,620		4,479	508	34,400
Low: $12,200 Average: $34,000	158	1,112	21,275	6,789	3,400		32,735	22,546	3,326			3,167	906	31,289
7000–4001 High: $45,297	22,000			500	1,500	1,000	25,000	18,000				6,000	200	24,500
Low: $7,500 Average: $25,000	130	410	27,022			1,500	29,062	27,500				632	285	29,062
4000–2501 High: $24,000	16,500			1,620	1,525		19,795	14,180				3,894		18,226
Low: $5,532 Average: $18,000		2,621	11,260	895	4,882	150	19,868	12,223	320	265		4,810	1,440	19,411
2500–2001 High: $26,700	10,362	1,143		2,094			13,599	7,576	1,176	3,113		500	770	13,564
Low: $6,950 Average: $14,000	11,700	1,980		2,960			16,640	11,800	935			1,100	1,370	15,606
2000–1501 High: $27,324	2,400	1,000	6,900	1,000			11,300	9,000				1,500	500	11,300
Low: $7,211 Average: $10,000			10,000			338	10,338	8,400				1,345	74	10,063
1500–1001 High: $15,079		1,335	7,617	705		458	10,116	7,024	804			1,471		9,229
Low: $6,015 Average: $9,000	900	2,650	4,400	2,535		50	10,485	7,950	325			600	25	9,105
1000–751 High: $11,232	900	2,395	3,013	275	100		6,683	4,800				1,000	75	6,679
Low: $3,771 Average: $6,700		400	6,842				7,292	5,698				406	115	7,140
750–501 High: $22,500	20	2,200	4,200				6,420	5,500				700	150	6,350
Low: $3,775 Average: $6,500	384	3,287	3,451			170	7,293	5,377			3	1,235	27	6,744
500 less High: $9,729			4,545				4,545	2,478				1,300	500	4,278
Low: $2,600 Average: $4,200	2,254	650		600		790	4,294	3,838				85	55	4,188
Junior College High: $13,135	4,875	805					5,680	3,290	317		29	815		4,693
Low: $1,050 Average: $4,600	2,640	1,800			440		4,880	3,380				1,000		4,680

The various miscellaneous expenses must be estimated carefully, also. Although each item in this category might be small, together they are relatively important and necessary. They include such items as office supplies, receipt books, advertising contracts, postage, freight, photography supplies, office equipment, and, on the larger college yearbooks, salaries for staff members.

Example of a Budget

Here is an example of a budget for an average high school. The figures are, of course, theoretical, and should not be interpreted to mean that this budget will apply to any school.

```
Estimated Income:
  1,000 books at $5.00  . . . . . . .  $5,000
  Sale of advertising space—
    20 pages at $50   . . . . . .    1,000
  Space sold to organizations—
    20 pages at $20  . . . . . . .      400
  Profit from class play  . . . . . .    150
          Total  . . . . . . .  $6,550      $6,550

Estimated Expenditures:
  Printing, covers, binding  . . . . .  $5,300
  Photography  . . . . . . . .          500
  Miscellaneous . . . . . . . .          200
          Total  . . . . . .  $6,000      $6,000
          Balance  . . . . . . . . .      $  550
```

As will be noted, a sizable balance of income over expenditures is provided in the budget. A margin of 10 per cent should be planned. This safety reserve will take care of unforeseen expenses that may arise, or of estimated income not obtained.

Activity Fee To Support the Annual

Some of the larger high schools and many colleges and universities have adopted an activity fee plan to help pay the cost of producing the annual. This system has many advantages which aid the yearbook staff in putting out a book of top-notch quality. Some of the advantages are:

1. The staff will know at the beginning of the year how much subscription money is available.

2. The staff members can plan a definite yearbook and proceed with their work. They will not be forced to wait until a book-sale campaign is conducted, the advertising is sold, and space sold to organizations before going ahead with the production of the book.

3. The yearbook is cheaper for each student, since the production cost per book is lowered when a large number is printed. Also, every student is assured of getting a book.

4. Each student will take more pride in the book because pictures of more students will be included. In short, it will be a better "memory book."

5. A more complete history of the school year can be presented because work can begin immediately after the previous book has gone to press.

6. If the activity fee is high enough to cover most of the cost of the book, it will not be necessary or desirable to charge for space in the annual. This makes it possible for the editor to allocate space to organizations and activities on a basis of their relative importance instead of on the basis of how much space they can afford to purchase in the book.

Be Alert To Get Your Share of Fees

If the yearbook at your school receives support from an activity fee, you must be alert at all times to see that the share of the fee that has been traditionally allocated to the annual is not diverted to other school activities. Often the amount allocated to various activities is changed from year to year and you must submit a budget for the yearbook requesting a certain amount of money.

Then, too, you may need to help collect the fee at enrollment if it is optional. Because of the increasing cost for most activities, the activity fee is increased from time to time. The yearbook staff should see that an increase is made in the amount it is to get if it is needed. The adviser can be quite helpful in this matter.

Budget Control Important

Too many editors and business managers think the budget can be forgotten after it is prepared. The truth is, a yearbook staff must watch income and expenditures as closely as any businessman. A budget can be a great aid—*if it is followed.* It is necessary to take inventory now and then to see where the budget stands.

The best time to do this is during Thanksgiving vacation. The staff has been busy with all the things that go into the hurly-burly of putting out a yearbook. Then comes vacation and things quiet down. Take advantage of that break.

First of all, check the income. The sales campaign should be in its final stages and getting set for a "clean-up" drive. How many books have been sold? Were there as many as originally anticipated? Will the income set up for book sales in the budget be as much as expected?

Advertising is another big problem. Has the business staff sold as much space as the budget called for? By the first of the year most of the advertising should be sold. If there is still a long way to go, make a memo to urge ad salesmen to make a special effort when they return from vacation.

On the other side, how are the expenditures going? If expenses are crowding the budget, remember there are still many pictures to be taken and that practically all of the costs of printing are still ahead. If there has been some radical change not foreseen when the budget was planned, it may be necessary to cut out some pages or add others.

The general idea is to find out just where the yearbook stands in regard to finances. Don't stop finding out. Check again during Christmas vacation and at least once more before the book reaches its final stages. Don't wait until it is too late and then attempt to cut expenses or to increase income. The enterprise will be in the red, if this is done. Only by practicing strict budget control can the yearbook be operated in the manner the staff wants it to be.

Use of Representative Budgets

Often the business staff of the yearbook will find it useful to have available detailed budgets from other schools. If, for example, it becomes necessary to increase the subscription price of the annual because of increased production costs, the student body has to be convinced the increase is necessary.

If the price currently charged is below the average collected by other schools, then the use of selling prices in comparable schools is a good argument for raising subscription rates. On the other hand, if the price charged is already higher than average, you will have to use quality rather than school by school comparisons.

The same kind of argument and many others can be presented for increasing advertising rates or space charges to organizations. For this reason a careful study of information contained in Tables 14.1 to 14.7 may be useful to the business staff of the annual. Be alert to studies as they are released by NSPA and ACP. Printing, photography, and other primary yearbook costs change rapidly—and usually upward.

Financial Survey of 227 College Annuals

In a study of 227 college yearbooks compiled by Mrs. Fran Compton and reported in "ACP Helps," approximately 30 per cent depended on subscription sales as a *major* source of income. The same survey showed 64 per cent of the 227 books receive *major* financial support from activity fees and that over 79 per cent receive some fee or school support other than book sales. Sixty-six per cent sold advertising space and 52.4 per cent charged organizations for space in the annual. In some cases only larger groups, such as fraternities and sororities, are charged for space in the yearbook.

Outside Sources of Income

In summing up sources of income Mrs. Compton says:

Many college yearbooks have sources of revenue other than subscription sales, activity fees, advertising, etc. Although ACP cannot provide details on these additional means of raising money, we hope the following list will give searching business managers some new ideas. Many of these methods raised several hundred dollars. When considering such a project, be sure you do not undertake such a complicated or extensive venture that the other yearbook business (and editorial) activities suffer.

1. Sale of senior photos, faculty photos
2. Auction of miscellaneous action photos used in previous book
3. Sale of plastic covers for book
4. Dance
5. Sale of books to school for public relations use
6. Class grants
7. Concessions at athletic events
8. Open houses, fashion shows, card parties, informal social affairs
9. Sale of beauty queen photos or sale of space in book for special queen photos.

Budgets Show Total Figures

In explanation of typical budgets shown in Table 14.7, Mrs. Compton states:

Now that each segment of the means of income has been studied in detail, we will present some *typical budgets*. In selecting these budgets, we have taken the range of total spent in each enrollment group and then tried to find a typical book in the middle range. These were not presented as perfect but rather as typical of each group. When there is no amount listed for cover costs, it is included with printing and paper figures in the first column on the expenditure side.

The left-hand column of Table 14.7 lists the enrollment group, the highest budget, the lowest budget, and the average budget for that group. Detailed budgets are given for two that are typical of the average for each enrollment group.

Keeping Complete Financial Records

Every successful business, regardless of its nature, needs a complete, accurate record of all financial transactions. The business of producing a school annual is no exception.

A simple, workable bookkeeping system is a basis from which the yearbook business manager or adviser can efficiently analyze and direct the business transactions of publication. The size of the annual and its financial resources may determine to a certain extent just what bookkeeping devices are necessary to maintain complete financial records. However, even the smallest book operating on a limited budget should have a system of keeping records.

It is not the purpose of this book to teach methods of bookkeeping. But, emphasis is given here to the value of keeping records and to presentation of forms that help one keep adequate records. Fundamentally, complete records for a yearbook consist simply of a written record of all money taken in from various sources and of all disbursements.

Receipt Forms Needed

For the average yearbook, depending on its size and systems of raising money, three receipt forms are needed, also a standard advertising contract, a set of file cards, and a ledger.

FIGURE 14.1. **This standard photograph receipt can be issued to each student who pays for an individual picture in the annual. A carbon copy is retained in the receipt book for use by the staff.**

Sources of yearbook income may be divided into four general divisions for bookkeeping purposes. These are (1) Sale of books (2) Sale of advertising space (3) Income from individual photographs (4) Miscellaneous income such as that from sale of space in the book, payments for group photographs, and money received from promotional activities. A separate form for recording individual transactions is required for each general source of income.

A receipt suitable for use in the book-sale campaign and a sample advertising contract, used in selling yearbook advertising, are shown in Chapter 15. Each of these forms plays an important part in assembling the yearbook's financial records. Both should be made in duplicate. The copy retained by the staff should be given to the bookkeeper. Book-sale receipts should be numbered consecutively. As in the case of the receipt forms discussed later, information contained on the book-sale receipt or the advertising contract must be transferred to the ledger as a permanent record.

Issuing Photograph Receipts

In addition to the two forms discussed in Chapter 15, photograph and general receipt forms are necessary. Figure 14.1 is an example of a standard photograph receipt used by many yearbooks. These receipts are numbered consecutively and made in duplicate with the duplicate bearing the same number as the original. For convenience in handling, they can be bound in books

✳ ORANGE AND BLACK – Photograph Receipt

Name _____ No. 4899

Home Address _____

School _____ Class _____
Insert Picture in the Following Sections:

Which Class _____ $ . . . .

Name of Fraternity _____ $ . . . .

Name of Sorority _____ $ . . . .

　　　　　Amount Received _____ $ . . . .

　　　　　　　　　✳ ORANGE AND BLACK

Date _____ 　By _____

of 50 or 100. Thus, when an entire book of receipts has been issued, the duplicates will still be in the bound form. In such a form, they are easily accessible, and can be filed easily.

As shown on the sample photo receipt, the section of the book in which the picture is to appear should be indicated, along with any other information the editorial staff may need in preparing the copy.

In some cases, it may be the policy of the yearbook staff to allow the photographer who takes the individual photos to issue the receipts and collect the money. However, this is not recommended since the staff has no assurance that complete and accurate records will be kept. It is a better policy for the photo receipts to be sold directly by the staff, and the money collected at the yearbook office. If this is done, the business manager has a complete record available at all times, and there is less opportunity for errors that result in omitting a picture that has been paid for.

Use of General Receipt

A general or miscellaneous receipt form is also essential. Figure 14.2 is an example of the general receipt issued when space in the book is sold, when a group picture is paid for, or when money is received from any other source such as candy sales or class plays.

General receipts also are numbered consecutively, made in duplicate, and bound in books of 50 or 100. These receipts are handled in much the same manner as the photograph receipts. In both cases, each receipt issued is recorded in the

ledger when the money is deposited in the bank. After a book of receipts is filled, the information is transferred from the receipt to a file card, which is discussed later.

All of the receipts are entered in the ledger as a permanent record. The ledger entry includes the name of the person or organization to whom the receipt was issued, the number of the receipt, and the date it was issued.

When ordering the various forms at the beginning of the year, make a careful estimate of the number of each type that will be needed. No two receipts, regardless of their intended use, should be numbered the same. For example, suppose the staff decides that they will need 1,000 book-sale receipts, 1,500 photograph receipts, and 200 general receipts. They can all be numbered consecutively with numbers 1 to 1,000 assigned to book-sale receipts, numbers 1,001 to 2,500 assigned to photograph receipts, and numbers 2,501 to 2,700 set aside for the general receipts. These numbers can be seen best if placed in the upper right-hand corner of the forms.

Use of Card File

A comparatively simple device and a valuable time-saver is a card file. In most cases a 4- by 6-inch card or a 3- by 5-inch card is suitable. Each person who buys a book or has a picture in the annual is listed on a file card.

The cards are filed alphabetically in a small cabinet. Information from the various receipt forms is transferred to the file card along with any material judged necessary by the staff. All of the information appearing on the card should be typed for legibility.

Figure 14.3 shows a recommended type of file card. Spaces are left for receipt numbers, money

FIGURE 14.2. A general receipt form can be used to record miscellaneous cash received from such items as sale of space to organizations, sale of pictures, etc.

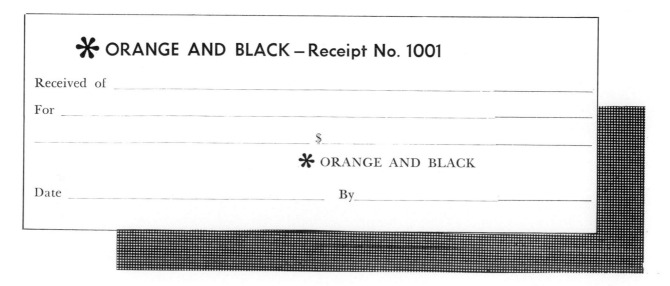

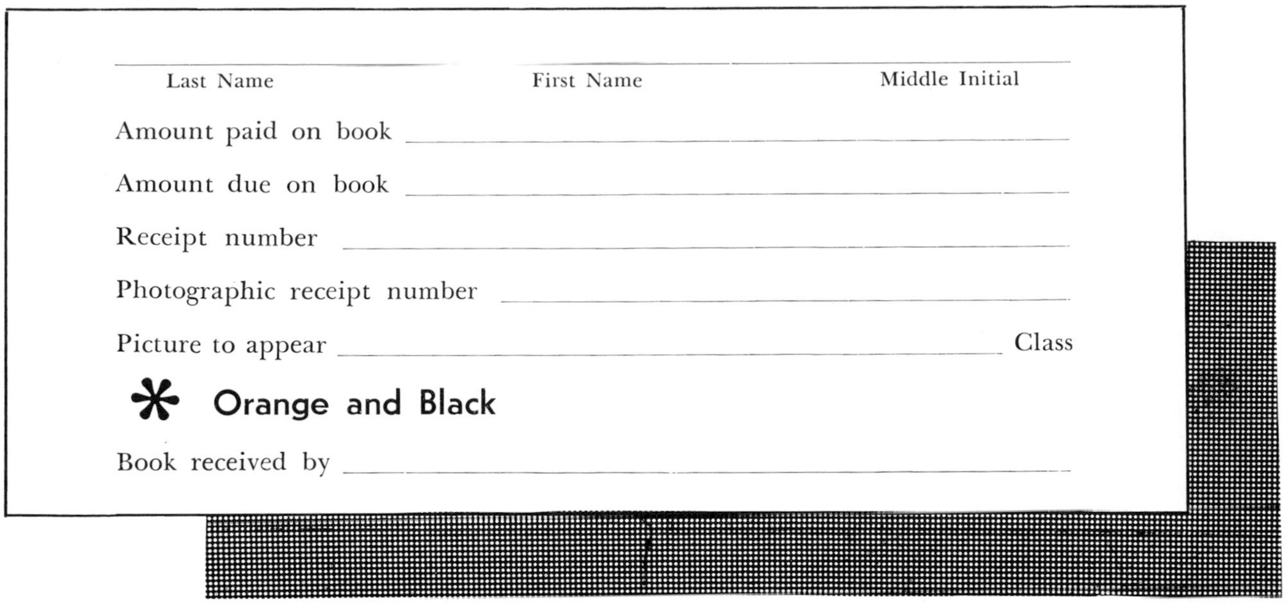

```
_____      _____      _____
   Last Name             First Name           Middle Initial

Amount paid on book _____

Amount due on book _____

Receipt  number  _____

Photographic receipt number _____

Picture to appear _____ Class

  ✳  Orange and Black

Book received by _____
```

FIGURE 14.3. A file card for each individual who buys a book or has his picture in the annual is a valu- able time-saver. It can be used when compiling an index and for each subscriber to sign as he gets the annual.

paid, money due, and for the signature of the person receiving the book. In addition, the numbers of the pages on which pictures of the card owner appear can be recorded in the margin of the file card. This is a marked aid in indexing the book. With the cards already filed alphabetically, it is simple to assemble the index by copying the name of the person and the page numbers from the card. Similarly, the card file-system makes it easier to compile almost any special list in alphabetical order such as a list of all seniors, juniors, or sophomores. The number of the original photo receipt issued to each individual also can be included to make it easy to order prints from the photographer.

Receipt numbers on the file card make it possible for the staff members to make a rapid check when a student comes to the office and announces that he has lost his receipt. Without the file card, all of the duplicate receipts might have to be examined to find the information desired. The system can be valuable in conducting the book-sale campaign as well as in other ways. A salesman can make a rapid check of file cards to see who are still prospective buyers.

The Ledger As a Permanent Record

Each financial transaction recorded in the various receipt books eventually is transferred to the ledger as a permanent record. Thus, the ledger is actually the only book required in this simple system. Many bookkeeping systems use a cashbook-journal as well as the ledger. However, the bound volumes of duplicate receipts serve the same purpose as the cashbook-journal and may be properly substituted, on a small annual, to simplify the system.

Into the double-entry ledger goes a permanent record of all income and all disbursements. Separate sections in the ledger are set aside to record book sales, sale of advertising, individual photograph receipts, and miscellaneous receipts and disbursements. Often it saves time if an index to these various sections is entered in the front of the ledger.

The staff should consult an experienced bookkeeper before making entries in the ledger. In a large college or university, some member of the business office may be an excellent source of advice. In high schools, the commerce teacher is usually willing to assist.

In any case, no yearbook staff should set out to produce an annual without having a complete system of records. Careful planning at the beginning of the school year often will save valuable time and prevent crises later. Many times, the efficient use of bookkeeping aids, such as the card file, will prove to be the difference between meeting and not meeting the final deadline.

Chapter 15

Make advertising pages a part of the complete yearbook by introducing the section with an interesting sub-division photograph. A picture showing a parade, a pep rally, a street dance, or student shopping in the business area of the city will lead readers into the advertising section and thus include the merchants in an annual that is treasured by the entire community.

Raising Yearbook Revenue

PUBLISHING an annual costs money, and raising the revenue necessary to pay the expenses involves a carefully planned program. It is the job of the business manager to see that the necessary income is provided, for even the best editorial staff cannot do a good job without adequate financial resources. Thus, the business manager and his subordinates play an indispensable role in producing an annual, even though outsiders may not realize this fact.

As shown by surveys of college and high school annuals discussed in Chapter 14, the two most important sources of income are sale of books and advertising space. In some schools they finance the entire book. Of course there are other activities that provide income. They include sale of space to organizations, sale of pictures, dances, plays, and candy sales.

The staff should not undertake too many business ventures. It is advisable to select three or four sources for major emphasis. Financing the

book must not become a burden to the students, faculty, or the city. A well-planned program is businesslike and thorough and will give subscribers and advertisers value received for their money.

Selling the Yearbook

In schools where the annual is financed by an activity fee, yearbook sales campaigns will not be necessary. Under this system, every student who pays an activity fee is entitled to a copy of the book, and the staff knows at the beginning of the year how much money is available and how many books are required.

In most cases the sale of books provides the largest source of income and should receive major emphasis. It is difficult to estimate how many books can be sold, but the business staff *must* sell the number planned for in the budget.

If the campaign to sell books is to succeed, the staff must have a plan that will:

1. Make it advantageous to the prospective buyer of the annual to subscribe during the campaign.
2. Provide receipt books that will insure accurate records.
3. Organize a sales force that will contact all prospective buyers.
4. Insure adequate and effective publicity and timely advertising.
5. Reach prospective buyers away from the campus.
6. Include an effective sales force for a clean-up campaign.
7. Provide supervision and instruction of the sales force.

Promoting Early Sales

The sales campaign should be conducted early in the year so that the number of books needed can be determined before the editorial staff gets far into the actual production of the annual. There must be time for adequate publicity about the campaign so the student body will be anticipating the sale. Most of the books should be sold before Thanksgiving, with a clean-up campaign just before Christmas.

A plan that makes it advantageous to the buyer to purchase an annual during the sales campaign is practically mandatory, and one that presses the prospective subscriber for immediate action makes selling much easier.

There are several methods of promoting early and prompt buying, foremost of which is a beauty or popularity contest. Time and again, this method has proved effective. When it is used, a buyer is allowed a certain number of votes for the queen if he purchases his book before a certain date. This induces friends of each candidate to buy books early. In many cases, the contest may reach such a fervor that friends of candidates become the best possible solicitors.

Some staffs use graduated price schedules to encourage early buying. At the beginning of the campaign, for example, the price of the book may be $4.50. At the end of the week, it may jump to $4.75. During the last week of the campaign, the price might be increased to $5.00.

Another system, used less frequently, is the rebate plan. This involves an agreement with the printer whereby a minimum number of books is to be printed and a reduced rate given for additional copies.

Suppose the contract with the printer calls for a minimum of 1,500 books. Then the staff sets the "goal" at 2,500. A thermometer drawn on a large cardboard may be erected for recording daily or weekly sales. When the sales reach 2,000, the price of all books is reduced 25 cents. If the "goal," or 2,500 mark is reached, the price is reduced 50 cents. This plan stimulates sales because the students who buy early become boosters, and thus aid in getting others to subscribe. The disadvantage to this system, however, is the considerable extra work for the business staff in making refunds.

Competition between classes or organizations is another method of stimulating early buying. This type of campaign often is conducted through home rooms, and a sales captain is selected for each room. The prize can fittingly be a special

FIGURE 15.1. Contract form for use in selling subscriptions to the annual. These are printed in duplicate and one copy given to the subscriber.

FIGURE 15.2. A ballot for beauty queen may be printed on the same sheet with the subscription receipt.

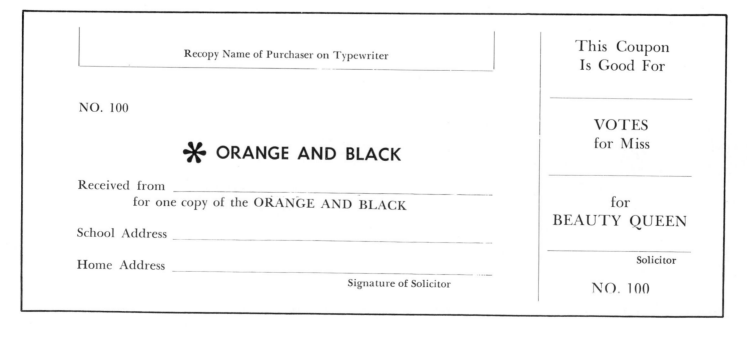

feature page in the yearbook for the room that wins or a free copy of the annual for the home room teacher.

Another variation of this method is recognition of individual solicitors. A special page can be devoted to the "Top Ten." Pictures of these workers, plus a few words of praise are often inducements enough.

Certainly the staff must not attempt to use too many selling devices. The method or combination of methods bringing best results should be discovered and adhered to.

Keeping Records of Sales

Whatever method is used, a contract form is necessary for good record-keeping. Figure 15.1 shows such a form. Usually the contracts are numbered and stapled in books of 25 or 50. Each solicitor is held responsible for the contracts in the book issued to him.

These forms are made out in duplicate and the original copy given to the purchaser. The buyer then has a receipt. Usually, the two forms are printed on paper of different colors.

After the campaign, the forms are filed alphabetically in a card file. Thus, a complete record of purchasers is available. If a space is left at the top of the form for the purchaser's name, the clerical force can do a better job of filing.

A coupon can be added to the contract form when the beauty contest type of campaign is used. Figure 15.2 illustrates how this is done. A blank space should be left for the number of votes allowable, the number depending on the date of purchase.

Several of the large printing houses specializing in yearbooks furnish free contract forms for book sales. These forms save the staff the cost of printing special receipts. If the forms furnished by the printer are used, they must be carefully numbered by the business manager before they are checked out to salesmen. It is essential to have a system that will insure getting the money for every sale made, as well as the name of each student who is entitled to a copy of the yearbook.

Aggressive Sales Force Needed

An aggressive, fast-moving sales force is highly desirable. Haphazard methods lead to defeat. A plan that will insure enthusiastic and complete soliciting is a must.

In small high schools a contest among the classes often works best. The classes are divided into home rooms, and a captain is selected for each. Then the yearbook adviser, editor, or business manager gives a short talk to each room, telling the students of the special features of the annual and the need of urging every student to be a purchaser.

In some prominent hallway, a large poster with thermometers for each class can be displayed so that students are constantly reminded of the contest. At the end of each day, home room captains can report to the business manager and the thermometers kept up to date. A campaign of this type in a small high school should usually last one or two weeks. It should not be extended over a long period lest students lose interest.

Longer Campaigns for Large Schools

In a large college, the campaign may be extended over a longer period, usually a month, so that the entire student body can be solicited. Every student is a potential buyer, and no one should be overlooked.

In many colleges, the beauty or popularity contest campaign is used. Fifteen or twenty candidates may be selected either by the business staff or by petitions from the student body. From this group, the "Queen" and her attendants are selected by votes of purchasers, and the winners' pictures are featured in the beauty section.

Details of the contest should be announced clearly and repeatedly in the school newspaper. Names of the candidates, voting places, time limits, and other pertinent facts should be publicized. Students should be informed of the progress of the contest by news stories or by means of the thermometer system in a student union or other popular place.

Another sales system often used is paying commissions to salesmen. Good results are obtained in this type of campaign only if solicitors are selected to cover areas where they are well and favorably known. It is much easier to sell a yearbook to a friend than to a stranger.

Publicity for the Campaign

One essential of a book sales campaign is publicity—lots of it. Cooperation with the school newspaper is extremely important from the publicity angle. The staff needs the paper to print special announcements and to advertise the yearbook. Surveys show that 96 per cent of the students read their school newspaper.

If the editor or business manager of the yearbook is not a member of the newspaper staff, it is a good idea to appoint someone to act as "press agent" or publicity director for the annual. Stories are more likely to be printed if prepared by someone who knows the facts and does a good job of writing. If the school prints a daily newspaper, two or three articles a week are sufficient. If the newspaper is a weekly, the paper should contain some story in nearly every issue.

A short news story is best. Announcements of staff appointments, progress of the beauty contest, naming outstanding salesmen, and stories about the work on the yearbook are always interesting.

Feature articles have their place, too. The amount of paper and ink required to produce the annual makes a good story. The number of pictures being printed, description of the theme, and comparison with other annuals in the past are other feature ideas. It is important to get the name of the yearbook in print as many times as possible so that every student will be constantly aware that there is a yearbook to be bought.

Printers Furnish Sales Material

Leading yearbook printers have worked out excellent sales campaigns to help the staff sell subscriptions to the annual. These plans should be studied carefully by the staff and used when the appropriate time comes. Clever color posters with effective sales messages are furnished by several printing houses, and these can be used in the halls and on bulletin boards to promote sales. Student artists can often contribute excellent sales posters, and they should be encouraged to help out.

Many schools use the assembly as a medium for advertising. If it can be arranged with the person in charge of assemblies, the business manager should make it a point to have some interesting announcements about the yearbook made frequently.

Special Assembly To Publicize Annual

Sometimes a special assembly can be arranged to publicize the yearbook. When this can be done, the editor and business manager should give short, interesting talks. A still better idea is to have some type of entertainment, with the theme built around the yearbook. This can be a short play, written by some member of the staff, or a variety show with prominent members of the student body participating. An outstanding example of how to present an assembly program that will arouse interest in the yearbook is shown in Figure 15.3.

Buttons, tags, or ribbons are other effective means of advertising the yearbook. Buttons are better than tags or ribbons, for they can be worn longer and displayed more prominently.

A slogan pertaining to the annual should be inscribed on the button to draw attention to the yearbook. Inscriptions such as "I'VE SUBSCRIBED," "I BOUGHT MINE," or "BUY AN ANNUAL," are examples. Sometimes an appropriate design can be worked out.

Buttons, ribbons, or tags worn by students who have bought annuals help salesmen. During a campaign, when solicitors are anxious to secure votes for queen candidates or to put their class on top, persons not wearing identifications can be pursued by solicitors on all parts of the campus.

Drawing Names Keeps Interest High

Interest and enthusiasm can be kept alive during the campaign by having a drawing each day of names of persons who have subscribed, the winners to have their names printed in gold on the cover of their annuals.

One enterprising staff staged a giant drawing at the close of its subscription campaign and gave an automobile to the lucky winner. The used car given away was donated by one of the dealers in the city. The car was parked on the lawn of the school during the campaign and new signs advertising the annual were painted on it each day.

In some schools, a permanent display case is set up in the student union or hallway of a central building. Each week, pictures of events that have taken place on the campus are displayed, always with the name of the yearbook. At other times, copies of previous yearbooks, samples of layout sheets and page proofs can be shown. Although it does not sell yearbooks directly, this type of publicity keeps the annual in the public eye.

There are many other ways of publicizing the yearbook: bulletin board announcements, handbills, descriptive folders and booklets, movie slides, and program advertising. All types of publicity should be directed toward one goal—to present the annual in the most favorable manner possible.

Selling Subscriptions at Enrollment

As previously mentioned, quite a few schools,

$\longrightarrow$

FIGURE 15.3. This complete page is reproduced by courtesy of the *Scholastic Editor* and describes the special assembly program presented at Broad Ripple High School, Indianapolis, Indiana.

"Riparian, Yeh, Yeh, Yeh." The entire cast gathers onstage cheering for the grand finale song.

Wildly waving signs, delegates parade down aisles to their seats as the band strikes up a lively tune. Marchers provided the first spectacle of the program.

"If you vote Lyndon, I'll vote Very." In his Texan drawl, Lyndon Byrd Baines extols the merits of the 1965 Riparian yearbook as Very Rightwater, with his slippery-nosed glasses, impatiently waits his turn to speak.

Try a Convention To Sell Subscriptions

By Ellen Bucek

Screaming, sighing, fainting females characterized the discovery of the "Bedbugs" in the Broad Ripple High School auditorium. Ripple's latest singing group, the "Bedbugs," along with a peppy band, exuberant convention delegates waving giant signs and two chorus lines highlighted the auditorium program which kicked off last year's *Riparian* subscription campaign.

To promote subscription sales of the *Riparian* newspaper and yearbook of Broad Ripple High School in Indianapolis, Ind., the auditorium program September 30 was a takeoff of the then current national political campaign.

After preconvention festivities Lyndon Byrd Baines expounded upon the values and awards of the yearbook. To prove his point, he presented his campaign song, sung by a talented cast member, after which a chorus line of yearbook staff members clad in cardboard yearbooks danced to the music of "Hello Dolly." As Lyndon Byrd thanked his performers and sat down, his backers roared wildly.

Introduction of the next speaker, Very Rightwater, brought cheers from the right-wing newspaper section. Very urged members of the delegation to vote newspaper in 1964-1965. A *Riparian*-style "Hey Look Me Over" sung by an attractive female Rightwater backer supported his views. At the conclusion of the song 10 newspaper-clad girls kicked their way through a gay 90's chorus line routine.

Since the delegates needed a composure-gaining period, the "Bedbugs" were introduced. With this, the entire house engaged in an uproar. Their first song, "Riparian, Yeh, Yeh, Yeh," sent screaming delegates into fainting spells.

Before the final newspaper-yearbook vote was taken, the three queen and three king candidates for Miss and Mr. Riparian were announced. The king and queen were to be crowned at the Riparian Dance to take place later in November after the campaign.

> *While the political theme used here is now dated, the ideas may help enterprising staffs to boost sales. The author is a student at Broad Ripple High School.*

Royal Purple Receives 29 All-Americans

The most valuable book a student can buy at K-State this fall will be one that isn't even printed yet.

Furthermore, it probably will cost less than any other book he buys.

But if tradition means anything, the student will keep the book longer and use it more than any book he buys during his college days.

Senior Pics In Color For '66 RP

Senior pictures in the 1966 Royal Purple will be reproduced in full, natural color for the first time in the 75-year history of the famous yearbook.

Editor Carole Fry announced this month that special arrangements had been made with the Royal Purple printer and photographer to provide color pictures of seniors at only $1 extra cost.

Seniors will select the picture they want to appear in the Royal Purple from prints made in full, natural color by Blaker's Studio in Aggieville.

The cost for senior pictures will be $3. Underclass pictures will cost $2.

Miss Fry emphasized that these prices include the sitting charge, a selection of poses and the price of a finished print for the Royal Purple.

Students will select the pictures to be used.

"We are confident that the reproduction will equal or surpass that in the 1965 Royal Purple," Miss Fry said.

The Royal Purple printer made a test run on a panel of colored pictures earlier this summer to perfect lighting and reproduction techniques.

Miss Fry said black and white prints will be made from the color negatives for seniors who may also be pictured with residence hall or fraternity or sorority groups.

There is no extra charge for the second print.

The book, of course, is K-State's Royal Purple, the nation's most consistent All-American.

The RP's record of 29 consecutive All-American awards is unequaled.

The 1965 Royal Purple, which is now being judged, could become the 30th All-American.

The 1966 staff, of course, hopes to continue this winning tradition which was established under the advisorship of C. J. (Chief) Medlin back in 1936.

Medlin has retired as Graduate Manager of Student Publications, but he will be available for staff consultations.

What makes the Royal Purple the winner it is?

The answers are simple: complete coverage, excellent pictures, good editing, and a dedicated and energetic staff.

Each year five or six yearbooks in the large university class are named All-American, but only one, The Royal Purple, is consistently at the top.

This amazing record was established under the guiding principle of providing the Kansas State student body with the best possible printed record and memory of one year of a student's college life.

What goes into an All-American Royal Purple?

* More than 600 pages of pictures and copy.
* More than 8,000 individual pictures.
* More than 100 group pictures.
* More than 1,000 pictures of extracuricular activities.
* Pictures of K-State administrators, faculty and visitors.
* Thousands of hours of time from the K-State students who serve as staff members.

Yes, The Royal Purple has fashioned an amazing record—one that can be shared by every student.

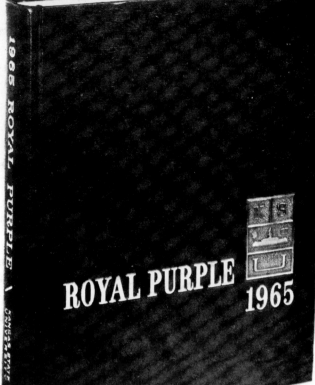

ALL-AMERICAN—Anyway you look at a ROYAL PURPLE, it's an All-American. The tradition of 29 consecutive All-American awards is an important one to K-State students and especially to yearbook staff members. These students have been working on the 1966 Royal Purple since the '65 book (pictured) was delivered in May. Editor Carole Fry believes the 1966 Royal Purple will live up to the All-American tradition.

Simple Two-Step Procedure To Order Yearbook, Picture

A simple two-step procedure will make it easier this year for students to order a Royal Purple and to schedule an individual picture.

Students going through the enrollment line will receive a blue IBM card requesting information for the University Directory.

In the upper right-hand corner of the card will be two statements:

1. Order my 1966 Royal Purple—Yes   No.

2. Schedule my RP individual picture—Yes   No.

Step one is for students to check the box indicating their wishes.

Step two is for students to pick up receipts for the 1966 Royal Purple and their class picture at the Royal Purple station at the end of the enrollment process.

Students will pay $4 for the 600-plus page yearbook that will be delivered in May.

By enrolling as a full-time student, individuals receive a $4 credit on a yearbook through the activity fee.

Students who are enrolled for fewer than six hours each semester must pay the full price of $8 for a Royal Purple.

Underclassmen can purchase a class picture for $2. Studio appointments will be announced in the Collegian shortly after classes begin.

Seniors, who will be pictured in full, natural color for the first time, will pay $3 for class pictures.

Students will select the picture(s) to be used in the RP from several poses.

(Advertisement)

STUDENT PUBLICATIONS, INC.—Royal Purple and Photograph Receipt

Name.. Class Fr So Jr Sr Grad

Last   First   Middle   Please circle correct class

Hometown.................................... State.................................... Curriculum....................................

Name of campus living unit..

Dormitory, Fraternity, Sorority, Jardine, Scholarship House, Off-Campus

Order my 1966 ROYAL PURPLE—$4.00   ( )   ( )

Yes   No

Schedule my Royal Purple class picture
Seniors (full color) $3.00; Underclassmen $2.00   ( )   ( )

Yes   No

Watch Collegian for Studio Appointment

By..   TOTAL....................................

No. 66 10000

STUDENTS who order a 1966 Royal Purple and/or individual picture to appear in the yearbook will pick up a receipt like this at the end of the enrollment line this fall. The process of ordering yearbooks and individual pictures was simplified this year to make it easier and faster for students to clear the enrollment process. Students are advised to check the Royal Purple boxes on the University Directory card (see story at right) and pick up a receipt at the end of the enrollment line to ensure receiving the most colorful book in Royal Purple history.

particularly colleges, are making an all-out effort to sell yearbook subscriptions to students during fall enrollment. This plan provides the staff with information on the number of books needed and the amount of money available from this important source, so they can plan the annual in detail without further delay. It also allows the business staff to concentrate its effort on selling advertising, collecting for organization space, or taking care of other business matters.

Royal Purple Sells 7,000 Copies

The staff of the 1966 *Royal Purple* sold more than 7,000 subscriptions at $4.00 each during fall enrollment.

More than 5,000 students paid the photograph fee for individual studio pictures at the same time. The campaign required careful advance planning as well as adequate publicity.

A story telling about the sales plan was published in the *Collegian*, student daily paper, the previous year, just before school was out. During the summer a special "University Edition" of the *Collegian* was printed and sent to all new students who had applied for admission to the University.

←

FIGURE 15.4. A full-page advertisement printed in the Kansas State *Collegian* emphasizes the excellence of the *Royal Purple*, its important new features, and how to subscribe for it during enrollment.

FIGURE 15.5. This order form used by the 1966 *Royal Purple* during enrollment is printed on NCR (no carbon required) paper so that three copies are made when the

The staff inserted a full-page advertisement printed in two colors in the edition, telling about the importance of subscribing for the annual and paying the photography fee during fall enrollment. A reproduction of the advertisement is shown in Figure 15.4. A copy of the special paper was placed in each dormitory room, and enough copies for all members were delivered to all fraternities, sororities, and rooming houses the day the houses opened for the fall semester.

Special Subscription Form Used

A sample of the form each student would be asked to fill out to order his annual and picture during enrollment was printed actual size in the advertisement so students could study it before receiving the actual order blank, while in the enrollment line. The form is shown actual size in Figure 15.5. Each student who wished to order a *Royal Purple* or class picture or both filled out the form and gave it to *Royal Purple* staff members and paid the amount due.

In a final effort to sell students on placing their orders during the enrollment process, the *Royal Purple* staff prepared the elaborate sign shown in Figure 15.6, and displayed it prominently in the area where students received the order blank. The display is so constructed that it can be stored and used with desired changes in future years.

student fills in the requested information. One copy is for the student, one for the staff, and one for the yearbook photographer.

STUDENT PUBLICATIONS, INC.—Royal Purple and Photograph Receipt

Name_____ Class Fr So Jr Sr Grad
      Last   First   Middle   Please circle correct class

Hometown_____ State_____ Curriculum_____

Name of campus living unit_____
               Dormitory, Fraternity, Sorority, Jardine, Scholarship House, Off-Campus

Order my 1966 ROYAL PURPLE—$4.00 .... ☐ ☐
                                  Yes   No
Schedule my Royal Purple class picture
   Seniors (full color) $3.00; Underclassmen $2.00 .... ☐ ☐

Watch Collegian for Studio Appointment

By_____   TOTAL_____

No. 66 8985

FIGURE 15.6. A special four-color display 3½ feet high, calling attention to six outstanding features of the yearbook, was used by the 1966 *Royal Purple* to help sell subscripions during fall enrollment.

Selling Yearbooks off Campus

Yearbook staffs often overlook potential buyers away from the campus. Business and professional men in the community frequently buy yearbooks. A great deal of their business comes from students, and they have a real interest in school activities.

Such professional men as doctors, dentists, and lawyers have use for a school yearbook in their waiting rooms. Their patrons, members of the community, are anxious to keep up with the school. A long wait in the office often passes more quickly by the revival of memories of school days. Former students and those who have sons or daughters already graduated from the school are frequently interested.

Alumni of the school, especially recent graduates, are another source for book sales. Through the principal's office or alumni secretary, addresses of former students can be obtained. A newsy, carefully circulated letter describing the book and giving the pricc often results in sales.

Parents of prospective students who are

known in advance often like to buy a yearbook "to get better acquainted" with the school before their son or daughter enrolls.

Clean-up Campaign

Just before the Christmas vacation begins, a clean-up campaign should be conducted. By checking the card file, a list can be compiled of those who have not bought. In the campaign earlier in the year, several salesmen will have proved their ability. These are the ones to use in the clean-up campaign.

Persons who have pictures in the annual are especially good prospects. The book has a special, personal meaning to them. In years to come they will be glad they have such a memory book for their families and friends.

Since the campaign is to be conducted near Christmas, parents are often potential buyers. A letter to the parents of students who have not purchased yearbooks, suggesting they give the annual to their son or daughter as a Christmas present, often brings good results. A better idea is to have a solicitor call on the parents.

The school itself is another potential buyer, purchasing copies to send to prospective students and supporters of the institution. The various departments featured in the book may be interested in buying copies.

Prepare a Sales Talk

Few yearbooks will be sold by the salesman who approaches a prospect with, "You wanna' buy a yearbook?" It takes real salesmanship—the same as in selling automobiles or magazine subscriptions. Thus, it is important that the business manager instruct his solicitors on how to sell.

Reasons why students should buy annuals can be incorporated into a sales talk. The reasons must not be recited as if they were memorized; each solicitor should put them into his own words, possibly using such sales points as:

1. It is a complete record of the school year, a record of the year's activities that cannot be obtained elsewhere.
2. In years to come, the yearbook will be valuable in recalling old classmates.
3. By taking a yearbook home, students can show their folks pictures of friends and of various school activities.
4. The student is loyal to the institution.

FIGURE 15.7. Collecting *Royal Purple* subscriptions and photograph fees kept the staff busy at enrollment. More than 7,000 copies were sold during the period.

5. The price of the book is low in relation to what the student receives in return for his money.
6. The yearbook is the student's book, a record of *his* school edited by *his* schoolmates.

Sale of Advertising

Advertising revenue usually provides the second laregst source of income for the yearbook, but selling advertising for a school annual is often difficult. It is one of the most important jobs in the financial program, and the responsibility for selling advertising must be given to those who realize its importance. Friendliness, willingness to work hard, tact, and a pleasant approach are the requirements for a good advertising solicitor.

The campaign to sell advertising should be conducted early because the business peak is reached in the fall. With students coming back to school, trade is good and businessmen are more willing to advertise then than after Christmas.

Advertising Agreement

It is wise to have a signed agreement with each merchant who purchases space. This will eliminate misunderstanding about the size of the ad or the amount charged. It is probably better to call it an agreement or an order for advertising space rather than a contract. Some merchants balk at signing a contract, but do not hesitate in signing an order.

FIGURE 15.8. Advertising agreement forms for space in the annual eliminate any chance for misunderstanding about the size of the ad and the amount charged.

The advertising agreement can be printed in duplicate and bound into books of 50 for the convenience of solicitors. The original copy is given to the merchant, and the carbon is used by the advertising manager. A good form of such an agreement is shown in Figure 15.8. Rates charged for space should be printed in the agreement to assure the merchant that he is getting the same rate as other advertisers. Advertising agreements often are furnished by the printer.

Some merchants refuse to sign agreements for advertising space, but are willing to buy an ad. It is not essential that an agreement be signed. All that is necessary is for the salesman to get the copy and have a clear understanding of how much space is wanted and the amount to be paid.

Give the Advertiser a Good Proposition

As in selling yearbooks, it is important that the advertising staff have a proposal making it advantageous for the merchant to contract for space early. Some staffs request extra proofs of ads from the printer. One is posted on the bulletin board where students can see it. One is sent to the advertiser with a notation that his advertisement is also being displayed on the bulletin board.

A sign with "PATRONIZE OUR YEAR-BOOK ADVERTISERS" will draw added attention. Eight to ten ads can be displayed at one time, usually for a week or so. Displaying advertisements in this manner pleases the merchant. He pays only for space in the yearbook, and the bulletin board displays are an added free service.

Another plan often employed is to run an ad-

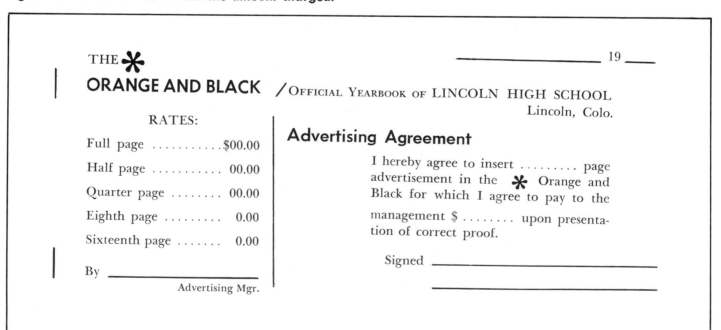

vertisement in the school newspaper naming all merchants and firms who have purchased space in the yearbook. A headline reading *"These Merchants Are Helping To Make the 1966 Orange and Black a Success—The Yearbook Staff Urges All Students To Patronize Them."* will indicate that the whole community is interested and will increase the advertisers' business.

Pictorial Ads Have Wide Appeal

Pictorial advertising is being used by more yearbooks each year. Students usually read pictorial advertisements, especially when the pictures show friends and acquaintances buying, wearing, or examining a product in the merchant's store. Usually, the advertiser leaves it to the discretion of the advertising manager to select the students to appear in the ads, and the manager should choose neat, popular students.

As indicated by the examples of pictorial advertising shown in Chapter 12, such yearbook advertising can be made to appeal to almost any kind of business. It also affords the staff a variety of approaches to regular advertisers as well as firms that have not had space in the annual previously.

For this type of advertising an agreement should be made with the advertiser concerning an extra charge for engraving if the book is done by letterpress. In most cases, the advertiser pays the cost of the cut, which is returned to him after the book is printed.

If the yearbook is being produced by lithography, the charge may be omitted for reproducing photographs, drawings, cartoons, or signature cuts. Many lithographic printers furnish a book showing cartoons, trade names, and entire advertisements prepared for different businesses. These items can be clipped and used at no extra cost.

Another device to attract attention to the advertising is to make it another division in the annual. One large college yearbook, for example, has used a heading and chapter number in keeping with the theme throughout the book. A colored picture of the business district opened the division and other pictures of business activities, parades, and modern store fronts "dressed up" the section. After the book was published, many students commented on the attractiveness and appeal, and merchants were greatly pleased with the results. Some schools give a copy of the yearbook to each merchant who buys a page or half page in the annual. However, if a $5.00 annual is given to each merchant who buys $10.00 worth of space, advertising revenue will not offset the cost for printing the section, much less produce a profit for the yearbook.

Selling Out-of-Town Advertisers

An advertising field that is becoming more profitable and should not be overlooked by business managers is that of out-of-town firms that do business with the school. Although some of these firms do not sell directly to the students, they do a large volume of business with the school itself. A list of these concerns and their addresses can be secured from the treasurer of the board of education or purchasing agent of the school.

Another profitable source of revenue is merchants in nearby large cities. If the cities are relatively near and travel facilities are good, students probably do much buying from these merchants. A letter to some of the larger firms, giving details as to the number of students in school and how much trading they do annually, will often result in sale of space.

Power and light companies, telephone companies, and transportation firms are excellent prospects. The presence of students means extra income and ordinarily these businesses are willing to advertise.

Selling the Local Advertiser

Most of the advertising space in the yearbook will be bought by local businessmen. Every prospective advertiser should be solicited. This includes outlying stores, factories, mills, and airports.

The classified section of the telephone directory will provide prospects who might otherwise be overlooked. This section of the directory in one city of 15,000 population lists over 500 business concerns and professional men, all of whom are potential advertisers. The listing gives the name of the firm, its street address, and usually the name of the owner.

Every man who buys space in the telephone directory believes in advertising. Probably 50 per cent of the firms have never been solicited by anyone from the school. In many cases they will feel flattered by the call and happy to place an advertisement in *their* yearbook, published by *their* children. Don't pass up the *little man*. He will want to be in the *permanent record* (the school yearbook) with other progressive merchants of the town.

Often it is wise to have several solicitors selling advertising space. The list of prospects can be divided among them; however, greater efficiency will result if the community is divided among several salesmen, each taking three or four blocks. Outlying concerns can be given to those who have cars and can make the calls in a minimum of time.

Advance Preparation

It is important for advertising salesmen to prepare carefully before calling on prospective advertisers. They should know the name of the concern, the owner's name (or in case of a large store, the name of the advertising manager), the merchandise handled, and how space in the annual will help sell it.

They should know whether the prospect has advertised previously and how much space he has used. In some towns, merchants who are in the same line of business and have an association take a full page and list the members. In one annual examined, a full page was printed listing all the dry cleaners who were members of the association. Other pages were purchased by the lumber dealers, service station operators, banks, and real estate agencies. This advertising is not so productive of income, but it often is a good long-term investment because students quickly mature and become prospective customers.

A carefully prepared layout of the proposed advertisement will help the solicitor. Advertising layouts are prepared in much the same manner as for other pages in the annual, but the work should be done by some member of the staff who has special aptitude for ad design. Often the journalism teacher will cooperate by having his classes prepare advertisements for prospective advertisers.

Conducting the Interview

Courtesy will sell more advertising than high-powered sales talks. The solicitor should not interrupt the merchant while he is waiting on a customer. If the store has a rush of business, it is better to see some other prospect and return later. If the store is a large one, the person in charge of advertising will be in his office. If the office door is closed, knock; if he has a secretary, ask for an appointment.

As soon as the salesman has gained the attention of the prospect, he should state his name and business. "Good morning, Mr. Jones. I am Bill Smith, on the business staff of the Central High School annual. I have been sent by the school to talk with you about advertising with us this year."

Always ask for the ad in the name of the school. Merchants do not like to say "no" to

schools. Inexperienced salesmen should first interview several regular advertisers because sales are fairly certain and the salesmen will gain confidence. After a few interviews, the new salesmen will be more self-assured and skillful.

Filling Out the Order

As soon as the merchant has agreed to purchase an ad, the salesman should fill out the agreement and have it properly signed. It is often unnecessary to give the entire sales talk. Salesmen sometimes lose orders by talking too much. If the merchant says, "Put me down for the same size ad as last year," the salesman can immediately reply, "Thanks very much, Mr. Jones. I will fill out the order." As soon as the order is signed (don't call it a contract) and before it is torn out of the order book, the salesman can say, "Mr. Jones, we are planning a pictorial advertising section this year and perhaps you will want more space." Show him in detail what is planned. The order can always be changed or a new order written.

Answering Objections

The advertising salesman must be prepared to answer the merchant's objections to advertising in the annual. His objections may not be serious. He may say, "It's too early, come back and see me later. I don't have my advertising budget made out for next year. I haven't made up my mind." Whatever the reasons given, the salesman should listen courteously (don't interrupt) and answer each objection in turn.

Don't try to win an argument. Get on the merchant's *side* and get an order for space. If he says, "It's too early," the salesman could reply, "Yes, Mr. Jones, I suppose it is a little early in the year to be talking about advertising in the annual, *but* this year we have worked out a plan at the school that we believe will give you your money's worth. We want to get your ad set up early and post proofs of it on the bulletin board and urge students to *patronize you.*" Keep the tone of the talk positive.

The instant the first objection has been answered, present the prepared layout of the proposed ad. It will convince the merchant that the salesman is really interested. If it is impossible to get the order on the first call, ask the prospect to think the matter over. Ask for a future appointment, and be sure to thank the merchant for his time.

Advantages of Yearbook Advertising

The advertising salesman of the school annual must be fully familiar with the advantages of yearbook advertising over other types available to the merchant.

Some of these are:

1. The life expectancy of the ad is greater in the annual than any other medium. Newspapers and magazines are read one day and thrown away the next. A yearbook is kept year after year—and is often re-read. For the price, the annual is the most permanent means of advertising.
2. Advertising in the school annual reaches young people who have not formed buying habits. They have a lifetime of buying ahead of them and in years to come will purchase homes, food, clothing, furniture, automobiles, and many other products. Merchants can build good will for tomorrow's business.
3. Students buy many products and greatly influence their parents' buying. Big corporations realize this and spend millions of dollars each year on advertising directed toward the 12 to 21 age group. Local merchants can also appeal to this group through the yearbook.
4. The enameled paper used in most yearbooks makes it possible to obtain excellent photographic reproductions. School annual ads are more attractive.
5. The yearbook advertisement is part of a complete book that is treasured by the entire community. It is often kept in waiting rooms of local professional men.

Miscellaneous Sources of Income

When the sale of books and advertising does not pay for all the expenses in the production of the yearbook, other means of obtaining income have to be planned. The business manager must be careful, however, in selecting the type of venture, since it may prove unprofitable from the standpoint of expense and effort necessary to stage such programs.

Selling space to school organizations is an important source of income. Under this plan, various organizations and classes are charged a fee large enough to cover the cost of the space devoted to their groups.

Most staffs charge each student for the cost of having his photograph made for the yearbook. If such an expense were borne by the yearbook, it would probably wreck the budget.

Added income sometimes can be earned by selling photographs after the yearbook has been printed. Although most of these pictures will appear in the book, many students want the original photographs and are willing to pay for them. The price should be low. Usually, a flat rate of 10 or 20 cents is charged for each photograph. As much as

$300, or more, can be earned by this method in larger schools.

One of the commonest sources of extra income for the yearbook is the class play. In schools where the yearbook is published by the senior class, proceeds from the senior play often go to the yearbook fund. Sometimes the annual staff produces an all-school play for the same purpose.

Probably the most popular means of securing added income is the yearbook prom. If the results of the beauty contest are announced at the prom, it should increase attendance. However, business managers should be careful in planning a dance of this type, since it is easy to spend more than will be gained.

Other sources of income include candy sales, a circus or carnival, or benefit movies. All are minor so far as the amount of income derived from them, but occasionally they prove to be a necessary part of the revenue-raising plan. It is important to remember that these miscellaneous sources involve extra work, and it is doubtful if they are worthwhile if they require the attention of the staff when its efforts should be devoted to more profitable ventures.

Closing the Yearbook's Affairs

Once the annual has gone to press, the editorial staff can catch up on lost sleep and neglected studies. Such is not the case with the business staff.

A good business manager often uses the lull between the final editorial activities and the distribution of the books to take care of the financial affairs. With his assistants, the business manager can use this period to collect all outstanding accounts and start a final financial report. At the same time, he must begin arranging for efficient distribution of the books.

Many advertising accounts can be collected in advance of actual distribution of the books if the advertising salesmen make necessary arrangements with the printers. Often, three or four of the complete advertising signatures can be obtained as soon as they come off the press. When they are folded and trimmed, these signatures will show the advertising pages as they appear in the finished book.

Provided with these finished sections, the business staff of the yearbook can collect for most of the advertising before the annuals are delivered. This plan of collecting will allow the business staff to get important work out of the way before becoming involved in the rush of distributing the books. At the same time, the plan of advance collections will help bring the financial records of the book up to date so that a complete financial statement can be prepared soon after the final flurry of activity.

Have the Books Audited

The final duty of the business manager of the annual is to leave on file with school authorities a complete statement of receipts and disbursements. In all cases, the books should be audited to protect all parties concerned. If the school does not employ an auditor, the business manager will be justified in asking that a committee be appointed to audit the books of the annual.

A simple statement, which is easy to understand but includes all necessary information, is sufficient. Figure 15.9 is one form of financial statement that might be prepared by the business manager from the financial books he has kept throughout the year.

Help the New Staff

While the yearbook staff members will be eager to complete their duties and close the book's affairs as soon as possible, they have a moral obligation, if nothing else, to offer to help the new staff for the coming year.

Once the new staff has been appointed, it is the duty of the retiring members, who are familiar with the problems of producing a yearbook, to get the new staff members off to a good start.

If the old staff lends a hand before bowing out, the new book is bound to be improved. Let the new staff profit by the errors of the old. It should be a standing policy that the retiring staff does its best to see that the new staff has advantages that the old staff did not have. Progressive action of this kind will insure improvement

THE 1966 ORANGE AND BLACK

(Annual Publication of the Student Body)
Statement of Receipts and Disbursements
June 1, 1965 to May 31, 1966

CASH RECEIPTS

Orange and Black Sales:		
1,402 at $4.00 to students	$5,608.00	
120 at $5.00 to non-students . . .	600.00	
	$6,208.00	
Share in activity fund	150.00	
Advertising space	404.50	
Sale of space to organizations	310.00	
Senior pictures	415.00	
Class play	71.50	
TOTAL CASH RECEIPTS	$7,559.00	$7,559.00

CASH DISBURSEMENTS

Printing, binding, and covers	$6,044.50	
Photography	224.00	
Prizes for book sales	25.00	
Postage and express	18.20	
Telephone and telegraph	5.60	
Office supplies and expenses	12.45	
Key awards to staff members	36.00	
Refunds $8.50		
Refunds 4.00		
Refunds 2.50		
$15.00	15.00	
Unclassified items	6.40	
TOTAL DISBURSEMENTS	$6,387.15	$6,387.15
Cash balance in bank, 5–31–66		171.85
Represented by:		
Bank balance per statement, 5–31–66		180.25
Less check No. 38 outstanding		8.40
Cash balance as above		$ 171.85
Business Manager		

1966 ORANGE AND BLACK

FIGURE 15.9. A simple financial statement that gives a comprehensive summary of all financial transactions for the year is a must for yearbook staffs.

of the school's annual each year. The retiring staff's helping the new staff should become a tradition at each school. Also, to cover a full year's activities, there should be no lapse between succeeding editors.

The book's affairs can thus be closed in a businesslike and efficient manner. Every record of the past year should be permanently kept on file and made available to the incoming group.

Appendix

STYLE BOOK

If the yearbook is to have uniform style, the the editor must adopt a "style book" and follow it carefully. As an example of points covered by such manuals, parts of the *Style Book* used by student publications at Kansas State University[1] are reprinted here and can be used for most yearbooks, with a few alterations if they do not have one of their own.

A Manual of Style, published by the University of Chicago Press, is accepted as authority by many publishers and by the publisher of this book. A copy of this manual can be consulted by the annual staff on matters not covered in the booklet mentioned above.

ABBREVIATIONS

1. **State names**—Abbreviate state names only when they follow names of cities. Do not abbreviate state names of five or fewer letters (Iowa, Maine, Ohio). Do not abbreviate Alaska, Hawaii, or Samoa. Write out Puerto Rico and Philippine Islands the first time you use them after the name of a city; thereafter use the abbreviations P. R. and P. I. Use these forms after names of cities:

Ala.	Hawaii	Mich.	N.M.	Texas
Alaska	Idaho	Minn.	N.Y.	Utah
Ariz.	Ill.	Miss.	Ohio	Va.
Ark.	Ind.	Mo.	Okla.	Vt.
Calif.	Iowa	Mont.	Ore.	Wash.
Colo.	Kans.	N.C.	Pa.	Wis.
Conn.	Ky.	N.D.	R.I.	W. Va
D.C.	La.	Neb.	Samoa	Wyo.
Del.	Maine	Nev.	S.C.	
Fla.	Mass.	N.H.	S.D.	
Ga.	Md.	N.J.	Tenn.	

---

[1] Printed by courtesy of the Department of Technical Journalism, Kansas State University, Manhattan.

2. **Titles**—Abbreviate faculty, military and professional titles when you use them with first name or initials, but spell out the titles when you use the last name only: Prof. R. C. Jones . . . Professor Jones; Gen. William C. Westmoreland . . . General Westmoreland.

EXCEPTION—For the President of Kansas State University, first name and initials are rarely needed for a local story. Even the last name is sometimes unnecessary when it will be clear who is meant: "President McCain said . . . ." or even "The President said . . . ." The same thing is true in writing of the President of the United States in a story about the federal government.

Titles used after the name are spelled out and written lower case: Dr. Charles E. Cornelius, dean of the School of Veterinary Medicine . . . The dean said . . .

Army abbreviations—Pvt., Pfc., Cpl., Sgt., Sgt 1/C, M/Sgt., Lt., Capt., Maj., Lt. Col., Col., Brig. Gen., Lt. Gen., Gen.

Navy abbreviations—Ens., Lt. (jg), Lt., Lt. Comdr., Comdr., Capt., Rear Admiral, Admiral.

Air force abbreviations—AB, A3/C, A2/C, A1/C, S/Sgt., T/Sgt., M/Sgt.; commissioned ranks same as army's.

3. **Months**—Spell out months except in headlines and datelines.

4. **Streets, avenues, organizations**—Spell out and capitalize such words as avenue, railway, company, building, county, association, corporation, where used as part of a name: U. S. Steel Corporation, Fifth Avenue, Story County, Press Building.

5. **Christian names**—Spell out such names as William, Charles, George.

6. **Names of well-known government and private agencies**—Write out completely the first time you mention certain well-known agencies and organizations, but thereafter use initials only, without periods: TVA, SPC, NBC, CIO, AFL, REA, ROTC, KSC, AAUW, UN, UNESCO, VA; but U. S., U. P., where initials form a word.

7. **a.m. and p.m.**—Use these lower case abbreviations rather than "morning" and "afternoon" or "night." But spell

out midnight and noon rather than using m. and n. with the number.

EXAMPLE—From 5 p.m. until midnight.

8. **College degrees**—When used after a name abbreviate and capitalize.

EXAMPLES—John Mason, B.S. '49; George Johnson, Ph.D. '50; Stanley Atlas, D.V.M. '35. If only the year is used with the name, omit the comma: Stanley Atlas '35 visited . . . .

CAPITALIZATION

1. **Political parties**—Capitalize names of political parties but not words that indicate general political beliefs, doctrines, or principles.

EXAMPLES—a Democrat (member of the party); a democrat (any believer in democratic principles); a Communist (member of the party); a communist (one who believes in Marxian principles).

2. **Regions**—Capitalize regions of the country and adjectives referring to them but not points of the compass or words that refer merely to direction.

EXAMPLES—The Middle West, Midwestern, but "He drove east" (in direction).

3. **Names of places, institutions**—Capitalize schools, churches, halls, and other public buildings when used with a distinguishing name: Iowa State University, First Christian Church, Lyon Hall, Memorial Union.

4. **Names derived from proper nouns but now used as adjectives**—These are not capitalized: A panama hat, an oxford shoe.

5. **Common nouns that by campus usage have the status of proper nouns**—These when used alone should be capitalized: the College, the Library, the Auditorium, the Stadium, the Union, the Field House.

6. **Parts of buildings, services**—Names of parts of campus buildings or of college services should **not** be capitalized: the cafeteria, the post office, the dairy sales counter, recreation center.

7. **Schools, departments, other divisions**—Capitalize all schools, experiment stations and the Extension Division. Do not capitalize departments and other subdivisions.

8. **Titles**—Capitalize when used before names but not after them. Check your school's catalog to be sure the title is given accurately.

EXAMPLE—Prof. John F. Helm, Jr., of the department of architecture and allied arts . . . or John F. Helm, Jr., professor of drawing and painting . . . (**not** professor of architecture). (Also see section Titles and Names.)

9. **College legislative and administrative bodies**—Capitalize these: the Board of Regents, the Faculty Senate, the Student Council, the various school councils, the Tribunal, the Board of Publications.
But do not capitalize subcommittees or subdivisions of such bodies: the faculty council on student affairs, the student planning committee, the counseling bureau, the registrar's office.

10. **Governmental divisions**—Capitalize these: the President, Congress, the Senate, the House, the Supreme Court, the Legislature, the United Nations, the Security Council, the General Assembly and no others.
Do not capitalize subdivisions of the above, such as the army, the federal bureau of investigation, the ways and means committee, the legislative council, the federal court, the department of agriculture, the soil conservation service, the veterans administration.

11. **Names of nationalities and races**—Capitalize such words as Indian, Negro, German, Caucasian. Use these identifications in news stories only when the information is neces-

sary to the story.

12. **Distinguishing words in names of holidays and special occasions**—Capitalize these: Homecoming Weekend, Fourth of July, Engineers' Open House, Hospitality Days.

13. **Common religious terms**—These are down except "Bible," which is the name of a book: gospel, scripture, heaven, biblical.

14. **Names of studios, courses, curriculums**—Capitalize language words as French, Russian and the names of specific courses as Survey of American History I, but not general terms as sociology courses, the home economics and journalism curriculum.

15. **Extracurricular organizations**—Capitalize such permanent groups as the A Cappella Choir, the Band, the College Players, the Purple Pepsters. Do not capitalize the meat judging team, the basketball team, the social and recreation committee, the senior class, the alumni, the faculty.

16. **The definite article in publications**—Capitalize it only if it is capitalized in the flag of the publication: the Kansas State Collegian, the Ag Student, The Kansas City Star.

17. **Titles of books, lectures, pictures**—Write these up if used in full: "The Idea of Nationalism."

18. **Music compositions**—Capitalize and quote titles of all music compositions except for arias commonly known by their opening phrases: "Symphony in E Minor," "My heart at thy sweet voice."

FIGURES

1. Spell out cardinal and ordinal numbers from one to nine inclusive, except sums of money, ages, time, votes, scores, percentages, temperatures, the number and opus in works of music, dimensions and general statistical matter.

EXAMPLES—Of nine (cardinal number) men, the ninth (ordinal number) man, 3 years old, at 3 o'clock, lost by a 4–8 vote, won by an 8–5 score, 2 per cent, 5 degrees F., Sonata No. 5, Opus 6.

EXCEPTION—When a number under 10 and one over 10 are used comparatively in the same sentence, both should be figures.

2. All cardinal and ordinal numbers of 10 or more should be written as figures **except as noted.**

EXCEPTIONS—Ordinal numbers that are **proper names** should **always** be spelled out.

EXAMPLES—Twenty-fifth street, the Big Seven; but the 25th in line, the 53d anniversary.

Names of military units should follow military practice: Armies, air forces and fleets spelled out, corps and wings in roman numerals, and divisions, squadrons and lesser units in arabic numerals.

EXAMPLES—The Twentieth air force, the Fifth army, II corps headquarters, the 2d Armored division, the 45th (Thunderbird) division.

Spell out common fractions used alone but use figures for fractions when they appear with a whole number.

EXAMPLES—One-quarter of an inch, five-sevenths of the required work, 24 1–8 feet, 24 feet, 1 1–8 inches.

When two figures are used in reference to the same thing, avoid confusion by making the first a figure and the second a word.

EXAMPLES—16 two-story houses, 73 twelve-inch boards.

3. The number **always** should be spelled out if it is necessary to start a sentence with it.

EXAMPLE—Ten men were trapped. (**Do not** start sentences with numbers that will be long and awkward if spelled out.)

4. General or round numbers such as one hundred, one

thousand, one million, or one billion may be spelled out as words rather than figures.

5. Always use the dollar sign when referring to a specific amount of money. **Do not** use zeros after even dollars.

EXAMPLES—$352.78; $100.

6. **Ciphers**—Drop unnecessary ciphers except in statistical tables.

EXAMPLES—It is $50, not $50.00. It is 1 p.m., not 1:00 p.m. In general use the most easily grasped form: 50 billion dollars, rather than $50,000,000,000. Ciphers are too easily dropped between the reporter and the presses or the microphone. Drop cents whenever feasible.

EXAMPLE—$4,453, not $4,453.23

IDENTIFICATION

Names of college students should be adequately identified.

EXAMPLES—John Doe, TJ Jr., Salina; Bill Smith, EE Soph., Topeka. See Student Directory for curriculum, classification and home town.

PUNCTUATION

The two most common punctuation marks, the period and the comma, frequently are misused. The period is not used enough. The comma is used too frequently. Most reporters make their sentences too long. They get involved in compound sentences that wander on endlessly, confusing writer and reader alike.

News style calls in general for short, terse sentence structure and compact, brief paragraphs. Few sentences should go beyond 15 words. Few paragraphs should exceed 50 words. But some variety in length is desirable. A news story made up entirely of 5- to 15-word sentences would be choppy.

A sentence that requires the use of a great many commas usually is a poorly constructed sentence. The copy reader should edit the material so the thought is clearly expressed with a minimum of punctuation. When the use of a comma is doubtful and no change in the meaning would result through its omission, the best policy is to omit it.

1. **The apostrophe**—The apostrophe is used to indicate the possessive case of nouns, a contraction or the plurals of letters.

EXAMPLES—"It's" for "it is," class of '37 for 1937, A's, John's house.

NOTE—The possessive **its** does not use an apostrophe, nor does the plural of figures—15s.
When the name ends with an "s" put the apostrophe after the "s" and do not add another "s."

EXAMPLE—The possessive of Mr. Adams is Mr. Adams', but the possessive of Mr. Adam is Mr. Adam's.

The singular possessive is formed by the addition of an apostrophe before the "s," the plural by an apostrophe after the "s."

EXAMPLE—"The boys' coats" (plural), "The boy's coat" (singular), "The boy's coats" (one boy with more than one coat).

EXCEPTION—The "s" after the apostrophe is sometimes dropped where its use would make for an awkward pronunciation, such as "for conscience' sake" or where the sibilant sound of a double "s" would result, as in "Kansas' son, Moses' behalf," etc. Avoid such usages if possible.

Do **not** use the apostrophe in such common contractions as varsity or phone.

2. **The hyphen**—The hyphen is used as a connecting link in some compound words. Many words formerly hyphenated are now used either as separate words or as one word without a hyphen. Prefixes such as **ante, anti, extra, inter, intra, mis, multi, non, over, out, post, pre, ultra** and **under** usually combine into the word without the use of the hy-

phen, except in cases where a double vowel results or where the second part of the word is capitalized. Since there is disagreement as to the use of the hyphen in specific instances, follow the usage of Webster's Collegiate Dictionary. When words are combined to form an adjective, they are connected with hyphens, unless the first word is obviously an adverb.

EXAMPLES—A 10-year-old boy, a 6-foot 2-inch man, the 100-yard dash, a 2- by 4-inch board, a quick-starting halfback, but a quietly spoken warning, a widely known speaker.

3. **The comma**—Do not put a comma before "and," "or" and "nor" connecting the last two elements in a sequence of three or more. Always place a comma before "etc." and "viz." and a comma (or semicolon) before "namely," "i.e." and "e.g."

EXAMPLES—Tom, Dick and Harry are all here.
He saw neither the owner, the agent nor the tenant.

Use a comma before "of" in connection with residence.

EXAMPLE—Roy E. Coe, of 1515 Tenth Avenue.

When the name of the town and state are both used, set off the name of the state with commas.

EXAMPLE—Tulsa, Oklahoma, and a Washington, D.C., visitor.

Point off with a comma all numerals of four figures except street numbers, year numbers, box numbers, tabulations and astrophysical and botanical numbers.

EXAMPLES—1,240 students, 1240 Main Street, 1940 A.D., Box 1240, 1240 species.

Do **not** use the comma or colon with the dash.
Use the comma between the name of a man and "Jr." or "Sr."

EXAMPLE—John E. Smith, Jr.

4. **The colon**—Use the colon after a statement introducing a direct quotation of one or more paragraphs, and begin a new paragraph for the quotation.

EXAMPLE—The speaker gave this six-point platform:
"First . . . etc."

5. **The semicolon**—Use the semicolon in a list of names and addresses in which commas are used to separate the name from the address.

EXAMPLE—Those honored included George Johnson, Kansas City, Mo.; John Adams, Junction City; and William Jackson '39, Wamego.

6. **The dash**—Don't use the dash where the comma will do the work. It may properly be used to set off parenthetical words, denote an abrupt break, indicate a significant pause.

7. **The period**—Do **not** use the period after "per cent" or after nicknames.

EXAMPLE—It is 9 per cent too much.

8. **Punctuation with quotation marks**—Periods, commas and semicolons coming at the end of the quotations **always** go inside the quotation marks. Other marks of punctuation go inside quotation marks if they are part of the quotation, but outside if they punctuate the entire sentence.

EXAMPLES—Have you read "Gone with the Wind"? The books were "The Pioneers" and "The Last of the Mohicans."

QUOTATIONS

1. When you use passages from a speech or interview verbatim, put quotation marks around them. Quotations sprinkled through a newspaper column attract readers. But do not use long, rambling verbatim passages where the phraseology or content has no particular interest or value. If those passages are needed to give a clear and fair idea of the speech or interview, put them into your

own words in order to summarize. Sometimes only a word or phrase or clause that accurately or vividly conveys the speaker's idea may be lifted and put in quotes in a summarized paragraph.

2. **Conversation, statements, testimony**—Use quotation marks for testimony, conversation and direct quotations from speeches or interviews, except when preceded by a name and a dash or by Q. or A. (Question, Answer) and a dash.

   EXAMPLE—James Smith—I have no comment.
   Q.—Where were you June 14, 1948, at 11 p.m.?
   A.—Looking at etchings.

3. **Titles**—Quote the titles of short poems, pictures, sculpture, short musical compositions, radio and television programs, lectures, sermons, unpublished theses, papers. Quote toasts, mottoes, chapters of publications, subdivisions of books (except books of the Bible).

   EXAMPLES—"Mona Lisa," "Venus de Milo," "Star Spangled Banner," Genesis. "How To Use Atomic Dust," "People Are Funny."

4. If you use verbatim several successive paragraphs from a speech, begin each paragraph with quotes, but use end quotes only after the last paragraph. If you are using verbatim only part of a sentence, do not indent it for a new paragraph. Put quotation marks around it within your own summarizing paragraph.

   EXAMPLE—The speaker said he was "not going to be swindled into supporting the plan."

   In such a case, do not use a capital letter for the first word.

Crediting Quotations

5. **Direct quotations**—You need only one reference to the speaker for a single quoted passage, even if that passage is 10 paragraphs long. You can put that reference in either the first or the second sentence. Have the reference **open** the statement if you feel that the reader will be confused otherwise.

   EXAMPLES—"Kansas State University definitely is to have air conditioning before the year 2000." This was the statement made today by John Doe at_____.

   Sheriff J. L. Jones said, "Richard Roe definitely is the man we want."

6. **Indirect quotes**—In general have only one reference to the speaker for each paragraph of indirect quotation. If there is danger of the reader being confused as to source of the statement, however, refer to the speaker more often. Refer to the speaker or source only as often as necessary to keep the reader aware of the source.

SPELLING

1. When in doubt, consult *Webster's Collegiate Dictionary*.

2. Follow American rather than British style: color, defense, insure, program.

3. The "United States Official Postal Guide" governs spelling of cities, states and countries.

4. Spell out "and."

5. Spell out "per cent" except in statistical tables.

6. Check names with student-faculty directory, telephone directory or city directory.

TITLES AND NAMES

In general newspaper usage the titles "Mrs.," "Mr." and "Miss" are used as a mark of courtesy and are applied in writing of people to whom the title would be applied in ordinary conversation.

1. Use the "Mr." only after the man's full name has been used in an earlier reference: Leland Stowe, veteran newspaper correspondent, arrived today . . . Mr. Stowe said . . .

2. **Titles and names of women**—Use the woman's first name, never initials alone. Refer to a faculty woman by her title if she has professorial rank, as you would in a story about her male colleagues; by "Miss" if she is an instructor. Prof. Lois Schulz, chairman, said . . . Professor Schulz went on . . . Sarah Smith, foods instructor, said . . . Miss Smith added. . . .
   For a woman student use her full name the first time, then "Miss": Chairman is Jane Black, TJ sophomore, Topeka . . . Miss Black asks . . .

3. **Names**—Write them as their owners do:

   EXAMPLES—James A. McCain, R. F. Gingrich, Arthur D. Weber.

   Always use the full name the first time it appears in a story. Use the last name with the proper title, if any, when it appears later. Nicknames should be used rarely unless they have distinct value in identification; or refer to a child; or are used in a story distinctly informal in tone; or are in sports copy. Same applies to headlines. When the nickname is used with the full name, it should be in parentheses: Laurence A. (Moon) Mullins.

4. **Clergymen**—Never use "Rev." alone. Always precede it with "the." Always follow it with first name or two initials (the first time you mention the man), or with Mr. or Dr. or "Father," depending on his degrees and the church with which he is connected.

   EXAMPLES—For the Protestant denominations if a man has a doctor's degree—the Rev. John B. Jones . . . Dr. Jones . . , or the Rev. Dr. John B. Jones . . . Dr. Jones.
   For Protestant denominations if a man does not have a doctor's degree: the Rev. John B. Jones . . . Mr. Jones.
   For the Episcopal or Catholic church: the Rev. John B. Jones . . . Father Jones.
   For the Jewish clergyman: Rabbi Samuel S. Wise . . . Rabbi Wise. Distinguish between a rector, a minister, a pastor, a priest. The words are not synonyms.

5. **Academic titles**—The general catalog gives ranks of staff members. Be **sure** you get them right!

First Reference	Later Reference
Prof. John L. Jones	Professor Jones
or	
Dr. John L. Jones, professor of agronomy	Professor Jones or Dr. Jones
John L. Jones, associate professor of agronomy	Professor Jones
John L. Jones, assistant professor of agronomy	Professor Jones
John L. Jones, instructor in agronomy	Mr. Jones
John L. Jones, graduate assistant in entomology	Mr. Jones
John L. Jones, assistant dean of Agriculture	Dean Jones
Dean John L. Jones of the School of Agriculture	Dean Jones
Dr. John L. Jones, dean of the School of Agriculture	Dean Jones or Dr. Jones

GENERAL INSTRUCTIONS COMMON USAGE

1. Collective nouns take the singular verb.

   EXAMPLES—News is interesting. Politics is barred. A series of three addresses is scheduled.

2. The name of the state is unnecessary and is not to be used after the larger cities or after towns that would not be confused with other communities.

   EXAMPLES—New York City, Topeka, but Kansas City, Kans.

3. Two singular nouns connected by the conjunction "and" take a plural verb, but two singular nouns connected by the conjunction "or" require a singular verb.

EXAMPLES—John and Mary are coming. John or Mary is coming.

4. When a singular noun and a plural noun are connected with the conjunction "or," the verb must agree with the noun closest to it in the sentence.

    EXAMPLE—The mother or her children are coming. The children or their mother is coming.

5. Make the pronoun agree with its antecedent in number and person.

    EXAMPLE—Each of them has his own way but all of them cannot have their ways.

6. Do not separate needlessly the parts of infinitives or verbs.

    EXAMPLES—To go quickly, **not** to quickly go. It probably will be, **not** it will probably be.

7. Use "per" before a Latin word, "a" before an Anglo-Saxon word.

    EXAMPLE—A day, a week, per diem, per annum.

8. Do not confuse "over" and "more than." "Over" means above in a physical sense.

9. "Farther" refers to distance. Don't confuse with "further."

10. Do not use the verb "secure" for "obtain." Bookcases may be "secured to the wall (that is, fastened) but they are "obtained" when purchased.

11. Do not use "contact" or "feature" as verbs.

12. Avoid simplified spelling unless the simpler form is used by a considerable number of prominent authors.

13. Familiarize yourself with the college catalog and the student directory. The catalog gives much information concerning departments and schools, curriculums, courses, academic calendar, registration schedule, Board of Regents, officers of the college, names and purposes of student organizations, loan funds, scholarships, prizes, enrollment statistics and number of degrees conferred. If in doubt about any of the information in the catalog or directory, check with the proper official source on the campus.

14. Avoid using "are as follows," or "the following attended."

15. Avoid "shown in the above picture," or "pictured above." Save words.

PREPARATION OF COPY

1. Use copy paper.

2. Write on one side only.

3. Type all copy.

4. Double-space all copy.

5. Set your typewriter for a 65-stroke line (15–80) in order to make copy-fitting easier. Four such typewritten lines will make one column inch in the *Collegian*.

6. Indent paragraphs at least 10 spaces.

7. Write your name, the subject of your story, your home telephone number and the date in the upper left-hand corner on the first page of all copy.

    EXAMPLE—John Jones
    FFA Meeting—2
    Phone 3150
    October 3

8. Write your last name, the story slug and the page number in the upper left-hand corner of all succeeding pages of all material turned in.

    EXAMPLE—Jones
    FFA Meeting—2

9. **Always** begin a story one-third of the way down the first page. This leaves room for the headlines.

10. Write "more" at the end of a page if the story is to be continued.

11. Keep your copy as clean as possible but **never** at the expense of accuracy. Reasonably clean copy with faults corrected in pencil is far better than spotless copy with errors. Always edit every story carefully before handing it to your editor or your instructor.

12. **Never** attempt to cover an error in typing with the correction. Cross it out and rewrite.

13. End each page with a complete sentence or paragraph.

14. Always put an end mark at the end of a story or report. The most commonly used end marks are 30 and # #.

15. If you make corrections on a news story in longhand, underline every a, u, w and overline every o, n, m. These letters are easily confused.

16. BE ACCURATE IN EVERY DETAIL.

Index

COPYREADING SYMBOLS

	HOW THEY ARE USED	WHAT THEY MEAN	HOW TYPE IS SET
TYPE SIZE and STYLE	Lansing, mich.—	Capitalize.	LANSING, Mich.—
	College Herald	Small caps.	COLLEGE HERALD
	the Senator from Ohio	Change to lower case.	the senator from Ohio
	By Alvin Jones	Bold face.	**By Alvin Jones**
	Saturday Evening Post	Italicize.	*Saturday Evening Post*
PUNCTUATION and SPELLING	"The Spy"	Emphasize quotes.	"The Spy"
	Northwestern U.	Emphasize periods.	Northwestern U.
	said, "I must . . .	Emphasize comma.	said, "I must ...
	Johnsons'	Emphasize apostrophe.	Johnsons'
	picnicing	Insert letter or word.	picnicking
	theatre	Transpose letters.	theater
	Henry Cook, principal	Transpose words.	Principal Henry Cook
	days	Delete letter.	day
	judgement	Delete letter and bridge over.	judgment
	all right	Insert space.	all right
	those	Close up space.	those
	Geo. Brown	Spell out.	George Brown
	100 or more	Spell out.	one hundred or more
	Doctor S. E. Smith	Abbreviate.	Dr. S. E. Smith
	Six North Street	Use numerals.	6 North Street
	Marion Smythe	Spell as written.	Marion Smythe
POSITION	Madison, Wis.—	Indent for paragraph.	Madison, Wis.—
	today. Tomorrow he	New paragraph.	today. / Tomorrow he
	considered serious. / Visitors are not	No paragraph. Run in with preceding matter.	considered serious. Visitors are not
	But he called last night and said that he	No paragraph.	But he called last night and said that he
	]Jones To Conduct[or ⟨Jones To Conduct⟩	Center subheads.	**Jones To Conduct**
MISCELLANEOUS	He was not unmindful	Bridge over material omitted.	He was mindful
	one student came	Kill corrections.	one student came
	or more	Story unfinished.	
	30 or #	End of story.	————————

PROOFREADING SYMBOLS

	SYMBOL	EXPLANATION	EXAMPLE	
			MARGINAL MARKS	ERRORS MARKED
TYPE SIZE and STYLE	*wf*	Wrong font.	*wf*	He marked the proof.
	x	Burred or broken letter. Clean or replace.	x	He marked the proof.
	ital	Reset in italic type the matter indicated.	*ital*	He marked the proof.
	rom	Reset in roman (regular) type, matter indicated.	*rom*	He marked *the* proof.
	bf	Reset in bold face type, word or words indicated.	*bf*	He marked the proof.
	≡	Replace with a capital the letter indicated.	*H* ≡	He marked the proof.
	lc	Set in lower case type.	*lc*	He Marked the proof.
	sc	Use small capitals instead of the type now used.	*sc*	He marked the proof.
	⊘	Turn inverted letter indicated.	⊘	He marked the proof.
PUNCTUATION and SPELLING	ℰ	Take out letter, letters, or words indicated.	ℰ	He marked the proof.
	#	Insert space where indicated.	#	He marked theproof.
	r	Insert letter as indicated.	*r*	He maked the proof.
	⊙	Insert period where indicated.	⊙	He marked the proof
	∧	Insert comma where indicated.	∧	Yes he marked the proof.
	∨	Insert apostrophe where indicated.	∨	Mark the boys proof.
	/=/	Insert hyphen where indicated.	/=/	It was a cureall.
	?/	Insert question mark where indicated.	?/	Who marked the proof
	em	Insert em dash, implying break in continuity or sentence structure.	*em*	Should we can we comply?
	n	Insert en dash, implying the word "to."	*n*	See pages 278 93.
	ᵛ/ᵛ	Enclose in quotation marks as indicated.	" "	He marked it proof.
	spell out	Spell out all words marked with a circle.	*spell out*	He marked the (2nd) proof.
	out, see copy	Used when words left out are to be set from copy and inserted as indicated.	*out, see copy*	He proof.
	stet ...	Let it stand. Disregard all marks above the dots.		He marked the proof.
	⌒	Draw the word together.	⌒	He marked the proof.
	tr	Transpose letters or words as indicated.	*tr*	He the proof marked
	?	Query to author. Encircled in red.	? *was*	The proof read by
POSITION	¶	Start a new paragraph as indicated.	¶	reading The boy marked
	No ¶	Should not be a separate paragraph. Run in.	*No* ¶	marked. The proof was read by
	=	Out of alignment. Straighten.	=	He marked the proof.
	⊔	Indent 1 em.	⊔	He marked the proof.
	⊔⊔	Indent 2 ems.	⊔⊔	He marked the proof.
	⊔⊔⊔	Indent 3 ems.	⊔⊔⊔	He marked the proof.
	eq. #	Equalize spacing.	*eq.* #	He marked the proof.
	⊥	Push down space which is showing up.	⊥	He marked the proof.
	[or]	Move over to the point indicated. [If to the left; if to the right]	[	[He marked the proof.
			]	He marked the proof.]
	⊔	Lower to the point indicated.	⊔	He marked the proof.
	⊓	Raise to the point indicated.	⊓	He marked the proof.
	∪	Less space.	∪	looks better